BLACK SUN

GEOFFREY WOLFF is the author of three other works
of nonfiction—*The Art of Burning Bridges: A Life of John
O'Hara*; *The Duke of Deception*, a memoir; and *A Day at the
Beach*, a collection of personal essays—as well as six novels,
most recently *The Age of Consent*. In 1994 he received
the Award in Literature from the American Academy of
Arts and Letters. Mr. Wolff is the director of the graduate
fiction program at the University of California, Irvine.

BLACK SUN

THE BRIEF TRANSIT AND VIOLENT
ECLIPSE OF HARRY CROSBY

GEOFFREY WOLFF

NEW YORK REVIEW BOOKS

New York

This is a New York Review Book
Published by The New York Review of Books
1755 Broadway, New York, NY 10019

Library of Congress Cataloging-in-Publication Data

Wolff, Geoffrey, 1937–
  Black Sun : the brief transit and violent eclipse of Harry Crosby / by Geoffrey Wolff.
    p. cm. — (New York Review Books classics)
Includes bibliographical references and index.
  ISBN 1-59017-066-0 (pbk. : alk. paper)
  1. Crosby, Harry, 1898–1929. 2. Poets, American—20th century—Biography.
3. Literature publishing—France—Paris—History—20th century. 4. Americans—
France—Paris—History—20th century. 5. Paris (France)—Intellectual life—
20th century. 6. Publishers and publishing—France—Biography. 7. Suicide victims—
United States—Biography. 8. Photographers—United States—Biography. I. Title. II.
Series.
  PS3505.R883Z95 2003
  811'.52—dc21

                                          2003013642

ISBN 1-59017-066-0

Printed in the United States of America on acid-free paper.
10 9 8 7 6 5 4 3 2 1

September 2003
www.nyrb.com

To Charles and Nancy Taplin,

in gratitude and friendship

Life itself is but the shadow of death, and souls departed but the shadows of the living. All things fall under this name. The sun itself is but the dark simulacrum, and light but the shadow of God.

—*Garden of Cyrus*,
Sir Thomas Browne

Contents

Preface

The notes at the back of this book may be consulted for the sources of all quotations not fully attributed and dated within the text. I have reserved for my bibliography a full description of the invaluable resources made available to me by a number of libraries, most notably those of Southern Illinois University and Brown University.

I first read about Harry Crosby fifteen years ago, in Malcolm Cowley's *Exile's Return*, and the story Cowley told was so striking, its implications so resonant, that I felt certain someone must have written it at length since 1934, when Cowley had finished his few chapters about Crosby's suicide. (He revised them in 1951.) But no one had in fact told Harry's full story, and most of those who had written about him, or about the Black Sun Press, treated him as merely a footnote, and borrowed either from Cowley or from Caresse Crosby's untrustworthy autobiography, *The Passionate Years*; so I finally decided to have a go myself at a full account of Crosby's remarkable life and suicide.

I have received generous support in this project: in the first, and enduring, instance from Joseph Fox, my editor, and at crucial moments from both the Committee on Research in the Humanities of Princeton University, and the National Endowment for the Humanities; the former financed a research trip to Europe, and the latter's generous Senior Fellowship gave me a year free to complete the writing of *Black Sun*.

In addition, many people gave abundantly of their time, permitting me to interview them in person, by telephone or through correspondence. I would like especially to thank Malcolm Cowley,

Archibald MacLeish, Elizabeth Beal Hinds, George Richmond Fearing, Kay Boyle, Adelaide Sohier, James Grew, Stanley Mortimer, Stuart Kaiser, Ruth Ammi Cutter, Polly Peabody Drysdale, Joseph Clark Grew, George Weld, J. Brooks Fenno, Lawrence Terry, Maria Jolas, the Earl of Portsmouth, Howard Hare Powel, Alexander Steinert, the Duc de Doudeauville, Edward Bigelow, Andreas Brown, John Nicholas Brown, Scott Burns, Mrs. Bernard Carter, André Magnus, George Rowe, Porter R. Chandler, Clarence C. Pell, Rev. John Crocker, Gen. Pierre Hamilton, Francis Lothrop, R. W. B. Lewis, Rev. G. Gardner Monks, Henry S. Morgan, Helenka Pantaleone, Mrs. William Ellery Sedgwick, Alice S. Wohl, Esther Grew Parker, Robert Snyder, Frances Steloff, James Thornton Sykes, Mrs. Sigourney Thayer, Benjamin C. Bradlee, Sylvia Whitman, Robert Choate, Mrs. Alexander Wheeler, Brian Swann, Betty Parsons, Warren M. Hoge, Dr. Michael Baden, Mrs. William Aspinwall Bradley and Murray Weiss.

Edward Weeks gave patiently and unfailingly of his time and recollections, and permitted me to read his memoir—*My Green Age*—while it was still in typescript; he led me to many sources I could not otherwise have found. So too did Harry T. Moore, who told me of the nature and scope of the Black Sun Press Archives at Southern Illinois University, and eased my way to them, as did Beatrice Moore. I am grateful to Rufus King, the executor of Caresse Crosby's estate, for permission to quote from the Crosby papers, and for much else besides. I was given extraordinary liberties with the Black Sun Press Archives, much of the material as yet uncatalogued, by Kenneth W. Duckett, Curator of Special Collections at Morris Library. He, together with David V. Koch, Rare Books Librarian, granted me favors without number. Ralph Bushee was kind enough to let me look at his catalogue of the collection, as yet unpublished.

James M. Wells, Associate Director of Chicago's Newberry Library, was generous in his support of my research, as was William S. Dix, Librarian of Princeton University, who opened many doors for me. The staff of the Harris Collection at John Hay Library, Brown University, especially Mary Russo, did me many and valuable kindnesses. Donald C. Gallup, whose direction of the American Literature Collection of Yale University's Beinecke Library is legendary among scholars, was kind and helpful.

Robert Lescher, whose friendship and support have mattered, read early drafts of *Black Sun* and brought to them a prosecutor's hard intelligence; his labor on my behalf was exceptional and valuable. Professor A. Walton Litz, whose student I was and shall continue to be, also read this book in typescript and suggested crucial changes that I have had occasion to act upon. He and Professor Carlos Baker, colleagues while I taught at Princeton University, encouraged me in this project from its beginning, and past its end. I would like also to thank my brother Tobias and Lynn Strong, my copy editor, for their close attention to the details of this book.

Priscilla helped me in more ways than I will ever know, or be able to repay.

Geoffrey Wolff
Warren, Vermont
September 17, 1975

BLACK SUN

"... to make the Last Thing Perfect."

—Harry Crosby's notebook

This time Harry had gone too far. It was one thing to fashion one's life as one pleased, and keep one's own gait; it was quite another to trifle and play the fool with the most powerful man in New York, to keep J. Pierpont Morgan, Jr., waiting at teatime. Now, going on 5:30, Harry Crosby was thirty minutes late at the Madison Avenue town house of his uncle, obliging that great man to make small talk with his sister-in-law, Harry's mother, and to try to put Harry's wife at her ease, meantime stealing glances at the library clock. It was December 10, 1929, a busy day in a busy social season, and an exacting time for Morgan, who was mobilizing a banking pool to raise a quarter of a billion dollars to support stock prices after the Great Crash. Matters of greater moment had claim to his attention than the capricious rhythms of an outlaw nephew.

Harry had made the appointment to deliver a Christmas gift, an elegantly bound copy of his new book of poems, *Sleeping Together*. His Uncle Jack, charmed by the young man, didn't know what to make of him: he walked around town like a dancing master, without a hat, with lacquered fingernails, wearing a black cloth flower in his buttonhole. Mr. Morgan had found a job for his nephew Harry at the Morgan bank in Paris, and Harry had repaid him by neglecting his work and then quitting without so much as a by-your-leave. Now he broke appointments. Harry's mother insisted that it wasn't like him, not at all; hadn't he won the Punctuality Prize at St. Mark's School? Harry's wife, Caresse, said there must be some proper explanation. But by 6:15 no more was to be explained away, so the ladies left the huge house and returned, bewildered and angry, to their rooms at the Savoy-Plaza Hotel.

Harry had spent his morning looking at sculpture and buying steamship tickets for his return with Caresse three days later to France, where they lived. After an early lunch he showed up at the Hotel des Artistes, 1 West 67th Street. His friend Stanley Mortimer, a portrait painter and—like Harry himself—a man of the world, kept a duplex studio on the building's ninth floor, and he had given Harry a key because he wanted a place to meet his girl friend privately when she came down from Boston.

Often Harry and the girl would arrive at Mortimer's separately, but today they arrived together. Some people said they looked like brother and sister, Harry and Josie, Henry Grew Crosby and Miss Josephine Rotch, both of Back Bay, Boston. Now she was Mrs. Albert Bigelow, having been married six months before to a Harvard hockey star. Harry called her his Fire Princess. They both had beautiful skin, like parchment, skin that people noticed, and eyes sunk beneath strong brows. Her mouth was sensuous and her lips full, and like hers his lips would quiver when he was excited, and like her he was frequently and easily excited. Harry was thirty-one; Josephine, twenty-two.

Mortimer was discreet: "When he popped in Tuesday with Miss Rotch—Harry always called her Miss Rotch in my presence—I knew he was going to ask me to leave. The two of them went up to the balcony. I was at my easel downstairs, working at a painting. They leaned over the balcony rail and kidded me." Harry had a bottle of Scotch. Josephine was wearing an orchid. "Crosby gave me a signal and I got on my street clothes and went out."

Caresse and Harry had lived in Paris since their marriage in 1922, but they returned to America from time to time, at first to please Harry's mother, later to please themselves. Their 1929 reunion had not been satisfying; Harry and his father had quarreled again, and bitterly. Mr. Crosby, an investment banker, had not yet recovered from his son's drunken cable a few months earlier: PLEASE SELL $10,000 WORTH OF STOCK. WE HAVE DECIDED TO LEAD A MAD AND EXTRAVAGANT LIFE.

When his parents had begged him to behave like a grown gentleman instead of some layabout Oriental prince, he had lectured them: "For the poet there is love and there is death and infinity and for other things to assume such vital importance is out of the question and that is why I refuse to take the question of money seriously." Harry hated money ("Why in hell won't they transact business with gold coins instead of with those filthy germ-ridden paper bills?") and he hated the getting of it. He overdrew his account at the State Street Trust, which in Boston was the equivalent of desecrating an altar. He and Caresse bought race horses, gambled and entertained on an imperial scale at their Paris apartment and nearby country place. Just a little bit too much was just enough for them.

Sometimes Harry's rebellion against Boston—"Drearytown," he called it, "the City of Dreadful Night"—seemed almost mathematically pure: in his response to his family's expectations of him, 180 degrees off course seemed always to be his setting.

He and Caresse had sailed on the *Mauretania* on November 16. He was determined to return to Boston in time for the Harvard-Yale game a week later in Cambridge; he had enjoyed the occasion the year before. Not the game itself—what did he care about football?—but the wildness of the event, its supercharged character, the drunkenness around him. He appreciated waste, and liked the casual way cars were abandoned in their owners' haste to get to a party somewhere—anywhere—after the game: New York or Long Island or Florida or California. Harry liked crowds. He was himself reserved in his manner, but he cherished the irrational: noise, energy, danger. Especially danger. During the past few years, his favorite occasions had been the hysterical reception at Le Bourget for Charles Lindbergh, when the crowd had torn to shreds the fragile wings of *The Spirit of St. Louis*, and the institutional carnality of the Four Arts student balls every June in Paris. Caresse had realized that her husband was not rushing home merely to attend a football game; she knew what had drawn him home. But she had not argued with him: what was the point? When Harry wanted to do something, he did it, and *no regrets* was her motto as well as his.

They had had a miserable crossing. A storm put them into New York a day late, and in their party was another Boston lady, now a countess, one of Harry's special girls. Caresse was falling out of patience with Harry's special girls, but she understood that it was late in the day to change their mutual regulations and liberties; she, after all, enjoyed her own courtiers. Besides, among princesses, she was still

Queen. When Harry wasn't passing time during the gray, rough passage playing baccarat with his girl friend, or receiving cryptic and conspiratorial cables from Josephine and yet another lady, he was laboriously copying by hand, as a tribute to his wife, a fair copy of *Sleeping Together*, his "dreams for Caresse." He wrote the poems without a blot in a book of blank pages bound in Paris by Gruel, a fabrication of rose vellum, gold-embossed.

The dreams in the book were weird, perhaps not the words J. P. Morgan would have selected with his brandy to warm him in front of the library fire:

> I have invited our little seamstress to take her thread and needle and sew our two mouths together. . . . I have arranged with the coiffeur for your hair to be made to grow into mine and my hair to grow into yours. I have persuaded (not without bribery) the world's most famous Eskimo sealing-wax maker to perform the delicate operation of sealing us together so that I am warm in your depths, but though we hunt for him all night and though we hear various reports of his existence we can never find the young wizard who is able so they say to graft the soul of a young girl to the soul of her lover so that not even the sharp scissors of the Fates can ever sever them apart.

This dream from his new book was prophetic, for it showed that Harry finally understood what Caresse had only dimly guessed: that they could be cut off, one from the other, by even such cliché-ridden hags as those "sharp scissors of the Fates." They had always liked to talk and write of their souls, and of their indivisibility. As far back as 1921, when Caresse was Mrs. Richard Rogers Peabody and Harry was a student at Harvard, and they were in love but unable to marry, he had cooked up a scheme to rescue them from their frustration. If Caresse didn't get a divorce, he promised her, he'd take the train to her in New York "and kill you and then myself so that we can go right to Heaven together—and we can die in each other's arms and I'll take the blame so you won't have to worry, Dear."

Josephine was quick to quarrel with Harry, and violent in her emotions. She had an ugly temper, and was jealous, and unlike Caresse she did not hesitate to tell Harry that his attentions to other women were intolerable. No sooner had the *Mauretania* docked in New York than Harry and Caresse had come up on the Midnight Express in the company of the Bostonian Comtesse de Jumilhac, and Josephine had hand-delivered a letter to 95 Beacon Street, Harry's parents' big Georgian house at the corner of Arlington.

Josephine had been educated at Bryn Mawr, where they taught a composed manner, smooth transitions, logical ordonnance. But her syntax in her letters, like her character, was all bounce and flash, crazy. She jumped from a diatribe against countesses to a diatribe against her fellow matrons of Back Bay to a frenzied declaration of love. A rival for Harry's affection had described her as a "strange wild girl who delighted in saying things to shock people." She rode Harry hard, and he did not like being ridden hard. By her lights he was in her debt; she had run grave risks for him ever since they first met two summers earlier in Venice, and she obliged him to appreciate her and—within the limits of his duties to his wife—pay exclusive attention to her. She suffered the legendary torture on the mistress's legendary hook: If he had betrayed his wife for her, would he not betray her for another? A sound suspicion; their appetites were cancerous, for each other, for novelty, for theatrics. They drank too much together, and Harry taught her to use opium—"black idol," he called it. Harry had a name for everything beneath the sun that mattered to him; he was a wizard with figures, conceits, lists, correspondences. His hair was fine and yellow, as yellow as sunlight, and sometimes he seemed not of this world.

Caresse, at The Game with Harry and his father, noticed Josephine's pale face staring at them, or she came later to believe she had noticed it. Her husband and his lover had met a few hours earlier, and they met again the following day in Boston, and the day after, and the day after that. Caresse left for New York as soon as the game ended, and checked into the Savoy-Plaza, Room 2707, and wrote to Harry, promising him he would relish the city if only he would join her:

> You will adore this room. Lying in bed I can watch the tugs nosing up the East River—see fly-like men against the skyline making towers of steel, and thrust through it all the most amazing phallic skyscraper, very straight and proud. . . .
>
> This is a marvelous city all energy and hardness and keenness, but I like France best, but we must come here *every* year . . . and after lunch Hart Crane and I have a rendez-vous under Brooklyn Bridge! Mac-Leish is in Conway but gets back Wednesday morning. . . . I adore you my darling darling darling! I sleep with "Sleeping Together"—but I want quickly to sleep together with you.

That was good enough for Harry; it never required much to seduce him away from one lover to another, back and forth. He joined Caresse on November 29: New York, he wrote, was a "madhouse," and he approved of madhouses wherever he found them.

On December 7 Hart Crane threw a party for them in Brooklyn. He liked the Crosbys, and was much in their debt for favors they had done him in Paris. Harry had established, with Caresse, the Black Sun Press, and he admired Crane's verse enormously and, as ever hospitable to his enthusiasms, was preparing to publish *The Bridge* within a couple of months. Crane, pulling out all the stops to please his guests, had invited William Carlos Williams, E. E. Cummings, Malcolm and Peggy Cowley, the photographer Walker Evans, and a crew of homosexual sailor friends to his flat within clear view of Brooklyn Bridge. The guests fell drunk, and someone holding a pack of cards urged Harry to select one, and he prophesied he would draw the ace of hearts. He crossed himself, picked blind, and drew the ace of hearts.

Crane was astounded, and chanted a line from one of Harry's poems about the Nile: " 'Let the sun shine! And the sun shone!' " Crane believed that he recognized a poet in his friend, who was his own man, who gambled and was quick to choose and to act, who could never be argued from a course he had set himself. Before the party wound down, Crane and the Crosbys decided they weren't yet ready to say goodbye to one another, and Harry invited his host to join them for dinner and the theater three nights later. They would see the tour de force called *Berkeley Square*, a comedy in which Leslie Howard returned from the dead to have a look at a later generation. The play was a touch slick for Crane's taste, but he accepted the invitation. Harry's mother was to be in New York, across the hall from Room 2707, and despite Crane's eccentricities—or more likely because of them—Harry wanted her to meet his most recent literary discovery.

Harry's mother and Caresse hurried back to the hotel from Morgan's house. There had been no word from Mr. Crosby, the clerk said. Distracted and alarmed, the ladies dressed for dinner and hoped that Harry would at least show sufficient courtesy to join them at the Caviar. Hart Crane was already there when they arrived, and he too was puzzled. Harry's mother kept the talk flowing; she was gracious, not one to buckle easily or to spoil a gentleman's meal by her nervousness. But Caresse could not force herself to eat. Harry went where he willed, and for as long as he willed, but he always told her what he was up to, at least in general terms; he would not upset her needlessly, and even less would he treat his mother with such disrespect. After the first course had been withdrawn, Caresse left the table to telephone Stanley Mortimer at his mother's apartment, a communication out of keeping with the rules of distance and propriety she and Harry played by. But she was badly troubled, and Mortimer agreed to pop over to his studio and look around for Harry.

The headlines next morning added up the lurid sum: TRAGEDY & DISGRACE. Decades later, a distant cousin of Harry's, Clark Grew, read something at Harvard about his notorious kinsman, and from curiosity asked his grandmother about the poet, till then unknown to him: "She just froze when I mentioned his name. She was in New York with my grandfather to go to the theater, and they came out of the theater at eleven o'clock, and there was some guy selling the local rag: '*Extra! Extra! Poet found dead in apartment with Boston girl!*' My grandfather turned to my grandmother and said: 'We will never mention his name again.' And they didn't."

Since it was almost 10:00 before Mortimer found them, the story was not likely to have hit the streets by the time the theaters let out, but Mrs. Grew's recollection was surely accurate in its drift, if not its details. For years Harry had thumbed his nose at Boston, and at his own people, and at first they had tried to understand him, and possibly even accommodate themselves to his oddities for a time, till he found himself. But he did not find himself, and would not listen when some of them warned him that he was drifting toward shoal water. Now this . . . this infamy, a humiliation past the reach of forgiveness. For many in his family he was deader than dead, a nullity, a never-should-have-been, a never-was.

They were discovered lying together in the bedroom upstairs off the balcony, beneath a silk coverlet and dressed except for their bare feet. Mortimer had reached the studio shortly after 9:30 and tried the door: it was bolted from inside, and no one answered his knock. He called for the building's superintendent, who broke in with a fire ax. Harry was gripping in his right hand, as though for dear life, a .25 caliber Belgian automatic. There was a bullet hole in his right temple, and a bullet hole in her left temple. His free arm was wrapped languidly around her neck, and their left hands were clasped. They faced each other. She was still wearing her orchid.

Among his clothes police found the Cunard Line steamship tickets he had bought that morning for his return home with Caresse. And in cash, $523.75. And several artifacts fashioned from the gold in which he had invested so heavily with his metaphors. These objects were translated by the language of the death report into: "yellow metal chain containing 17 parts, one yellow metal letter A." Most resonant of all, they found Harry's sun-ring, which he had sworn to Caresse never to remove. This "yellow metal ring" was found on the bedroom floor, stomped flat.

The police also found a telegram from Josephine, addressed to Harry on the *Mauretania*: CABLE GEORGE WHEN YOU ARRIVE AND WHERE I CAN TELEPHONE YOU IMMEDIATELY. I AM IMPATIENT. In his pocket was another cable from another girl; it said simply, YES, Harry's favorite word. The police noticed that the toenails of Harry's bare feet had been painted bright red, and that the soles of his feet were tattooed with a Christian cross on the left and a pagan sun-symbol on the right.

Caresse would not go to the studio to witness the carnage. Instead she telephoned Archibald MacLeish, who was in town from his Massachusetts farm to see his friends from Paris. She begged MacLeish to take charge; when he was admitted as Mrs. Crosby's ambassador to the ninth floor of the Hotel des Artistes, the first man he noticed was Dr. Charles Norris, the medical examiner: "He was pacing up and down like a tragic figure in a Sherlock Holmes story. 'That's quite a friend you've got there.' He was fascinated by Harry's looks, thought he was wonderful-looking." Norris told MacLeish that Harry had let himself live at least two hours longer than Josephine.

If Harry and Josephine had dreamt they would be married by blood, they could never have imagined to what degree their death would polarize their survivors. Albert Bigelow knew his wife had been murdered, and Josephine's friends supported the widower's judgment. Hadn't Mrs. Bigelow said to some of them only a few weeks earlier that her married life was "terribly happy"? And hadn't she been in high spirits that very morning when she left the Park Avenue apartment of Margaret Burgess, an old school chum with whom she was staying? And why shouldn't her spirits have been high? Hadn't she made an enviable match with Albert Bigelow? He was handsome, intelligent, young and enormously popular. Besides, Mr. and Mrs. Burgess had planned a party in her honor for the very night she died, and she had seemed to look forward to it; surely she would not have selected the night of a party in her honor to fulfill a suicide contract . . .

On the other hand, one of Harry's lady cousins thought he had been misled and ruined by Josephine, merely a "passing fancy" for him. One of Harry's closest friends, Gretchen Powel, had had lunch with him the day of the bloodletting, and her recollection supports the notion that Josephine was merely a "passing fancy": "Harry said the Rotch girl was pestering him; he was exasperated; she had threatened to kill herself in the lobby of the Savoy-Plaza if he didn't meet her at once. He agreed to see her, reluctantly."

What puzzled the police, and impelled the newspapers to write follow-up stories through the week, was the absence of a suicide note. The newspapers looked high and low—very low—for clues to what that note would have said had Harry only been thoughtful enough to write it. They tried disappointed love, with a boost from Stanley Mortimer: the couple had died of frustration; Society, barring their divorces for the purpose of marrying each other, had killed them. Then alcohol was tendered as a likely suspect, since it was known that the lovers had finished most of a bottle of Scotch together. (The papers never thought of headlining drugs, though this would not have led them much further than love or drink.) It was suggested that immoral times had killed the couple—that European influences had pulled the trigger twice. ("Mr. Crosby, who had lived several years in Paris, held suicide preferable to life in America.") The New York *Daily News* put its theoreticians to work and reached a novel conclusion regarding the cause of Josephine's death:

CROSBY POEMS CLEW IN DUAL DEATH
Passion Verses Secret Reading of Slain Bride

The story, a crazy-quilt of fictions, would have pleased and amused Harry, for it suggested that the poet is a wizard of deep powers who can lead his beguiled readers where he will:

A Puritan of the Puritans, the 22-year-old June bride . . . neither smoked, drank, nor used cosmetics more extensively than a touch of rouge at her lips. Yet at the climax of an affair with the 35-year-old [sic] Crosby which, as far as her friends were concerned was absolutely clandestine, she was found in death beside a lover who wore a black carnation in the lapel of his jacket, and whose toes, tinted a flaming crimson, peeped from beneath a coverlet.

Crosby's poems of passion, whose mood was as exotic as some of their author's preparations for death, were found by members of the amazed family in the home of her aunt. . . .

Harry certainly believed that poems could seduce and transform; perhaps they could even destroy. Years earlier, he had composed a histrionic sonnet on the subject of his own "dissolution," and had titled it after one of his own dark influences, "Baudelaire":

> ... *Within my soul you've set your blackest flag*
> *And made my disillusioned heart your tomb;*
> *My mind which once was young and virginal*
> *Is now a swamp, a spleenfilled, pregnant womb*
> *Of things abominable* . . .

The better to solve the mystery of the gunshots, the *Daily Mirror* consulted authorities on aberration: "Profoundly moved by the double tragedy which carried the Byronic Harry Crosby, society esthete and Great Lover, to his death . . . psychologists yesterday [December 11] probed further into the young man's writing, seeking there some new reason for the rash adventure."

Now they were getting warm. Indeed, Harry's writing was no more nor less than a prolonged suicide note; he had often, and in every imaginable manner, composed its thesis: Death was *"the hand that opens the door to our cage the home we instinctively fly to."* Death was a "Golden Future" and "a land where nothing was amiss." By his writings he instructed himself in it, arranged its form, provided for himself the whip to lash him home. It inspired him, literally; breathed life into him. Death was a goal he ran toward full tilt. He was a poet of final stanzas, or so he liked to believe, and that last shot was no more than a punctuation point, a dot smaller than his smallest fingernail, a hard period, full stop.

Harry's experience of art, and its most dangerous risks and sensations, was deep. For the sake of art, it was his preposterous ambition to translate himself from a Boston banker into a genius. He studied geniushood as his school friends studied the conventions, or contract bridge, and he decided, with terrible calculation, to short-cut his way to genius by way of madness. Harry Crosby is an entire laboratory wherein may be studied the terminal consequences of the religion of art. Almost alone among the outlaw artists of his time, he translated every aesthetic notion—so long as it was sufficiently wayward, outré and violent—into acts. In his heart he lived a dangerous metaphor: Art is magic. The magician is a god. Gods can do anything, and never mind the cost.

But literature, art, like Josephine, was only Harry's accomplice in murder. Death had been his master long before he began to write, even before he began much to read. He loved death. And during those two hours alone with his still lover and himself and his odd, familiar friend, Harry must have studied the dead girl, trying to find in her smile some clue to where he was about to take himself. A clerk at the Savoy-Plaza believed he saw Harry wandering in the lobby while his mother and wife were at tea with J. P. Morgan, just after he had fired the first shot. More likely the clerk had seen a phantom; more likely Harry simply lay beside Josephine trying to recollect himself, so that he would finally know, before he finally left, where he had been.

2

A BOSTON BOY

Harry Crosby was born at home in Boston's Back Bay in 1898, June 4, under the influence of Gemini, whom we represent as the twins Castor and Pollux, whom Egyptian astrologers represent as a pair of goats, whom Arabian astrologers represent as peacocks. Geminis are said to be quick and restless, mutable, not to be depended upon. Harry's mother was a pious Christian and would not have interested herself in such a vulgar and pagan custom as belief in planetary influences. Still less would his father, who kept his eyes on the ground, who would have hooted down such notional nonsense as faith in lucky stars. But both of them, Henrietta and Stephen, believed in the shaping power of lucky circumstances, in the predisposition of people born into a favorable setting to rise high and let their light shine down on others. Harry's parents provided in abundance what they regarded as fertile nurture—money, position, authority and generosity.

A convention, often tiresome, calls upon biographers to precede an account of the subject's childhood with a genealogy, taking the relentless inventory of his great-aunts and infamous cousins. But in Harry's instance a table of pedigrees, distinguished name upon distinguished name, is fundamental to his story. Harry's ancestors, Van Rensselaers and Grews and Morgans, at first inspired him, then reproached him, and finally shamed him, as he shamed them. His destiny was in hostage to their ambitions and judgments, and they never willingly paroled him from the genetic prison into which he was born. When at last he broke out, the carnage was awful.

By his birth certificate he was fashioned Henry Sturgis Crosby. His maternal grandfather was Henry Sturgis Grew, a Bostonian much admired for his philanthropies, who had married the owner of another name prized in Boston, Jane Norton Wigglesworth. (The Sturgis line was patrician enough, but soon after Harry was born his parents elected to change his middle name to Grew.) Henry Sturgis Grew had a son, Edward, and three daughters. Elizabeth Sturgis Grew married Boylston Adams Beal, of Boston; Jane Norton Grew married John Pierpont Morgan, Jr., of New York; Henrietta, named for her father, married Stephen Van Rensselaer Crosby, of Albany, whose bloodlines were no less noble than his wife's. His maternal grandfather was Gen. Stephen Van Rensselaer, the last patroon. The family had received from the Dutch government in 1629 a land grant of twenty miles along the Hudson River, and they ruled it like a duchy. Stephen Crosby's mother was the great-granddaughter of Alexander Hamilton, from whom his father too was descended. They also shared descent from a Revolutionary War general, Philip Schuyler, who became a United States Senator. William Floyd, a signer of the Declaration of Independence, was Stephen Crosby's paternal great-great-grandfather.

Col. John Schuyler Crosby, Stephen's father, was much publicized for his exploits as a soldier and big-game hunter. He served heroically in the Civil War with McClellan in the Army of the Potomac, and during the Indian campaigns with Sheridan and Custer. He was Governor of Montana from 1882 to 1884, and he liked to shoot bear and buffalo in the company of his friend Bill Cody. In Albany, where his son was born in 1868, he and his wife stood high.

Stephen Van Rensselaer Crosby went to St. Mark's School, graduating in 1887, and then to Harvard, graduating four years later. At St. Mark's he won the Fearing Athletic Prize; he was short and light, but he was also tough and determined: he played football and baseball, and ran on the track team. He prized excellence, and at St. Mark's and Harvard, in his time as in Harry's, excellence in athletics was valued above all excellences. At Harvard, Stephen Crosby was captain of the baseball team; as a freshman he tied for victory in the one-hundred-yard dash; as a junior he was treasurer of the Track Association and won the half-mile run; as a senior he coached the freshman football team and was a halfback on the undefeated varsity team, which scored 555 points to its opponent's 12.

Although there is no published evidence to support it, the impression left upon people who knew him much later in life was that Harry's father had been "quite a football star at Harvard," that "he had made some phenomenal run that established him forever as one of the great backs of Harvard's history," that he was the "lightest fellow ever to play football for Harvard." Whatever his success at the game, it nourished him; his niece, Betty Beal, said he "lived on it."

Stephen Crosby was plucky, he wasn't odd, and his social credentials were impeccable. Accordingly, he was elected to several Harvard Clubs: Deke, Hasty Pudding, the Institute of 1770 (the latter two weren't yet joined), and finally the A.D. As Bentley is to Rolls-Royce, so is the A.D. Club to Porcellian (and St. Mark's to Groton), as good as the best, perhaps even better than the best because quieter in the announcement of its excellence. He never ceased to take an interest in the A.D. and its members: his loyalties were deep and persistent, and when he left Harvard (having achieved the distinction of being named Third Marshal of his class), he gave the football stadium its first automatic scoreboard. He worked for the Boston & Albany Railroad at home for a year after college, and then left for Boston where he joined F. S. Mosely, a brokerage and old-line investment banking firm, retiring after thirty-five years, just ten months before Harry died.

As a man he had grown nervous, explosive, tightly coiled, sometimes distant but more often sociable, always generous with gifts. He liked the ladies, and was easy among men, at least among those of his taste and class. He intimidated some of Harry's kinsmen and chums ("He used to scare me to death," in the memory of a female cousin), and a few, thinking him cruel or indifferent or uncultured, didn't like him at all. But people liked to be liked by him. He went about wearing a silver whistle attached to a silver chain, and when a comrade said something that amused him, within the bounds of clubly decorum, he'd blow it, and his friends, pleased with themselves, would laugh. He was supremely clubable, and despite the misfortune of his birth beyond the territorial frontiers of Boston, he was taken into that city's sanctum sanctorum, the Somerset Club. Stephen Birmingham has written that John Marquand's election to that club meant more to him than the critical and commercial success of his books, more even than his Pulitzer Prize. Steve Crosby would have taken his own election for granted.

He married Henrietta Marion Grew in the autumn of 1895 in Manchester, on Boston's North Shore. Harry's mother was as serene as her husband was edgy. One of her son's childhood friends recalls her:

"I was playing at Harry's house. I remember one time, for no reason at all, she brought me a present. And I just instinctively threw my arms up around her and kissed her. I thought, *That was a strange thing to do.* But she made it a natural thing to do." She was quiet, but not mousy; pious, but not strident in her faith; gentle, but not plastic. She was too sensitive and feminine in her manner to qualify as that most Bostonian of female creatures, the low-heeler, the aristocratic, gutsy, plain talker. But like low-heelers, she was without guile or pretension. She liked to play golf, and to read seriously, and to travel far to see strange sights. (She once remarked, in an uncharacteristically scatterbrained sentence: "It's interesting—things that are interesting interest me.")

Her passion was for flowers—especially wild flowers—and she wrote about them for *Nature*, and lectured on botany. She was a founder and president of the Garden Club of America, and sent her gardener to agricultural school, and her greenhouse at The Apple Trees, the Crosbys' great white summer place in Manchester, became a botanical marvel. People from all around Boston who were not related by blood to her knew her as Cousin Rita, later as Aunt Rita, and it is not recorded that she ever in her life did anyone intentional injury.

Her husband was a man of sudden changes, like his son, and his character was a patchwork of paradoxes. He was known as the Napoleon of the North Shore, and that bigger little man was his idol. He never passed through Paris without visiting the Emperor's tomb at the Invalides, and he liked to quote a fellow admirer's inflated apostrophe to their hero: "He cast a doubt on all past glories, he made all future renown impossible." In matters of reputation, the figure that a man cut in society, Harry's father regarded himself as a very Roman, imperial and consequential.

But in his personal affairs he was petty, fussy and fretful. He would pack his bags days before he left on a trip, and arrive at the station hours early, and refuse to leave a train in transit for fear of being abandoned. When his wife traveled alone—which was often—he forever pressed instructions upon her, who was more willing to run risks, and more curious: "Be careful not to slip on the wet decks! Keep your passport buttoned to your chemise!"

He was frequently a stuffed shirt, but toward his son he acted without formality, and allowed himself to be addressed in a spirit of bonhomie, so that an illusion of intimacy between them persisted long after they had failed—to their mutual sorrow—to understand each other. In one matter of taste, however, they understood each other perfectly and forever. They were excited by pretty girls, and intolerant of plain ones.

As a grown man Harry wrote his mother, who was plain (though not, perhaps, to his eye), a letter about a friend's wife that must have drawn a drop or two of blood from Henrietta Crosby: "She looks like nothing at all. When I first saw her three years ago she was quite pretty—now she is dreadful looking. I wouldn't stay ten minutes with a girl if she wasn't pretty."

In his stimulations and interior commotions, Harry's father liked to flirt, and a peculiar social convention of his time and city afforded him an occasion and license. In Boston it was considered at least marginally correct for ladies to entertain gentlemen who were not their husbands at tea during "calling hours" every afternoon, between four and six. Stephen Crosby took liberal advantage of this indulgence to visit many ladies, and one in particular, the wife of a bank president.

It is not known whether he indulged in what we would call an affair, but certainly he preferred the company of many girls, and many women, to the company of his wife. Esther Grew Parker, the niece and goddaughter of Harry's mother, did not care at all for Stephen Crosby: "He had no intellectual character; in fact, he was quite snobbish about intellectuals, and I think Rita was rather understanding about them. I really loved her, more even than my own mother. She did all sorts of things for me. She was forceful, in a gentle sort of way, humorous and close to her children, because her marriage wasn't particularly happy." Mrs. Parker's brother, James Grew, is blunter: "Steve Crosby was very much a man's man, very popular with my father, and my father's friends, and all that generation, and I could never see why. She was such a marvelous person; he didn't measure up at all. They had one of those marriages that today wouldn't have lasted, but they belonged to another era."

They did indeed. Harry's mother was surely wounded by her husband's various affections, but like him she was pledged to things as they had been, were, and must remain. So that, supported by her wit and generosity, and fortified by her self-persuasion that her husband and his lady friends confined their intercourse to tea and gossip on the ground floor, she endured Stephen Crosby's reluctance to concentrate his attention exclusively on her. And Harry, who repaid her love with high interest, was her consolation.

Three years after Harry was born, the Crosbys' only other child came along, Katherine Schuyler Crosby, called Kitsa, and soon after that the family moved from their comfortable house at 304 Berkeley Street—between Beacon and Marlboro—to a big place nearby at 95

Beacon Street, on the northwest corner of the Boston Public Garden. The backyard went down near an esplanade beside the Charles River (till Storrow Drive effaced it) and shrubs bordered the large site. The views from the house, along Beacon Street, and of the Public Garden, and up and down river, were remarkable. Sometimes the Charles froze hard enough for the family to skate clear across it.

The house was lavishly furnished and huge, with a dance floor big enough to accommodate one hundred and fifty guests. A portrait of Gen. Van Rensselaer hung in the library, and there, among volumes bound in leather, dark blue, dark green, dark red, dusted and oiled, Harry would sprawl on a couch, his head in his mother's lap while she read to him: *Ivanhoe, The Talisman, Henry Esmond*. A fire always burned in winter, and the chairs were deep, stuffed with goose down. When he was still very young, his mother, whom he called Mammy-Gu, recited verses to him, and her favorite, and his, was the first stanza of "Songs of Seven":

> *There's no dew left on the daisies and clover,*
> *There's no rain left in heaven.*
> *I've said my "seven times" over and over,*
> *Seven times one are seven.*

His father gave him rewards and prizes for learning poems by heart; "Sheridan's Ride" and "The Death of Napoleon" were required material. During Stephen Crosby's freshman year at Harvard a lecture had been delivered by Col. T. W. Higginson called "Literature as a Profession." It is unlikely that Harry's father bothered to attend it, but surely the kind of literature the Colonel discussed was not the kind Harry came to write. It was not unknown for the sons of Brahmins to make their way by words, and through ideas, as long as the ideas were respectable and the words chaste. But literature was by no means a profession of choice. The members of Stephen Crosby's class, two hundred and eighty-nine of them, reported five years after graduation on their callings and inclinations. There were two fiction writers in the class of 1891. *The Atlantic Monthly*, whose offices are within sight of 95 Beacon, was acceptable in a pinch, but the periodical in which Stephen Crosby wished to find his son's name published was the Boston *Evening Transcript*, on the page given over to business, or society. And the book of books was the *Directory of Directors*.

Like most children, Harry did not much confide in his father, but neither did he bridle against his father's view of the world or his father's ambitions for his son. When he was twenty, Harry wrote his mother from the war in France, without irony, to still her worry about his behavior and ambitions: "Don't think for a moment that I don't take your advice or at least give it very careful thought, and there's nothing that I value more in this world than yours and Pa's advice." Her advice was to heed the Scripture, to act with generosity, to behave with decency, and to live within his income. His father's advice was to be brave, to charm, to have a lively concern for the good opinion of his peers, to join the A.D. when he reached Harvard, to make his way in business, and to live within his income.

Harry was a mischievous boy, who liked to throw water bombs from the upstairs Chinese room, with its intricately lacquered ceiling, and black carpet, and exotic flowered wallpaper, and black lacquer bed, and red flamingo set in a black picture frame. Sometimes the butler would be obliged to look down his snoot at wet victims standing enraged on the stoop at 95 Beacon, and explain to them that they were not wet, as they believed, and that if they were, their discomfort had nothing to do with Mr. Crosby's well-ordered household. Finally, Mr. Crosby himself fell victim to the stunt, and Harry's practice ceased for a while. He liked to tease his plump sister, and pull the girls' pigtails; he was still throwing water bombs from high places the month he died, and he continued to pull the girls' pigtails, too, after his fashion.

His portrait hung in the salon: his hair was gold, and he wore a white smock and white socks and white slippers, and held a large India rubber ball. His lower lip drooped in a pout, a legacy from his father's mother.

Every Thanksgiving a huge feast would be given at Harry's Uncle Ned Grew's house, and Harry's grandmother would appear from Albany, tall, grave, gaunt, nervous, dressed in black, a foreshadowing of the deathly figure Harry himself later contrived to cut. The Thanksgiving dinners were so populous that some of the guests, though kinsmen, were strangers one to another.

Such good people as the Crosbys and Grews and Beals would also gather at weddings and coming-out parties, but funerals were the social occasions of choice, and going to them was a Boston habit and hobby. The late Lucius Beebe wrote of this odd and durable custom: "Boston has always been a funeral-going town, and a service of importance at Trinity or Emmanuel is sure to find the first citizens out in force with wide bands on their top hats, happy in an impenetrable, but for all that thoroughly enjoyable, atmosphere of gloom. The custom is rooted in respectable antiquity and the gentlemen of the town once counted the number of times they had participated in such pomps as most young men today take pleasure in the number of times they have served their friends as best man or usher."

For the Crosbys, later for Harry, death was a familiar, nothing that held terror, something that enticed, something to roll over in the imagination, and test, and look at from across the fence, close up. When he was twenty-nine, Harry wrote in his notebook, without much amazement: "I ponder death more frequently than I do any other subject, even in the most joyous and flourishing moments of my life."

During the summers the family would retire to Manchester, on the North Shore, about twenty-five miles from Boston. It was a beautiful town, with heavy woods and rocky headlands alternating with long stretches of white sand. The Apple Trees was a grand house built well back from the road on what had once been an enormous orchard. Behind it was a barn and a greenhouse, and in front was a high wall, called the Morgan Memorial, built with an endowment from Uncle Jack Morgan's father to isolate J. P. Morgan, Jr., from public view, and protect him and Aunt Jessie from any possible embarrassment.

Weekdays the fathers of boys and girls like Harry and Kitsa commuted to town on a private train called *The Flying Fisherman*, pulled by the Boston & Maine. Sometimes Harry would go with his father to watch a Red Sox game, but mostly he stayed at the shore, swimming at Coffin's Beach or his favorite, Singing Beach—so called because its fine white sand gave off an odd tune, something like a whistle, when it was stepped upon. He especially cherished foggy days, and liked to hear the horn boom off the point that protected Manchester's harbor, which was busy with pleasure boats. He swam, if he could get away with it, when it was forbidden to swim, when the surf was high and there was undertow. They flew flags at both beaches, red for warm water and blue for cold, and he liked blue best. He liked green, for medium temperature, least: he was never one for in-betweens.

The children rode in pony carts, and rolled hoops, and wore sailor hats, and their hair was cut in bangs. Just as Stephen Crosby had the Somerset Club, and his wife the Chilton Club, the children had a place called the Montserrat Club, run by Mrs. Jackson, whom Harry would torment by walking in golf cleats upon the mahogany table. Mrs. Jackson called him the Sultan, but the nickname didn't stick: something in him even then did not invite liberties.

There was a crowd of kids at the shore: George Richmond "Tote" Fearing, Philip Shepley, George Weld, Francis Lothrop, Lawrence Foster. Harry was the gang leader, the one who bestowed nicknames and led everyone into scrapes. George Weld was Harry's especially close friend, and together they built a tree house in Manchester and decorated it with baseball cards of the dramatis personae of the Red Sox and the Braves, and together they bedeviled Kitsa when other action was slow. There was always something doing, swimming or golf or tennis. The little children had governesses, but manners were easy and the kids went barefoot if they wished.

There were, however, social regulations, and for a young man of Harry's station they would come to have a character as inexorable as gravity. The clubs where he played—the Essex County, the Myopia Hunt, the Montserrat—were closed to members of the world's exotic races. For the matter of that, they weren't open to many Protestants, either. Exclusion in Boston, the Family City, had—continues to have—a calculated quality, as though it is performed for the sake of legend, to build a record.

Only a few thousand people (the Crosbys, Grews and all their friends among them) were listed in the *Social Register*; nevertheless, one gentleman objected that the studbook had become a "damned telephone book." To assure that bloodlines never blurred, the Boston *Evening Transcript* published, every Wednesday, the most comprehensive genealogy column in existence. The story is told of a young Bostonian eager to make a dollar or two in the commercial hurly-burly of Chicago, that odd place without history, beyond the antipodes. His prospective employer sent to Boston for letters of recommendation, and such was the nature of the replies that were returned that the employer felt obliged to explain that "we were not considering using your young man for breeding purposes." Until 1905 newspapers in Boston printed the names of undergraduates elected to Hasty Pudding, a club less exclusive than Porcellian or the A.D., and thus more socially confusing, in the order in which they were desired and selected, so that some decent hierarchy could be maintained among the young men. Indeed, till the 1800's, freshmen at Harvard College were listed in rank according to their social standing.

All this was in the air, the given of election and privilege, but gentlemen didn't discuss it much. Mrs. Crosby instructed Harry in charity, and piety, and perhaps even a kind of tolerance that extended to those less socially fortunate than herself, her husband and their children, as long as those less socially fortunate remained content and in place.

Mrs. Crosby studied the Bible, and under her influence so did her son. Together they would often drive the family Lancia through the Essex Woods, or along the shore to Coffin's Beach, stopping for a picnic to admire the view toward Plum Island and down along the white flat stretch of sand. Mrs. Crosby permitted her son, when she was alone with him, to take liberties with the character and habits of her husband, a practice that encouraged intimacy between Harry and his mother, and subverted his regard for his father. Together they would joke about Mr. Crosby's loud voice, or his vanity and fussiness, or his readiness to pontificate. Harry and his mother laughed at the memory of Mr. Crosby's dissertation on the art of shaving, delivered the first day he discovered a whisker growing on his adolescent son's chin. They would laugh at Mr. Crosby's homilies ("More flies are caught by honey than by vinegar") and at his anxieties, expressed again and again in the catch-question "What will people say?" (Mrs. Crosby, out of sight of her son, cared every bit as much as her husband what people said about her family.)

Harry was permitted to call his father, to his face, "the Old Rodent," a familiar endearment that Mr. Crosby tolerated because he felt so secure in his conviction that Harry respected him and was intimidated by his high place in the world. And also because he loved his son, and wished to be his friend. But Harry's easiest and deepest friendship was with his mother. They played a great deal of golf together, and tennis, and Mrs. Crosby could spot her son 30–love every game, and whip him despite the handicap. When he was still a boy, she knew him back and forth: "Do you remember you would always win the toss by holding the golf ball in your left hand? I would invariably guess the right hand?" *He* remembered, many years after their games, when she could no longer decode his messages, when he wished she could.

At night there would be dances for the young people, or Harry would play auction bridge with his parents and his sister. Then he'd climb the stairs at The Apple Trees to the sleeping porch and listen for the foghorn. He liked it best when summer turned, and leaves began to give up and fall, and the sky went to clouds. All his life he looked forward to autumn: not for its crispness, but for its sadness, and black and gray were his favorite colors. It was a taste that his family, with its fascination with dead times past, and dead ancestors buried in family plots, and the end of things, could appreciate.

Not that Harry was gloomy as a boy, or death-obsessed. He was cheery, hospitable to mischief, energetic, well-liked and quick to take friends, attractive to the girls around the North Shore and attracted to them, especially to two of them, Ella Snelling and Sister Caswell, whom he called Goldenhair. He made a single exception to his rule that any girl in whom he took interest must be comely. His cousin Betty Beal, the daughter of his Uncle Bob and Aunt Elizabeth Beal (who was said by some to be Boston's foremost snob), was plain. She was also Harry's closest girl friend; he confided in her as in few boys, or none, and called her while she was still a child "Auntie E," perhaps causing her no pain by such a spinsterly title, even though he was by two years her senior.

As a child he had gone to Noble and Greenough's School, which at that time was situated downtown in Boston. In the autumn of 1911, when Harry was thirteen, his parents decided it was time to send him away to St. Mark's, an hour from Boston, in Southborough. He would have the company there of many friends, of Gardner Monks and Tote Fearing and Ned Bigelow and Brooks Fenno, and he would have an opportunity to observe the manners and mores of children from such far-off territories as New York and Greenwich and Philadelphia's Main Line and Lake Forest, maybe even Santa Barbara. He wasn't eager to leave Manchester for what he immediately called The Monastery, but he wouldn't have dreamt, then, of quarreling with what he knew he was obliged to do.

Years later, in September, 1929, after a happy weekend at the Moulin du Soleil in Ermenonville, just before quitting his country place for Paris, Harry found a magnum of champagne in a corner of the sitting room, where he had overlooked it the night before: "So for good luck I poured it over and rubbed it into my hair as I used to rub sand from the beach into my hair before going to school." Harry was always a boy who believed he could stop time dead, at just the perfect moment.

3

"From prison to prison . . ."

—Harry Crosby's diary

Saint Mark's School was founded in 1865 to educate young gentlemen
sufficiently in Greek and Latin and mathematics and rhetoric to get
them into Harvard College or, in the infrequent instance of a boy's
lesser ambition, Yale or Princeton. Beyond this, the school instructed
its boys in good manners and manliness, and above all sought to lead
them toward such grace and piety as might be required to secure their
admission into a Protestant Heaven. The catalogue assured parents that
Southborough (or Southboro, as it is also called) was "singularly free
from objectionable features," and that the "school's order and management are in conformity with the principles and spirit of the Episcopal
Church." Prayers were said daily, under the charge of the headmaster,
Rev. William Greenough Thayer.

Father Thayer had become headmaster of St. Mark's in 1894, while
Harry's father was president of the Alumni Association. During the
ripest era for boarding schools—from before World War I till the
decade before World War II—he was one of a patriarchal group of
Great Headmasters (Frank Boyden of Deerfield, Endicott Peabody of
Groton, Father Sill of Kent, George St. John of Choate, one or two
others) who believed that the nation's best interest was served by the
cultivation of a Christian elite. To Dr. Thayer, "distinction of brain

and physique, opportunity and personality" were what made "this world worth living in." The distinction he had in mind must have been between social class and social class rather than between one of his students and another, because personal quirks and singularities were not encouraged at his school, which embraced as a principal virtue the repression of peculiarities, the smoothing of rough edges, the correction of eccentricities.

The fathers of Gardner Monks, Brooks Fenno and Harry Crosby ponied up the tuition of a thousand dollars, and the three chums from Noble and Greenough's went up to St. Mark's in the fall of 1911 to take their entrance examinations. The Latin textbook at their old school was markedly different in vocabulary from that at the new, so all three failed the exam in Latin and were obliged to enter as first-formers rather than second; thus they were the oldest members of the class of 1917.

The roster of names from Harry's time at St. Mark's reads like an American *Almanach de Gotha*: Bradlee, Sears, Dewey, Bigelow, de Gersdorff, Pell, Lowell, Codman, de Rham, Whitney, Huntington, Iselin, Winthrop, Beal, Grew, Morgan, Van Rensselaer. On the school's fiftieth anniversary in 1915, when Harry was a fifth-former, or junior, the trustees issued a report commending St. Mark's for its excellent works, but taking some note of other people's criticisms of the place: "Some of the graduates were disturbed because St. Mark's was becoming more and more a rich man's school." These subversives even wanted "competitive scholarships, or something of the sort." Not a chance. The report committee observed that "similar experiments in other schools had not been markedly successful. The Committee believed very strongly that the influence of the Headmaster was so wisely exerted that the boys at St. Mark's were in little danger of becoming snobbish, or of laying undue stress on the mere matter of wealth."

Meantime, the school newspaper and literary magazine, *The Vindex*, ran advertisements from Brooks Brothers for liveries suitable for "stable, garage, or club," or for "menservants." In 1914, an anonymous member of St. Mark's Missionary Society, unwilling to identify himself perhaps for fear of the ridicule his sentiments would have invited, wrote for *The Vindex* an article titled "Town and Gown." He was distressed that his schoolmates lorded it over the local lads, and he proposed, modestly enough, that town boys be invited once or twice a week to use the St. Mark's gymnasium. "I suppose," he wrote, "that this proposal will shock and startle some of the more conservative readers of *The Vindex*." But he gamely soldiered along, attempting to argue the merits of his notion. His article is a masterpiece of good intentions colored by unconscious condescension, a manual of arms for those who would comprehend the meaning of *noblesse oblige*:

> Here in this town there are many boys who, for lack of proper treatment and of a place where they may get some wholesome exercise and amusement, are forced either to hang about the streets or to visit the cheap shows of Marlboro. . . . The majority of the boys in this School are the sons of wealthy or well-to-do parents, at any event they are members of the so-called "upper classes." Many of us will be called to positions of responsibility and importance in various commercial organizations, such as railroads, mines, and newspapers, in our after life. Very few of us will be forced to the misnamed degradation of manual labor, and will consider ourselves superior to and will hold positions of authority over the laboring classes. We are evidently on the verge of another social upheaval, like those which have troubled the course of history since the earliest ages. . . . It may even break out into the horrors of an inter-class war. . . . How much better it will be for us to learn to understand the other class now! An understanding of the laboring classes will do much to remedy and smooth over difficulties in the future . . . it may do much to prevent the impending cataclysm of socialism.

But "the impending cataclysm of socialism" wasn't much on Harry's mind, not then, not ever. At school he made no mark as a rebel, reformer, regular fellow, or much of anything. *The Vindex* shows that he took mandolin lessons, was a timer in a hockey game, managed the Glee Club and gave three (required) extemporaneous speeches. A gregarious leader with his mob at the North Shore, he made no new or lasting friends at St. Mark's, and some of his classmates recall him best as a loner. His indifference to the boys he found at school is not out of character: he always responded with warmth and generosity to people who surprised him, and no one, no thing, surprised him at St. Mark's. He took little interest in team sports, just as in his mature life he disdained communal enterprises—unless they were wars, riots or parties. But if he failed to catch fire at St. Mark's, neither did he entertain a wish to burn the place down. He kept a diary of which only a few pages survive, all from the end of his fifth-form year. The entries show a cheerful boy, empty of introspection, pleased enough with his lot:

> *Sunday, June 11, 1916*: Church. Studied. Got elected to the Boston Dance Committee for the Sixth Form Dance. Missionary Society Meeting.

Monday, June 12, 1916: School. Spring Sports. Got 2nd place in ½ mile run.

Wednesday, June 14, 1916: School. Went in swimming twice. Played 4 sets of tennis in the T[ennis] T[ournament] Doubles. Fenno and I beat Fearing and Thayer 6–3, 6–0. Got 3rd in the 120 yd hurdles and 220 dash junior. Studied for exams. Peach of a day!!!!!!!

Thursday, June 15, 1916: Exams. Got a 60 in Latin and a 55 in Math. In the T.T. beat Harris 6–2, 6–4. Won the junior ¼ mile in 57½ seconds. . . .

Saturday, June 17, 1916: Exams. Got a 61 in English and a 65 in French. Had a haircut. Won the Mile Run doing it in 5min 10sec and got my running stripes. Best day ever!!!

Monday, June 19, 1916: Came down to Manchester!!! Prize Day!!!!! Took a Latin Comp. exam. Swimming. Fenno and I won the S.M. School Tennis Tournament Doubles by beating Fuller & Weld 6–3, 6–4, 6–2. Got a Punctuality Prize for not being late for 2 yrs. Motored home with A. Shaw.

Tuesday, June 20, 1916: Saw Pa. Swimming. Drove the car 40 miles. The new French maid is a queen! Some pep!

Thursday, June 22, 1916: Motored down to New London. Went on board the Corsair. . . . [Harry does not specify which *Corsair* he boarded—Uncle Jack's 250-foot schooner or his twin-screw steam yacht, longer by five feet than a football field.]

The jottings tell Harry's whole story at St. Mark's, less a detail or two, and the story is oddly commonplace.

Despite the advantage of his superior age, Harry did not distinguish himself academically. Once only, in February of 1912, was he able to report a good record: "Dear Ma—I ranked second in my form and 18 in the school. I am going to have my hair cut." Otherwise, his grades were in the cellar: he was graduated from St. Mark's two places from the bottom of his class, but with perfect marks for conduct and punctuality, and on Prize Day he was awarded a citation for having contrived to arrive at appointments on time to the minute—a virtue he enjoyed for the rest of his life. Still, good conduct and punctuality didn't make for much to take home to his father. Not that Mr. Crosby would have objected to the boy's rotten grades, so long as they got him passed along from form to form, and into Harvard.

No, what must have stuck in Mr. Crosby's craw was his son's indifferent performance in team sports. Harry had no career in football, nor in hockey, nor in baseball. His classmate, and closest friend at

St. Mark's and at war, Tote Fearing, recollects how things were meas-
ured in those days: "The heroes were football players, and Harry
wasn't big enough or strong enough to play football."

That Harry was good at golf and tennis, and loved to run, hardly
mattered. "Running," as Gardner Monks recalled, "was pretty far
down the list of things that were esteemed." As a boy, Harry would
run a mile along Singing Beach every day, and at school he was remembered by Richardson Dilworth, the late Mayor of Philadelphia and
Harry's classmate, for one thing only: "He was a passionate cross-
country runner, and every day we would see him slogging off across
the hills by himself, seven days a week, rain or shine."

Porter Chandler was Gardner Monks's roommate both at St.
Mark's and at Harvard, and the two alternated academically between
best and second-best in their form at school, with Chandler graduating
at the top of his class. Chandler remembers Harry as "an amusing
companion, with a genius for finding reasons for *not* doing his homework." Since Harry took no pleasure from such dreary business as
Latin and Greek, he appealed to Chandler for informal tutoring in
those subjects, and to Monks for help with science and math. Irregular
verbs and the proper use of the subjunctive were sovereign mysteries
to him, and he saw no profit to be had in mastering them when another
fellow had done so sufficiently to serve them both.

Years later, in 1923, when Harry was at Morgan, Harjes & Co. in
Paris, neglecting his banking chores in order to study words in the
dictionary and write letters to improve his style, he recalled Porter
Chandler: "As the head of the class used to do all my Greek for me at
school, and as Goopy used to look after my ambulance for me during
the war, so now Vicomte du Mas (deux mots if you please) occupies
himself with what work I am supposed to do."

Gardner Monks had been as close as any boy to Harry before they
went to St. Mark's ("I was constantly in his house"), but once at
boarding school the two friends drifted apart. As a child Harry had let
himself be steadied by Monks, who had once by only the thinnest
margin of time managed to talk him out of setting fire to a house.
Monks was responsible and prudent, and must have lost patience with
Harry's antic bursts of energy and his counterpoint stretches of torpor.
Once Harry took a one-mile run and invited Monks at the end of it to
read his pulse: "Needless to say, it was high, and he swore up and down
that he would run no more for fear of damaging his heart. . . . It is
perhaps typical that he hadn't the foggiest notion as to what would be

the normal heart beat at the end of the mile." Today, looking back, Rev. G. Gardner Monks finds even Harry's piety "in keeping with his unpredictability: every so often he did things very intensely."

Tote Fearing had not known Harry as long as Monks had (though the Fearings and Crosbys were close friends in Boston), but his style was better suited to Harry's. He was, and is, a partisan of plain talk, intolerant of hypocrisy, earnestness and self-importance. He has wit and irreverence; he is a sensualist, and likes to throw people off balance with his candor. He has been called by more than one of Harry's Boston friends "outrageous," but always with either affection or envy. He has always placed a great premium on courage and endurance.

Fearing introduced Harry to Edward FitzGerald's translation of *The Rubáiyát of Omar Khayyám*, the work that joined the Bible in Harry's literary pantheon, and continued among his touchstones through his life. Omar's epigrammatic quatrains—passionate and direct, expressive of the kind of pessimistic fatalism that young men use to justify their self-indulgence—seeped into Harry's fancy, and soon began to control his character. He was, simply, seduced by these verses:

> *Come fill the Cup, and in the Fire of Spring*
> *The Winter Garment of Repentance fling:*
> *The Bird of Time has but a little way*
> *To fly—and Lo! the Bird is on the Wing.*
>
> *Ah, make the most of what we yet may spend,*
> *Before we too into the Dust descend;*
> *Dust into Dust, and under Dust, to lie,*
> *Sans Wine, sans Song, sans Singer, and—sans End.*

St. Mark's was rule-ridden, and a friend recalls that Harry, though not outwardly rebellious, never liked to be "squeezed" by regulations. He called the school "the monastery"—"with complete justice," in Fearing's memory. "If we were caught smoking during vacation, we were put on probation, and if we were found smoking at school we were fired. And so it went. It was stricter than anything, stricter than West Point is today." The school catalogue warned parents that "boxes and packages of all kinds are forbidden without the express permission of the Headmaster. Whenever it is necessary that a boy should go home in term time, the reason must always be stated in advance; but leave of absence will not be granted except under extraordinary circumstances. Important letters and telegrams should be addressed to the Headmaster." Harry managed, when he felt the urge, to smoke, as well as return to Boston. Years later, he wrote his mother that "home is the *only* place to be sick in. How I used to rush back from St. Mark's! Do you remember?"

His parents would come to Southborough one Sunday each month and he would go with them to lunch, but, as Richardson Dilworth correctly recollects, "he never invited anyone else to go along." He liked even then to be left alone, and would sometimes turn inward, and his mood might darken for reasons no one understood, or cared to understand. Dilworth never saw him again after graduation, but upon hearing that Harry had killed himself he began to think about his old classmate, and ask other St. Markers about him. They could make no sense out of what Harry had become: "It is very clear from Harry's subsequent career that none of his classmates had any idea such a time bomb was ticking away inside of him."

"He hates noise," a friend told his sister Kitsa while Harry was a schoolboy, "and does not care a rush what people say or think of him so long as they leave him alone." Still, with Tote Fearing, and the gang at the shore, he was energetic, wry, ironic, an inventor of what he must have thought were sophisticated apothegms. His favorite, recollected to this day by four of his friends, was the instruction that "people who live in glass houses should not take baths in the daytime."

Perhaps under the spell of Omar Khayyám, and subsequently of Schopenhauer, La Rochefoucauld and Wilde, Harry was fatally attracted to epigrams, and in his youth these were either cute or domestically homiletic. When Kitsa was made president of Miss May's School in 1917, Harry, Polonius-like, wrote her from France a letter that, coming from him, was a thesaurus of hypocrisies. It would be comforting to believe he choked on his laughter while he composed it, but its cautionary tone is typical of his manner during those sad occasions when he succumbed to good resolutions:

> That's damn fine your being president of the school and if you work hard you have a chance to do Miss May's a lot of good. What you and your class does and how it acts bears directly upon the actions of the rest of the school. If you set a good example it follows that the younger girls will hold to your examples. Therefore take a lot of interest in your new position and don't let up your interest till next June. . . . Good luck to you. . . . Get a good start and keep going—in other words acquire PEP which is the secret of all good work.

The full harvest of Harry's own PEP made for slight nourishment at his father's table, so that when war fever began to rise at St. Mark's as the United States came closer to joining the fight, Harry was in the vanguard of those who wanted to leave school. Beginning with the fall term of his last year, he chipped away at his parents to let him go to battle; he wanted to sail for France on the first tide.

During that term there were lectures on aviation and preparedness, and war maps placed in several buildings on the campus were kept current by the students—whose restlessness during Harry's final year was so extreme that Gen. Leonard Wood (who had established the camp for officer training at Plattsburgh, New York, to which many St. Mark's boys went, and who led all men in his eagerness to bring America into the War) sent a telegram urging Harry's schoolmates not to leave St. Mark's before the government's plans were announced. Most families believed their schoolboy sons were too young to go to battle, and urged them to enter college; the majority did their parents' bidding.

Harry was insistent, and while his mother and father failed to say yes to his pleas, neither did they say no. They saw the merit of his proposal, recognized his need to do something beyond the little he had so far done. And not just his "bit" for America, though they all wanted to serve their country well, no gentlemen would wish less. Harry wanted more, to test himself against death, to brush against it, maybe to outface it, or maybe even let it outface him. Why shouldn't he at least take a hand in writing his own timetable? Besides, if he hadn't won a letter in football, or hockey, or baseball, he could at least win his letter at war.

So St. Mark's students would often gather during Harry's time at the school to hear lectures from graduates recently returned from the war zones of Europe, or to see moving pictures of the American Flying Corps or the American Field Service Ambulance Corps. They would also assemble to listen to ghost stories told by one or another of the masters, and on an evening early in 1916 they sat at Robert Frost's feet in the library while he read "Mending Wall," "The Road Not Taken" and "The Death of the Hired Man."

Though Harry was remarkably alive to the poetry of his time, almost prophetically so, he never in his life referred to Robert Frost, or read him, so far as is known. Perhaps Frost, by "barding around" (as he so sweetly had it) with schoolmasters and their pupils, had cast his complicated, worthy self beyond Harry's poetical pale. Or more likely, given Harry's inclinations at the time Frost read at St. Mark's, the poet did not register on the boy. It is not surprising that Harry was indifferent to academic work, though he later satisfied the enormous appetite of his curiosity by studying, with discipline, such subjects as astronomy, anthropology, aesthetics, philosophy and architecture. He did not begin systematic work, however, till he was safely clear of his obligation to study at school. His utter lack of response to literature while he was at St. Mark's is, however, more curious. He used the *Rubáiyát* as he used the Bible, not for literary pleasure but for utility, as an instruction manual to fit conduct.

During the summer before his fourth-form year, Harry's collie died. His master buried him, and erected above his grave a stone, with a tribute cut into it:

> *EASY*
> *a faithful friend*
> *Born Feb. 13, 1903*
> *Died Aug. 14, 1914*

The loss moved Harry to write the only piece he submitted to *The Vindex* while he was at St. Mark's. It opens with "a heavy bank of dense fog . . . slowly drifting in over the long, crescent-shaped beach, enveloping all in its damp, grey shroud." Such fogs and such beaches— indeed, such envelopments—have done sturdy service for many a schoolboy's poetic or fictional installation, but in Harry's case the images were prophetic of his mature symbolic preoccupations, not to mention his lifelong seasonal preference. Breaking waves "fill the air with a weird, humming sound." The bizarre and fantastical presence, perceived before understood, plays on Coffin's Beach, that place so suggestive to Harry of childhood's freedom and, by its name, of death. Friend Seagull (has a beach yarn yet been spun without him?), "a lone seagull, flying somewhere in the mist utters raucous cries. . . . A mass of damp, slippery rocks suddenly confronts you, rising ghost-like on the sand. . . ." And what waits down the beach, beyond the mist and the ghostly, slippery rocks? A log cabin, with a cheerful fire in the hearth. And keeping *you* company all the while, a true ghost, summoned from his grave by his master's imagination, a collie dog, Easy, as good as alive for as long as the fiction lasts.

Why then was he not more interested in writing? It is true that excellence in athletics, in team athletics, was a certified way for a boy to make his name, and academic excellence was a possible way, but creative excellence was no way at all. Nevertheless, Harry had always been willing to navigate for himself, despite the wanderings of the fleet, so it cannot be that the fleet's low opinion of literature would have had a disruptive bearing on his own. He merely came to writing late, a course and schedule by no means unprecedented. By idling, and waiting for literature to take him unawares, Harry suffered the commonplace consequence of late conversion, a crippling intensity about his calling and an intolerance for those not yet delivered from illiteracy. Seven years after he left St. Mark's, Harry wrote his mother a letter so stiff and stilted, so foreign in tone to his own voice, that it seems to have come not from him at all, but from a malicious schoolboy masquerading as an eighty-year-old retired headmaster, senile, mumbling into the night's last glass of port. The letter's bona fide author, sowing wild oats all over Europe, scolds his old school:

> On rereading certain years of my life as set down in my autobiography this morning I see for the first time how at fault is the educational system in our private schools. It is wrong to standardize young boys and girls who are born of aristocratic parentage. . . . I cannot overemphasize that the literary tastes of the young at home are abominable, nor are the tastes of their fathers and mothers very superior. If ever I ran a school I should compel each pupil to read any one classic every week, to write a criticism of this classic, and furthermore to discuss this book with me personally. This classic reading is all important and other branches of literature as well as athletics should be subordinated to literature. . . . It would be a school which would develop the younger generation along ideals of thought, whereas more than three-fourths of our boys and girls receiving diplomas from private schools are colorless, standardized and commonplace morons. . . .

Gargantua and Pantagruel Harry's letter is not. Nor does it reflect an alternative to his own education. The fact was, Harry had had a mighty dose of the classics at school, force-fed, including, in French, a shot of Rabelais. He had read Macaulay, Defoe, Pope, Scott, Swift, Byron, Southey, Milton, Tennyson, Dickens, Addison, Chaucer, Spenser, Dryden, Browning, Wordsworth, Gray, Shakespeare and the author of a lasting impression, De Quincey.

Stephen Galatti, a graduate of St. Mark's with the class of 1906 and second in command of the American Ambulance Corps in France, appealed in the spring of 1916 to the school for a donation of a Ford ambulance, costing a thousand dollars. He noted in his letter to *The Vindex* that such ambulances, emblazoned with the name of the donating school, had already been given by Pomfret, St. Paul's, Middlesex and Andover. The students of St. Mark's immediately drummed up two thousand five hundred dollars and sent it to the Field Service of the American Ambulance, care of the Boston banking house Lee, Higginson & Co., for the purchase of two ambulances.

The head of the Ambulance Corps (familiarly called simply the Ambulance), A. Piatt Andrew, was a friend of Harry's mother and father, and when he wrote to thank the school he gave a teasing hint to the boys of high adventure waiting at the Front:

> Gifts of this kind are particularly welcome at the moment as a considerable number of our cars have been destroyed during the past few weeks. At the very moment, when we are hoping to enlarge our service in response to the invitation of the French Army, we've had 125 cars working in the vicinity of Verdun during the great battle, running up very close to the lines, and over roads pitted with shell holes and much encumbered by motor trucks and the whole paraphernalia of war, running for the most part in the obscurity of the night. This work has told heavily on our equipment. . . .

Mrs. Crosby was active in the American Field Service, which sponsored the Ambulance Corps, and her husband, feeling as he did about the Emperor Napoleon, and clamor, and manhood, sympathized with Harry's ambition to test himself under the gun. There had been talk for a couple of years by Teddy Roosevelt about raising his own private regiment, so Mr. Crosby wrote him on behalf of his son and Gardner Monks. Though he received an encouraging reply, the plan to take a club of gentlemen warriors into battle against The Hun washed out when President Wilson forbade the organization of private regiments.

Tote Fearing, who had been born in France and yearned to get into the thick and muddle of things there, wanted to enter the Lafayette Escadrille, but he was an only child, fighter pilots lived by short odds, and his parents thought it unfair for him to die and leave them alone—however little value he put on his own life. He struck a bargain with them, and they let him enlist in the Ambulance Corps. The Crosbys then let Harry, too, have his head, providing he stayed at St. Mark's through his sixth-form year and successfully completed his entrance examinations for Harvard before he left for war.

At graduation most of Harry's class, upon the urging of teachers and headmasters and parents and deans, entered Harvard. Harry hung around Manchester for a few weeks, practicing at the wheel of his

Studebaker and his father's Lancia, managing to worry his mother about drink and excess, looking through fated, doomed eyes into the eyes of quite a few young ladies, kissing most of them, flying high on dreams of high deeds. On July 6, with Tote Fearing and another classmate, Charles Merrill Chapin, Jr., he sailed from New York aboard the *Espagne* for Bordeaux, from monastery to combat, "from prison to prison," as he liked to say.

The *Espagne*, flying French colors, crossed in ten days. It was a hot passage, troubled by greasy ground swells in the Gulf Stream, and the liner, with seven hundred passengers, lay too low in the water. Harry's stateroom, which he shared with three other volunteers, was cramped and stuffy, and its porthole had been sealed and blackened to hide light from the periscopes of German submarines. He preferred to sleep on deck, and so did most of the other two hundred Field Service volunteers bound for the war.

A newsclipping from a Boston paper reported that Harry would be the youngest ambulance driver in France, but this was not true: at nineteen he was a year older than the minimum age required for enlistment in the Corps. Volunteers were expected to know how to drive and repair cars; they were obliged to buy their own uniforms and to pay for their transportation to Bordeaux and Paris, eighty-five dollars going and, with luck, eighty-five coming home.

Crossing with Harry and Tote Fearing and three other St. Mark's boys was Stuart Kaiser, a Harvard senior Harry had met the summer before at training camp in Plattsburgh. Kaiser was wise and quick, and wore a face like Eeyore's, speaking with resignation and incapable of dissembling—except at poker and bridge, at which he was a shark. Ted Weeks was another card player, a merry, pocket-sized fellow who had recently survived an untimely but amicable divorce from Cornell University. Like Harry, like Tote and Stuart, he was on the hunt for adventure and distinction, both of which had eluded him at home. He was energetic, eager, and quick to take the drift of things. He was a gentleman, and Harry liked him, and captured his affection utterly and at once.

To this day Edward Weeks, who later became editor of *The Atlantic Monthly*, can recall his first sight of Harry: tall, with light hair which he did not part in the middle, according to the fashion of the day, but cut short in some streamlined manner singular to him, perfectly fitting him. Weeks remembers Harry's skin, how clean it looked, its luster and quick blush. And Harry's mouth, curling quickly from a pout to a winning smile, and back if something displeased him. He was struck by Harry's Boston accent, and his French, almost as fluent as Fearing's, which he used to joke with waiters or with French officers returning to the war from promotional missions in Washington and New York.

Also aboard were Harry's cousin Betty Beal and her mother, bound for London, where Boylston Beal, Uncle Bob, had been posted at the embassy. A gushy lady named Virginia Lee, writing "From Somewhere at Sea" for the August, 1917, *Town & Country*, described the play from her own peculiar vantage: "Very jaunty were the débutantes and superdébutantes; very excited most of the painfully youthful 'Field Service-ers' and ambulance drivers; very apart Mrs. Boylston Beal and her daughter. . . . We have every sort and condition of man and woman in the crowd on board; brides, fiancées, divorcées, widows and girls who are ripe to be any of these."

Harry flirted, and necked in the lifeboats, but he guarded himself. If he did not treasure his virginity, he nevertheless protected it—across the ocean, through the war, during many leaves in Paris, back across the ocean—and regretted his lost pleasure forever after. Ted Weeks recalls his own private vow "not to lose his cherry." And Stuart Kaiser endured a similarly chaste history; in his diary he moaned and laughed at himself, at his bad luck, or the will-o'-the-wisp of manly priggishness that afflicted him and his comrades. One night, Kaiser noted, Harry discovered a boy and girl busy in a lifeboat, and admonished them to be good. "Why should I?" the girl asked.

During the month before the *Espagne* sailed, several troopships and a hospital ship had been torpedoed, with terrible and much publicized loss of life. Now the passengers were jittery, and jumped at people careless enough to light cigarettes on deck at night, and searched the horizons. The third day out, there was a submarine scare when a lookout spotted something that resembled a conning tower with a flag flying from it. Kaiser wrote in his diary of waiting for the torpedo that didn't come, and from that moment till he was safely home he continued to wait for it.

Rumors flourished, and died young. Someone heard that an important man was locked in a stateroom, another that the *Espagne* was in convoy with troopships, another that she was a decoy to divert ships from troopships. It was told that she was laden with explosives, or inestimable gold, that the Germans would spare nothing to bag her. It was told on good authority that a *very* important man was locked in his stateroom. (Yes, we heard). But have you heard who he is? (Who is he?) The German ambassador, being returned in exchange for an important American. (What can it mean?) The Germans won't want to sink us. (Won't they?) Past mid-Atlantic everyone's nerves had been badly chafed; Harry was warned rudely by a sailor to leave off wearing his radium-faced wrist watch on deck at night; its glow might be noticed by the enemy below.

The *Town & Country* lady offered a melodramatized version of the mood eight days out from New York:

> The ship moves patiently on. She knows nothing of what the night holds. We know nothing. It seems that danger lurks all about us in the waste of water, each phosphorescent wave of which may spew up our death. What is slipping along under the sea's surface slowly making ready to destroy or maim each person of us and plunge to her grave the ship? Each wave may know; we do not. . . . There are giggling, jerking bursts of laughter out of the black shadow; there is a spasmodic attempt to sing some college songs; it fades and dies. There are sullen, quiet figures waiting for they don't know what, immovable upon the uncomfortable chairs; there are nervous-moving talking men, and silent, shivering, nervous women. There are careless persons of either sex who have ordained to stifle thought with drink, poor careless persons!

In fact, Harry and his comrades passed time by looking astern, at their boyhoods back there. Tugger Fay, a year ahead of Harry at St. Mark's, and a great athlete, wondered how the school would do a season hence against Groton. Harry talked with Betty Beal about his girl friends on the North Shore, his "Janes," and he wondered whether any would wait for him, and whether any of them cared for him as much as they said. And Betty teased him, and they traded gossip about innocent scandals at coming-out parties. London had been bombed from the air two days before they sailed, and fifty-seven had died, but she knew better than to speak aloud of her anxiety. Cole Porter was aboard with a contingent from Yale who were everywhere, singing his wised-up songs, playing the piano, or a kind of zither rigged up with a keyboard. There was a lecture by someone Kaiser called "Scudder of Yale" (pronounced as though the three words were one) to Field Service volunteers on the subject of disorderly conduct.

The last night out is usually raucous. But that night on the *Espagne* was not. The French coast was near. Passengers were barred from their staterooms and made to sit on deck wearing life jackets, ready to take to the jolly boats. There was little drinking, or card playing, or loving, or talk. At first light, July 19, the *Espagne* worked into the mouth of the Gironde, clotted with vessels building up courage to go out to sea. Presently she was tied to France, and Harry, though he didn't know it then, cast off Boston forever.

4

"... horrible, terrorstricken fright, until of a sudden the
gloriousness of the thing struck me and I threw back my
head and sang. ..."

—Harry Crosby's *Diary*

Mr. and Mrs. Crosby had taken Harry to Bordeaux during a European
trip the summer of 1912, and now, writing his first letter home the day
after he arrived in France, he began at once to lead them to sights and
circumstances more amazing than any they had shown him. The streets
were clogged with soldiers and heavy weapons. He imagined all single
women to be widows. He noticed a Moroccan rifleman dressed in red
trousers with "a blue bandana wound round his waist and with his head
covered by a red fez with the half moon engraved in gold."

Throughout his twenty months abroad, Harry wrote hundreds of
letters and kept a diary, which was evidently lost or destroyed. He was
meticulous in his inventory of such details as that "half moon engraved
in gold"; he kept track of precise times and sequences, and listed in his
letters such placenames and statistics as the censor would allow. From
his first letter home he began to function as a writer, as though things
could have no substance unless they were written down, just so, as
though he would pass unnoticed unless he took events by the tail as
they passed him, and caged them in words. The idiom he selected was
exact rather than fanciful, the language of history rather than poetry—
at least in the beginning.

With Fearing and Weeks and Kaiser he shared a cramped train

compartment, and a sleepless, clamorous trip to Paris—the second in his life by third class, the first having been his crossing on the *Espagne*. His excitement and curiosity were high, and when a Belgian trooper entrained somewhere along the route, Harry quizzed him about his experiences and asked whether he knew firsthand of war atrocities. The Belgian told him that he had seen Germans advance using women and children as a shield against enemy fire: "He also saw them cut off the hands of children at the wrists. How he hated the 'Boches'!" For a couple of months after arriving in France, Harry went in heavily for this kind of thing, wearing fright masks picked up secondhand to terrify his parents and raise the temperature of his own blood. Later, after he had carried buckets filled with amputated human pieces, he learned to husband his most morbid battle yarns, to write about carnage only when he had in fact seen it, from up close, and to write about it precisely, coldly, as though from a great distance.

Of all that the friends saw their first day and night in France, nothing touched their interest as much as military decorations: "I must have seen over fifty men who had the 'Croix de Guerre' and quite a few who had the highly valued 'Légion d'Honneur.' A few sported the 'Médaille Militaire.' " This last was the best of all, and beyond Harry's dreams. But the Croix de Guerre was not, and he meant to win one.

A. Piatt Andrew had a Croix de Guerre *and* the Médaille Militaire. Col. Andrew welcomed the volunteers at American Field Service Headquarters in suburban Paris, at 21 rue Raynouard. "Old 21" was a château set at the top of the hill of Passy, in a five-acre park. The château had been loaned to the Field Service by the Comtesse de la Villetreux, and served volunteers as a mail drop and clubhouse when they were back from the Front; it looked down past terraces and formal gardens, through huge chestnut trees, to the bank of the Seine.

Andrew had been a professor of political economy at Harvard before he founded the volunteer ambulance and transport sections in 1915. The war had worn him out and the strain showed, but he spoke to the new recruits as though he had not given the same speech dozens of times before and his manner was cordial if grave: he wished to treat the volunteers decently, but not at the cost of failing to serve France. At his discretion, drivers were assigned either to trucks or to ambulances. Within a few months of Harry's arrival, the Field Service camions had carried more ammunition than would be used by the entire American Expeditionary Forces during World War I, but to the volunteers trucks were considerably lower in prestige than ambulances.

Half a million wounded had been driven from the trenches to dressing stations and field hospitals in Field Service Fords and Fiats. Because the work was even more hazardous than truckdriving, it was more desired.

Col. Andrew promised that assignments would be made within a couple of days, and explained that the volunteers would have the rank of *aspirants*, which put them above enlisted men and below noncommissioned officers. In return for their work they would receive a nickel a day and a generous ration of miserably offensive red wine. He warned them against getting into public mischief in Paris.

As soon as they had been sworn in, Harry and Stuart Kaiser registered at the Crillon, which was perhaps not the class of lodging that Col. Andrew had in mind when he told the volunteers they could expect to spend fifteen dollars per month for their incidental expenses. A few days later they learned from Steve Galatti, the St. Mark's graduate who served as the Colonel's second-in-command, that strings had been pulled and that Crosby and Fearing would be together in a section of ambulances, and that Kaiser and Weeks would join them. Each section consisted of twenty-five ambulances, and there were seventy-one sections. Harry and his friends were assigned to the seventy-first, which they immediately called "The Cootie Section."

They took tea at Rumpelmayer's that afternoon, and Harry and Fearing treated the others to dinner at the Café de Paris. Later, they celebrated their deliverance from mere truckdriving at the Folies-Bergère, which bored Kaiser and mystified Weeks, who could not comprehend the argot spoken onstage and felt like a greenhorn among officers on leave from the rigors of trench life. Harry and Fearing were relaxed, and Harry bantered with the bar girls, who looked, in Weeks's disapproving phrase, "so used." Next morning, they left for a training camp twenty miles north of Paris.

It was quickly discovered that Weeks had bluffed his way into the Field Service, that he couldn't drive worth a damn. The motor skills required to cause a Model T to move from place to place were none he possessed, and he turned to Fearing and Harry for help. Both drove well, so well that Fearing was temporarily promoted to the rank of instructor and Harry was exempted from driver training. He had quick reflexes, and could tease a reluctant engine to life, sweet-talking or threatening while he cranked. From the time he had begun to drive, during the summer of 1914, he had driven recklessly. Gardner Monks tells of a time when Harry drove him to St. Mark's in the family Lancia: "He delighted in scaring the daylights out of me by driving fast, and shaving some pedestrians whom he didn't like as close as he dared."*

They were in training only a week, but during that short time Harry managed to find himself a girl friend. He wrote Kitsa about her: "Did I tell you of the cunning Belgian Jane who kissed me and gave me her only ring? She is very nice and of a *highly respectable* family. . . . Of course, I have fallen hard. She has promised to write me at the Front. You ought to hear your brother 'tutoyer.' Some class. She is *pure, innocent* and talented. Plays the violin." If the letter was meant to alarm his parents, it did. In fact, the girl was a beet digger Harry had met while he was swimming naked in a canal, and after writing Kitsa of his infatuation he never mentioned her again.

When training ended July 28, Harry's request that he have Ted Weeks as his co-driver was granted, and Weeks was grateful that he'd learn to drive from someone as patient and gifted as Harry. Section 71 was bound for the Somme Sector of the Front, the scene of "the Great Fuck-up," in which 70,000 of the 110,000-man British attack force were slaughtered on the morning of July 1, 1916. The volunteers passed through Paris, picking up Lt. Roland Speers, their commander, a twenty-three-year-old Stanford graduate whom they took to at once. The following morning, hung over, they joined the French Army's 158th Infantry Division, which had recently lost a thousand men in the battle at Chemin des Dames.

The division was exhausted, *en repos*, and right away Harry learned the miseries of hanging around camp, waiting for something to happen. He visited with French officers and enlisted men; he collected horror stories, and retailed them at home. He waited for letters, and got more of them than anyone in his section—from girl friends, from Boston pals and almost every delivery, from his mother—and replied by return of mail. He was sent the Boston papers, got them many weeks late, and read them as though they held the secret of eternal youth. He would even read the fine print advertising a Jordan Marsh furniture sale, months after the event.

One day, to break the monotony, Harry organized a soccer match between the Americans and the French, who won easily. Ted Weeks remembers Harry's energy and stamina, the easy way he ran during the match, his elbows close to his body, shouting encouragement: *Come*

---

* In one of his holograph notebooks, at Southern Illinois University, Harry refers elliptically to the time "a boy jumped directly in front of our car—within four days a satisfactory settlement was made." The entry was written in 1928, about his St. Mark's years, but it is not known who was driving "our car."

on, you rodents! (He ran almost every one of those dog days, long runs to somewhere; his friends usually let him run alone.)

The Fords had been light and nimble, if unforgiving, but now the section was issued new Fiats, heavier, harder to crank, with solid iron wheels, sturdier transmissions and better brakes. They lumbered into headwinds and sank deep into mud. And Harry and his friends passed time learning what could be made of the monsters. They taught themselves to hang hammocks in the stretcher compartments, where they could sleep protected from the mud and rats that plagued them in their tents. They shaved in hot water drawn from the radiators. They tinkered with the Fiats' engines, and sunned themselves on their roofs, the few days the sun shone.

Fearing tells of a wild night following a frustrating, empty day. Members of the section began an impromptu road race: "It was really a pretty even thing till Harry and the others started driving on the sidewalks with their sirens going full tilt. Out of twelve cars I think seven arrived at our destination, more or less together. And the others, with inferior driving ability or luck, were strewn in ditches along the way...."

Harry was reading two or three chapters a day of the New Testament, which he at first preferred to the Old, and began a lifelong habit of writing his mother to tell her where in the Good Book he was, so that she could read along with him. He had even taken to singing hymns to himself, and his favorite *mirabile dictu*, was the St. Mark's anthem, "Sun of My Soul." He went to church whenever he could get free of a Sunday, and on that day his thoughts would run home: "I can imagine you as clear as day sitting in church listening to Rev. Carey preaching when it is 4 p.m. here."

One afternoon Harry and a friend went walking and came upon a church that had been blown apart by a German shell.

> The wooden pews were smashed to atoms. Fine looking marble pillars lay in pieces on the floor. The pulpit was filled with bullets. The altar was a heap of ruins. Bibles and psalm books were strewn about on the floor. One nice painting had been ripped out of its frame and then left to rot away. The only thing left untouched was a beautiful statue of Christ, just behind the altar. His hands were out-stretched in such a fashion that he seemed to say to the congregation: "Look and see what the Germans have done to my temple."

Jesus in simulacrum, miraculously spared, is a chestnut, one of the staples of Christian soldiery. The letter is fascinating not because of its

workaday piety and jingoism, but because of the way its author warms
to the task of describing sacrilege. If there was one thing Harry learned
to love more than the sacred, it was the sacred in ruins.

Life at war was deliciously low-down, even behind the lines. Harry
ate his meals, sometimes of horsemeat, with a knife, moreover one that
had "killed two Germans." The young gentlemen blew away time
hunting rats with pitchforks and baseball bats, or cleaning their ambulances, greasing them and changing tires, or beating back cooties with a
powder called "knock 'em stiff." He found a kitten and gave *it* fleas;
likewise a dog, Bohunk. (Harrison's lice pomade was a specific against
other vermin.) Most of the time, even at the Front, was wasted preparing for inspections, or boozing, or scrounging for food they never
found. Kaiser grew a mustache. Harry had a "convict cut," so close to
the scalp that at first his friends didn't recognize him. When it began to
grow cold at night, he looked to his comfort, and hugged the wood
stove in their tent. One Saturday, Kaiser wrote in his diary that Crosby
appeared "in the most wonderful costume ever beheld by mortal man.
Among other things he wore 4 layers of socks, wooden shoes, countless
layers of clothes with a pongee pyjama coat on the outside of all, a red
cigarette holder, and a cap. He went to sleep with everything that he
possessed on top of him, including one pie plate and one frying pan."
He liked to smoke gold-tipped Shepheards.

Other volunteers called their tent "The House of Lords." Harry
gave his mother a group portrait:

> First there's May, the camp dude, who appears in a new turnout al-
> most daily. His best effort is his regalia composed of a tam o'shanter
> "capote" tilted at a rakish angle, à la New York débutante, over one
> eye, an English sport military coat, very chic and racy looking, but
> utterly useless as far as warmth or protection is concerned, with a
> leather belt outside, and with a cigarette (he is never without one)
> dangling nonchalantly from his mouth. . . . Then there's Brother Block
> from Arizona or some western state nearby, who's over here to spend
> his "jack" as he terms his wealth, and to get a good idea of the country
> here in general. . . . Rogers, another Western sketch . . . is a great lover
> of the Champ Agony bottle, as are most Westerners, so I have found,
> but there isn't much drifting round here, and at $1 a bottle!!! . . . Phelan,
> before coming over, was a master in some N.Y. Kindergarten, and
> looks the part. Lewis, his driving partner, is one of these fellows who
> has gone a little daffy over "Blighty," as he expresses it. He wears Eng-
> lish clothes, smokes English coffin-nails, and is actually commencing to
> use an English accent. . . . Moran and Bliss are a pair! They are the

naughty boys of S.S.U.–71 and I'm afraid they went astray in gay Paree. Samuels, the camp Yid, inherits the customs and manners of his race. I believe that he was a hack driver in N.Y. before joining the service. He is one of those scouts who talks out of the side of his mouth, à la Bowery, in this wise "Aw, quit yer kidden" or "Sling over the jack." Some boy! Paul Weingartner is another boy of Jewish propensities, but he's all right. He comes from the University of Pennsylvania and belongs to some prominent Jewish fraternity there."

He appears to have felt no embarrassment writing about Jews in this manner to his kind and gentle and tolerant Christian mother. In fact, he wrote her again, two weeks later, suggesting that she and Mr. Crosby make every effort to secure a copy of the latest *American Magazine*, which offered its readers a nasty little fable called "Pearls before Klein," whose racial vulgarities had much amused him. Despite their safety behind walls of social exclusion that had not yet begun to tremble, let alone fall, Boston's best people were as quick to bait the Jews as was any vulgar bigot. Harry, true to the stereotypical form in these matters, numbered many Jews among his closest friends at war and later (though not all of them announced their racial heritage), and a charitable judge might fairly conclude that his apparent contempt for the "camp Yid" carried less conviction than his innocent affection for almost everyone else, that it was a casual expression of received habits of dismissal and discrimination. A few days before the above letter was written to his mother, another was sent to his father: "Over here you learn a lot. Above all, democracy. It would be impossible to ever be snobbish in any way after living here. There are some scouts that I have met who probably don't earn more than ten or fifteen cents a day who are the straightest, finest cleanest specimens of men I've ever known." The way was labyrinthine through the social and pietistic standards he had had pressed upon him since childhood. It is no great wonder that he lost his way in Boston, and lost his will to find it.

Harry carried his first wounded soldier August 8, one month less a day since he had sailed from New York, six weeks after Prize Day at St. Mark's. He drove, while Ted Weeks tried to comfort the soldier, holding his torn leg so that it wouldn't bang against the stretcher's frame while the Fiat bucked and pitched around huge shell holes scooped out of the muddy road. Weeks recollects watching the man bleed through his bandages, and there began that night a routine that would repeat itself throughout Harry's war, at St.-Quentin and Verdun, in the Argonne sector and at St.-Mihiel. The wounded would lie in the back, beating their fists against the metal sides of the compartment, screaming *Doucement, doucement!* as though the ambulance by going any slower could reduce their misery. Sometimes, if they were hurt very badly, they'd beg anyone within hearing to shoot them.

"You were always aware of the suffering," Ted Weeks remembers. "Really, I think the suffering was worse than the death. The carrying of the wounded was absolutely traumatic. Now, it's a series of dreams . . . those lurching black nights. . . ." Usually, the wounded were evacuated under cover of darkness after night patrols had brought them back from the battlefield to heavily fortified underground dressing stations, called *abris*. From there the ambulances, running without lights, would take them to hospitals; the driver's orderly was often obliged to walk in front of the ambulance with a white handkerchief on his shoulder, leading the way around shell craters.

The Germans zeroed in on crossroads, and when the shells came down the wounded would scream in terror, and scream again when the French replied. Sometimes the concussion from a nearby impact, or from a mighty French 75, would stall Harry's ambulance. He'd curse, his wretched cargo would plead for deliverance, he'd crank the damned engine till it started again, or didn't. The German artillery impressed him. He wrote his father that from far off they sounded like trolley cars tearing out of the subway by Arlington Street: "Then they sort of screech—followed by a boom like dropping two huge iron plates together. . . . Suddenly a battery of 75s started barking in a salvo. They sound like the cracking of a great whip—short, snappy, and with a punch to them." Anyone nearby had to remember to hold open his mouth, lest his eardrum be shattered by the insane noise.

St.-Quentin was quieter than any sector where Harry later served, but he broke himself into service with a full portion of terror and gore. Most nights Harry and Weeks were obliged to make only a single ten-kilometer run from the Front to a hospital, and sometimes back. (At Verdun, however, he drove eight, nine, eleven, fourteen, *seventy* hours without relief.) They'd carry three stretcher cases in the Fiat, and as many as eight walking wounded who sat squeezed beside the driver or hung from the running boards. If a wounded man seemed likely to die, a priest would accompany him—if he was an officer.

There were frequent collisions that early autumn, especially with horse-drawn munitions wagons. Harry was near-sighted, and when his fear overcame his vanity he wore eyeglasses, but the ambulances had no windshields and in the downpours of August and September and October he frequently drove blind, or gave the wheel to Ted Weeks. Then

Harry would talk to the broken soldiers, and cushion their heads, and worry about whether he was as brave as they had been.

His descriptions of the wounded in his letters home began vividly, with anatomical detail:

> I saw the most gruesome sight I've ever seen. Lying on a blood-stained brancard was a man—not older than twenty I afterwards ascertained—suffering the agonies of hell. His whole right cheek was completely shot away so you could see all the insides of his face. He had no jaws, teeth, or lips left. His nose was plastered in. Blood was streaming all over. Under his eyes the skin was just dead blue. . . . It took us an hour driving between two or three miles per hour to get him to his destination. Of course he couldn't yell as his mouth or what was left of it was a mere mass of pulp. For a while I was afraid our ambulance was to be turned into a hearse, but he was still alive when we got him there. Of course in typical French fashion the doctors held their usual debate of questioning whether it was the right hospital or where his papers were.

According to Ted Weeks, Harry successfully frightened them into accepting the wounded man for treatment. The man then died, immediately, and the episode provoked from Harry an outburst of jingoism: "In America the man would have been on the operating table within a minute after his arrival but in this rotten country they had to hold their usual delayed 'toute de suite' conference. . . . I suppose it's too much to ask of them to come out of their dream and show some 'pep.' Well, thank God I'm an American. I'm prouder of it every day. So is everyone else here."

Each day presented some mutilated caricature of humankind worse than yesterday's worst, more gruesome than "the most gruesome sight I've ever seen," till the blood clotted the arteries of Harry's observation and response, and he left off sending home anatomy lessons.

The drivers and orderlies frequently slept at the Front, or tried to sleep, on stretchers stacked like berths on a Pullman, deep down in an *abri*. The stink beneath the mud was awful, and it was so cold that in midsummer a man could see his breath, and the dampness leaked in everywhere. The trenches were lit by kerosene lamps and candles. And by such uncertain illumination Harry wrote home, wishing the Red Sox well, begging for news about coming-out parties and tennis tournaments and girl friends. He put a brave face on his life at war, and worried whether it was hard enough to suit his father, and to make certain that it was hard enough to suit him, and risky enough, he began to embark on hazardous and unnecessary adventures with the men he met in the *abris*.

Once he went into no man's land with a French infantry captain willing to satisfy Harry's wish to "go over the top," as they said. The captain quite understood: it wouldn't have done to leave the war without having been fired upon at close range. The German lines were two hundred yards away, a star shell lit the night sky, machine-gun bullets whined above Harry's butt, he escaped with his short life, and wrote home at once, proudly confessing his daredeviltry.

He idolized the pilots, everyone did; he would never forget lying on his back on the hood of his Fiat, watching them duel. They began about nine o'clock on a clear night, and he heard them "way off in the distance sounding like a small motorboat." They used port and starboard running lights, and searchlights. These resembled shooting stars as the planes rose and fell and banked, and Harry watched them flicker till he fell asleep with a far-off drone installed for good in his dreams: "When I awoke there were twelve just above us, flying at a dazzling speed. . . . Presently eleven more planes, looking like moths around a candlelight, flew by, their immaculate machines glittering in the rays of the morning sun."

He wouldn't rest till he had flown like them, putting his life at hazard to something not unlike magic, the power to defy natural law, to break free of gravity at will. He would have tried to transfer at once, save for his weak eyes. Instead, he charmed a pilot into taking him up.

The pilot was a peacock, blond, dressed all in black with a silver scarf; pilots could wear whatever they wished. Harry gave him champagne, and asked questions. When a matter touched his curiosity, his appetite for detail was relentless: he wanted to know what powered the plane, how it was maneuvered, what was its fire power, how fast, how high, would it climb, what was its range . . . The pilot surrendered, and Harry wrote home the same day: "I got nearer to heaven than I've ever done before." Five minutes aloft, above the trenches, and then "we swung round; the sun striking us broadsides and an exhilarating breeze, seemingly blowing your head off. . . ."

At the end of August, 1917, about four months after Congress declared war on Germany, news arrived that the United States Army would soon absorb the American Field Service ambulance and transport sections. Volunteers were offered a simple choice: to sign on as privates in the American army (at thirty-five dollars per month) for the duration of the war, or return home. The young gentlemen in "The House of Lords" did not care for the prospect of being translated into common soldiers, or having to wear G.I. issue. They would not be allowed to fraternize with officers, their social equals—some of them—in the U.S. Army. Kaiser and Weeks decided at once to sign on with the Army, however. Weeks recalls that Harry, "who had been crabbing at the food, the French, and the weather, said he'd be goddamned if he'd join." Fearing agreed with him. Both were influenced by Lt. Speers, who urged them to go home and begin at Harvard.

But on September 21 Kaiser noted in his diary: "Fearing and Crosby depart for Paris to join the U.S. Army. Crosby had sworn never to do so. Oh-well. . . ." The decision was not so casual as Kaiser made it seem, nor was it to have a casual influence on Harry's history and character. In an autobiographical narrative he composed after the war, he recollected the dilemma:

> I was young and inexperienced and dreadfully forlorn, and my judgment was swayed to the point of resigning by homesickness. Fortunately, some strong influence that I might have acquired by reading the Bible and praying daily to God came to my aid, and brought it about that in this quandry of indecision I was able to reject the inglorious alternative of going home, and accept the honorable *devoir* of enlisting as a private. Woe to me had I not, for it would have meant a life of failure and disappointment. And I thank God for saving me from the dishonour I so narrowly escaped.

As Harry and his chums never tired of repeating, there would be only two classes of men in America after the war: those who went, and those who did not. Even today, some of Harry's childhood friends and schoolmates feel obliged to justify having stayed at home; they had no brothers and sisters, so their parents refused to let them go, or they were certain the war would not have ended by the time they had finished up at Harvard, they meant to serve, later, really. Harry was infuriated when Brooks Fenno, his St. Mark's roommate and tennis partner, wrote and asked, "Is War really so terrible and cruel as one is led to suppose?" Harry instructed his mother to "tell him to come over and see. Then, I think, he'll be 'led to suppose' it's hell. He also states that in one week he'd been to five dances, two dinners, and various other fetching parties." Tote Fearing remembers the letter, and Harry's violent reaction to it: "We hadn't had a bath for two or three months, and we were crawling with fleas, and Harry's profanity was something else. . . ."

Harry never forgot Fenno's question about war, and later dreamt that the brain of his former friend was fuzzy and round and white, like a tennis ball. Of a couple of other boyhood pals, spending the summer at Manchester, Harry wrote his mother that "they ought to be ashamed of themselves." And after he enlisted in the Army Ambulance Corps, he wrote home that "it is time for us to come out of our dreams and get into the game," that the "lounge lizards of the Back Bay" were shirkers.

At the end of October, Section 71 gave up its Fiats, again took over Fords and left for Verdun, where it regrouped as Section 29, attached to the 120th French Division. Ted Weeks left for another group, also at Verdun. The Fords were usually sent out without co-drivers.

Harry arrived November 3 at the place where a year before the Germans had taken more than three hundred and thirty thousand casualties, and the French about twenty thousand more than the Germans. Nothing had been settled, both sides had been bled white, but the French had plucked from the carnage a nourishing motto—*ils ne passeront pas*—and it had sustained them, had been picked up and broadcast around the world as a call to arms. A poem by an otherwise unrecollected English versifier named Harold Begbie was clipped and pasted in Stuart Kaiser's diary to remind him of the legend of the First Battle of Verdun:

> *She is a wall of brass:*
> *You shall not pass! You shall not pass!*
> *Spring up like Summer grass,*
> *Surge at her, mass on mass,*
> *Still shall you break like glass,*
> *Splinter and break like shivered glass,*
> > *But pass?*
> *You shall not pass!*
> *German, you shall not pass!*
> *God's hand has written on the wall of brass—*
> *You shall not pass! You shall not pass!*

So bracing the motto, so stirring the memory, that it inspired a Second Battle of Verdun, which began as Harry arrived. He wrote his father about the approaches to the Front the evening he drove in:

> Here we are at Verdun, the most famous place in the history of the World. . . . As far as I could see was a long line of huge camions,

troops on the march, huge 280 cannons, ammunition trains, *ravitaille-ment* wagons, kitchen carts, and racy staff cars. Way back for miles and miles this seemingly endless column stretched till it dwindled completely out of sight on the horizon. . . . Aviation hangars, vast motor parks, artillery barracks, dug-outs, every conceivable shelter. Everything was camouflaged—from tiny staff cars to the huge caterpillar-wheeled motor tractors dragging immense cannon. . . . Mud-bespattered dispatch riders, tearing staff cars, rattling artillery trains rush along these roads. This is War all right. I've never been so impressed in all my life. . . . There's a ravine near here twenty kilometers wide and ten deep where the Crown Prince lost 300,000 men. There isn't a square yard that isn't pockmarked with shell craters. The Valley of Death I should call it. It is thrilling living amidst such surroundings and taking an active part in events that are making history. . . .

The work at the Front was gruesome and exhausting. Salvos from the French batteries would "almost blow you out of your seat," and they continued without respite for forty days. The sky above that boneyard was like lead, the mud oozed or froze, there was no end to gore and terror, nor to valor. John Dos Passos was there, and for years after saw in night-visions a distorted sun falling into blackness: "In a dream in Verdun as I looked the sun was filmed over like a bloodshot eye and began to sway and wobble in the sky as a spent top sways and wobbles and whirling rolled into the sea's vermillion ways so that pitchblackness covered me."

Tote Fearing sums up the experience as "pure terror. Verdun was very rough. I think anybody who has sensitivity and imagination isn't particularly afraid of being killed, but they are afraid of being hurt, and we ambulance drivers were alone always, at least in our Fords. Cowards could always smash a spark plug and say their car wouldn't run, and others, with a sense of duty, would take their places." About a year after Verdun, Fearing lost half his lung in the Argonne Forest and returned to his section despite his right to return home: "I was scared perfectly pissless. But that didn't stop you doing what you were supposed to do."

The Fords were fragile: "They have papier-mâché sides behind which I should hate to be when the éclat is coming," Stuart Kaiser wrote, as soon as he took charge of his. In a period of forty-eight hours, six cars from Harry's section were smashed. Ted Weeks, attached to a nearby section, remembers: "We were all scared: it was very dangerous business to come and go. You were on duty hour upon hour without relief, and you had to go down the road in the full throat of the Germans, and they could see every damned thing, especially if you kicked up dust, even if you didn't kick up dust. It was grim."

Harry wrote home on November 11, to his sister, that on that day "we carried more wounded for the length of time we worked (from 7 a.m. till 4 p.m.) than have ever been carried by any American Field Service section." (Two hundred and sixty-five, according to Kaiser's count, and it was common for at least one of the three stretcher cases to be delivered dead, according to Weeks.) Harry continued: "Wouldn't I love to get what they call a *blighty*, that is, not a very serious wound but one that would let you get home to the States. . . ."

Shortly thereafter, November 22, a Thursday, came the trial whose anniversary he would never neglect to note, the most important day of his life, his first death-day. November 22, 1927, he wrote his mother from Paris: "Ten years ago today on the hills of Verdun and the red sun setting back of the hills and the River Meuse and the black shells spouting up in columns and the roar of the barrage and Spud was wounded and the ride down and the metamorphose from boy into man on November 22, 1917 I shall never never forget. . . ."

He and Way Spaulding, a childhood friend from Haverhill, Massachusetts, and another old friend, Ben Weeden, had been ferrying many casualties between the dressing station at the Front, a post near Bras called Haudremont, and a field hospital several hilly miles away. The Second Battle of Verdun had officially begun two days before, and it gave every promise of being as bloody as the First. The Fords bucked and pitched on the hills, and punished the wounded when their drivers tried to shove them into a lower gear; when the gear gripped, the ambulance would shudder; when it didn't, the drivers would back down and try again.

Harry was returning to Haudremont under ferocious shelling, alone in his ambulance, No. 741. He hit a dangerous stretch, and big shells started coming in, sending up geysers of debris and foul mud, and a terrible stink, what the soldiers called "mackabby," from the French *macabre*, deathlike. Dead horses lay everywhere, and overturned wagons, debris of every sort. A huge hole was cut into the torn earth forty yards to Harry's right as he ground up the last hill to the dressing station. He arrived, took on wounded, and began to turn his Ford around when it stalled. Spud Spaulding's ambulance was just behind Harry's, and as he stood at the mouth of the *abri* laughing at his friend's shaky exhibition of driving, a shell burst ten yards from Harry, who dove to the floor of his ambulance, saving his life. "There was a deafening explosion and then flying rocks, éclats, mud, everything in sight shot past us." His ambulance was vaporized: nothing of 741 remained after the explosion except a few spare parts and a young man's untouched body and gravely injured imagination.

Spaulding had been hit by shrapnel; his chest was torn open just above the heart. "I saw a couple of Frenchmen lifting him in and laying him on the operating table." As soon as he had been temporarily patched up, Harry and Ben Weeden volunteered to drive him down the hill to the hospital, together with two other wounded men. Weeden drove, and Harry comforted his friend, who had been shot full of morphine. The Ford stalled behind a truck, and then the shells started coming in again, and Harry got out and pushed his miserable cargo up hill. "Spud got it again, an éclat passing through the brass name-plate on the car." Harry and Ben began to sing, terrible noise at full volume, "I Never Raised My Boy to Be a Soldier" and "America, Here's My Boy." They made it safely, and Spaulding survived, after six months in the hospital, three listed as "critical."

Everyone agreed that Harry's deliverance was miraculous. Kaiser said so, noting that "he was sitting in the only place in the car that wasn't touched, and only a yard from Spaulding." Ted Weeks came back sun-tanned from leave in Villefranche two days after the episode and visited Section 29, finding Harry more "nervous" than he had ever seen him. Harry was wearing sabots—heavy wooden clogs—and a thick sheepskin coat. The shell had "by some miracle" left him unharmed. A friend looked at the backboard against which Harry should have been leaning, ventilated across its width by shrapnel, and called out, *Jee-sus!*

As Harry, too, in different voice, had called out His name. Harry believed that God had delivered him. "God: A gray-golden light in a sky dark-gray. . . . Then Hell's Corner, a sharp climb to the dugout entrance, and a friend frantically beckoning.—Thrrr-ump, an arrivée exploded. Dense swirling smoke, the acrid smell of powder, and the limp body of my friend. The operating table, a surgeon, morphine, and the boy's face ashen-pale. A coarse candle stuck in a bottle. 'He must be taken down to the hospital.' 'Let me,' I said, 'afraid to be afraid.' . . . I took an oath that should I escape from this peril I would ever after lead a virtuous, uncomplaining life." He led no such life, but he believed, for a long time, that he should; because he believed he had died, and been reborn, re-created by God's merciful hand. "God only knows why the shell didn't hit me," he wrote Kitsa, "and now right here I want to tell you that faith in God is the most powerful factor in the entire world. Strange coincidence, I was reading the Bible yesterday morning and I noticed a passage (Romans X, 13: 'Whosoever shall call upon the name of the Lord shall be saved.' And a few hours later I was praying as I've never prayed before. In my mind there's not the slightest doubt but that faith in our God pulled me through. I never hope to come next to Death like that again. . . ."

From the day of his near scrape, till he came home from war, Harry raced through the Bible. His friends took note of his reverent spells, Fearing nicely describing them as "lapses into piety." He inclines to the opinion that Harry no more than demonstrated the veracity of the old saw about atheists and foxholes. Weeks deflates the importance of Harry's pious moods, explaining that even under the influence of the Bible he underwent no change in character, he simply thought in terms of God and the Ghost rather than in terms of friends and ladies. "As long as I knew him he never tried to proselytize me for anything except to go to Harvard." Weeks believes Harry was merely a commonplace product of the Episcopal training he received at St. Mark's.

But in the autobiography which he or someone close to him mutilated, there is a reference to another red-letter day in his life, September 22, 1917. He was in Paris, signing on for the duration of the war with the United States Army: "I knelt down upon the floor in the little room at the hôtel and gave thanks to God. In this way were born my first religious thoughts." He never shared this event with any friend, nor did he write his mother about it or celebrate its anniversary later in his life. Yet it was precisely in his character to perceive events as watersheds, to invest all his loyalty and energy in magic: at first, the approved magic of established religion; later, the witchwork of poetry and sun worship; finally, the black mass of violence. The later, darker manifestations of his faith in a higher principle are paradoxically easier for the imagination to accommodate than this early, unstylish plunge to his knees "upon the floor in the little room." Yet it has been noted that in court cases where a proof of legal insanity is sought, nothing succeeds like prayer aloud, or public citations of Biblical wisdom, or warnings against the miseries of hellfire. A barroom brawler or child-beater is as sane as you or I, but unordained preachers are looked on as eccentrics and bores, and knowing this Harry must have been as eager to disguise his crisis of conscience and imagination as his friends were eager to ignore it.

Surely, he became what they called in those days "nervous" after his providential near-miss. Hours after he returned from Spaulding's hospital room in Beaulieu, he was seen running, more or less in circles fifty yards in diameter, lap upon lap without purpose or destination. He became, naturally enough, preoccupied by death, and at first he squeezed scripture till its pips squeaked. On the day following Independence Day, 1918, Harry sent his mother an unwitting pledge of allegiance to cosmic platitudes. The occasion that provoked his words was his successful completion of the New Testament: "You were mighty wise about unnecessary risks. Hereafter no more for yours truly. Of course, as you said, if you're sent 'Theirs not to reason why'. . . . Life seems to me to represent a race. The start is your Birth. 'All men are created equal.' The race is Life. The finish is Death. To the winners, those who have led a straight, clean life, comes Eternal Life and God's Love—for those who lose—those who have sinned, etc.—the penalty is Hell."

In this same odd, silly *dogma summa*, Harry assured his mother that "you need never worry about me becoming a confirmed boozehound, as beer is the only stuff I like, and you know that this French beer is very light and does one no harm. It takes the place of orangeade or sarsparilla. . . ." The fact is, Harry had been drunk unto oblivion only the night before, on champagne, and he was drunk once again hours after completing his discourse on The Meaning of Life's Laps.

In the process of surviving one crisis after another, Harry continued to receive prodding letters of encouragement and scolding letters of advice from his parents, letters urging him toward what they conceived to be manhood, and he—incredibly—tolerated them, often managing to play Laertes to his father's Polonius. Just before he left for Verdun, he received a letter from home encouraging him to reflect more on life's goals. He wrote his mother, who spoke in such letters with the voice of his father: "What you said about thinking is absolutely true. At home all I did was tear frantically around from one amusement to another thinking only of the present and living in a rut about two inches wide. . . . Before the War the U.S. might be exemplified by the song "Yaadie Kadie Koo" and vaudeville in general. All most people thought of were their own petty affairs—and dancing. . . ." He wrote his sister a wistful letter recalling St. Mark's: "Them were the happy days! If only one could appreciate the academy more before those blissful schoolboy days are over and it's too late. . . . But time allows no one to ever turn back. Always forward. . . ."

Rather than show a new face to his parents during the war, he constructed, with great effort, a mask that resembled—even caricatured—the face of a St. Mark's Boy. He wrote his mother that "if I get home I really ought to be fitted to amount to something instead of drifting through life in an aimless fashion thinking only of things ephemeral. I shall read the thirteenth chapter of the Corinthians today." Just what she hoped he'd read: *When I was a child, I spoke like a child, I thought like a child, I reasoned like a child; when I became a man, I gave up childish ways. For now we see in a mirror dimly, but then face to face.*

His letters home usually heaped respect upon affection. To his mother he wrote: "You and Pa all my life have done every conceivable thing for me and you may not know it, but I certainly appreciate it all right. It is absolutely impossible for me to half thank you or Pa for everything you've done for me in such an unselfish way. If I could but half follow in your way I would make good anywhere." He neither questioned their wisdom, nor challenged their authority. Yet in his transactions with his parents there was nothing falsely formal or distanced. Early in the war, he had pressed the advantage that his status as a knight-errant offered him vis-à-vis his father. Within a month he had been translated from a schoolboy, obliged to tug his forelock in deference to his elders, into a warrior at the Front, full of beans, entitled to address his father man to man. He tried, anyway: "Have you seen Miss de T. lately? She's sure some warm baby!!! Lead me to her. Here's looking at her with a full glass. . . . Goodnight, Steve, you old racer, lots of love to your lady friends. . . . On les aura. Best of luck. . . . Over the top with the best of luck, and give them hell. . . ."

Mr. Crosby did not discourage his son's liberties, but neither did he write as often or as warmly as Harry had hoped. And when Harry held a finger to the air, he felt the breeze blowing from his father to be frostier than he might have liked. The chill between them was at first no fault at all of Harry's. In January of 1918 Mrs. Crosby had sailed to France to work in a soldiers' home at Lunéville, and her husband resented her desertion of him. A story from the society page of a Boston paper tells some of the tale:

SOCIETY WOMEN PROVE THEY ARE NOT SLACKERS BY EARNEST WAR WORK

Society is destined to get on as best it may without Mrs. Stephen Van Rensselaer Crosby, who is entering with enthusiasm upon her trip of mercy to France, where she is to do canteen work with the Y.M.C.A. The Crosbys, the Beals, the Morgans and all that family, you know, are nothing if not keen as regards the war. . . . I feel justified in saying that Mrs. Crosby will have something of a task to keep up with the record which her son Harry has established both for industry and for bravery. Harry Crosby, in fact, must be one of the very youngest of the ambulance drivers, for he went abroad with Richmond Fearing in June, just after he was graduated from St. Mark's, without so much as a preliminary canter at Harvard, where, in accordance with all family traditions, he should be disporting himself today.

His mother was meant to sign up for six months in France, and Harry was pleased that she had come, of course, but in so doing she had robbed Mr. Crosby of her companionship and a bit of his manliness; he was reduced with sister Kitsa to the role of stay-at-home, a mere major in the home service. As Mrs. Crosby deprived Harry of the theatrical effect he wished to work on her when she discovered him, home from war, grown full up, as in an instant. They had companionable leaves together in Paris, and Harry was happier dining with his mother than he was raising hell. But the six months passed, and she was still in France, stuck on her son, and her husband did not like it. Harry was afraid she would never leave, and he wrote her July 18, laying down the law: "Now, I'm sorry to say—this is going to be a lecture letter. . . . It's about going back to Manchester. You practically promised me you'd start back late in August—or at the very latest in September. Now I receive a letter saying you're . . . thinking of staying on till November. I think it's damn foolish, that's all, for many reasons. . . . It's really and truly time for you to go back to Pa and K. . . . When Pa says he thinks I want you to stay—he's entirely mistaken. You know just as well as I do there's no one in the wide, wide world I love more than my own Mammy-Gu—but that has absolutely nothing to do with it. . . ." Mrs. Crosby finally sailed at the end of August, but by then some space had opened between Stephen Crosby and his son that neither of them would ever successfully close: he treated Harry like a rival from that time forward, and Harry behaved like one.

Certain bad battle dreams never let go of Harry and his friends. Ted Weeks's punishment has been to redrive in his dreams a piece of road upon which a French captain bled to death, perhaps because Weeks drove too slowly or roughly. Harry's own awful dream, many times written out in his notebooks, was of Verdun, where nothing would grow again, where everything had been smashed and the future tense abolished. The following overwrought version, from a 1927 notebook, shows signs of having been poeticized, but Harry never managed to beat this particular melodrama into literature:

Water, water, a dying soldier drinking cold wine from a steel helmet; a dead man flat upon his back in a wheatfield, swollen, vermin-covered, rotting in the sun; a cowardly corporal shooting himself in his dismay; the charred remains of an aviator brought down in flames; the frenzied flogging of prisoners; and the mutilated body of a girl strapped backward upon a board, her legs dangling, her loveliness defiled, and a dagger plunged to the hilt in her soft bosom.

And little children, little innocent boys and little innocent girls sitting death-pale at a long, low table, their shrivelled hands nailed to the boards; a detachment of artillery hauling their guns into action over the bodies of living wounded; captives of war bound to blazing trees, burning to death in the night, human torches as in the days of Nero; seven women crucified in a lonely swamp-wood with seven ravens pecking out their brains; and a hirsute, shell-shocked, madman squatting on his heels over a group of unburied corpses gouging out their eyes with his long thumb-nail and swallowing the rotten, pulpy fruit as one might swallow oysters.

It was not until later years, after Harry took up literature, that Nero, together with Poe's ravens, invaded his nightmare; nor is the reference to "little innocent boys and little innocent girls" to be taken on faith: by 1927 Harry no longer believed in innocence, and he had never given two sticks for the fate of any child. Nevertheless, this was no counterfeit dream; mutilation, vermin, cowardice, relentlessness, insanity, hysteria and cruelty played in the theater of his imagination from the time of Verdun till the end of his life, and they were prompted by war.

He wrote of Verdun that "Death's hand is written over it all. In spite of all this foreboding evil scenery embodies a certain fascination, a sort of lure that acts as a magnet." He was learning to cherish extreme situations, and especially extreme waste. His gravest introspections he saved for the subject of death, its bracing charge, its consoling, everlasting peace, its theatrics. Harry Crosby and Ernest Hemingway shared a few things: mutual admiration, an affection for French customs and places, a religion based on literary principles, suicide, and a special fondness for the words Feeble wasted upon Falstaff in *Henry the Fourth: Part Two: By my troth I care not, a man can die but once, we owe God a death. . . . An't be my destiny, so; an't be not, so. . . . And let it go which way it will, he that dies this year is quit for the next.* Except that Harry did not want to be quit for the next. He wanted to dwell on his death, because everlasting reflection upon it emptied it of terror, tamed it and liberated him. He wrote in his notebook the words of another man ("It is significant that there has always been about me, notwithstanding all my experiences, that something untouched and apart, that stamps those marked for early death"), and beside the entry, penciled large, twice underlined, his own, single judgment: "YES."

In fact, Harry and his friends came through the war with singular good luck, to judge the matter simply and statistically. Only three men from the two sections Harry served with died on ambulance duty. The Field Service lost a total of one hundred and fifty-one volunteers, of whom the largest number of university graduates or students were from Harvard (twenty-one) and the best-represented state was Massachusetts (twenty-nine). Twenty St. Mark's students—the size of one class—were killed, most of them in France. One-half of the thousand and some living graduates of the school served, and one-third were decorated, provoking the author of *A History of St. Mark's School* to observe that "it may properly be added for the purposes of our history that a comparison of this record with the records of the public schools is very reassuring to those inclined to question the democracy or the patriotism of such private schools as St. Mark's."

Saint Mark's School in the War Against Germany, edited by Albert Emerson Benson of the class of 1888, and privately printed in 1920, gives the sense of Harry's time, its exuberant innocence, and reverence for the dead. No doubt about it, to die—especially young, and most especially by gunshot—was to be raised high, in the eyes of Society, perhaps in the eyes of God. An account of the death of Holyoke Lewis Whitney, one class ahead of Harry, killed while cleaning his own pistol, extols his "magnificent manhood" and records his great faith: "Plunged from all he loved into an apparently senseless, hopeless welter of good and evil, his sensitive spirit rose cleanly and strongly above it and surveyed it with the undeceived eye of the Soldier of Christ. He says in his letters 'the whole business is sensible' and 'I believe that God ordains that all things have their reasons, and that He allows nothing to be wrong at last. . . .'"

Richard Mather Joplin, class of 1912, a bookish fellow whose heart condition prevented him from making a name for himself at St. Mark's in games, was salvaged by death, a mysterious death following severe shell shock. Described as a "gentle, earnest, but almost over-modest boy . . . who watched quietly at the side-lines at football games, who spent hours by himself in the music room, and wrote poems for *The Vindex*," he was on the instant translated into a hero. If "his manhood and courage had not the opportunities for display which are given to most boys," death redeemed him. The lesson was not lost upon the living; how else could Great Wars be fought? One of Joplin's last *Vindex* poems was bang in the mainline of his schoolmates' belief, and mordantly prophetic of his own end and revision:

Spirit of the school! Live in us yet
That thy earnest, fearless ardor let us feel
That each disheartening combat may be met
With boyish zeal.

Then onward still, never thought of rest,
Till all the tumult of the world is past,
That with a conquering courage in our breast,
We may be men at last!

Stuart Kaiser noted in his diary July 1, 1918, that the Boston papers had brought "news of more deaths of boys I know. Kaiser, get busy!!" Late in March of that year, an old friend of Harry's, Dick Fairchild, had been killed driving an ambulance on the Italian front; he was eighteen. Then another, better friend died, Oliver Ames. And finally, around Christmas time, Aaron Davis Weld was reported missing in action; then he was reported dead, and his death had a lifelong effect on Harry. Together with his own near miss, Harry noted the anniversary of Davis Weld's death every year. He gave a church bell in Weld's memory at a memorial service in France. Yet Weld was older than Harry, the older brother of Harry's friend George, and George to this day has been unaware of Harry's fixation on his late brother: "We, his family, were very touched at the gift of the bell but I think he never or rarely spoke of [Davis'] death to us when he returned."

Harry's interest in Weld was literary. Not that he was incapable of registering, and expressing, personal sorrow; rather, he understood the utility of an objective correlative before Eliot gave it a name. Harry did not know, had not even guessed by 1918, that his calling would be to letters, but he had a proper hunch that it would be to death. His flow was usually toward the abstract, which is why he was so brave, and sometimes so cold, but he understood that death in the abstract could teach him nothing. And so he formed his closest and most enduring friendship with a corpse, the brother of Harry's friend, just as later he would nail the photograph of an anonymous soldier's corpse to his study door in Paris, and give the unknown fellow a name.

Harry's judgment of war, its purpose and meaning, suffered wrenching alterations throughout his time at the Front. He could write disapprovingly of the French enlisted men that they drank too much, and had been turned into "very low beings, morally." Yet he was often sympathetic to them: "They don't seem to think there's any kindness left in the world. 'A quoi bon la guerre!' they all say—and yet they never lie down but keep scrapping right up the finish. They all say that the courage and willful destruction is beyond all barbarity. . . . Life here makes every paltry amusement and pleasure seem petty trivialities." From Verdun he wrote his mother that "the French here are a fine lot and I take back what I said about them some time ago. They are brave, fearless, and resolute. . . . That God ordained this War is beyond the slightest doubt and when it's all over the world will be a finer, cleaner, and squarer place. This War is all for bettering men and women, but the cost is tremendous." A few days earlier he had written, evidently without irony: "God surely meant this War or it would never have happened. . . . It makes you feel that there's a Power above that is willing this struggle for the betterment of humanity and the world will be a much finer place when it is all over." How so? "A man who pulls through this is twice as efficient and useful as before."

This is not a simpleton writing home, after all. Harry was young and innocent, and he had been rained upon with mumbo jumbo from editorial-page warriors and boarding school preachers. But the true provocation for his acrobatic solecisms, for the specious claptrap that he sent home disguised as right reason, was his honor. A fellow volunteer one night left Verdun drunk, and laughing, and he drove his ambulance to Paris, and there he sold it, and with the money from the sale stayed drunk till they found him. Harry did not want to drive off drunk to Paris, and he tried—awfully hard, too—to dream up some reason why he shouldn't. The reason held, for a while.

On the last day of 1917, Stuart Kaiser reflected upon the war, Whither and Why: "Here we are—another year gone—three and a half years of war. Let the war be soon finished, but let not that which has gone by have happened in vain. And as for myself, let me live the kind of a life I think I ought to over here. . . . *Vive la victoire et la paix.* . . ." Then, on the morning of the first day of 1918, he scribbled in dark ink across the passage above: "Aw Rot! Wake up!"

Harry had written his father that winning the "coveted Croix de Guerre" was "much like winning [an] 'H' at college, only infinitely more difficult and dangerous, requiring tremendous nerve and skill." Stephen Crosby had only a few H's, but Harry had nothing at all, even after Verdun, and he was worried. He tried unsuccessfully to transfer into the tank service, to increase the probability of being shot at to his greater glory. He wrote his father again: "I'd give anything in the world for the Croix de Guerre or would be perfectly willing to be wounded to get it." A year later he was obliged to report to his mother that four good friends, Tote Fearing among them, had won the honor: "Wish to God I had one." The bronze cross, with a green and red ribbon, had been given to ninety-seven Field Service volunteers, but it was never given cheaply. Finally, August 23–25, 1918, during the Battle of the Orme, Harry's section carried two thousand wounded, working night and day, and was cited in the field a few days later by Gen. Gassouin for "disdaining danger, without regard for fatigue . . . carrying on without pause the evacuation of the wounded in violently bombarded zones."

The ordeal never let up till the Armistice, November 11, 1918, and Harry, in the words of this same Gen. Gassouin, Commander of the 17th Infantry Division, fighting in the Ailettes and around Laon, was *toujours montré plein d'élan et de courage*. So much so that on March 1, 1919, the vital and courageous young son of Stephen Van Rensselaer Crosby could write in his diary, "Oh Boy!!!!!! won THE CROIX DE GUERRE. Thank God." More exclamation marks than for his Punctuality Prize at St. Mark's. More heartfelt thanks to his Maker than for his deliverance at Verdun. Now he could go home, and not have to apologize for coming back alive.

Like every other soldier, Harry wanted to leave for home half an hour after the Armistice had been signed, and after waiting a month to receive his sailing orders he wrote his mother asking her to pull strings to spring him: "Now about Uncle Jack. Do your best to get him to try and get me a discharge. Anything can be done by means of graft. Any amount of men are trying to get mustered out. You ask me what my plans are. Impossible to answer. . . ." J. P. Morgan was in a fair way of becoming his nephew Harry's oracle: "When does Uncle Jack think the War will end?" asked the volunteer, after Verdun. "I'd very much like to know his real opinion as it ought to be very valuable." In 1914, J. P. Morgan & Company had gambled one and one-half billion dollars in loans to the Allies for arms to be used against the Germans. Thus Harry was guilty of no overstatement when he remarked that "Uncle Jack usually has some pretty keen dope on the world's affairs." He aspired to his uncle's power and achievement, and to his manner as well. J. Pierpont Morgan was a great gentleman, but a man forward in his opinions, strongly held. He was intimidating, gruff but polite, generous, knowing, expansive, and fond of his nephew and godson.

So it was that on April 5, 1919, having sailed sixteen days from Brest to Philadelphia, having been demobilized at Fort Dix, Harry stopped off in New York, on his way to Boston, to visit his renowned uncle. Who wasn't at home. Harry took dinner at the Madison Avenue mansion anyway, *solus*, at the head of a huge table, along with "detectives and footmen." He ate a magnificent dinner, and noticed "lackeys" and "menials" and ancestral portraits, classifications that he had begun to forget in France. He "poured down the ancient wine till I felt the room reel round," and was carried to Grand Central in a limousine, and caught the midnight express north. "The next thing I remember was a colored porter shouting *Back Bay* and I half-stepped, half fell off the train into the arms of my family."

5

"It was like the Magdeburg spheres; the pressure
outside sustained the vacuum within
and I hadn't the nerve
to jump up and walk out of doors and tell them
all to go take a flying
Rimbaud
at the moon."

—John Dos Passos, *42nd Parallel*
(about his years at Harvard "under the ethercone")

Face to face with his parents on the platform at Back Bay, Harry saw
two guides he was no longer to follow. He would love them if they let
him, but he would never again, even briefly, reflect them. They saw a
son they had tried to prod into manhood, who was hurled into manhood despite them, by experiences and black visions they couldn't have
imagined. They looked at their boy: mussed, sleepy, drunk, all his
visible parts accounted for, no boy at all.

Homecoming was a brief transport, followed by Harry's steep
downhill slide in Boston's esteem. Even as he had been dragged by the
war away from his childhood assumptions, he had dug in his heels, and
sustained himself with fanciful visions of a future in Boston matched to
his mother's and father's past. He had been homesick, and bits and
pieces from his letters home reflect his longings and resolutions: "Gee
I'm glad we're Americans! Best country in the world!" . . . "After this
War you'll have to get a derrick to get me out of Massachusetts. No
more travelling for yours truly. 'Home Sweet Home' is my motto."

Less than three years later he left for Paris, intending never to return, declaring "to hell with most of Boston." His about-face strained his navigational instruments, and confirmed him in a lifelong habit—a *versus* reflex—of casting alternatives as polarities. He could never contemplate both Boston and Paris; it must be Boston versus Paris. Partly, this was provoked by personal circumstances, by his contest with Boston's iron laws of decorum, but his alienation from the people and customs of his city and country was also a function of social forces that have been often enough described and analyzed: the riptide of anxiety, anger and restlessness that carried thousands from his generation back across the ocean to Europe.

The Great War, regarded from Harry's vantage, was not what it seemed to his mother and father. For him, and for his comrades, it was everlasting; for the parents of an eligible young gentleman, it had been a successful adventure—an affair to be bound in leather scrapbooks and memorialized on Armistice Day. Thus, no sooner was he home than they pressed him for his plans: When would he begin Harvard? What would he make his life's work? Business or law? Harry was in no rush to decide or do anything, save loaf. He longed for "the life deluxe." In fact, no sooner had he arrived in France than he announced that "I certainly intend to be pampered for a month or two after this War and my conscience ought not to hurt me about it." He dreamt of "normal life again where people and things are clean and pure and white."

During the war Harry and his father had struck a bargain: Mr. Crosby would buy his son a Stutz runabout in return for his matriculation at Harvard. Mr. Crosby welshed on his half of the deal, and Harry tried to welsh on his. He had decided almost as soon as he arrived in France that his experience there would be a sufficient initiation into manhood, that he would return too old for college hijinks, and after strutting herolike about town for a while he planned to find himself a job. He worried that his contemporaries were stealing a march on him in the marketplace, and when the time came for wives to be drawn he would not be able to afford a good one.

His father regarded the matter from a different perspective and longer view. He subscribed to the judgment made by Edmund Quincy, the son of a Harvard president. While tapping the sober binding of the *Harvard Triennial Catalogue*, Mr. Quincy had said, "If a man's in there, that's who he is. If he isn't, who is he?" Mr. Crosby wanted his boy's name printed in that book, and even more he wanted his boy in the A.D. Club—so much so that he agreed to let Harry quit college as soon as he gained membership.

Since Stephen Crosby was still the master of his son's actions, if not of his son's inclinations, Harry entered Harvard midway through the spring term of 1919, almost as soon as he returned home, and by attending summer school that year he was given a "War Degree" at the conclusion of the academic year 1920–21. (To further confuse his status, Harvard listed him as a graduate of the class of 1922.) Such accelerated courses of study as Harry's were offered by Harvard as a reward for soldierly service and an inducement to gentlemen veterans hesitant to play out the post-adolescent destiny that had been scripted for them by their schools and their families. Nevertheless, many young men of Harry's age and background, who would in the normal course of things have entered Harvard, never bothered with college at all. Or, if they did, they stayed only a year or so, to play football, or join a club.

Harry's work load was light: he was obliged to carry six or seven courses during each of the two full years he was at college, and two courses during the summer of 1919. Of the nineteen courses he took at Harvard, six were in French—which he spoke and read fluently—and six in English literature. The others were in fine arts (four), music, Spanish (the only course he failed) and social ethics. His grades were B's and C's, with twice as many of the latter as the former.

At some unfixable time during his odd career at Harvard, Harry's fascination with literature became serious, and obsessive. But he hid it carefully, from almost everyone. He did not consort with writers, nor did he write for the *Advocate*, or even the *Lampoon*. In his classmate Tote Fearing's recollection, "If he was interested in literature at Harvard, I wouldn't know it."

During the war, Harry's reading had wandered all over the place. He would pick up whatever came to hand: *The Atlantic Monthly* and *The Saturday Evening Post* were his favorite periodicals. He read Douglas Fairbanks' lightweight memoir, *Laugh and Live*, and judged it "a book of philosophy and really pretty good." And in the touching tradition of spies who lie awake reading spy novels, and whalers who once read *Moby Dick*, he huddled in the trenches of France reading books about the trenches of France. He read war poetry, and took especially to Kipling and a new favorite, Robert Service, whose *Rhymes of a Red Cross Man* made a superficial impression on him that at the time seemed profound: a new enthusiasm for Harry always, in his youth, effaced all previous enthusiasms, while one of the boldest marks of his postwar years was his capacity to love more than one idea, and one girl, at one time. He tried one of Tolstoy's journals, but it defeated him; he found it "pretty deep literature." More to his taste was Winston Churchill's *Richard Carvel*: "Have you struck?" the British commander asks Jones, who replies, "Sir, I have not yet begun to fight." He continued to appreciate *The Rubáiyát*, and marked a favorite passage:

> *Some for the Glories of the World; and some*
> *Sigh for the Prophet's Paradise to come;*
> *Ah, take the Cash and let the Credit go,*
> *Nor heed the Rumble of a Distant Drum.*

But Harry's first systematic self-education in good poetry came through his reading of *The Oxford Book of English Verse*. He had bought a copy, and sent his mother a duplicate for Christmas in 1917 so that they could correspond about the poems they enjoyed together, as they corresponded about the verses in the Bible that they shared.

At Harvard, Harry's single institutional association with matters putatively of the mind and the spirit was his membership in the Cercle Français. Each year the Cercle performed for Harvard students a classical play from the French repertory, and although Harry was not drawn to the stage he grew close to two fellow members of the group: Alexander Steinert, a neighbor from the North Shore whom Harry first met at Harvard (Steinert was a composer who had many times encountered Harry's mother at the Boston Symphony, whose Friday afternoon concerts were one of Back Bay's most enduring cultural and social institutions) and Helenka Adamowski, like Steinert an intellectual, and as well a great beauty.

Steinert knew nothing about Harry's attraction to literature: "He was in the *fun* department. I think of him in the category of gaiety, an aristocrat to his fingertips. He was quick-witted, zany." Helenka Adamowski recollects a different young man: "Harry was an incredibly sensitive, high-strung, poetic individual who was wound up to such a pitch that even in those early days I wondered whether he would survive the year." She knew him as "grave," yet "full of mischief . . . a sort of mercurial being." So it was at Harvard that Harry began to play parts, swapping masks and manners with the easy speed of Mercury, baffling friends and the recollected apprehensions of those of his survivors who have tried to decipher him.

Steinert noticed no moodiness; quite to the contrary, Harry was "a witty-looking character with his crew cut, and a ducklike nose. He made me laugh. He had a very clipped manner in his speech, nervous, and he chopped the air with short gestures. He was thin, almost emaciated, very aristocratic. Always moving, on the jump, like his father: jittery, a go-getter. His mother seemed remote, very much within herself. Like her he had a curious quality in his voice, a chesty quality, hollow and metallic. The Crosbys' houses, on the North Shore and in Boston, were always open to young people; there were clambakes, dinner dances, theater parties. I don't know how we ever got any work done."

Steinert and Harry were hardly ever at Harvard, so busy were they with parties: "Suddenly, when midyear examinations came, Harry and I knew we were going to flunk. So we went to a wonderful man called the Widow Knowland, a tall grey-haired fellow who ran a tutoring school near Harvard Square. You went to him before exams because he kept track of all the exams in every course. He knew virtually what questions would be asked. So we went to him, paid him, and crammed, and that was the only time any of us concentrated on what we were meant to know. That was the order of the day, that was how we got through." (Steinert was graduated magna cum laude.) Harry's investment in Harvard's academic resources was so casual that less than six years after his graduation he could not recollect whether he had in fact studied under a professor of English mentioned by his mother in a letter, nor whether he had ever been enrolled in a course called The History of the Printed Word. (He had not.)

Harry divided his friends between the many from whom he hid his anxieties and interests, and the few with whom he shared them. He realized that an extreme affection for poetry was laughable in his circle, as was an extreme affection for God, or for anything. For the time being, his transactions with books and ideas was almost silent. Almost. Helenka Adamowski recalls that Harry used to take her to a friend's house on Cape Cod. One "soft, foggy weekend" Harry sat "by the hour outside leaning against the cottage wall and philosophizing. He had a deep spirituality and interest in poetry."

Stephen Crosby never tired of reminding Harry that the point of his college enterprise was his election to the A.D. Club. Harvard's club system was and is a complicated, many-tiered system of social progress through what are called "waiting clubs" toward the Valhalla of a "final club," such as A.D. or Porcellian. As soon as he matriculated, Harry was eligible for membership in the Hasty Pudding Club, a nonexclusive mob of young men whose pleasure it still is to dress up like counterfeit ladies and perform counterfeit musical comedy. Harry was in the kick line of *Barnum Was Right*, written by Robert Sherwood and Alex

Steinert, not because he cared for such gambols but because to proceed to the A.D. he was obliged to go along with the system. His next step toward the summit of clubland was election to the Institute of 1776, and then to the Dicky. An item in *The Crimson* reported that as part of his initiation to the Dicky (so named because of its past tie to D.K.E.) Harry was seen on Boston's Franklin Street

> wearing a fashionably cut suit about five sizes too small for his large frame. A high hat and a cane completed his ludricrous make-up. In his arms he carried a rag doll about the size of a real baby. As the candidate paraded Franklin Street an immense crowd gathered, and several telephoned to police headquarters that an insane millionaire was loose in the financial district. A squad of officers was sent out, but before they arrived on the scene state guardsmen had seized Crosby, and were piloting him to the station. At the station house Crosby explained that he must not be detained as his evening's program called for the measuring of Franklin Street with a fresh mackerel, and then shaving in the ballroom of the Copley-Plaza.

Of all the episodes in Harry's various life, this was surely the least in his character. He was no clown, no fraternity boy; he loathed kid stuff. Still, he moved along to the next level, a waiting club called S.K. And then something went wrong; he should have been invited to join the A.D., but he wasn't. His bona fides were all in order: he knew the right people, had been to the obligatory schools and was confirmed in the obligatory church; he summered at a fit summering place, enjoyed elegant manners and a striking, if odd, appearance. He was charming. He hung out with the gay blades, to his credit with clubmen. He had plenty of money, which was useful because such clubs as the A.D. and Porcellian were expensive. Most important, Harry was a "legacy"; his father and any number of Grews had been members of the A.D., and his father's interest in the club was as high as that of any of Harry's contemporaries.

Marquand's Late George Apley wrote his son a letter about Porcellian that might have been a Stephen Crosby monologue directed at Harry in the library of 95 Beacon Street, over Upmanns and Remy Martin, on the subject of the A.D.:

> I am still quite well-known around the Club, you know, and your first object must be to "make" the Club. I believe that everything else, even including your studies, should be secondary to this. . . . I don't know what I should have done in life without the Club. When I leave Boston

it is my shield. When I am in Boston it is one of my great diversions. The best people are always in it, the sort that you will understand and like. I once tried to understand a number of other people, but I am not so sure now that it was not a waste of time.

In fact, Harry was himself coming to be numbered among the "other people." He seemed always to go too far. There was danger that he might, at any minute, show up in the newspapers, the only sin Harry's father's Harvard could not forgive. He was passed over for the first final club election for which he was eligible. "Let's say," says one member, "that Harry Crosby was not clubable." Nevertheless, after three election rounds, Harry was finally invited in 1921 to join the A.D., certainly because of his father. Cleveland Amory, a social meteorologist in possession of the most delicate available instruments to measure Boston's hierarchical weather, writes that for those Harvard boys chosen late for such clubs as the A.D. it is a "dubious honor, since such boys sometimes go through life with the feeling that while judged socially presentable enough to be seen on the occasions when they may as graduates return to club dinners, they were deemed hardly worthy of close fellowship during their undergraduate years."

So what cast Harry to the edge of outer darkness, by his father's measure? The offense closest at hand is excessive boozing, but the most clubable of Harvard's young gentlemen, the members of Porcellian, as a regular matter drank themselves insensible. They celebrated an occasion they called "the Day of the Book" by drinking, before breakfast, a martini, and during breakfast a quart of champagne. Then they drank one martini per hour till lunch, and during lunch another quart of champagne; the regimen ended at midnight. Yet the excesses of "the Day of the Book" were committed behind the walls of the club, beyond public view. (Indeed, so insulated were the members of Porcellian from the mass of common folk that they looked out their club window by means of a mirror in order not to be obliged to behold the *demmed people* face to face.) Harry, on the other hand, performed his stunts in full public view. At Betty Beal's coming-out party he tripped and knocked his aunt to the dance floor. Caught by another girl's mother spiking the cider at a tea dance, he was asked to leave. "Harry's drinking was causing trouble" in Ted Weeks's understated memory of his friend's Harvard years.

Harry trained for the cross-country team, and at first did well, as a newsclip from a 1919 issue of *The Crimson* tells: "TEN HILL AND DALE MEN SELECTED FOR YALE MEET. Coach Eddie Farrell announced yesterday the addition of H. G. Crosby '22. Crosby's addition to the team is due to the improvement he has shown during the fall. . . ." Harry would recruit Weeks to run with him, beating lap after lap around the wooden track of the Harvard Field House till Weeks's lungs gave out. Harry was good; he beat all comers at Harvard in the mile run with a time of four minutes, forty-one and a half seconds. But the night before the Yale meet he broke training, "went on a bender and the next morning, still hung over, followed the race in a roadster, cheering, 'Come on, you poor bastards,' at the teammates he should have been laboring with." Weeks, who tells the story, also recalls that Harry later showed up at the victory dinner, again drunk, and ate some camellias from the table's centerpiece before he passed out.

Ted Weeks stood witness to many of Harry's most notorious performances. By the agency of his friendship with Harry, his name had been put on "the List" of eligible young gentlemen selected to attend coming-out parties in Boston and New York. In the autumn of 1919 he made his way to The Apple Trees for the first of them. After tennis on the grass courts of the Essex County Club, Harry and Weeks took a few drinks with Mr. Crosby before the dinner party (despite prohibition), and then more, and more, through the night, whiskey nipped neat from flasks. After the dance there followed the obligatory high-speed drive in the obligatory Stutz (Tote Fearing's), and then "the Hounds"—as the veterans of war had taken to calling themselves—showed up at dawn at the house of a chum who removed from beneath his pillow a sheer, black silk stocking, he wouldn't say whose. After which there was another high-speed chase to the house of another friend, whom they found before breakfast driving golf balls into the sea; floaters had been attached to the balls in consideration of the gardener, who was sent to fetch them from a rowboat.

As soon as they returned home from the war, Fearing, Crosby, Weeks and Kaiser had formed an association called "the Triumverate," whose title referred to the three sober members of the group of four. They would go to parties together, where one of them was licensed to drink himself to the pass-out stage while the others cared for him. Like many of his colleagues, Harry had begun to drink hard as soon as he arrived in France. The French enlisted men and stretcher-bearers attached to American ambulance units were most often too old to fight, and by virtue of their age and rough wisdom they influenced such young men as Harry and Tote Fearing and Ted Weeks in the way of diabolical and subversive godfathers. If Boston elders instructed that a gentleman did not drink in the business district or before the stock market closed, their French counterparts advised that a young man should drink wherever he happened to find himself, and as early in the day as suited him. On Christmas Eve, 1917, Stuart Kaiser noted that Crosby, "who always looked harmless, got drunk and performed wild antics. The Frenchmen stayed up late and got drunk, and saw a cat, and killed it and cooked it, and ate it. Wow!" (Kaiser learned to ration his exclamations, for such havoc soon became commonplace.)

When Harry's mother arrived in France, she immediately became alarmed by the amount he was drinking. Pretty soon he was obliged to reassure (and mislead) her. On August 29, 1918, he wrote her that "you needn't worry about the liquor question as to-morrow we start out toward Villers-Cotterets. Can't even get beer out that way so yours truly for two or three months on the water-wagon." Less than two months later: "I'm still on the water-wagon (not even Pinard or Beer, since Oct. 1st) but November 1st I intend to call off this resolution." Harry made resolutions to quit boozing for years thereafter, and broke them always, usually within days.

Harry's family and prewar friends were shocked by the kind of postwar attitude Tote Fearing expressed: "I came back with the idea that three meals a day were about all that I wanted out of life. I was alive; I wanted to live." Gardner Monks felt that the change that overcame Harry in France had the force of a religious conversion: "He was an entirely different boy after the war experience and a much more confused and impulsive one. . . . He was wild as blazes." Helenka Adamowski, with a reluctance fueled by affection, concedes that "there were indications of instability even in those days in the Twenties." (She also, however, recollects the "electricity about him that made him exciting.") Harry once took her to the Harvard-Yale boat races in New London, hired an airplane and insisted that the pilot essay some aerobatic stunts. The pilot refused, but "Harry did succeed in getting him to fly low and at one point we cleared a flagpole by what seemed to be a matter of inches."

Harry was in a fair way of becoming a public nuisance in Boston, than which there was no greater abomination. Brooks Fenno, Harry's roommate from St. Mark's, was under the impression upon meeting Harry several months after he returned from the war that he had been "shell-shocked," and noted with no little revulsion that he had had his fingernails painted black. Harry's clothes were correctly cut, but uncommonly stark: he had already begun to dress almost exclusively in black, double-breasted suits. He quickly won himself a reputation for self-indulgence and carelessness. He struck sparks with his sister, who, like her father, cared greatly what people thought about her family. Kitsa was shocked, embarrassed to the point of tears, the first time she saw Harry drunk dead to the world at a party, carried out like a corpse. Her brother regarded booze with affection, thought of it as magic, remembered his discovery during the war of heavy drinking and celebrated its "subtle power which, in the days to come, dragged me to strange depths and carried me to equal heights. It was the end of the ordinary and the beginning of the extraordinary."

"The extraordinary" is not Boston's favorite realm, nor Harvard clubmen's, not even for brief holiday visits. Harry was not himself, his old friends decided; they blamed the war for his odd behavior, and he let them. But in truth the war had merely forced his character, not altered it, and he knew as much. Betty Beal felt that battle traumas had caused an absolute break in his even disposition, a malign disruption, and there began an estrangement between them that was never healed. She began to find Harry peculiar, perverse, *odd*. George Weld believes "when his ambulance was bombed, tearing up the front and rear and leaving him unhurt on the front seat, that had a major effect on his character." Gardner Monks called him a "war casualty. The traits that made him chafe against society—I don't mean *high society*—were enormously accentuated." Mrs. Monks thought Harry was a "hell-raiser," and she knew, by going to the same dances he went to, that he had a terrible reputation. Henry Morgan, Uncle Jack's boy, remembers the Harry of Harvard as "incapable of coherent thought or speech."

The miracle is not that he missed election to the A.D. first time around, but that he got in at all when one blackball could have kept him out. Lord knows Harry was no toady: he was as indifferent as ice toward people he didn't like, especially toward the self-righteous or vainglorious. A college friend who later became a writer and teacher, William Ellery Sedgwick, recalled Harry's rapid energy, his wit, his coiled, nervous quality, his provocations and menacing disorder. "His energy appeared in an intolerant sincerity. In his serious moods he was simultaneously fantastic and deeply touching."

Toward people like Sedgwick, who excited his admiration or appetite for mischief, he was warm and eager. And he was generous: all during the war he had given money and presents to soldiers who for one reason or another were having a hard time of it. His letters home are full of instructions to send a parcel to this address in Algeria, or ten dollars to that one in Belgium. Ted Weeks has never forgotten Harry's many kindnesses to him when he took his friend's advice and enrolled after the war in Harvard. Harry's introductions formed the basis of lifelong friendships for Weeks in Boston.

But Harry could hate with enthusiasm. He despised noise, and "people whose voices are tin cans thrown into back alleys." He hated people who were afraid of mirrors, people who talked about having been seasick, whose noses ran, who expected beggars to thank them. The perfect clubman was one who was congenial to his clubmates' expectations, avoided grades above C, hair that was very long or very short, eccentric dress, and a passion for anything, especially literature. Harry's passion for literature, though not yet manifest, must have been sensed. He did not counterfeit good fellowship, nor conceal his intolerance of people who believed that only pederasts had their fingernails manicured, who made jokes about ping-pong and croquet, who were transparent, who liked to organize events, who had gold teeth. His greatest contempt of all was for people who wanted to meet people. In short, he didn't give a damn about the A.D., or its members, or their opinion of him.

A fellow member, Lawrence Terry, recalls that Harry was a "charming, moody, private person. . . . I can't remember ever seeing him in a group. I have on my wall a picture of the class of 1922 in the A.D. Club and he is in it. But I don't remember seeing him in the building and I doubt if he came in more than two or three times in his life. . . . It's fair to suppose that he was elected because of affection for his father and that he accepted to please his family."

By the time of his election to the A.D. and his graduation from Harvard, Harry had gone far beyond mere indifference to the conventions and expectations of his club and college. He was determined to marry Polly Peabody, who was married to someone else. He was about to spit in Boston's eye.

6

"Bostonians hate her (the lost lady) so I hate Bostonians."

—Harry Crosby, *Shadows of the Sun*

Harry first met Polly, then Mrs. Richard Rogers Peabody and later Caresse, on Independence Day, 1920. Writing in her autobiography, *The Passionate Years*, Caresse fixed the date as Harry's twenty-first birthday, June 4, 1919, but his diary proves her wrong. The occasion was a shore party laid on by Harry's mother for some dozen of her son's friends, dinner at a roadhouse followed by a visit to the amusement park at Nantasket Beach. Mrs. Crosby invited Polly Peabody, who was twenty-eight, to accompany the young people as their chaperone. It was a thoughtful gesture: Richard Peabody was at the time in a sanitarium, drying out, and Mrs. Crosby rightly guessed that the pretty young lady was restless.

Harry called for Mrs. Peabody in the family Lancia, and at dinner she sat at his right. He was obsessively attentive to her and ignored the girl on his left, to Polly Peabody's visible embarrassment. A few hours later, in the Tunnel of Love, he told her he loved her. Her reaction was not at all unusual among people upon whom he turned his attention: "Harry seemed utterly ruthless." In Caresse's mature recollection of their meeting, "to know Harry was a devastating experience."

He pestered her to let him see her alone, a proposal that was unthinkable to a correct Boston matron—let alone to the wife of a handsome young ex-officer who carried one of the city's three proudest names. But she saw him again. And again. And two weeks later, July 20, Harry wrote in his diary: "Church with M. & K[itsa]. Beach. Goodbye to Ma, Pa & K. Started up to Boston with Polly Peabody. . . . Kissed her. She read to me. O God we slept together all night. She lay in my arms." Two days later he was to sail to Europe, with a college friend who had been an ambulance driver in Italy, for a summer tour of the battlefields. He took Polly Peabody with him as far as New York, and on July 21 he wrote in his diary: "New York. Rushed around, passport etc. Belmont with Polly. Lunch together at the Ritz. . . . Belmont room 943—Polly—together again. Pink intimate night-gown. Over the top with Polly. Marvellous. She slept in my arms. I love her. God bless her. . . . Kissing loving. Said goodbye to Polly. . . ."

What they had just done for each other, and to each other, was exceptional, and before they were finished with Boston and Boston with them, they were held up for contempt and ridicule. By their courtship they had managed to violate Boston's three most fundamental codes: theological, sexual and social. And if his rebellion was part of a calculated briar patch strategy—*Please don't make me leave Boston for Paris, anything but that!*—hers was not. For if any single quality characterized the life of Polly Peabody before her marriage to Harry Crosby, it was her appetite for the approval of other people.

Which she enjoyed in happy measure. Strong, aristocratic bones formed her face, and all her social ducks had been nicely lined in rows by her fond mother and father. She was born in New York, and spent her childhood in a house at the corner of 59th Street and Fifth Avenue, where the Plaza now stands, and her girlhood in Westchester County. Her father was not successful in business, not rich, but he lived high: he had been brought up to "ride to hounds, sail boats, and lead cotil-lions" in Caresse's summary recollection. The accuracy of her memory is seldom dependable, except in the drift of things, in their surfaces and significances. Never mind: it was by precisely such external contours that Boston judged her to be at first acceptable, and later a Jezebel. She understood the game perfectly, while Harry did not. Harry did not lie, or even amplify, except so far as his own signals and reception were amplified by his peculiar intensities and sensitivities. In her autobiogra-phy Caresse uses the kinds of symbols and social shorthand to draw herself that one gossip-ridden matron might use to draw and quarter another matron while at tea with a third. "I grew up in a world where only good smells existed," she remembers. So that in her reconstructed childhood she recalls as the greatest horror of her adolescence the time that she let a roast beef sandwich go bad in her desk at Miss Chapin's school, till she was too embarrassed to remove it publicly. The anecdote smells of fancy and glue, but it's just right, better than true, a parable of fastidiousness and shame.

Her maiden name was Mary Phelps Jacob, and her paternal ancestors had lived a thousand years on the Isle of Wight, in Chale Abbey. Polly Jacob's mother, Mary Phelps, was descended from Governor Bradford, first governor of Plymouth Colony, and from Robert Fulton, developer of the steamboat, and Polly grew up in an atmosphere of privilege and expectation. She was served by Delia the nurse, Tony the handyman and Katie the cook. (The Crosbys also had a Katie to cook for them.) "What I wanted usually came to pass."

She was taught to skate, because young ladies were obliged to know how to skate. As she was taught to ride, having first been fitted out by de Pinna with a bottle-green riding habit, at Dorland's Riding Academy on Manhattan's West Side—"a part of town only suitable for horses." As she was taught to dance at Mr. Dodsworth's Dancing Class for Young Ladies and Gentlemen. She went away to school at Rosemary Hall in Greenwich, where she later remembered herself as a school leader, the fastest girl around (on the running track) and America's first Girl Scout (by virtue of a visit to the school by Sir William Baden-Powell, founder of the Boy Scouts, and his wife, founder of the Girl Guides in England). A classmate, Adelaide Chatfield-Taylor, recalls Polly Jacob at school: "If ever there was a sweet, dear little girl, it was Caresse at Rosemary Hall with me. I can't tell you. Of all the people I've ever known, I'd say she was the freshest, sweetest, nicest, dearest. . . . She certainly changed."

Years later Caresse recollected her schooling as having been neither notably happy nor unhappy. She admitted to having learned nothing in the academic sense, yet characteristically claimed, without merit, to have ranked second in her class. She had no interest in history, in facts and chronologies, or in the past. Reality did not bind or attract her, and she lived her life in dreams.

One such dream, retailed in her mature years as reality, was of the King of England chasing after her bonnet at a royal garden party at Windsor Castle. The putative occasion for this *tableau vivant* was a reception given for young ladies recently presented at court, and Polly advertised herself as having been the only American débutante of that spring social season of 1914, when she would have been twenty-two, considerably long in the tooth for a presentation of her maidenhood to the King. She had had a coming-out party in New York at Sherry's several years earlier, but it pleased her in her later life to tell a pretty tale of having been taken to Paris for the fabrication of her gown, of having flirted with princes and barristers at Oxford's Eights Week, of having ridden to hounds, and of having cheered for Eton against Harrow at Lords. (Polly was something of a snob of the common school, preoccupied with bloodlines and pedigrees, and she recalled without much irony that Mr. Dodsworth's Dancing Class was even more successful than the *New York Social Register* had been at weeding Jews from his rolls.) Presently she tired of England, and turned homesick for the one American boy she cared much about. He was a Bostonian.

Polly had then known Richard Rogers Peabody six years, having met him in 1908 at an elegant summer camp on the Upper Saint Regis in the Adirondacks, where Polly had gone with her aunt and uncle. She met Dick Peabody sailing Idem Knockabouts on the lake: they were the same age, fourteen; he was a Groton boy with charm and poise, and without self-consciousness. What first seemed to be his shyness was in fact indifference, attractive then but later repellent to Polly. Over a sweet kiss or two, he invited her to marry him in seven years when he finished with Harvard: "I said yes. I love to say yes."

Incredibly enough, he called in their contract, just as he had promised—but a year earlier, in 1914, the August that the Great War began. Polly came home from England, met with what passed for approval from the Peabodys, who regarded all New Yorkers as Hottentots, and in January 1915 she and Dick were married by "Uncle Cottie," the legendary Rev. Endicott Peabody, headmaster of Groton. They lived in Quaker Ridge, New York, for a year while her husband commuted to the City to work for Johns-Manville, a building supplies company. He wasn't much of a go-getter, didn't care about business or much of anything, except booze and fires; he loved to watch buildings burn. Their son was born February 4, 1916, William Jacob Peabody, and the three moved into New York. Richard Peabody was a reluctant father. He didn't like childish noise or childish mess, and he wished for Polly to remain his playmate. Domestic responsibilities were for him both an offense and a rebuke, and he took to leaving the house at all hours, and coming home drunk. Polly did not miss him: the thought of nursing and caring for her son beneath the gaze of her husband filled her with revulsion. Dick quit his job, just as he had quit Harvard, and decided to go into the shipping business for himself; Polly invested her father's legacy in the enterprise, and it went bust.

Her husband then enlisted as an officer in Boston's aristocratic Battery A, and headed for the Mexican border to help quell The Troubles there: "My nest egg was gone and so was Dick."

Polly lived, miserably, with her in-laws. Her husband returned from one war, gave her a daughter, Polleen, born August 12, 1917, and left for another war in France. (The sight of his newly born baby girl had sent him off on a bender.) Life with Col. and Mrs. Peabody, Jacob and Florence, was dismal and mean. The old man was preparing to go to war himself, and the house in Danvers, Massachusetts, was as full of battle as St. Mark's School had been in Harry's last year there, with huge display maps set here and there, the day's advance or retreat marked with colored pins, and implements of war laid out and at the ready. Boston loved the war, with its discipline and its agon of retribution and sacrifice.

Florence Wheatland Peabody had been a great beauty in the Nineties, and had then "unsensationally" married Dick's stern father. Now she was an invalid, wearing nun-black nightclothes, and much given to sotto voce complaints about the thoughtlessness of her daughter-in-law. The house, brought brick by brick from England by an ancient shipowning Peabody, was kept shuttered. Polly rolled bandages like a fairy-tale stepdaughter, and recalled that only Uncle Jack Morgan—Dick Peabody's godfather, too!—said a kind word or two to her.

One can imagine with what relief and joy she greeted her husband home from the war. Whole he was, and wearing the Croix de Guerre. The young couple found an apartment on the seamy side of Back Bay, and prepared to be happy together. But Dick, out of uniform, found jobs scarce, and his experience in France of no use in finding them. He was indifferent to the realities of marriage, and whiskey was close at hand. Dick began to drink so compulsively that frequently it was necessary that he be watched day and night by a nurse. His only delight during those postwar days was to chase fires: he had installed a fire gong above their bed and arranged with the fire chief to have all major alarms rung there. He kept a full fireman's outfit—hip boots, rubber coat and helmet—ready on a chair, and was considering the installation of a pole to the garage below their bedroom. Polly said it was "unnerving." When such private arrangements as his were banned by the municipal authorities, he sought and found excitement in roadhouses. At the urging of J. P. Morgan, Polly took him into the country during the winter to try to cure him, but he managed, as always, to get hold of a bottle. He lost his job at the State Street

The Grew family, together with inlaws: Crosbys, Beals and Morgans: c. 1906. *(With permission of Ruth Ammi Cutter)*

KEY

Top row: 1—2—3—4—5—6—7
Middle row: 8—9—10—11—12—13—14—
15 (in lap)
Front row: 16—17—18—19—20

1. Stephen Van Rensselaer Crosby
2. Junius Spencer Morgan
3. Henrietta Marian Crosby (Aunt Rita)
4. Boylston Adams Beal (Uncle Bob)
5. Jane Norton Morgan (Aunt Jessie)
6. Elizabeth Sturgis Beal (Aunt Elsie)
7. John Pierpont Morgan, Jr. (Uncle Jack)
8. Edward Wigglesworth Grew
9. Ruth D. Grew, Jr. (Cutter)
10. Jane Norton Grew ("Gramilee")
11. Henry Sturgis Grew

12. Henry Sturgis Morgan
13. Henry Grew Crosby (Harry)
14. Ruth Dexter Grew
15. Helen Grew (Birdsall)
16. Jane Norton Morgan (Nichols)
17. Elizabeth Sturgis Beal (Hinds)
18. Katherine Schuyler Crosby
(Choate-Wilkins)
19. Jane Norton Grew (Angell)
20. Frances Tracy Morgan (Pennoyer)

Henry Grew Crosby: Independence Day, 1900.

Henrietta Grew Crosby. *(With permission of Sylvia Choate Whitman)*

The Apple Trees: Manchester-by-the-Sea. *(With permission of Sylvia Choate Whitman)*

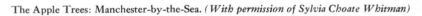

Harry Crosby, about six years old. *(With permission of Sylvia Choate Whitman)*

Harry, about eleven years old, a student at Noble and Greenough.

Senior class, St. Mark's School, 1917: standing, Gardner Monks (third from left); seated, front row, George Richmond Fearing (second from left) and Harry Crosby (second from right). *(With permission of G. Gardner Monks)*

Lanchy, near the Somme, August 23, 1917: "Crosby and Fox have their hair cut off with a singularly weird effect," according to Stuart Kaiser. *(With permission of George Richmond Fearing)*

Harry, with chums and Ford, shortly before catastrophe at Verdun, November 22, 1917. *(With permission of the Morris Library, Southern Illinois University)*

Harry (second from left on bench) with comrades in Ambulance Section 641, at the Somme, summer of 1917. *(With permission of George Richmond Fearing)*

The Hounds, photographed with decorations following Armistice Day, 1919, in Boston. From left, Philip ("the Vulture") Shepley, Harry Crosby, George Richmond ("Tote") Fearing, Stuart Kaiser.

Harry and Polly Crosby, soon after their marriage in New York, photographed in Paris, September, 1922.

St. Moritz, February, 1924, with Caresse (seated between unidentified woman and Harry's mother) and unidentified man wearing mustache: "Dislike the hemmed-in feeling one has in the mountains. Was never meant for a cage . . ." —*Shadows of the Sun (With permission of the Morris Library, Southern Illinois University)*

Caresse: North Africa, winter of 1925. *(With permission of the Morris Library, Southern Illinois University)*

Harry in the Sahara, at Touggourt, with opium pipe and Zora, a Berber girl, thirteen: "Two gaunt musicians and beer and hashish and little Zora removing layer after layer of the most voluminous garments, the last piece being a pair of vast cotton drawers, such as clowns wear, and which was gathered about her slender waist by a huge halyard. Then she begins to dance, slowness at first with curious rhythms of her ventre and then convulsive shiverings (two matchless breasts like succulent fruit) and wilder the music and more serpentine her rhythms . . . and O God when shall we ever cast off the chains of New England?"
—*Shadows of the Sun* (February, 1925)

Walter Van Rensselaer Berry ("Cousin Walter"), friend of Henry James and Marcel Proust, companion to Edith Wharton, surrogate father to Harry, to whom he left his library and the residual legacy of his fortune: "Lady Ribbesdale told me that it was said in Paris that, unlike some gentleman callers who left their hostess with a baby, Berry left them with a book . . ."
—Louis Auchincloss (*With permission of the Morris Library, Southern Illinois University*)

Harry and Caresse, 1925: "But the best picture is that one of you and me at Etretat. It is perfect and if we ever get to be famous we should destroy all our other pictures in favor of this one . . ."
—Harry to Caresse, three years later

Trust Company, run by friends and relations of the Peabodys; he was hospitalized. And Polly met Harry.

She wasn't coy with him. She was his elder, and her compassion for her husband was deep, but Harry overwhelmed her, frightened her, excited her, won her: "My love for Harry blinded me like a sunrise." For a few days she refused to meet with Harry alone, to betray Dick. But Harry pounded away at her, showered gifts on her children and flowers on her. The Peabodys' modest walk-up at 37 River Street was not far from 95 Beacon, where Harry was living during his second year at Harvard. Mrs. Crosby was in Switzerland for the winter, and her son intercepted the gardenias, camellias and lilies brought to town from her hothouses in Manchester and had them sent to Polly. On one occasion, when Mr. Crosby wished to give a dinner party, the Crosbys' butler was obliged to borrow back some plants to adorn 95 Beacon.

From the day he first slept with her, Harry pursued Polly with the kind of fanatical purity of intention that was his virtue and vice, his bold signature. No sooner had she spent a night with him at the Belmont Hotel in New York than she got a letter from Paris: "I don't know what to do and I suppose it would be better if I were killed. You're my religion and everything I look up to. . . ." Talk of death and religion, such a natural coupling for Harry, must have alarmed and baffled her.

Harry's attitude toward the ladies of his generation was confused. Tote Fearing recalls a Harvard lecture on social ethics after which Harry rose and "said he'd rather kiss a nice girl than screw a chippie. . . . The line in those days was finely drawn between nice girls and chippies." Marriage had been much on his mind during the war, and so, naturally enough, was sex. But he had, after all, given his mother certain assurances. She was anxious about her lamb's immortal soul among the stews of the immoral City of Light; she had pressed him to reassure her that he would be good, and he did: "Paris certainly is the city of temptation—especially for those who heretofore have been inclined toward gaiety of all sorts and who haven't been warned sufficiently of the tremendous risk and dangers that abound. However don't you and Pa ever have any qualms about me for you can count on Private Crosby to keep his word—that you may be sure of." To his regret he kept his word.

Harry's serial sexual adventures during the last seven years of his life should be understood as acts committed not only in the service of pleasure but against self-government, of which decorum was the most visible symptom. His seductions were acts of anarchy—and they were thus perceived by the Brahmins, whose social arrangements he labored to subvert. But however he might thumb his nose at Boston by seducing its women, or its men's women, he managed to worship the purity of whatever young lady might find herself his temporary partner. The values that he received, and wished to disrupt, are nicely condensed in a letter written by Elizabeth Cabot, from Boston, at the turn of the century:

> We are moral over the breakfast table and moral the last thing at night, and moral all the hours in between. We moralize in society and at home, and I confess to an unsatisfied longing, occasionally, for a little of the harmless and graceful superficiality of the French. These, however, are the natural sensations of a girl brought up in the most moral of cities and belonging to the most moral family in that city, and I have no doubt that if I tried the superficial system a while, I should seek refuge from a still deeper discontent.

By the time Harry had met Polly, and decided to woo and win her, it was arguable that the Peabodys had displaced the Cabots as "the most moral family" in the "most moral of cities." Harry expected Polly to divorce her husband, quickly, just like that. What a program to impose upon a socially conscious young maiden, wise to Boston's rules if not to the point of the game, moreover a young lady who had been sealed in matrimonial oaths by none other than "Uncle Cottie"! The views of Rev. Endicott Peabody on the subject of divorce were notorious in Boston. Frank D. Ashburn, in his *Peabody of Groton*, reproduces a letter Dick Peabody's uncle wrote in 1916 to a middle-aged graduate of Groton who had announced to his former headmaster his marriage to a divorcée:

> Dear ——
>
> I feel obliged to tell you that the contents of your letter from Bermuda have brought me great distress. I have been informed that Mrs. —— obtained a decree of divorce from her husband for some other reason than that of unfaithfulness on his part. This being the case, she was not in my judgment free to contract another marriage.
>
> The step is directly contrary to the teachings of Christ and strikes at the very foundations of family life.
>
> Aff yr friend,
> (signed) Endicott Peabody

A book of etiquette from the early nineteenth century suggested that young ladies should reject a gentleman's offer to touch their hands, and offered "many other points of delicacy and refinement" to ward off "that desecration of the person, which has too often led to vice." The Bostonian view of woman as either an unpolluted vessel or a "chippie" had not changed since Mrs. John Farrar composed the frosty instructions above, in 1836. But Harry and his colleagues in war knew all about the "desecration of the person." They had carried buckets filled with amputated hands and legs, yet they were asked to regard hands and legs, attached to women, as mysteries too sacred to clasp.

Yet for Polly to indulge her passion seemed equally impossible. From time to time during late 1920 and early 1921, when the pressure on her to decide—or her guilt—became unbearable, she would run off to New York for asylum. And Harry, stuck at Harvard "for the family's sake," would pursue her with letters. Often the difference between them in age and situation became for him almost intolerable. There she was, seven years his elder, moving freely through the world, while he, a college boy, was expected to prepare a speech arguing the pros and cons of prohibition to deliver before his class in social ethics the following morning.

> I'm in the most horrible state of depression this evening. Cambridge on Sunday night is like a morgue. And I haven't seen you for so long, dearest. Sometimes life is absolutely unbearable without you and tonight is one of those times. You write me and tell me that I must be all happy and cheerful but God don't you see that this is impossible seeing that I can never hope to marry you whom I love and adore and who means life itself to me. . . . You also say that it is better for us not to see each other if I'm unhappy, but can't you see that this would be even harder to bear? The hours spent with you and my memories of you have meant everything in the world to me they have been the happiest and most perfect times. My life really began when I first met you and it will end if I ever have to say farewell to you.

From the beginning, he never let up with his talk of death and love, the two always mixed in his imagination, with mutual suicide apprehended as the most sublime of couplings. His letters are full of his curious fixation:

> I promise you that whenever you want we shall die together and what's more I am perfectly ready now or will be anytime. With the

absolute Faith that we shall be One in Heaven as soon as we die forever and ever it is a great temptation to foresake this life. . . .

. . . if worse should come to worse and you couldn't get a divorce . . . I'll come down [to New York, from Boston] and kill you and then kill myself so that we can go right to Heaven together—and we can die in each other's arms and I'll take the blame so you won't have to worry, Dear. . . . If by any chance I should die or be killed (I promise you never to kill myself unless you die or unless I kill us both together) I hope you'll end your life and come to me right away so we can be together as One in Heaven. . . .

I still and always will feel that we are so close and near to each other that Death at any time for us both will bring us such happiness as we've never dreamed of and which will last forever. And someday Darling I pray that we shall die together. I can think of nothing more sacred or beautiful. . . .

Assuming by the face of all available evidence that Polly Peabody was in no hurry to die, and enjoyed no conviction that she would meet her lover in worlds to come, it is clear that she was a brave woman. To love Harry she was obliged to believe in his seriousness: his talk about death, and his eagerness to die, would have been merely contemptible were it not meant. And if he meant what he said, what assurance did Polly have that he would not act upon it, let the hammer fall according to his whim, despite her wishes?

Moreover, she found herself late in 1920 married to an alcoholic and in love with someone who gave every appearance of becoming one. There were some things about Boston she never understood, but the part that liquor played in the city's moral system she comprehended with subtle exactitude. Alcohol had been important to the social life of Harvard, and, as Polly understood, its importance continued thereafter. Dick and his friends had roistered at roadhouses, and they still roistered at roadhouses, and in the company of fast women, from whom a decent wife was meant to save them. Forgiveness and promises of reform were the exchanges of courtship between a Boston gentleman and a Boston virgin, and they gave to one's love, as Polly said, "an evangelistic aura."

For Harry, Polly was his sacred savior, and how he repented—and sinned that he might repent—on her behalf! He created a prayer for them each to say at bedtime, and illustrated it with the first of many signs he designed for them: *Thank You O God for Pollee. I pray Dear God that our Love shall be immortal. I pray Dear God that we shall*

*have a perfect marriage together. God bless us and take care of us.
Grant O God that our two souls shall be together as One in Heaven.
Forever. Amen.*

He prayed twice each day in front of her photograph, morning and
night, after purifying himself in a cold bath: "As I wrote you & believe
implicitly 'more things are wrought by prayer than this world dreams
of' and 'are not two prayers a perfect strength?' I ask God to make me
worthy of You and pray God to grant you Happiness. My faith in You
is my faith in God and my religion is You and God and for our Souls
to mingle and be as One protected by God." This pious declaration
comes from Harry's June 2, 1921, forty-page leviathan, wherein he also
offered to murder his beloved and himself on behalf of their passion, a
course neither his Church nor any other would be likely to sanction.
But Harry had managed to translate bloody self-slaughter into a rite of
holy sacrifice.

Back and forth he went, from piety and innocence to cruel self-
indulgence. Polly was forever pushed off balance by his violent trans-
formations of humor and character. He especially upset her with his
black moods. A funeral-going Bostonian once remarked that "melancholy, Sir, is the one passion of my life," and it was surely the control-
ling passion of that time in Harry's life. Years later he would recall his
courtship of Polly Peabody, and his battle with Boston and his family
on her behalf, as the darkest period of his history, worse by far than
his sentence under the guns in France.

In letter after letter he threw himself upon her mercy: "I'm very
happy to know that in spite of my rotten behavior you have stuck by
me and have put me back on the path of decency and strength. . . . To
have caused you so much pain makes me miserable and unhappy. O
Bunny Dear I pray you on bended knee to forgive me." For drinking
too much, and doubting her loyalty to him, and picking at her to leave
her husband, and blaming her for his unhappiness. He was even capable
of accusing her of having defiled him: "I was a young unsophisticated

virgin that time we loved together in N.Y. and it wouldn't be fair to forsake me now that I am so hopelessly in love with you." Within the same letter the wronged and abandoned virgin would whipsaw his seducer into his redeemer: "You have saved me and pulled me up to heights I could never have reached."

Surely, Polly enjoyed the "evangelistic aura" that Harry's theatrics provoked from her passion, and Harry understood this as well as she did, and played upon it, committing a full inventory of sins the better to have a lively one to confess: "I'm so repentant Bunny and oh so lonely that if you could see me you'd want to mother me and be all mine." But his hard drinking bothered her greatly, and she begged him to quit; she also worried about his affection for the girls he had known before they met. So from time to time he would offer for Polly's benefit a program of assurance and reform: "You'll probably hear rumors about me rushing Sis or Sue or drinking too much but after all you know me Dear and I promise you it won't be true. I can't help seeing people at dances and drinking once in a while but I have drawn up a list of what I call 'Moderation' rules dealing with (1) drinking (2) gambling (3) fast driving and (4) smoking, all conducive to quietness. I shall practically cut out drinking except on Saturday nights." But he did no such thing. Rather, Polly's requests that he quit drinking angered him, and he would get drunk to spite her. Only his mother managed to extract a contract of abstinence from him. Early in 1922 he noted in his diary: "Today Mamma gave me a hundred dollars for going a month without drinking. Wasn't worth it."

Harry pestered Polly to tell her husband about their affair, and then divorce him, and finally she did confess. Dick accepted the fact of his cuckolding with grace and sympathy, and offered his wife, without bitterness, a divorce, late in May of 1921. Harry begged her to grab it: ". . . and dear, you know that although it's terrible now for Dick that he is the type that will get over it—whereas we never could have." The single condition imposed upon her—by her mother—was that she forgo seeing Harry for six months, beginning in June, 1921, while she tested a separation from her husband. She agreed to the arrangement, and left Boston for New York.

It might have seemed to them for a moment that their prayers were to be answered. They had fallen in love: very well, at the end of half a year they would be free to marry. But they had not reckoned with Boston, with the Peabodys' rage and humiliation, with the Crosbys' contempt, and most crucially with their own uncertainties of intention and emotional tempests. During the following year and more, they would set dates for their marriage, break them, set new dates, quarrel violently, resolve to have done forever one with another, reconcile. Polly was at once proud of Harry's violent recklessness, and frightened of him; Harry was at once proud of her worldliness, and ashamed of it. It is true that the very pain provoked by their many unions and sunderings was bracing for them: as believers in pearls, they were also believers in the irritations that produce them. But those irritations were valuable only when they were internal and organic. Polly and Harry were perfectly willing to stage a two-character melodrama to play out their love, but they never counted on such a hostile audience as they were obliged to endure.

In the Crosbys' best judgment Polly-Jacob-from-New-York had wormed her way into poor Dick Peabody's heart, and after his heroic service in the war had abandoned him, trading him in for a newer model Brahmin, their own son, in whom they had invested such high ambitions. She had acted as his chaperone, and perverted the trust that Mrs. Crosby had placed in her out of pity. To the Crosbys, Polly Peabody was dishonored and corrupt, and for their son to love and honor her was absurd, without dignity or sense, wholly unthinkable. She was an adultress, about to become a divorcée, no better than one of the dance hall girls that Harvard boys might use for a night or two.

And not only was she an adultress; it was clear to the Crosbys that she had led their son astray. She was seven years older, after all, a mother! Betty Beal had no liking for her, Kitsa despised her; even Tote Fearing held her in contempt: "She married Harry, and wrecked him. I always disliked her, because I felt that she wrecked Harry. I felt that he was an orthodox Bostonian who had been exiled to Paris by his family because he wanted to marry a divorced woman, and that seemed a good place for them. And from then on he was on the great slide down." Even after the fact, one of his St. Mark's classmates, studying for the ministry, wrote Harry in Paris about his bride, so hard-won: "Pray God you will be able to lift her up!"

Polly, who believed that upon her marriage to Dick Peabody she had been accepted by Boston, was stung by the savagery of her former friends once she was known to be considering a divorce from a Peabody. She recollected years after the event that "the entire 'shore' ganged up on me and were plotting to move in for the kill." A luncheon was given in her honor in the same house where she and her husband had announced their engagement, with the same guests that had been there on that previous, happier occasion: "If I refused the invitation I was to be branded without benefit of trial; if I went I knew I must defend myself or sink." It is characteristic of Polly's self-certitude, and Boston's killing courtesy, that she believed she had performed a *coup de théâtre* by flattering each guest in her turn. "It worked, my Lord, it worked."

It did no such thing.

The first edition of *Etiquette*, by Emily Post, was published in 1922. Under a rubric called "The Instincts of a Lady" there appears the following regulation: "As an unhappy wife, her dignity demands that she never show her disapproval of her husband, no matter how publicly he slights or outrages her." For Polly to divorce her husband was in Tote Fearing's recollection "unheard of in those days, even among Boston Episcopalians." Mrs. Crosby could not bring herself to discuss the disgrace with her son. The possibility of his marriage to Polly Peabody was, literally, unspeakable. And so was it at first for Stephen Crosby. He threatened Harry, and bribed him, finally buying him the Stutz he had promised him, to put him in a happy and sensible humor.

But Harry would not budge from his intention. That his generation considered itself betrayed by the aftermath of World War I is one of the most often-told tales of American social history. F. Scott Fitzgerald's characters are forever complaining that the homeland repudiated them by refusing to stand at moral attention for them after the war.

Ten minutes of heavy shelling, or the first whiff of gas, taught young men to distrust old men, if they were prepared to distrust anyone. Harry was too young, when he docked in France, to distrust the people he knew, whom he innocently believed he could comprehend. He clung fiercely to his innocence during the war, perhaps because he had had a glimpse of the territory one generation beyond, and hadn't liked what he had seen. But if he managed, by heroic disregard of the evidence, to accept his elders as models and guides, his slightly older and more sophisticated comrades regarded them as tin preachers and lost idiots. John Dos Passos wrote home from the war what Harry came to swallow whole while he was courting Polly:

The fellows on the section are frightfully decent—all young men are frightfully decent. If we only governed the world instead of the swag-bellied old fogies in frock-coats that do! oh what a God-damned mess they have made of organized society, the bankers and brokers and meat-packers—and business men. Better any tyranny than theirs. Down with the middle aged!

In Boston even the young aspired to the condition of the middle-aged, and Harry began to rebel against everyone who disapproved of his lady—and his love for her. "Bostonians hate her (the lost lady) so I hate Bostonians," he wrote from Paris after his contempt for his home-town had congealed. Earlier, during their courtship, he wrote Polly in a tone of anger provoked by hurt and betrayal: "To hell with most of Boston. Why can't they mind their own business? They all go to church and are sabbatarians and think [they're] damned righteous. Then why don't they help us instead of hinder or at least stay neutral and not concern themselves with other people's private affairs. They're for the most part sexless, hypocritical busy-bodies. . . ."

And none more so than Dick Peabody's father. Col. Peabody tried strenuously to injure both Polly and Harry, and to that end made a monstrous strategic blunder. On January 4, 1922, Harry wrote Polly in New York that Col. Peabody "came to see Pa today but I don't know what about. I hate him. Pa however refused to discuss our situation with him. The old man I feel sure now is right back of us. . . ." In fact, Mr. Crosby, in one of the abrupt turnabouts that characterized him, decided, very reluctantly, to give his son whatever support and love he could muster at a bad time for them both. He was starchy, he was a snob, he wanted the approval of Society. But he loved Harry, and wished him well, and would not be pushed around, not by Dick Peabody's father, not by anyone. Harry understood his father better than his father understood himself when he wrote Polly that "my old man is peculiar but he will stick right back of us no matter what happens. It's too bad he is so conventional and is so damned scared of what people will say, but I told him if I didn't marry you I'd commit suicide and that I nearly had already." Betty Beal remembers Mr. Crosby from the period of Harry's courtship with compassion both for him and for his son: "You couldn't help liking Steve, you really couldn't. In some ways I think he and Harry were too much alike, so they didn't get on from that angle. Their temperaments were alike; their points of view were not alike. He never got over his disappointment in Harry. He was always trying to get him back into the fold, to be a proper banker, or whatever, whatever he would have liked himself to have been. I don't think his father was ashamed of him, but he was certainly bitterly disappointed."

Col. Peabody was so outraged by Polly's repudiation of a Peabody son that he vilified his daughter-in-law everywhere, and so hysterically that Polly wrote Dick in desperation, begging him to intercede, to interrupt or at least slow the flow of malice from his father. Dick replied in some confusion: "I haven't seen anybody & don't know anything. There have been some good fires lately & I have been on the wagon & that is about all the news there is with me. You may be right in my old man's attitude of mind about you, but as far as his doing anything about it, I am positive you imagine it. . . . As for his hurting you in Boston, that is rubbish. He doesn't want to, & you are too well known for him to be able to if he did. . . ."

Dick Peabody behaved toward his estranged wife with impeccable consideration, and persistent affection. At the end of their trial separation, on December 11, 1921, he wrote her in Millbrook, New York, where she was recuperating from a tonsillectomy and from the exhausting strain of Harry's courtship:

> I feel sure that the hardest part of your trouble is over now. Your tonsils will make more difference than you realize, & with Harry adopting such a fine attitude, & with both of us doing all we can to help you, I know that life will soon take on a very different aspect. I can still start the water eyewards when I think of you, but if we grasp Harry & Jane firmly with our left hands we should be able to shake with our rights without any show of emotion and with a good deal of genuine pleasure. . . . [He had found a girl, who worked with Harry at the National Shawmut Bank, whom Harry did not know that Dick loved.]
>
> I am so glad Harry has made everything so easy for you & that you have decided to wait longer than April. Selfishly for me I can't think of anything better than your marrying him; & if after a year, during which time you saw what N.Y. had to offer, you still were in love with him I should really feel that it was a genuinely good thing & therefore be very happy about it. . . .
>
> I went on a drunk after seeing you but as I felt I had sufficient cause & pulled myself out of it all right after the game I decided to keep on drinking. Last week I went on another, without any cause & though I pulled myself out of it alone I am through for a good while. . . . It is hard of course to give it up especially as this time I really enjoyed myself hugely & wasn't sodden & stupid & drinking in bed & weeping the way I used to be—neither did I go nuts on one drink. . . .

By joining the Shawmut National Bank, Harry tried one last time to play his father's game by his father's rules. Robert Maynard Hutchens, who had been graduated from Yale in 1921, the same year Harry got his war degree from Harvard, recalls that his classmates were "overwhelmingly" Episcopalian and Republican, and that "their favorite poem [was Tennyson's] *Crossing the Bar*, perhaps because of some confusion about the meaning of the words." The great ambition of Yale and Harvard and Princeton men was to enter the profession of law if they were intellectuals, or if they were not, to make money as brokers, bond salesmen or investment bankers. Soon after joining the bank, Harry reported to Polly in New York that "I am reading with minute care a book on stocks and bonds and am learning everything I can about business in general as I want to someday be able to give you lovely presents and I want you to be very happy and have everything you wish for. I think in two or three months I'll get a better job in the bank. . . ." He would eat lunch every day with Tote and one or another of the business-bound "hounds" at Schrafft's, "where there are some pretty peppy waitresses." He went to Red Sox games, was subject to the affectionate concern of his friends, played golf and bridge, looked forward to the time when Polly would meet *The Flying Fisherman* at the Manchester depot in the gray Locomobile touring car his father, he hoped, would give them as a wedding present: "Can't you see the pretty Mrs. Harry Crosby driving down to the station with the kids to meet me? God it will be Heaven."

He was trying hard to fulfill the expectations of his father. Too hard, for Polly's taste, and he had finally to reassure her: "Don't worry that I'll become conventional or too practical as I can assure you it's not in my nature and it's only by the supremest of efforts that I am being quiet this winter. . . . Have you bought those fascinating black lace pretties yet? I saw a new kind here in a shop window today flesh colored with pink rosebuds on them—very charming. Thank God our love has so much of the spiritual in it."

At the end of her half-year trial separation from Dick, Polly accepted weekend visits from Harry in New York during the winter of 1921. After one of those visits, Ted Weeks bumped into Harry returning home to Boston in the sleeper section of the midnight train. Harry told him he "loathed" his job: "I recite the Rubaiyat as I jog across the Common to State Street, the one bright spot in my day." Harry, offering Ted "a snort from his flask, loosened his tie, removed his shoes and coat, and slid into the blankets the same impulsive, unorthodox kid." Harry's recollection of the occasion was bleaker: "Boozed scotch with Weeks on the N.Y. train, slept in clothes, cold and exhausted." His commutations to New York became increasingly miserable. Polly refused to promise to marry him. She tried for a while to forget Harry, even became casually engaged to some other men. She had accepted child support from Dick, but no alimony, and she felt pressed to find a career.

Harry's published diary, *Shadows of the Sun*, begins on January 1, 1922, and the early, brief, forlorn entries tell a good deal about the kind of life he and Polly suffered during those will-she/won't-she days:

> *February 9th:* Ashamed and unhappy and owe it to her to be a thousand times more dignified. . . .
> *February 10th:* Relentless remorse on my part; infinite weeping on hers. . . .
> *February 28th:* Tossed my sun-cross into the air to see whether to fight on or surrender. Fight on as it falls upon the floor sun upwards.
> *March 6:* Dark day of doubt.

Harry insisted upon regarding her as a frail vessel for his ethereal love, when in fact she was shrewd, tough, ambitious and worldly. "You're my religion and everything I look up to," he wrote her, soon after they first slept together. But the letter is addressed to The Fashion Form Brassière Company in Boston, at 2389 Washington Street, where Polly had a small sweatshop that manufactured the wireless brassière she had invented when she was a débutante, and whose patent she later sold to Warner Brothers Corset Company. Harry's letter continued: "You are so youthful and so trusting that I always feel you need protection." She neither needed nor solicited "protection." Harry loved Polly for her courage and resourcefulness, yet his training in the helplessness of undefiled ladies subverted his understanding of the woman he wished to marry. "You never can be terribly independent (thank the Lord) as you're too feminine and are not strong enough to battle in the world all alone."

Polly announced that she might make a career for herself as a writer, and Harry laughed at her, then was obliged to back off: "I think it fine of you to want to write books or plays and I won't laugh at you . . . but will try to help you to the best of my ability." Yet in the same letter he managed to condescend to her again: "You are so helpless that I worry about you in N.Y. . . . ." Sometimes his fussy concern for her welfare turned priggish, as when he insisted that she quit drinking cocktails "except when you're with me. They are too strong for you. And Dear never let your hair down your back except when you're alone." His jealousy in the days of their courtship and early marriage was fierce: he begged Polly not to see her husband after the separation, or write him, despite the amicability of their parting. He insisted that she destroy what photographs she owned of Dick, and that she give her engagement ring to her mother.

Polly was infatuated with the movies, and this caused awful friction between her and Harry. The possibility that his precious Polly might become the temporary possession of just anyone who had in his pocket the price of a movie ticket drove Harry wild: "You mustn't go into the Movies, Dear. You're too pure and decent and refined and so far above everyone that I should hate to think of you going into them. . . . I shan't let you go round with a Movie crowd under any circumstances." Well, she did, despite him. She always did what she pleased. She worked up a screen name that would disguise her, and save the Peabody and Jacob names from disgrace: Valerie Munro. She took screen tests, and boosted herself however she could, within decent limits, and Harry was obliged to swallow her determined ambition to put her name in lights: "How are the Movies going? I'm very jealous. . . . I hope you don't have to be seen in your 'pretties.' Do you? Answer me truthfully. I do hope you don't wander round with your hair all unloosened. . . ." He told her that the movies were "degrading." But the only reason she didn't finally make her career on the screen was that she couldn't; what she had, the movies didn't want. When she finally faced up to that sorry truth, Harry wrote her in relief: "You are most wise Dear to have stopped the Movies. Now that you have I can speak out and say frankly what I didn't want to before for fear of interfering. You have my wholehearted admiration for being so brave as to undertake it but the entire thing filled me with disgust to think of you who are so pure and clean and Dear associating with that type of person the greater part of whom are really no more than degenerates. . . . The movie sort of person is utterly worthless . . . the whole thing is cheap. . . ." For the rest of his life Harry avoided moving-picture shows. He wanted to marry pure, clean, helpless Polly, but sensible Polly wished to know what kind of life she could expect with him—what kind of economic future they would share. His job at the bank paid little. He had managed to make only eleven hundred dollars on stock speculations between July, 1921, and March, 1922: "Remember," he wrote her before he began his job, "in a short time we are going to have all the money we want. . . ."

He planned to take Polly to Europe for a while after they were married, and explained that his mother had given him thirty-five hundred dollars, and that two thousand more were due him from other sources. Not enough, she told him. (He noted in *Shadows of the Sun*, January 4, 1922, that in going over last year's accounts he discovered that he had spent seven thousand dollars: "More for charity than for gambling, more for flowers than for clothes, more for her than for myself." Seven thousand dollars at that time was a substantial sum, for a single man, living at home.) He tried to reassure her regarding his prospects:

> The financial situation isn't as bad as it looks. I'm to blame for giving you the impression that we wouldn't have enough. As I wrote you you don't know my family. They really are bully and if we really needed 20,000 they would come across. After . . . affairs here have calmed down (they are hectic at present and the family are pretty highstrung) I shall have a long talk with Ma about it all and explain to her that we'll need more. Then too Pa is always presenting K & me with 50 or 100 shares here and there and they're going to give us each a Cadillac (we could take the $4,000 instead of the car . . . if necessary). I won't mind cutting down on things. The only worry I have is that you shouldn't have enough.

None of it sounded right to Polly. Try as he might, Harry could not make her promise to marry him. She had no wish to remove herself from New York to the contempt of every person who mattered in Harry's hometown. Very well, Harry would live wherever she wished: "I hate Boston—but we could live on the Shore in summer & N.Y. the rest of the time. I've liked every friend of yours you've ever introduced me to," he lied, "and am sick to death of this blue-blooded régime." He assured her and reassured her: "We'll never live in damned old Boston." Still, she would not say yes; she said she would like more than anything to say yes, but she wouldn't.

Harry's diary entries for March, 1922, tell what it was like for him:

> *March 8th:* Her preciousness. Yet thrust deep into my heart is the sharp knife of despair. Adios. Shall never forget her eyes. Encountered my father. Pathetic attempt at sympathy. "Will give you a Rolls-Royce" and "People would never have approved." Whiskey and to bed. Cried all night.
> *March 12th:* Have not been to the Bank for five days.
> *March 14th:* Resigned from the Bank.

A week later Mrs. Crosby called upon her brother-in-law to help, and J. P. Morgan agreed to give Harry a position in Paris, for one year, at Morgan, Harjes et Cie. Harry's spirits lifted temporarily, and he even managed to reconcile himself to Polly's intransigent refusal to marry him. He wrote her that he had met with his Uncle Jack in

Boston: "I saw him alone for but five minutes yesterday and he was damn nice about you and me. The Morgans have certainly been great friends of ours during our many vicissitudes." Most of Harry's kin loathed Polly, but his Aunt Jessie Morgan liked her and so did her husband. J. P. Morgan had bought East Island, in Long Island Sound, from Polly's maternal grandfather, and renamed it Matinacock. He had helped Polly repeatedly to resolve her problems with his other godson, her husband Richard, and he was eager to help her to overcome whatever obstacles Boston had raised between her and her happiness. But he was merely mighty, not superhuman, and Boston would not budge, as he knew. So he arranged the exile of her lover.

Harry celebrated his resignation from the bank, and liberation from "Drearytown." The day he met with his uncle is recorded in his diary as "one of my wild days where I threw all care to the wind and drank to excess. . . . Result of being happier. At midnight drove old walrus' new automobile down the Arlington Street subway until we crashed slap-bang into an iron fence. A shower of broken glass, a crushed radiator, a bent axle, but no one hurt. Still another rotten episode to add to my rotten reputation." The next day, March 22, he noted "remorse and the usual gestures: a letter of apology, a cheque for damages, a gold resolution for the future."

It was past time for him to sail away from the City of Dreadful Night. And so he did—with Spud Spaulding: many wounds to share— but not before the city fired a final shot at him in the Boston section of a national society rag called *Town Topics*:

It looks as if the much-rumored engagement of Harry Grew Crosby and winsome and coy Mrs. Dick Peabody, one-time Molly [sic] Jacob, will not materialize into anything tangible for the present. The youth's father, Stephen Van R. Crosby, has just executed a neat *coup*, which, for the present at least, will put a stop to all possibilities revolving in the minds of this infatuated young pair by sending him off on the *Olympic* [*sic:* they sailed on the *Touraine*] last Saturday. With a responsible party, he is to visit the battlefields where he saw service with the French and, later, our armies. Crosby, only graduating last June from Harvard, was one of the youngest American soldiers to receive the Croix de Guerre from the French Government. The family and friends of the Crosbys are hoping this separation, with its new environment, will serve to break up this unfortunate love complication. . . .

7

"fantaisiste distingué."

—A senior Morgan banker's opinion of Harry Crosby

When his mother secured the bank job for Harry in Paris, Polly struck a bargain with him: she would leave for Europe also, and they would rendezvous there as long as he ceased to pester her about a wedding. He agreed to the terms: "When you come to Paris I'll promise not to keep urging you to marry me unless you want to and in that case we'll make a dash for the nearest eglise." (Harry had ambitions for a church wedding, and Polly didn't care for any kind of wedding at all. However, in the same mid-March letter, Harry took pains to remind her, before he left for Europe, that she had a contract to be fulfilled: "It was a pure gamble on my part as a year in Paris alone away from home and friends would be agony and I'd be miserable. Before taking this pretty decisive step I thought over all we had discussed and finally decided that you cared enough to come and live with me in Paris even if you wouldn't marry me. You told me you would do this."

And so she did. Polly sold a strand of pearls to pay for her passage to England, left her children in the care of her mother, and was staying with her aunt and uncle George Elin at their estate near London, Ardleigh Park, when Harry telephoned from across the English Channel the day he arrived in Paris, May 1. He was to begin work at Morgan, Harjes & Co. a week later, but his friend Philip Shepley, from the North Shore and American Ambulance Corps, had urged him to come to Turkey, so no sooner had he arrived than he "tossed the suncross to see whether to go to Constantinople to join the Armenian Relief or go to work at the Bank as I had promised Mamma. Verdict said stay. Instead flew to London."

His flight across the Channel was in those days a dramatic and expensive gesture (a one-way ticket cost seventy dollars) and it impressed Polly, who took leave of her alarmed relatives three days after Harry "dropped in from the clouds and swooped me up from the family nest." She flew with him to Paris, and Harry began work at the bank May 8. He gave as his address the Hôtel Métropolitan on rue Cambon, where he shared rent and lodgings with an American named Lou Norrie,* but he and Polly in fact lived together in a little room at the nearby Regina, on the Right Bank. He was hired at a salary of six hundred francs per month, plus a living allowance of seven hundred and fifty. With the franc at eighteen to the dollar, this came to seventy-five dollars per month. J. P. Morgan's instructions to his bank on Harry's behalf had made it clear that his nephew was to be hired "at a salary satisfactory to us as the boy has independent means." So he was, with the notation to his previous employer at the National Shawmut Bank that French salaries were not as high as American salaries, and that Harry "will be of no particular use to us for some little time." Shrewd guess, but optimistic: he was never worth a nickel to Morgan, Harjes & Co.

May and June in Paris were a lark. The couple walked together and lay together in the Bois de Boulogne. Harry took Polly to the battlefields he couldn't seem to stay away from: "And how I have changed but the land itself is little changed since the war and it is still The Waste Land." (Harry had read Eliot's long poem when it was first published, earlier that year.) On his twenty-fourth birthday at the fashionable Château de Madrid just outside Paris, he bribed a waiter to exchange clothes with him so that he could dance the tango wearing a dinner jacket. Afterwards, they swam in a pond in the forest, and then slept together between linen sheets.

One hot afternoon they hailed a taxi near the Place Vendôme, and when the cabdriver asked where they would like to be taken, Harry

* Seven years later, writing in *Shadows of the Sun*, Harry marveled that Francis Lothrop, his roommate for a while his first year at Harvard, had chosen the Métropolitan as the hotel to stay in with his wife: "Of all the dreary places and lousy with Bostonians."

said Deauville, hours away on the Normandy coast. And later, in mid-July, Harry wangled a leave of absence from the bank and took Polly to Venice, on the Simplon Express. They registered at Casa Petrarca, an orange-red hotel beside the Rialto on the Grand Canal, and used the names Vicomte and Vicomtesse Myopia, scoring a point off Boston's Myopia Hunt Club. One week later, they went to the Normandy coast again, to Étretat, and walked the bluffs and beaches, and Harry swam naked in the sea while Polly watched him from beneath a lace parasol.

Then, in Polly's words, "Boston trespassed into our Paradise again." Harry had flirted during the summer with a girl from Boston, and one day the girl's mother, "an indignant hyena-matron," visited Polly and told her she was ruining Harry's life, that Harry loved her daughter, and they wanted to marry but he couldn't break away from Caresse, who was furious, and told her she was leaving anyway and would sail for home the very next day. Polly left abruptly for America on July 22, and Harry was disconsolate: "Why did I let her go why why why O Sun-God tell me why." He was, oddly, more certain of their future than ever, "but there are sharp knives in the heart (to be withdrawn)." When the Boston girl left three weeks later, Harry did not even send her off: "Another closed book. She was like an appendix. Now she has been removed I feel strong and unafraid."

He took inventory of his recent history, found his values to be depressed, and resolved to reform himself. Nine days after Polly left for America, Harry wrote in his diary that the July just ending had been his "most unbalanced, unsettled, unforgiveable month." He pinned a chart on the wall, naming the evils he wished to conquer: "Thus Cigarettes (Smokeplums), Gambling (Pyramid), Girls (Masked Marvel), Talkativeness (Chatterbox). Each day is represented by a square. The race from start to finish is a hundred squares. Each day I abstain I shall advance the name (or horse) one square." Such lists and good resolutions were common symptoms among Bostonians, who were even quicker to detect the signs of sin in themselves than in others. For a week the chart seemed to work, and Harry wrote Polly on August 7: "I am more worthy of you now than at any time & so pure in heart and so much all yours that you would be a fool to marry any one else. . . . Reggie in the Ritz Bar the other day said My God Harry I've never seen you this way before. Keep it up as you're most attractive and dignified."

But Harry could never leave off breaking his good resolutions, any more than he could leave off making them. On August 9, Harry organized a carriage race, *"pour me distraire,"* down the Champs Élysées to the Ritz Bar, for a prize of five hundred francs: "At the Concorde the four hacks were well grouped and it was not until after the Rue de Rivoli that Joan and I were defeated in the final sprint by half a length, the others trailing behind. Brandy for the coachmen, cocktails for ourselves. . . . To make of life a race." And two weeks after he had begun his hundred-day race toward Goodness he gave an "elaborate luncheon at the Ritz (Extravagance moves back a square) then drove a virgin named Jeanne (she works in the Bank) to Deauville (Masked Marvel moves back a square) where I left her with her cousins and all night it rained and all night I gambled (Pyramid moves back a square) in the Salle de Baccara. What a spectacle! What avarice! What hunted faces! What folly! Smoked and drank and went to bed at five in the morning. (Smokeplums, Ritz Bar and Nocturne all move back a square). But I was morose and silent and Chatterbox advanced." One week later, he and Lou Norrie took five show girls to Deauville ("Masked Marvel moves back two and a half squares"), where he ran on the beach, played the horses, drank and gambled.

After such adventures he went to work and sat at his desk in a stupor, having too little energy even to eat lunch. He would torment himself with self-hatred, wondering what his mother, and Polly, would think of him if they could see him. On the reverse side of a Morgan, Harjes check, he composed further resolutions: "1/To behave—no hard liquor—no femmes 2/Not to get too involved 3/When we marry to promise to play the game no matter what happens." Then, after work, he joined his friends from the Ritz Bar in a high-stakes baccarat game, throwing empty champagne bottles out the window, barring their door against the angry proprietor: "Wilder and wilder, higher and higher the stakes; twenty louis a hand [one *louis d'or* piece, twenty-five francs, was worth almost a dollar and fifty cents], thirty louis, forty, fifty and the last few hands at a hundred louis. Won double what I lost at Deauville. Lucky in cards, unlucky in love. The hell you say."

Finally, on August 30, exhausted, sick with longing, disgusted, he wrote in his diary, "can't stand it any longer!" He sent a cable to Polly in Nantucket, where she was vacationing with her mother and brothers: BUNNY I CAN'T STAND IT ANOTHER DAY WITHOUT YOU. SAILING SATURDAY AQUITANIA STEERAGE DONT SAY A WORD TO ANYONE WILL MEET YOU AT THE BELMONT. HAVE BEEN SICK BUT BETTER TODAY. WILL HAVE COME RIGHT BACK. WIRE REPLY TO CAMBON. ALL MY LOVE. YOUR HARRY. He told the bank he was indisposed with the grippe and bet his roommate, Lou Norrie, who was sailing September 1, one hundred dollars that he could beat him to New York. Polly wired YES. Harry borrowed a hundred dollars to pay his passage and made his way to Cherbourg, where he was told he would have to remain a week in quarantine. He fell into an uncontrolled rage, then successfully bribed his way aboard the *Aquitania*. He had no money but snuck into first class and managed to win forty dollars at a game of cards, which he immediately spent on champagne for "a crowd of unfortunates (you can keep only those things which you give away)."

Three days before reaching New York, he bathed in the first-class swimming pool, and that night, dressed in evening clothes, "hair immaculately parted, shoes polished, gold-tip cigarettes, contrast to four days on the bow deck in an undershirt and a pair of torn trousers," he took a dinner of caviar and mock turtle soup and hummingbirds on toast with a lady and her two daughters, whom he decided were "pincushions." During coffee a steerage inspector tapped him on the shoulder and asked him by what right he had elevated himself to first class: "Would have replied 'love' had it not been for the pincushions. Thanked my hostess and departed without mortification. (I had eaten.)"

The *Aquitania* docked September 9, and Polly was at the customs barrier to greet him. The battle was over, he wrote, the race was won: "Felt like a marathon runner who has breasted the tape but who is on the verge of collapse." They met Lou Norrie's ship, collected Harry's hundred-dollar wager, and were married that afternoon in the chapel of New York City's Municipal Building. Leonard Jacob, Polly's brother, gave away the bride. They celebrated at the Belmont, Back Bay Boston's favorite New York hotel, then Harry telephoned his mother in Washington, D.C., where she was staying with her daughter and son-in-law, Robert Choate, whom Kitsa had married shortly before Harry sailed for France.

The *Aquitania* was to sail east in forty-eight hours, and the Peabody children had to be sent for, but Harry insisted on seeing his mother to explain why he had had to do what he had done. Kitsa answered Harry's telephone call and in cold fury told him that Mrs. Crosby was too upset to speak with him. Harry and his sister had never been close, and now they never could be. Harry demanded an audience with his mother, and that Polly come to Washington with him. Polly remembered later that Kitsa warned Harry to come alone, and that Harry replied, "Nevermore."

Together they took the midnight train to Washington, and arrived at the Choates' house in Chevy Chase in time for breakfast: "All of us were unnerved," Polly remembers. "It was a bad beginning. Harry's mother never addressed a word to me. Kitsa was cool; only Robbie was compassionate. We left on the three o'clock, nearly broken in spirit. Our glorious adventure had lost its shine. They made me feel like a two-year-old who had gotten into the forbidden jam pot."

The Peabody children were waiting with their nurse at the Belmont. When Harry saw them, he disappeared till it was time to sail next morning. It was, as Polly understood, Harry's "Gethsemane." Harry had moved heaven and earth to marry the woman he wanted, and like a man who has lifted too heavy a weight, or run too long a race, certain muscles had been stretched too far to function ever again at full strength. The first entry in Harry's diary following his marriage says only that he had just read *Les Désenchantées*, and asks, "Am I?"

In the midst of his most strenuous efforts to win Polly, he had noticed about himself that he had "the fox's fear of being trapped." Polly understood this, and resolved from the beginning to abjure from the Boston custom of shaming her husband into submission; she knew that he would accept neither the whip nor the cage, so she advised him to cease his promises of reform if they were made on her behalf. She had married Harry for what he was, rather than for anything she might make of him.

But however determined she was to leave her fox free, he felt trapped anyway. Suddenly he was not merely a lover, but a stepfather, and he did not like what he suddenly was. In his courting days he had heaped gifts upon the Peabody kids, and charmed them, and perhaps his expressions of affection were even sincere. He had offered Polly advice about their care during her separation from Dick: "don't pamper Bill," and "don't let little Polleen get too stubborn. She's a knockout. I hope they'll grow to love me." He spoke of the children as "our infants," but as soon as he married Polly the children became entirely hers. He wrote in his personal diary that Rimbaud and a Spanish bootblack he had recently met were the only children he should ever have cared to have. He began to uncover his authentic attitude toward Polleen and Billy even before the wedding, when Polly was in one of her willing humors and they were planning to marry: "We'll take the infants if you think best but of course for a honeymoon it would be better if we can go without them as we would be so tied down. . . ."

Harry wanted a married mistress, not a mother, and reminders of Polly's domestic condition, and his, offended him extremely. A few months after their marriage, the Crosbys were visited in Paris by some guests from Boston, Ellery Sedgwick and a couple of other Harvard classmates. Harry took them to the races at Longchamp while Polly, pleading exhaustion, remained at home to read. Or so she said. Instead, she gathered her son and daughter, dressed herself in a matronly robe they liked, and spent the afternoon playing with them on the floor. Harry and his friends returned winners from the track and wanted to fetch Polly away to the circus. When he discovered familial squalor on the floor of his sitting room, Harry was shocked. Seeing Polly at play with her brats, with a motherly fit upon her, he stormed in shame out the door, pushing his friends before him. He returned three days later, bearing toys for the children and a cloth-of-gold mandarin negligée for Polly.

The family first lived on the Left Bank at the Hôtel de l'Université, but at Morgan, Harjes' recommendation they moved to an apartment on the rue des Belles Feuilles, a fashionable and dowdy address on the Right Bank. The children were kept prisoners of their nursery. Twice each week, Polly allowed them to jump up and down on her bed while the maid changed the linen, and the children regarded these meager adventures as the high moments of their week.

Billy Peabody was rarely home, having been trundled off from childhood to one school or another, Le Rosey in Gstaad or Cheam in Surrey. He was on quite a formal footing with his mother, less so with Harry, who took some temporary pains to entertain him while the boy was on vacation, pulling pranks with him, taking him to horse and bicycle races, or to the circus. Harry was pleased enough to drop balloons filled with beer from the top floor of 19 rue de Lille on passersby to the delight of Billy and a school chum, but he remained set irrevocably against any hint of entrenched domesticity in his household. He and Billy were effectively friendly acquaintances, and Harry liked it best that way.

It was awful for the boy, and his misery was compounded by Harry's stubborn refusal to allow him or Polleen or Caresse to have any contact with Richard Peabody, who had cured himself of drinking with the assistance of a psychologist, and then had established his own clinic on Commonwealth Avenue. Long before the creation of Alcoholics Anonymous, Peabody was treating alcoholism with that institution's methods, rather than with drug therapy, the approved technique of the day. A newspaper article published in 1924 quotes him as saying: "If you expect to be shown how to drink like a gentleman you will have to go elsewhere for instruction. When I take on a drunkard, it's to cure him. When he's cured, he never takes another drink, as long as he lives. Once a drunkard, always a drunkard." This brave and gentle man, who abhorred liquor for the wreckage it had made of his life, nevertheless fought publicly against the Volstead Act, because he believed more in freedom than in sobriety. He had remarried in 1923, yet with the exception of a single secret letter to Caresse in 1924 after having surreptitiously met with his son at Mrs. Jacob's house in Watertown, Connecticut, it wasn't till 1927 that he was allowed to contact his ex-wife: "Dearest Pittons," he wrote Caresse, "I am so glad that Harry has changed his attitude about letting you see me. . . . It seems terrible not to have seen each other for so long." Four years later, he died in his sleep, shortly before the publication by Little, Brown in 1931 of his book, *The Common Sense of Drinking*, a pioneering study of chronic drunkenness.

Polleen recollects the first time Harry seemed to take notice of her, a year or so after she had come to Paris with him: "I was sitting on the steps taking off my shoes when he appeared. 'Why are you taking off your shoes?' he asked me. I said, 'Well, I'm not supposed to make any noise going through the flat, in case you hear me.' He thought that was great, and immediately put my shoes on, and rushed me off to the Ritz. I was given a glass of champagne and taken back absolutely blotto. I was about six. That was the beginning of our friendship. He thought I was funny, or something. . . ." The considerable resentment that Polleen (now Polly Drysdale) feels toward her childhood circumstances is directed more at her mother than at her stepfather. "I was ignored, kept out of the way. I looked scruffy: When she'd take me for a fitting she'd ask someone to brush me down. It was humiliating; she didn't bother. . . . There was a time when I had been kept back from school because I had been very ill; I was a frightfully nervous child, I never got fed properly, and I obviously was put through all sorts of traumatic experiences, which took their effect on me. Finally, some specialists were called in and they blew up at my mother, and really told her a thing or two. I was in bed in my nursery with books up to the ceiling, and Harry came down with a glass of champagne, and said, 'Oh, Wretch, I'm told you're going to die. You'd better have a glass of champagne.' That's the sort of thing Harry would say. He was unbalanced, no doubt about it, in a sort of extravagant, glorious way. He had a kind of child's mind. I could understand his sort of madness."

In a sense perhaps Harry was mad, even then. His refusal to adjust to any measure externally imposed might be judged a symptom of madness, or of heroism. So might his singleness of purpose once he had set a course. A student of normalcy would shake his head at Harry's absurd, quixotic intention to "strive for an unbroken consistency and unity of aim all my life." Normal chaps of Harry's age and background talked about the affairs of the day. Harry did not concern himself even slightly with politics, or matters of state. He did not care about the economy, except as it touched the exchange between dollars and francs (and because he loved the French, most of the time, he rooted for the franc to strengthen against the dollar, despite the hardship this would work on him) and the doings of his illustrious Uncle Jack. He disregarded the Sacco-Vanzetti case, though it was a matter for earnest debate in Boston, above all places. He made no written reference to trade unionism, or to the traumatic Boston police strike of 1919, or to Spanish flu, which carried away twenty-one million people during and after World War I.

By democratic and populist standards he was not much of a citizen. On June 18, 1923, he wrote in *Shadows of the Sun*, which he wished to have published after he died: "There are too many people in the world and Mount Etna is erupting and thousands of lives are lost. Let them be lost. Let them be lost." He had no fear of death himself, and felt no awe before its prospect. And when he reached twenty-five years, he announced that he was at his halfway mark and ran a mile to celebrate his announcement. Six months later, he discovered with Polly the Cimetière de l'Abbaye de Longchamp and decided to be buried there, "a *real* burying place." He had begun to speak of suicide again, and took as one of his central mottoes the declaration "It is better to be too soon than too late."

By late 1922, his friends were obliged to take him or leave him as an eccentric, someone who refused to be squeezed by rules, and many of them even believed he had married Polly for no other reason than to spite them and their conventions. He hated holidays because they were arbitrary periods of freedom which were given rather than taken, and because they were occasions for artificial merriment. He was an authentic dandy. He never let Polly wear false pearls; he wouldn't wear false anythings. He dressed impeccably, always in black, shaved scrupulously every morning, was repelled by the touch of strangers. He found it "disheartening to consider the ugly bodies that have washed in one's bathtub, to imagine the people who have been born, who have made love, or have died in one's bed. . . ."

While he enjoyed nothing like the common touch, he was financially generous with all sorts and conditions of people. He gave lavish gifts by reflex, and saved his greatest contempt for people who gave away hand-me-downs; he gave new and expensive clothes to his servants. He was never imperious, and was rude only to his social equals or nominal social superiors. So that from time to time he was called upon to perform in ways that made him uncomfortable. At the end of November, 1923, he was asked by a man at the Morgan bank to stand godfather to the man's son. The christening was performed "in a sordid part of Paris out by the walls":

A squalid wooden church that looked like a cardboard box and we could hear the rain pattering upon the roof and the dark and sinister-sounding words of the priest, and there was a smell of unwashed bodies, and the hero of the occasion snivelled and cried and drooled (I hate children) while I answered the questions of the priest. Afterwards on foot through the rain along a muddy alleyway, past dreary buildings to the uninviting entrance to a tenement house. A winding flight of stairs and a barren room and cooped up for three hours among food and smoke and bottles of beer. A Zola scene. The suckling of a child and more beer and at last a delighted escape and back again to the security of the Princess's.

This ceremony, as seen from Harry's peculiar angle of vision, might profitably be contrasted to the memorial service three weeks earlier that he had arranged in commemoration of his friend George Weld's brother, Aaron Davis Weld, whose death had so profoundly touched him. Although Weld had been killed by shellfire during the Argonne offensive, and was buried at Romagne, Harry chose Longpoint in the Aisne as the place where he wished to donate a bronze church bell and install a memorial plaque, because he and Davis Weld had been in Longpoint together, and had had a happy afternoon and evening there. The ceremony took place November 4, and the day before a brief item appeared in the Paris *Herald-Tribune* announcing it as a social occasion: "In view of the social prominence of the Weld family, as well as that of the Comte de Montesquieu-Fezensac [the mayor of Longpoint] and the Crosbys, the event is expected to attract a large number of notable persons." Indeed it did:

How natural to be once again in the great forest of Villers-Cotterets. How natural to be again in ruined Longpont! And how natural to be drinking brandy from a flask! It was pouring with rain and there were fifty people for luncheon including the Bishop of Soissons and all the clan of Fezensacs and [Polly] had the Bishop on her left and a Marquis on her right and I was between the sheets (imaginaire) with a Duchess, and a sumptuous repast with a great deal of wine and a speech by

Fezensac and a blessing by the Bishop. Then into the Chapel for the benediction of the bells. And the villagers came en masse, ignorant, curious, superstitious, pious, unspoiled by modern life—just as they were centuries ago, and there were three bells (ours and two that the Fezensacs gave) and I thought of Davis (five years now since he was killed in the Argonne) and of our friendship in the dawn of our youth when life was sunnygolden and war a myth. And the rain, always the rain pattering upon the roof and it was very dark with here and there a candle burning and the sing-song voices of the priests as they intoned their oraisons and incense fumed upon the altar and the air was warm with the breath of worshippers. And we had had so much wine— Drowsiness—Then to strike the bells with a small iron hammer (formality which ended the service). . . .

And now the manor house for hot chocolate and brandy and so back to Paris in the car, holding hands in the rain, and I smoked my pipe and thought of Davis (it must cold in the grave to-night) while behind us in the dark rang the three bells.

He considered himself an aristocrat; he was considered an aristocrat; he was an aristocrat. And he was a snob. A person's standing at birth was of no consequence to him (though it was to his wife), but a person's style was. He could not abide people in bondage, so until he and poets began to discover one another he usually avoided the poor. The perfect freedom he demanded, from time and circumstance, was costly, a prize taken only by the very rich, the very brave or the very careless.

It was like him to prefer the celebration of a corpse to the christening of a child. Death focused his bravery and carelessness. He sought the society of people who were exacting, and especially the society of exacting women because he found them rich in secrets. Harry enjoyed secrets: "When I like people immensely, I never tell their names to anyone. It is like murdering a part of them." He prized discretion highly, and was never happier than when people congratulated him for his taciturnity. He would not abandon his flirtations and love affairs, even at the very beginning of his marriage, but he hid them from Polly: "You only upset yourself by your sins, but you upset other people by your confessions," he wrote in his notebook not by way of rationalization—he never troubled to rationalize or explain—but as a legitimate article of his belief.

In her preface to the unpublished sequel to *The Passionate Years* (which begins in 1940, where her published memoir leaves off), Caresse Crosby wrote that "in 1922 Harry and I did what we did and went where we went because we wanted to. . . . 'No compromise' was Harry's theme song, 'Never have any regrets' was mine." Harry found no reason to compromise his often-repeated belief that "there is no reason why I shouldn't have a harem." So he had one. Neither did he feel he should surrender himself to the exactations of banking, which he despised. So he quit.

In *The Passionate Years* the date of Harry's leave-taking is given as 1927, off by four years. He quit the last day of 1923. According to Polly's recollection of the affair, Harry asked her if she wished to be the wife of a Morgan partner, as though such an outcome were probable, or even possible, when, as Harry well knew, it was not. For a brief time after he began at the Morgan bank, Harry entertained the illusion that after a year or so in Paris he would return to Morgan's home office in New York, there to prosper. But soon enough, as far as banking went, Harry was, as he said, "ambitionless." He preferred to gamble, or read. "As for banking it can go to H E double L," he wrote, with uncharacteristic coyness, less than a year after he began at Morgan, Harjes. He found his work "dreary-dull," and did not like being caged up among stocks and bonds and paper bills.

The bank, for its part, returned his want of enthusiasm at the highest permissible rate of interest. One of his supervisors reported to the personnel department's request for an evaluation late in 1922 that he did not wish even to consider Harry as part of his staff. Little wonder: Harry was late coming to work, or absent entirely, almost as frequently as he was on the job. Nevertheless, because of his nephew-hood, he was promoted on Thanksgiving of 1922 to the position of financial researcher, and was given a large desk, and stenographer, and additional freedom (but no additional pay). His supervisor in his elevated position had little to remark about Harry after a year, save that he was a *"fantaisiste distingué."* Harry obliged his friend the Vicomte du Mas to "occupy himself with what work I am supposed to do," while Harry read poems, and thought about writing them.

By the beginning of 1923, Harry wrote that he was "fed up with banking and the bank and if only I could summon enough courage to resign, only my family would strenuously object with sound, practical, commonsense New England arguments." Anticipating the character of these arguments, he found an article that sang the praises of duty and endurance and self-denial, and copied it into his notebook:

After the age of sixty-five most of us retire. The man who is called "successful" by his friends is the man who, during the period of his greatest productivity, has saved systematically. At sixty-five he has sufficient principal to meet his and his family's needs for the rest of his life. He can maintain the same club memberships. He still drives his favorite car. His family lives just as they did when he was in his prime. This is just as it should be. His life ambition has been achieved. He is content.

Below this extended homily Harry wrote, "Jesus Christ!" While his friends envied him his position at the bank (which was considered a fashionable place to cash checks and to work), Harry had nothing but contempt for a friend of his father's who was proud never to have missed a day at *his* Boston bank for forty years, and who had a son whose notion of happiness was "to defecate well every morning." Despite his contumely for such regular practice, Harry appreciated some of the logistical advantages of his place at Morgan, Harjes. The Ritz, after all, was directly across Place Vendôme from the bank at No. 14, and everyone in the world showed up sooner or later for lunch there, or for drinks in the Ritz Bar. But though Harry liked the Ritz well enough, the job that offered him an occasion to go there on his lunch hour, and after work, was becoming intolerable. He went to a banquet given on behalf of the bank's employees and judged it "a dismal affair. Poor people trying to enjoy themselves are more pathetic than rich people trying to have a good time for the poor are utterly defenseless whereas the rich are sheltered by their cynicism."

Harry was becoming cynical enough, but he was hardly rich, at least by his father's standards. He was, however, sufficiently rich to suit his own needs. He received an income of about twelve thousand dollars per year from the stocks given him by his parents. During most of his seven and a half years of life in Paris, the dollar traded for better than twenty francs, and briefly in 1926 a dollar bought fifty francs. On a typical day in 1924 Harry spent a total of four hundred francs: two hundred for lunch at Chez Philippe, forty at the Ritz Bar, twenty for tips and charity, thirty for taxicabs, the rest for odds and ends. He and Polly enjoyed the services of two maids, a cook, a governess and a chauffeur (who earned more from Harry than Harry made at the bank). What use to him was a salary of seventy-five dollars per month for a job he performed with neither skill nor pleasure?

On November 3, 1923, Harry wrote his father that "Uncle Jack said there would be no future for me in his office in N.Y. so that just about settles the business question for a while. He was very nice as was

Aunt Jessie and had us out to dine the first night they arrived and then lunched here with us a few days later. They both like Polly a lot and told Mr. Jay so who repeated it to me. . . ." Holding his breath for the storm he felt would answer his letter, Harry prattled on about Harvard's chances against Yale at football, and his gift of a cross-country cup to St. Mark's.

But the storm never came. Mr. Crosby already realized that his son was a professional failure, had shot his bolt at two banks, was hopeless. On the last day of November, Harry gave Morgan, Harjes a month's notice. He had decided to become a writer. He was neither cocky nor casual in his decision, under no illusions as to his gifts. He meant to serve a proper apprenticeship. He never pretended to be more, or even as much, as he became; he never announced himself, in the manner of Left Bank layabouts, a Poet. But he became a poet, single-mindedly worshiping both the sources and products of art.

As far back as their courtship, Harry and Polly had shared an ambition for a career in literature. Its manifestations are sparsely documented, but a hint here and there in their letters, and in Harry's diaries, suggests that Polly certainly, and Harry perhaps, dreamt of becoming poets. Like many another love-struck college boy, Harry scribbled verse to Polly; they kept a commonplace book together, of maxims and poems. On March 9, 1922, just after Polly had broken off one of her promises to marry him, Harry wrote her, more in desperation than from conviction, that "if you could be content to live very modestly I would take up writing. I think that with your help and advice and with your wonderful mind to help me that we have the ability to produce something worthwhile." Two days earlier, he had encouraged her to "keep on with your writings. We must compare notes. . . ."

Polly skipped from ambition to ambition. She always showed flair, was quick to catch the drift, but had no staying power. For a time she thought she'd make her way manufacturing brassières. Then she thought that writing might be just the thing for her. Then the movies. Then, upon coming to Paris to live in sin with Harry, she took to the notion that she should establish a line of French bathing accessories—"Paris le Bain"—to be sold in New York. Harry, chivalrous and eager to interlock his own affairs with hers in any available manner, wrote Polly August 1, 1922, from Paris to New York that he thought her business idea was "the best I've heard yet provided you get your numerous N.Y. friends to do the financing of it. I'll be a very efficient foreign agent and will provide for you all the softest and most luxurious bath salts and perfumes and such things. . . ."

After they were married, Polly abandoned commerce (till she and Harry established the Black Sun Press, in 1927). During 1923, while Harry worked at the bank when it pleased him, Polly decided that with all Paris available to her she should do more with her opportunity than housekeep, rhyme and dine. She decided to try to become an artist. To find an art school she asked the advice of Morgan, Harjes & Co., of all improbable authorities on investments in the imaginary. The bank recommended Julian's Academy, which had a section for men—with nude models, located in the Latin Quarter—and for young ladies, *without* nude models, located just off the Champs Élysées.

She signed up, and then transferred almost immediately to the Académie de la Grande-Chaumière, an atelier run by the celebrated sculptor Antoine Bourdelle, under whom she studied. There she met the sculptors Isamu Nogouchi and Alberto Giacometti, and the painter Fernand Léger, who also taught there, so that Harry met the first artists he knew through his wife. He urged his mother to come to Paris to see Polly at her work: "Nude girls & nude men around—but one gets used to them right away." (The Crosbys had managed to maintain their fury with Polly for only a year; Mrs. Crosby came to Paris for a brief visit, and saw that her daughter-in-law loved Harry as Harry loved Polly, and the two women, bound by their common love, became friends.)

People, especially men, were easily attracted to Polly. She was gay, at once irreverent and dignified. She had high color and fine skin, was pretty when young, and handsome later. An English admirer recalled that she was vain, but that her silk stockings were forever twisted, and he fell in love with her. But then he met Harry, and was even more powerfully drawn to him, for his odd, menacing charm. Harry was an outlaw, and Polly accepted his wildness, and they together created an atmosphere of hazard at high stakes that was irresistible to the Englishman.

Given the character Harry had cut for himself, he *had* to become an artist, or a monarch, or nothing at all. There were many times when it seemed he would become nothing at all. He never publicized his ambition, but confided it to his diary nine months after quitting the bank: "Oh that my words were now written! Oh that they were printed in a book!" When he left the bank, Harry was ill-equipped to reply articulately to his new calling. He was unpracticed at poetry, and not well-read. In 1921, finished with Harvard and its many courses in French literature, he wrote Polly that he had encountered a list somewhere of the ten best books in twentieth-century French literature—prose, poems and drama—and that he had read not a one of them, "veree bad. . . ." He continued to dig into the Bible and the *Rubáiyát*, he offered Polly a list of recommended texts in 1921—Cellini's memoirs, William James, *Richard Feverel*, Alan Seeger—and late in 1923 he discovered "The Ladybird" by D. H. Lawrence ("perhaps the best short story I have ever read"), but it wasn't till he had announced his intention to write that he began the extraordinarily concentrated study of religion, philosophy and literature that occupied the remainder of his serious life.

In mid-November, 1923, when he wrote his father and mother that he was breaking with the bank, he made no pretense that he had advanced beyond the beginning of his new career: "I'm thrilled at the idea of writing," he had told his mother, "but it is a game where one must be left alone for one or two or more years to work out the problem for himself." Mrs. Crosby tried to encourage her son, whatever her true feelings about his chances as a writer and his future as a man of affairs and consequence, now quite undone by his folly. Betty Beal recalled that his mother—"poor Aunt Rita"—adored Harry no matter what he did: "She was always making excuses for him, trying to explain away his peculiarities to people. His affection for his mother was very deep, and she tried to understand him, and didn't badger him." His father, on the contrary, was angry and humiliated by Harry's choice of career. Esther Grew Parker, Harry's cousin, remembered that Mr. Crosby discouraged his son, and laughed at him, and "was satirical about his poems." Harry put his father's contempt into the record late in August of 1924:

> Says that is is ridiculous for me to write poetry that the days of Shelley and Byron are over. "The idea of you writing poetry as a life work is a joke and makes everybody laugh" and "You will be a dismal failure and laughing stock if you take poetry writing seriously." Lastly, "I'm not cross with you (not very) but think it very stupid and shows that after two years you are still in the clouds and just as much a visionary as ever."

To which Harry replied cheerfully, "best praise he ever gave me. . . ."

8

"Walter's young cousin turns out to be a sort of half-crazy cad."

—Edith Wharton, about Harry Crosby

The legends of American literary life in Paris between the wars have been as remarkable for their durability as for their marketability. No sooner has one memoirist brought the news for the dozenth time of what Hem said to Scott than another retails what Scott said to Hem, same dialogue, same stale stuff eagerly bought and relished, a defiance of laws governing the conservation of energy, matter and curiosity. So that it is natural for such eminent survivors of the period as are today about the business of today—Kay Boyle, Maria Jolas, Archibald Mac-Leish, to name three—to have wearied unto death of the numberless rag and junk dealers eager to rummage through the attics of their memories for bits of the gossip and pieces of the glamour of that place at that time. And it is natural too, finding themselves reluctant prisoners of a legend, that they would if they could drive a silver stake plumb through the heart of Montparnasse, through the terrace of the Dôme, and through the ghosts of Lady Brett and Jimmy the Barman.

Today, when a player in the theater of the Twenties does consent to share a story, it is with an impulse toward deflation: Paris was nothing special, he might insist; we only went there because the exchange rate was favorable. One Paris veteran recollects that the serious

American writers of the time never—but *never*—discussed Literature and Art (though her own memoir contradicts her), and all deny they were café-goers, all refuse—understandably—to be paraded among the others for the sake of that most convenient fabrication, a literary generation.

Still, it cannot be denied that Paris in the Twenties was a place very special indeed in its intersection with a risk-taking time. No less sobersided an instrument of authentication than the *Encyclopaedia Britannica*, in its article on the city, certifies the passing of its unique character: "Once capital of the arts, Paris has become provincial. During the 19th century and halfway through the 20th, Paris was the great garden of creative talents. Painters and sculptors, writers, musicians, and dancers came from around the world, hoping to blossom in the incredibly propitious intellectual climate. By the 1970s, however, nothing was left but nostalgia."

A full-page color photograph has been appearing lately in glossy magazines. It shows a smoke-filled night club's dance floor, empty except for a languid couple moving to music played by a quintet of black musicians. The couple stare into each other's eyes. The trombonist is reaching for a high note, the trumpet player is lost in reverie. The girl's hair is bobbed, her partner's is grease-parted down the middle. Silver smoking paraphernalia signal their financial security. There is a caption, the point of the photograph: "1925, A FRAGRANCE CAPTURES THE WORLD LIKE LE JAZZ HOT. A transmuted sadness pours forth from jazz trumpets. The rhythms are compelling. It is the Jazz Age, and Guerlain creates a perfume of real power. Shalimar. Heady, exciting, as intoxicating as Prohibition itself."

An absorption in the past is often a repudiation of the present, not the least vice that nostalgia encourages, and a repudiation of the present, by distortion and false memory, is a repudiation of the self. But deflation is also a vice of repudiation. Myth-sellers sigh that the experience of Paris in the Twenties was at a pitch and intensity never again to be duplicated. Reason, and the enemies of nostalgia, argue against such limits and exclusions. Evidence supports the nostalgists.

Artists, especially American (and Russian) artists, commonly regard themselves as exiles. Subversion and rebellion are first principles of invention, since invention seeks to replace what has been given with another something apprehended as ideal by its inventor, and very often only by its inventor. The artist happily accepts his alien status. Perhaps too happily, for in his aggressive hunt for something singular, some piece of territory all his own—however barren—the outsider risks losing touch not only with his community but with himself. A poet, for example, needs a community, an audience, as much as they need him, and for much the same reason—to trade discourse. Yet the poet is most distrusted by his fellow poets when he is most of the world. A tyrannical mythology of genius rules, and even the good citizens of the stay-at-home republic insist that the artist conform to it: the poet must scorn social commerce as he does commercial success; he is a loner, sniping at society from its frontiers, a runaway. It is an odd arrangement. This rejection of a native public is above all to be announced publicly; a man tricks himself out as a poet, a genius, and announces, *I am an exile, thank God.*

For many artists it is enough to be a foreigner at home, in Seattle or Phoenix or Boston. But traditionally the climactic experience of the American writer—of Melville and Hawthorne, as well as of Pound and Hemingway—has been his first trip abroad. Gertrude Stein formulates the case in *Paris France*, that most excellent tribute to a city and its country's people: "After all everybody, that is, everybody who writes is interested in living inside themselves. That is why writers have to have two countries, the one where they belong and the one in which they live really." For Americans of Washington Irving's generation, the "other country" was Spain. For the American literary generations that came to maturity during the years before and during World War I, the country of choice was England: Henry James, Stephen Crane, Ezra Pound, Robert Frost, Conrad Aiken, John Gould Fletcher and of course T. S. Eliot were participants in an authentic cultural emigration from home; that is, they returned to England as to a source, of language and manners and system. But the generality of American writers who left for Paris in the early 1920's—Harry Crosby's own date of departure, 1922, was the peak year of the emigration—went to be among other American writers. From Paris they wrote not about French culture, or Western civilization, or European manners; they wrote about home.

Malcolm Cowley's *Exile's Return* is a provocative and deftly argued narrative that attempts to sell a thesis about American exile and homecoming during the time between the wars, a thesis with which a great many of Cowley's American friends from his Paris years, 1921–23, utterly disagree. Announced by its title, the book takes as axiomatic that such American writers as found themselves in Paris after the war—MacLeish, Boyle, Cummings, Hemingway—answered to the name exile, and that they left one country for another primarily because of principles rather than circumstances, because of an admiration for French aesthetic habits and a longing to duplicate them.

Cowley's thesis is not weakened, as some have argued, by the fact that in Paris Hart Crane wrote about the Brooklyn Bridge; Gertrude Stein spent her years there on *The Making of Americans*; Gerald and Sara Murphy called their house in the South of France "Villa America" and served flapjacks for breakfast and played jazz records for the entertainment of their guests. The Crosbys, too, from the beginning of their life in France, transported America to them, just as their countrymen might transport an Italian *palazzo*, stone upon stone, to Newport. (The Crosbys' Cordon Bleu cook, Louise, was obliged to fry chicken and make corn pone, to cream codfish, to cook fish chowder and to hash-brown potatoes.) An enhanced awareness—even an enhanced affection—for the homeland is characteristic among those who have left home, whether through choice or by obligation, as in war. For the artist this enhancement is something quite apart from homesickness, yet no less an ache: it is often the very motive for leaving, like walking from a room, shutting the door and looking through its keyhole back into the room, the sharper to see it. (Cowley himself was stout in his defense of his homeland: "America is just as god-damned good as Europe —worse in some ways, better than others, fresher material," he wrote his friend Kenneth Burke, an envying stay-at-home at the time. But he also doubted in a poem that he would ever return to America: "*I dipped my finger in the lake and wrote I shall never return, never, to my strange land.*")

Yet to speak with any surviving American writer who was there is to hear almost unison agreement with Archibald MacLeish: "In all the time I was there, in six years, I never met anyone you could call, by the remotest stretch of the word, an expatriate. I never met anyone, that is, who had exiled himself from his country because he couldn't take it. I went there because the franc was dropping, and you could live well in Paris for about half what you could live on in Boston."

Berlin was even cheaper, dramatically so; Matthew Josephson, on a salary of one hundred dollars per month (according to Cowley), lived with two maids in a duplex apartment with his wife, for whom he bought riding lessons, he ate gallantly, and was lavish with tips and handouts. In Josephson's own more modest recollection of the time he calculates that his hotel, meals, night clubs and theaters cost ten dollars per week. Why, then, didn't the American community settle its tab at the Dôme and entrain en masse for the better rate of exchange? Cowley says merely that Berlin offered "an insane life for foreigners . . . and nobody could be happy there." Then why not Italy or Austria, where the exchange rates were also substantially more favorable to Americans than in Paris? Shunning myth, why was France every American writer's "other country"?

The French are good to writers, and always have been. They name streets for them (every town in France seems to have its rue Victor Hugo, while in America you may find Hawthorn Drive between Birch and Elm, but you'll look in vain for Hawthorne, next street over from Melville). The French use a skin cream called Stendhal, and toy stores sell a wind-up mouse named Zola. "Paris was where the twentieth century was," Gertrude Stein said, and there's no arguing with her, any more than with the similar sentiment of the *Encyclopaedia Britannica*. V. S. Pritchett remembers that even as a very young man he realized that Paris was "built for Art and Learning, whereas my London was built for government and trade. At home I was a tolerated joke, 'the professor.' " In Paris he was *un homme sérieux*, at least in the deference paid his estimation of himself.

The French have elevated toleration of eccentricity to the estate of a creed. It is not that they are themselves eccentric, nor were they then: they are lovers of convention and form and balance, and after the war they especially longed for serenity. Rather it is that Parisians are so utterly cocksure regarding the wisdom of their own manners and purposes that they could afford to tolerate the fopperies and misbegotten pranks of their guests. Foreigners are nothing to them; they've seen them come and go; they regard strangers as neither threats nor inspirations, as invisible creatures.

Certainly there was little cultural intercourse between the hosts and their American guests. In fact, to read one after another the dozens of memoirs written about Paris in the Twenties is to notice immediately that very little that was French, save for food and artifacts and bodies, registered on American visitors there, least of all French fiction or poetry. If the cry from the French Line pier in New York was, as Cowley has it, "They do things better in Europe: let's go there," *things* did not include poems. When William Carlos Williams asked Robert McAlmon, who was at the dead center of life in the American village of Montparnasse, to introduce him to some French poets, McAlmon could not, because after years in Paris he knew none. Fitzgerald never learned French; Hemingway learned it, but preferred the speech and company of Americans.

Malcolm Cowley concludes his study of expatriation with the story of Harry Crosby because he believes Harry to have been a paradigm of Twenties "themes." He was a paradigm, sure enough, but not of the kind of exile and forced return Cowley describes. Cowley's chapters on Crosby are elegant and persuasive. They were written with no personal knowledge of the man save a single meeting at Hart Crane's party two nights before the suicide, but they assume a kind of reassuring authority. In many places Cowley's hunches are prophetic, but Harry Crosby was in truth in no way representative of the American literary migration to Paris.

A profile of the exemplary Montparnassian would include, tautologically enough, an affection for cafés of Montparnasse. Harry shunned cafés almost as resolutely as he disliked the seediness of Montparnasse. The typical American in Paris of Cowley's portrait went there to write. Harry left home to escape his parents, Boston and his lovelorn fix. He intended at the time to make a life of banking, and to return to Morgan's home office in New York as soon as possible. The typical American exile was from the middle class, and poor; Harry was from the upper class, and rich. The exemplary young American writer actually did little writing in Paris (Hemingway was an exception, of course, but he too was in no way typical of what is called the "expatriate" community); Harry Crosby, once he began to write, wrote steadily and obsessively.

Indeed, when he and Polly first began to dream of living in Paris, the impulse that propelled them owed more to the traditions of the Grand Tour than to the Great Escape. "We can become very cultured and improve ourselves," Harry wrote her. Later, after he had quit the bank, he began to hunt for and find more magical qualities in the city where he had been living more than two years. On Independence Day, 1924, while Polly was visiting her family in Nantucket, he wrote her from Paris: "O I wish you were here for Paris is the only city in the world with its charm, and its sparkle, and its ceaseless undercurrents of adventure. Aren't we fortunate Bunny dear to have this as our home? The weariness of the outside world is appalling today and I suppose that we are all tired children awaiting the hour of everlasting sleep—for us in golden blissfulness—for the others I do not know. . . ." And when he and Polly returned to Paris from one of their frequent trips to America or Central Europe or North Africa or the Middle East, it was always with exalted relief, and a sense of homecoming, and Harry would almost invariably write in his diary some sentiment or other of allegiance. ("Paris, and all other lands and cities dwindle into Nothingness. Paris the City of the Sun.")

Like the bohemian community of the Left Bank (which would never have dreamt of patronizing, even if its members could afford to, such Right Bank haunts as Harry enjoyed: the Ritz and Fouquet's), Harry's anti-American credentials were impeccable. He confided to his notebook, and to anybody who might care to listen, that "I doubt if anyone in Boston could do anything which would make a person in Paris even change his expression." He chafed against his notion of America's ruling slogan: *Not Allowed!*

Harry Crosby nevertheless confessed freely to frequent and painful homesickness, and marveled that Polly did not share his longing for Singing Beach and the Essex Links, the foghorn's moan, the fall of dead New England leaves. But even when most cast down by *mal du pays*, he could lift himself with work and mischief. Like many another American in Paris, he delighted in putting the sword's point to the fat American middle class and hearing it squeal. But unlike Malcolm Cowley's exemplary holiday exile, who would *épater le bourgeois* from within its ranks, or from below, Harry dropped water bombs of scandal on that hapless, much-abused class of decent folk from above. For Harry Crosby was no bohemian: the sorrows of Mimi, the pallet and the loft, short rations and immature wine attracted him not at all. And unlike his compatriots Harry was at home with the French, with their culture and language. And finally, he was authentically influenced by French writers more than any others—by Rimbaud, supremely, and by Baudelaire and Anatole France and Flaubert. In this he did indeed comform to the image of an American writer at worship in Paris, but he was all but unique in his conformity.

In common with many another American of his age who had refused to steady down and buckle himself into a respectable calling, Harry suffered the contempt of an anxious father, and this could not help—whatever brave face he showed his diaries—but cause him to doubt himself. When his father wrote him that "the idea of you writing poetry as a life work is a joke and makes everybody laugh," Harry must have been stung. But worse must have been his fear, uttered so bluntly by that same man of the world, that he would be no good at it: "You will be a dismal failure." Perhaps Harry would have taken solace from the company of a young Canadian, John Glassco, who was at the same time in Paris trying to write and receiving such communications from his father as this rebuke: "You have now been almost two months in Paris, and after further consideration of your project of a literary career I must once more express my disapproval. As you well know, I altogether disapprove of literature as a futile and unmanly pursuit and one that cannot but lead to poverty and unhappiness. I accordingly advise you that your allowance from now on will be halved."

Archibald MacLeish quit a pretty career at law with Charles Francis Chaote's Boston firm to come to Paris and write poems: "I was there in a situation that was deadly serious for me. I was over thirty; I'd given up my law practice; although my father and mother were understanding in the most miraculous way, my friends certainly weren't. There still are people in Boston who regard me in some way as a traitor to old Charles Francis Choate because I worked in his office and then left him. You don't *do* that in Boston." If MacLeish, who *knew* he was good, and had the encouragement of his parents, felt himself on the firing line, how must Harry have felt? A year after leaving the bank, he was still writing lines in his diary about home ("And the chains of New England are broken and unbroken") and still wishing to please his father, but fearing he never could. In that spirit, in 1928 he copied out some lines from Eugene O'Neill's *Strange Interlude*: " 'I couldn't understand him . . . what son can ever understand? always too near, too soon, too distant or too late. . . .' "

But he found someone else, a surrogate father, who loved and supported him, encouraged him to quit the bank and to write, gave him books and money and friendship, introduced him to everyone in Paris —French and American, but especially French—whom Harry could hope to meet, and did all this, subverting Stephen Crosby's influence, from the security of unblemished family credentials. The man, Walter Van Rensselaer Berry, was Stephen Crosby's cousin, a great and wealthy gentleman in Parisian social and literary circles, a friend to Henry James and Proust, a man whom Edith Wharton loved throughout most of her life.

Berry was born in Paris in July, 1859, the grandson of Gen. Stephen Van Rensselaer of Albany. He grew up in Paris and Albany, went to St. Mark's and then Harvard (where he was a classmate and good friend of Theodore Roosevelt), graduating in 1881. He took a law degree at Columbia, but soon after he began his practice in New York (where he first met Edith Wharton) he moved to Washington and developed a reputation as a first-rate international lawyer, representing the French and Italian embassies in the United States. Between 1908 and 1911 he served as a judge at the International Tribunal in Cairo. In 1911 he returned to Paris, from time to time took unusually challenging or remunerative cases at law, and acted as president of the American Chamber of Commerce in Paris from 1916 till 1923, the year that Harry and Polly first met him.

Berry was a lifelong bachelor, despite the clear wish of Edith Wharton that he marry her after her divorce. He was a man of striking elegance, in both manner and bearing, well over six feet tall and thin, with a small, delicate head and thick white hair and mustache. His eyes were set deep, and cold, lidded like a hawk's, and he had a hawk's fine beak and menacing attention to details. Caresse Crosby is characteristically casual in her inventory of the facts of his case in *The Passionate Years*. She has him graduating from Harvard in 1871 (ten years early), and dead in 1928 (one year late), and she recollects that when she and Harry met him he was seventy-six (he died at sixty-eight). But she accurately describes him:

> He was enormously elongated, slim as a straw and as *sec*; his small head poised erect above a high wing collar was birdlike in its sudden turnings and its bright quick glance. His most usual dress was a morning coat of Edwardian cut, striped trousers and highly polished black button shoes. His arms long, and his wrists like pipestems, he could have been exhibited as a sculpture by Lipshitz [*sic*]. His fastidiousness was part of his general allure. His speech was witty, and his knowledge worldly; his manner with women was most gallant and wicked; and to me he was utterly delightful. I could well understand his amorous successes even with the young belles of the day.

Friends of Edith Wharton were not so enchanted by Berry, and considered him a malign influence upon her. In part, ironically enough, because he would not marry her, and in part because his aloof and rational character was perhaps too strict a governor on her freer inclinations. For her own part, she worshiped him utterly. In her autobiographical account, *A Backward Glance*, she recalls her struggle with her first book at just the moment Berry entered her life:

> Walter Berry was born with an exceptionally sensitive literary instinct, but also with a critical sense so far outweighing his creative gift that he had early renounced the idea of writing. But though he was already a hard-working young lawyer, with a promising future at the bar, the service of letters was still his joy in his moments of leisure. I remember shyly asking him to look at my lumpy pages; and I remember his first shout of laughter (for he never flattered or pretended), and then his

saying good-naturedly 'Come let's see what can be done,' and settling down beside me to try to model the lump into a book.

She goes on to credit him as her writing master throughout much of her life.

Berry despised unnecessary ornament, and anything hackneyed. He was a man of patience, with an instinctive aversion to the ungainly detail. Even his enemies, such as Percy Lubbock, credit him with wit, an appetite for work and reading, skill at languages. Lubbock describes him as a "glutton of books," but maligns his "dry and narrow and supercilious temper." He could freeze half to death anyone he found vulgar or untutored. In his hauteur he was a Van Rensselaer, sure enough, and once he was safe in the ground people began to charge him with narrow-mindedness, snobbery (it was said of him that when he saw a duchess, he saw two hundred years of duchesses), dogmatism, selfishness, reactionary political principles and an unseemly contempt for Christian doctrines and metaphysics. One of Edith Wharton's biographers quotes a letter from an unnamed correspondent who admits in his first sentence that he had never met Berry, but unintimidated by such a niggling liability quite happily characterizes him: "He was a lady-killer. . . . I think he was what used to be called a cad. . . ." He certainly enjoyed the company and attentions of young and comely ladies, but he was, after all, in his sixties at the time he was meant to have been a "lady-killer." Louis Auchincloss, a more worldly Wharton biographer, prefers the opinion of Lady Ribblesdale, who told him that it was said in Paris, "Unlike some gentleman callers who left their hostess with a baby, Berry left them with a book."

What is beyond dispute is Walter Berry's extraordinary erudition and urbanity. He was a close friend of Henry James, who corresponded frequently with him and remarked Berry's "beautiful . . . insolently exquisite hand." Marcel Proust dedicated *Pastiches et Mélanges* to him. At his death many newspapers noted Berry's easy access to the French, to princesses and dukes, poets and painters and generals: in his house on the Left Bank, at 53 rue de Varenne (where Edith Wharton had been the previous tenant), he entertained Paul Morand, Paul Valéry, Jean Cocteau, the Duc de Gramont, the Duchess of Marlborough, Marshal Foch, and Harry and Polly Crosby.

In early November of 1923, in the letter to his father saying that Uncle Jack held out no hope of a transfer to New York, Harry first refers to Cousin Walter, with whom he and Polly had had lunch the day before: "He certainly is well educated and what a cynic—but who knows that he may not be an idealist at heart. . . ." Berry had advised Harry to follow his inclination and leave the bank to write, and when Harry jumped at such sound counsel and tendered his resignation a few weeks later, Berry wrote at once to congratulate him: "I'm so glad you chucked the bank! If this keeps up you'll have better things to your account than fat $$'s—" The friendship was struck, and within a few months Berry, no man for idle effusions, told his sister Nathalie that he wished he had had Harry as his godson. There began a remarkable fraternity between Walter Berry and his cousin, that only ended four years later at Berry's death, with Harry left in charge of the funeral arrangements for that proud man, and named as residual legatee of Berry's considerable estate (the money to come to him after the death of Berry's sister), and confirmed utterly in habits of temper and inclination that had been uncertain before he met Berry.

A measure of Berry's influence on his twenty-five-year-old cousin can be taken from a letter written to his mother shortly after Berry died. Harry had just had J. P. Morgan to lunch at home on *crabes indiens* in return for his uncle's having taken him and Polly several times to dinner while he was visiting Paris. Till Harry met his Cousin Walter, Morgan had been the world's mightiest citizen in his nephew's eyes. (In March of 1924, after the House of Morgan under the Dawes Plan loaned France and other war-ravaged countries almost two billion dollars, Harry's fervor for his uncle reached high water. He wrote his mother on March 14 that "Uncle Jack apparently has saved France. I have always considered him the greatest man in America. Now I rank him about the greatest man in the world. The franc has recovered a great deal of lost ground. Imagine one single man having the power to influence and change the trend of world affairs.") But now, Harry told his mother, "Uncle Jack is as unstimulating as Berry was stimulating. Uncle Jack is interesting to talk to but he is altogether devoid of that spark which inspires. . . . I am afraid you will not agree. . . ."

What could Mr. and Mrs. Crosby make of Berry's advice to their son, running as it did so contrary to their own? They could not deny that Walter Berry was an ornament to the family, a man of the world as well as of the spirit. He certainly took second place to no kinsman, least of all to his cousin Stephen Crosby, in the intimidating range of his friendships, or in the esteem in which he was held by the serious world. He had inherited a fortune, and multiplied it by his work and wit. And yet in all matters touching the conduct of Harry Crosby's life, he took sides not with the established father but with the dreaming son.

Not that Walter Berry was in any way a rebel, or enemy of social conventions. He cared at least as much as Stephen Crosby what the world thought of him. But rather than submit to his peers' opinion of him by trying in all things to conform to their expectations of a gentleman's conduct, Berry mastered their opinion, forced it to conform to his expectations of himself, looked down his elegant beak at the world and caused it to shake in its boots at his certain, disdainful stare; he *obliged* the world to adore him. He knew who he was, and was pleased. And to know himself, Harry studied the strange man and came to love him. Harry's other cousin, Betty Beal, who in many things reflects the judgment of Harry's mother and father, took consolation from Berry's influence: "I think Walter Berry had a good, and restraining influence on Harry because he didn't just wipe everything away, and say nothing's good."

What Harry—and Polly—brought to this gentleman, what needs of his that they satisfied, may be easily enough imagined. Berry responded to physical grace and beauty, and the young Crosbys had both in abundance. Berry enjoyed flirting with Polly, and enjoyed being teased by her. Harry's war record would have appealed to his elderly cousin: Berry had been instrumental in bringing America into the war against Germany, and after the war he organized and directed the Union des Colonies Étrangères en France en Faveur des Victimes de la Guerre, which gave money and succor to wounded French veterans. Berry had been made a Commandeur of the Legion of Honor, but he had never himself been in battle, and liked to share the adventures of someone like Harry who had.

Best of all, Harry was unshaped clay, and Berry's history with Edith Wharton—as her master, inspiration, editor without portfolio, and sometime bully—anticipated his moral and intellectual instructions to Harry, and to a lesser degree to Polly. Soon after he met his Cousin Walter, Harry began to gorge himself on the modern French literary masters so dear to the older man: Valéry, Verlaine, Baudelaire, and above all Rimbaud. Berry suggested that Harry write a biography of Rimbaud, a tribute to the high esteem in which Berry held his young cousin's capacity as a linguist and critic. And soon enough Harry was consigning cautionary homilies to his notebooks: "It doesn't do you any good to read if you don't apply what you read to your work WVRB."

Most of Edith Wharton's biographers agree that Walter Berry intimidated and even oppressed her, that in his hatred of anything that sniffed even slightly of the mystical he hounded her away from territories of the imagination she would otherwise have been free to explore, according to her inclination. Certainly he had no such dampening effect on his young, more impressionable cousin, for it was precisely as he was falling under the spell of Berry that Harry began his course of sun worship. One April evening Harry and Polly had dinner with Cousin Walter, and after browsing through his magnificent library, and finding book upon book dedicated to him, Harry listened to his host tell of the five men of five nations who went elephant-hunting in Africa, each of whom wrote a book upon his return: "The Englishman called his book 'The Elephant, his Life and Habits'; the Frenchman 'Étude sur l'Eléphant et ses Amours'; the American 'In Favor of Bigger and Better Elephants'; the German 'The Metaphysics and World-Weariness of the Elephant'; the Pole 'The Elephant and the Polish Question.' And I suppose I should have entitled mine 'Elephants of the Sun.' "

Harry's growing obsession with the rites and symbols of sun worship joined nicely with Walter Berry's preoccupation with Egypt, and its art and mythology. Harry longed to learn, and his cousin to teach: what the young man had neglected at St. Mark's and Harvard he began to mend beneath the Degas nude (to which Harry wished to make love) hanging in his cousin's dining room. One afternoon, Berry took his disciple to a Manet sale at the Hôtel Drouot, where he bought a lithograph to match "Un Corbeau," Manet's frontispiece to the edition of Mallarmé's translation of Poe which Harry had first read in the library at 53 rue de Varenne. Harry was experiencing literature and its artifacts from a privileged position, close up. On June 17, 1926, he first met Edith Wharton at Cousin Walter's, and they all took tea "in the dining room (where she wrote Ethan Frome, 'poor Ethan' as she called him)—and there was Paul Morand . . . and he was heavy and oriental with a pale opium face and there were the young Count and Countess de Noailles, and a pretty Comtesse de Ganay and a Mrs. Hyde and last but not least a delightful Abbé Meugnier who said he wished that someone would invent another sin, he was so tired of always having to listen to the same ones, and who remarked when he saw Narcisse: 'Mon coeur, c'est tout un jardin d'acclimations.' "

The Narcisse who inspired the Abbé to declare that his heart was one big zoo was the Crosbys' whippet, who, to the surprise and one might imagine disapproval of Mrs. Wharton, was not exiled to the garden, where it was suggested he might feel more at home; instead he was given pride of place beside Cousin Walter on a silk settee, "like a delta dog on a royal sarcophagus." The master indulged his handsome young disciples. He introduced them to Gerald Murphy, who was "going to Bâle to paint locomotives," and to Sinclair Lewis. He showed them his prayer shell from Tibet and his Egyptian stone cat and his Indian and Persian prints and his Gauguin landscape and a small Burne-Jones his friend Berenson had lent him when he was last at *I Tatti*. And there were always the books, "the books books books books and the bindings and the colors of the books."

If Harry was bedazzled by books as artifacts, his Cousin Walter kept his eye on the point of the enterprise, hectoring Harry to read and write: "Good advice from W.V.R.B. to set aside regular hours for work and to stick by them religiously. And how Anthony Trollope when he had finished a three volume novel at eleven o'clock, instead of stopping work for the day, began immediately upon a new book until his allotted time was up." Always there were anecdotes. One day Berry found his cousin sitting on a floor arranging books, and told him about a New England schoolmistress who put all male authors on one set of shelves and females on another. And he read Harry's poems, and encouraged him, and warned him against poets who "make up for the meagerness of the matter by the beauty of the typography."

In late April of 1925 Harry bought his cousin a letter from Baudelaire offering to sell the manuscript of *Les Fleurs du Mal* for four hundred francs (evidently the offer was not accepted by the letter's recipient, to Walter Berry's amused wonder), and used the occasion of gift-giving to announce that his wife would thereafter be known as Caresse. The Crosbys had written finish to the names Polly and Mary as too pedestrian shortly before Christmas of 1924, while Polly was preparing her first book of poems—*Crosses of Gold*—for a vanity printer. They were sitting together in bed, with the books of Rimbaud, Huysmans and Mallarmé piled around them, and Harry was absorbed by a cipher of Poe's. His wife was trying to choose between Mary and Polly as a name for the title page.

"Why not a new name?" Harry asked her.

"Why not?" she answered.

They wanted something from the C's to go musically with Crosby, and, under Poe's influence, Harry demanded an acrostic. They tried Charlotte and Clara, Clarisse and Clytemnestra, Clara and Cara. Harry liked Cara, but not the acrostic that could be fabicated from it. He told Polly that her name should sound like a caress. There it was: they Frenchified it with a final *e*, and fashioned the Crosby Cross thus:

```
              C
              A
    H A R R Y
              E
              S
              S
              E
```

They then emblazoned the colophon on their bookplates and letter-heads, and screwed up courage enough to try their reformed identity out on Harry's family. His first announcement was to his mother: "I have a list of girls nearly as long as Pa's! Caresse is amused by it. My two favorites are Constance and Ethel. Then there are many, many others—all save two in society—so that is quite creditable." If Harry thought to divert his mother's attention from the name Caresse by offering her gossip, mistresses and scandal, he underestimated her powers of discrimination. She replied that Polly's tarted-up change of name was like undressing in public. Betty Beal wrote, signing her name Baiser Beal. Harry's Boston friends snickered and sometimes hooted when they heard the dandified title. Walter Berry, however, deeply touched by Harry's gift to him, took the Crosby Cross in good spirits, gently joked about it, and from then on called his cousin's wife Caresse.

One year later Harry gave away his brown suits and announced that "from this day to the day of my death . . . I shall wear only dark blue suits and from this day a black knitted neck-tie ('asserted' by my pearl pin) and from this day in my buttonhole a black (artificial) gardenia. And always bareheaded." He announced these intentions first to Cousin Walter, who nodded, accepted, reminded Harry in the manner of a *cher maître* that the poetic person was important but that poetry was the point, the writing was everything.

On June 19, 1927, Berry wrote a codicil to his will, placing Harry and Nina de Polignac in charge of his funeral:

> At my death I direct that funeral services shall take place immediately (without waiting for the arrival of my sister from America) at the American Church or Cathedral of the Holy Trinity, 23 Avenue de l'Alma; that directly thereafter my body be cremated, and that my so-called 'ashes' be not taken to America for burial, but shall be chucked out anywhere.
>
> I request that my cousin the Marquise de Polignac and Harry Grew Crosby take charge of the funeral arrangements.

Cable my sister that my request is that she should not come over, either for my funeral or afterwards, as my will provides for all my property in France, and there is absolutely no reason for her to come.

A few months later, in August, Harry wrote his mother that Cousin Walter was alone near the Black Forest, and bored: "When I get that old I shall jump into the sea (body) and into the sun (soul). I am growing remote it is the only way not to be hurt. . . ." Within a few weeks from the time of that letter, Berry suffered a stroke in Paris that left him sharp of wit but unable to speak or read, and Mrs. Wharton sent for his sister, Nathalie Alden (whose husband, and therefore whose person, offended Berry), and sat beside him day and night, talking to him and holding his hand. On Wednesday, October 12, Harry and Caresse went to the races at Longchamp and returned in a friend's yellow Hispano-Suiza to receive the news that Cousin Walter had died that morning.

Harry wrote his mother: "Poor Cousin Walter I am afraid this last year he has suffered physically and even more morally. . . . He has been such a tremendously strong and good influence for me and he has left such a noble and brilliant example. . . ." Harry saw to the disposition of his cousin's body, dealt with the undertaker "in his lugubrious dress suit," watched the coffin screwed shut, and received from Berry's valet, Jules, a pair of onyx cuff links.

The funeral services October 17 were suitably grand. Harry insisted upon a procession of horse-drawn carriages, ornamented with plumes and silver, rather than the automobiles preferred by Edith Wharton. Among the honorary pallbearers were the French Minister of Justice—M. Barthou—and the generals Weygand and Pershing. The procession wound through the Left Bank, crossed Concorde Bridge, moved up the Champs Élysées (where Harry reflected on Berry's disbelief in an afterlife), and came to rest at the Church of the Holy Trinity on Avenue Georges V, where eight hundred mourners had collected to celebrate one of Paris's most noble ceremonial occasions. Foch was there, and Cocteau and Paul Morand and Valéry and the Comte and Comtesse de Chambrun, the Comte and Comtesse de Mun, the Comte and Comtesse de la Rochefoucauld. Harry listened to the "voice of the hypocrite minister (thank Christ I am not a Christian)" and then after the service, in accordance with the custom of the French, stood in line with what members of Berry's family were in attendance, and shook hands with those hundreds lined up to console him and look him over. He let tears fall finally when mutilated veterans—

some without legs—passed with generals and royalty in review of the corpse. Later he remembered the hands: "moist hands strong hands exquisite hands coarse hands hands gloved and ungloved left hands (parmi les mutilés) duchess' hands, generals' hands, the Count's hands, veuve Biron's hand, white hands, dark hands, limp hands, bony hands, shaking, shaking, shaking but cold and motionless are the hands of the dead." And later he wrote in his notebook, "never, *never, never* must have a funeral."

Then he and the body of his cousin were driven to the crematorium, where he was obliged to witness the reduction of Walter Van Rensselaer Berry to ashes. The mahogany casket with its bronze nameplate was opened, and Harry removed Berry's Legion of Honor from his neck, to give to Berry's sister, and then the body was sealed in a white pine box. "The master of ceremonies (he looked like a sommelier with chains round his neck) asked my assent and I nodded assent Yes to him and the door of the oven opened and the coffin slid in and the oven closed with a sharp metallic click and the master of ceremonies went away and all the men went downstairs to eat and I was alone listening to the crackling of wood." Like Meursalt, who smoked while he stood vigil over his mother's corpse in the opening scene of Camus' *l'Étranger*, perhaps to vacate death of its black magic, and domesticate it, Harry sipped brandy from a flask while his cousin burned, listened to the laughter of the coffin carpenters eating lunch in the cellar and drank a toast to Cousin Walter ("Dieu it must be hot inside"). Then the master of ceremonies returned and opened the oven door, and from the heap of hot red and white embers gave Harry what he fancifully believed were the ashes of Berry's heart, which the young man placed in a tiny gold box. The rest, what they call "the remains," were scooped into a white cement urn, which Harry carried to the car waiting outside, after first instructing the funeral director to place Berry's wreaths on Oscar Wilde's grave. The cremation had impressed him deeply, and thereafter he carried with him always instructions regarding the disposal of his own dead body: "Under no circumstances do I wish to be buried in the ground after my death scatter my ashes to the four winds. . . ." Beneath the rubric "Funeral Orgies" Harry listed the services and appliances—embalming and cremation, casket and flowers, the fumigation, in accordance with French law, of 53 rue de Varenne—he had purchased at a cost of one thousand four hundred and ninety-four dollars from the funeral director, Bernard J. Lane. He believed, rightly, that Cousin Walter would have been amused by the high nonsense.

As he might also have been by the comic opera scenes immediately played out around the person of Edith Wharton. She had requested Berry's ashes, and Harry, believing that his cousin's wish to be "chucked out anywhere" could as easily be satisfied by chucking him out on Mrs. Wharton's property near Versailles as anywhere else, readily agreed. He took the urn full of Walter Berry's combusted residue to Versailles, presented it to her, and on the instant there commenced a loud banging on her door. Two gendarmes had followed Harry to Mrs. Wharton's house to assure themselves that Berry's ashes be put in the ground, in accordance with the laws of France, rather than chucked into the air. Mrs. Wharton, close to tears because of the humiliating intrusion into her private grief, agreed with the earnest lawmen's demands, and bade them leave her in peace. She never forgave Harry for having witnessed the awful comedy.

Mrs. Wharton soon enough armed herself with further reasons to dislike Harry. As soon as Berry's will had been read, it was learned that there was a fourth article to its codicil, viz.: "All the rest of the books in my appartement (except those bequeathed by Articles First and Second above, and except those books which Edith Wharton may desire to take, as provided by Article Third above) I give and bequeath to my cousin, Harry Grew Crosby, of Boston, Mass."* In common with many another lawyer's, Walter Berry's will and intentions were a jumble. The aforementioned Article Third of its codicil said, "I give and bequeath to Edith Wharton, of Château Ste. Claire, Hyères, France, all the books (except those bequeathed by Articles First and Second above) in my appartement 53 rue de Varenne, which she may desire to take and as many of them as she may desire to take."

What was his purpose? To give the lion's share to his lifelong companion, and by her own reckoning his star pupil, or to give them to his most recent favorite, his young cousin? No biographer of Edith Wharton feels satisfied till Harry has taken his lumps in this affair. One accuses the Crosbys of an eagerness to throw Cousin Walter's cinders on the rubbish heap on their way to loot his library. Another asks, touching Edith Wharton's own delicate sensibilities, "What did the Crosbys care?"

In fact, a few days after Berry's death, Harry seemed to care a great deal about Mrs. Wharton's loss, and about her immediate future. He wrote his mother that "she is broken-hearted and it is she who is

* It is interesting, in light of such theories of expatriation and renunciation as have been contrived by writers like Malcolm Cowley, to notice that Walter Berry always described himself as being from Washington, D.C., temporarily [i.e., for several decades] residing in Paris, just as Harry was to him "of Boston, Mass."

suffering the most," and added that "she deserves [the ashes] for she has loved him faithfully since she was twenty a real, golden love I am excited about the books but wonder how many she will leave." It is clear that he understood his precarious legal position regarding the bequest, that Mrs. Wharton could if she chose take every volume, "as many of them as she may desire to take." On the other hand, Berry had left him many *objets d'art*, an elaborate inlaid wood and silver picnic set, his mink-lined greatcoat which Harry had so much admired and, to his sister Nathalie's dismay, his entire and considerable fortune upon her death.

The day after the funeral, which Harry believed to have been a success ("if you can call a funeral a success"), he wrote his mother again: "I never realized before how much Uncle Walter meant to us, how important his encouragement was in the dark days when I had just left the bank, how stimulating he has been, and how very generous to us. . . . Mrs. Wharton has been quite diffiult but I agreed with her—as often as possible. . . ." Six days later, he wrote again to his mother: "I wonder if Mrs. Wharton will take all the books—everyone says she will. Still she has a right to them but I do hope to have some of them." The next day the three women of Berry's life—his and Harry's cousin Nina Crosby (by marriage, the Marquise de Polignac), Mrs. Wharton and his sister commenced to quarrel over where the ashes, as yet unburied, should be put, and Harry wrote his mother:

> Women are very difficult Mrs. Wharton asked for Cousin Walter's ashes to scatter in her garden. Arrives Natalie wants ashes put out at Versailles Mrs. Wharton suggests American Church in Paris Nina Belleau Woods. Finally Natalie says Père Lachaise and here is where I step in and say *NO*. After all Nina and I are to decide and we have done all we could to please people to no purpose Natalie's husband is angry because he is not mentioned in the will (why in h—— should he be) and he has a tremendous hold over Natalie. I would be surprised at nothing he did I have never seen human nature in so bad a light the aftermath has been too disgusting. But if I say so I have "kept clear from what enslaves and lowers" and have acted for the best. The worse [*sic*] part is that people never think that it would be a nice thing to carry out the wishes of the person who has died (I hate the word "deceased") Nina is the nicest Natalie is pathetic and Edith Wharton worries only about what people will say. . . .

At about this time Mrs. Wharton was writing a friend that "seeing all the little people crawling over [Berry] nearly kills me," and on

October 28 she wrote another friend that Harry was "inexperienced and unmanageable." She had never liked him, and liked Caresse even less for the impertinent manner in which she had usurped Mrs. Wharton's high place within Berry's establishment. Nor did Mrs. Wharton care for the Crosbys' impulsive defiance of convention, their black whippet adorned with a gold necklace, his toenails lacquered gold, their damned youth and carelessness and irregularity.

Harry wrote his mother in mid-November that it had become evident to him that Mrs. Wharton would take all the books "and not leave me one I think it is disgraceful and she should damned well be ashamed of herself." He had developed an uncharacteristically grasping fixation about the Berry books, and decided to ask Mrs. Wharton "point blank" for half of them; if she refused him, "she is a bad sort." He did ask for half of them, and told her Berry had meant for him to have the library, causing her to write an English banking friend that "Walter's young cousin Crosby turns out to be a sort of half-crazy cad." She wrote Harry "an exceedingly cold letter," and he urged his father to write Mrs. Wharton, asking her to be reasonable. There is no evidence that Mr. Crosby, wise fellow, put his head in the lion's mouth.

In the event, Mrs. Wharton finally helped herself to only seventy-three books and sets of books, valued at almost precisely the cost of Berry's funeral (forty-seven thousand francs), and on May 8, 1928, the balance were delivered to the Crosbys' apartment at 19 rue de Lille:

> Books Books Books Books eight thousand of them crate after crate crate after crate borne upon the shoulders of solid men came cascading all morning and all afternoon into the house and my library is a pyramid of books and C's atelier is stacked high with books (I hope the ceiling won't fall through) . . . a leaf from the Gutenberg Bible two chained manuscripts from a monastery an illuminated Koran illuminated Psalm books and enormous Book of the Dead (the largest book I have ever seen) . . . a microscopic volume of old French songs (the smallest book I have ever seen) the Sacred Books of the East in fifty volumes an Histoire Naturelle in one hundred and twenty-seven volumes a magnificent set of Casanova with erotic plates . . . books on art (enough to constitute a library in itself) books with the bindings and arms of the Kings of France books with the arms of Mazarin and Richelieu of Napoleon of Madame de Pompadour of Le Roi Soleil and the signatures of Le Roi Soleil and of Henry Fourth and of Voltaire . . . every kind of book imaginable from the oldest Incunabula down to the most recent number of Transition for which treasures I offer thanks to Cousin Walter on the Book of the Dead.

Two days later Harry sold a pearl pin he had inherited from his Cousin Walter for one thousand dollars at Cartier to pay the taxes on that astonishing library that comprised the shrine wherein Harry came to worship words and the paper and typographical arrangements that show off words. But oddly enough, having succeeded in his unseemly attempt to prevent what Caresse ungenerously called Edith Wharton's "grab act," it became Harry's purpose to dispose of his books once he had read them. He decided to reduce his library from ten thousand volumes to one thousand to one hundred to ten to one, the one true book containing one true word. His reductive ambition was grounded both in conventional Christian doctrine—the man having least has most —and in some garbled version of Eastern mysticism.

For a while he considered going into the rare book business, but reading, writing and gambling left him no leisure for commerce. So he commenced to give away the books. Caresse later remembered watching in anguish as he took his leave from their apartment day after day carrying bags full of them. She tried to prevent him from giving them to taxi drivers and barmen and casual passers-by. "I loved those books but he loved them more and had this idée fixe about reducing the things that surround him. We had talked to a wise man in Egypt in 1928 who had said 'my wealth I measure by the things I do without' and Harry believed that so many books weighed him down." He pressed first editions of Baudelaire on anyone he met and liked, and finally commenced a pretty trick, smuggling rare volumes into Seine-side bookstalls, marking them with absurdly low prices, and leaving them among odds and ends, laughing to imagine with what amazement they would be discovered by browsers, and with what confusion the bookstall owners would respond to Harry's mischief. Cousin Walter would not have taken much pleasure from the stunt.

9

"The Renaissance knew of strange manners of poisoning—poisoning by a helmet and a lighted torch, by an embroidered glove and a jewelled fan, by a gilded pomander and by an amber chain. Dorian Gray had been poisoned by a book. There were moments when he looked on evil simply as a mode through which he could realize his conception of the beautiful."

—Oscar Wilde, *The Picture of Dorian Gray*

The book that corrupted beautiful Dorian Gray, and whose bane he passed along to anyone unlucky enough to touch him, was a yellow-backed novel, untitled by Wilde in his own novel but presented as evidence against him at his trial for homosexuality: Joris Karl Huysmans' *À Rebours*, called in English *Against Nature*. (The hero of this farrago of decadence, Des Esseintes, owes much of his own unnatural affection for sensation and perversion to the fancies of Baudelaire.) Wilde, through Dorian Gray, summarizes the spirit and effect of *Against Nature*:

There were in it metaphors as monstrous as orchids, and as subtle in colour. The life of the senses was described in the terms of mystical philosophy. One hardly knew at times whether one was reading the spiritual ecstasies of some mediaeval saint or the morbid confessions of a modern sinner. It was a poisonous book. The heavy odour of incense seemed to cling about its pages and to trouble the brain.

As Dorian Gray fell under the spell of Des Esseintes, so did Harry Crosby fall under the spell of Dorian Gray, and of his guide in hedonism, Lord Henry Wotton, known too as Harry. He first read *The Picture of Dorian Gray* at about the time he first met Walter Berry, and then he read it again, and again, copying out its passages and appropriating its paradoxes, eroticisms, worship of art, and explorations of the sensational for his own credo. Several times throughout his various notebooks and journals Lord Henry's instruction to Dorian appears:

"The mutilation of the savage has its tragic survival in the self-denial that mars our lives. We are punished for our refusals. Every impulse that we strive to strangle broods in the mind, and poisons us. The body sins once, and has done with its sin, for action is a mode of purification. Nothing remains then but the recollection of a pleasure, or the luxury of a regret. The only way to get rid of a temptation is to yield to it. Resist it, and your soul grows sick with longing for the things it has forbidden to itself, with desire for what its monstrous laws have made monstrous and unlawful."

Silly mischief today, a collection of aphorisms and chopped logic. But it acted catalytically on Harry's disenchantment with his received conventions, gave an expressive form to his appetite for novelty, and seemed to license any act he might wish to commit, so long as it was not stale. Under the influence of Oscar Wilde's overwrought, florid melodrama (in which, however, the sinner is as lovingly punished as in any soap opera), Harry religiously studied the articles of faith of the Yellow Book decadence of the Nineties in England, and earlier of the French Symbolists. Any bravo might have taken Des Esseintes' bait, but Harry was not merely some posturing dandy of the boulevards. He acted everything out—everything; there was no lag for him between thought and experiment. What Huysmans imagined, Harry performed.

He expressed his affection for artifice by the black cloth flower displayed in his buttonhole. Not content with meditations on the nature of corruption, he pushed past regulations and limits. He expressed his hedonism through an indulgence in whatever came to hand: opium, hashish, absinthe. He gambled recklessly, and spent his money and his health as though waste were his faith. If the morbid was a principle of decadence, Harry took himself to a bordello where he paid a thousand francs to see a girl flogged: "Would I have the courage to flagellate a girl, for in a queer way it would take courage." He did worse finally, but for the time being he was content to offer as many pretty girls as he fancied "a little touch of Harry in the night," and to follow Lord Henry in the lessons of misguidance. It pleased him that a lady, "Mademoiselle Fragile," told him that he reminded her of Dorian, so much so that he sprained his wrist by falling off a table on which he was performing acrobatics for another lady. At Étretat, on the Normandy coast in early July, 1925, he read *The Picture of Dorian Gray* for the second time, and reflected that "to corrupt the young is a temptation," and surrendered to the temptation with a pretty American innocent, an adolescent of full body, "Nubile," as Harry called her in his notebooks.

A couple of weeks later, back in Paris, he copied once again Lord Henry's lecture: " 'The only way to get rid of a temptation is to yield to it.' (tempest of applause.)" And two days later: "The sun is streaming through the bedroom window, it is eleven o'clock and I know by my dirty hands, by the torn banknotes on the dressing table, by the clothes and matches and small change scattered over the floor that last night I was drunk. Disgusting! And there is a cable on the mantlepiece (how long has it been there?) and it is from C and I am unworthy. This is the result of reading Wilde." Harry would have disappointed Lord Henry by his uncharacteristic remorse, and by his abdication of responsibility for his own actions. Lord Henry believed, with his author, that art could only please, not—as Doran Gray whined—corrupt:

> You and I are what we are, and will be what we will be. As for being poisoned by a book, there is no such thing as that. Art has no influence upon action. It annihilates the desire to act. It is superbly sterile. The books that the world calls immoral are books that show the world its own shame. That is all.

Harry Crosby would surely have endorsed the penultimate, but only the penultimate, sentence of Lord Henry's declaration. For books most certainly excited, rather than annihilated, his desire to act. Rather he annihilated all proprieties and inhibitions that fenced off desire from deed: "One's innocence deteriorates rapidly," he wrote. "In kindergarten was amazed to hear of kissing; at boarding school was shocked at lewd stories, during the war felt a revulsion on hearing of perversion; now worry very little about morals." Taking to heart the fanciful bravado of the decadents, Harry taught himself to become a law unto himself. But part of him answered to a more general call of his time, the elevation of mischief and play into a kind of creed. A life of riot was not uncommon for an American living on the Left Bank in the mid-

Twenties. What writer there was a stranger to booze, women not his wife (or men not her husband), indolence, petty crime? Harry was the author of a typical escapade late in August of 1923: he and a girl named Geraldine (who disappeared from his life as abruptly as she had entered it) had begun an evening with champagne orangeades at the Ritz Bar, then had danced in the Bois de Boulogne and later in Montmartre. They found themselves at seven in the morning in the markets of Les Halles, where they came to the bottom of a last bottle of champagne. Harry struck a bargain with a "sturdy peasant" to haul them to the Ritz in his vegetable cart: "and thus we reclined Geraldine in her silverness I in my blackness, upon the heaped-up carrots and cabbages while our poor man strained in the harness. A memorable ride with the strong summer sun streaming through the streets, she frivolous and gay, I pale as her dress, with champagne eyes and tousled hair. The Ritz, and a gift to the cuisine of our vegetable cargo, and a paying off of our man (too early to eat at the Ritz) and then she to a warm bath and I home to a cold one."

There was at this time a Mrs. Crosby, and where was she? Out of town, as it happened, but it wouldn't much have mattered to her husband. Lord Henry Wotton had explained to Dorian Gray that "the one charm of marriage is that it makes deception absolutely necessary for both parties." Not for Harry, who despised deceit, as he despised pretense. (It is important to note that however extremely Harry might be beguiled by an idea or by a book such as Wilde's novel, he rarely swallowed it whole, and would never violate his reflexive inclinations merely to bring himself into accord with a literary or philosophical precept.) He was not a man for confessions, believing that a confession of infidelity merely transfers discomfort from the guilty traducer to the innocent aggrieved. The disloyal husband who awakens his wife with the words *I can't sleep; I feel terrible; there's something I must tell you* augments the crime of infidelity: confession complete, he sleeps while his wronged wife lies miserably awake.

Harry did not bother to volunteer to Caresse what he was up to with his harem of pretty girls whom he so longed to revirginate. Neither was Caresse at liberty to ask. Harry would, upon request or need, read her the gospel according to Lord Henry: "If you want to mar a nature you have merely to reform it." That was the theory, and it was time and again put to the test of action. Like many a libertine, he truly believed that there was too much love in him to be contained—or absorbed—by any single woman, though Caresse was, as she knew, always his favorite. He had about him the pure, direct and unapologetic self-certitude of a fanatic, of an idealogue converting everyone to free love. This was potently mixed with an almost toxic dose of plain-dealing caught from his mother and father, from his headmaster at St. Mark's, and from those descendants of Hotspur whose company he had kept during the war. So little did he prevaricate about his appetites that he even wrote to his mother about the girls he enjoyed, and shared with her his fantasies: "I should like to have a harem, no girl to be over fifteen except Caresse." In response to a friend's curiosity about her evident indifference to Harry's infatuations, Caresse wrote that "no one girl seemed more important than the preceding one to me, and I never thought of them as Harry's *women* only as *decor* . . . they really didn't worry me—only Constance [Coolidge] and [Nubile], because she was only 14."

Yet sometimes Caresse would revolt, as Harry wrote in his diary, "against anyone sharing with her the queenship of my heart and she is tragic and unbalanced. . . ." On one occasion he noted the "shadow of a disaster" because Caresse believed that she should enjoy her own physical independence (as she soon enough did), and that woman was "the equal of man I believing that woman is dependent and the slave of man." There were awful tempests from time to time, especially when Caresse finally began to take lovers of her own, but they were remarkably short-lived and infrequent. Later, she explained the success of their odd balancing act: "We were each free to do as we wished, alone if not together, but *alone* was never really as well as *together*. We were restless out of one another's sight and Harry was forever telephoning to tell me where he was, and neither of us ever came late to a rendezvous with the other. Only the devil or death could keep us waiting."

She trusted him, finally, and in his extravagant love for her he seemed to give her cause. During July of 1924, while she was in America visiting her family, Harry wrote her almost daily from Paris. "I worship you. I have just been kneeling before your miniature which I have arranged in a sanctuary on my desk and before which I burn incense while repeating Our Prayers over and over again before God. . . . It is the most beautiful and wonderful thing to realize that we are to be together irrevocably forever and ever and eternity. And what happiness this foreknowledge of our immortality brings." (In Harry's persistent calculations about death and suicide, he never abandoned his belief in an afterlife. Neither did he regard suicide as a sin that would condemn him to an eternity smoky and hot. Walter Berry's contemptuous disbelief in eternal life and the Elysian Fields shocked and saddened his otherwise adoring young cousin.)

Harry and Caresse were not often apart, but when she went home to the stability and decorums of American family life she endured the disapproval, even horror, that her mother expressed in the discovery on a Nantucket beach that her precious Polly had let hair grow beneath her arms. Caresse had no affection for American customs, and in for a pound more than a penny she managed, with rare lapses, to abide by the plunger's rules: "By our background we were privileged," she later wrote, "by our actions we were ostracized; but we stood stubbornly on ground which we knew to be our own and which gradually came to be recognized and envied." They wanted so badly, as she said, to be themselves.

The literature of decadence was perfectly suited to Harry's needs at the time he left Morgan, Harjes. It gave him license to rebel against the common sense of his parents, and honored his retreat from workaday life as a blow struck on behalf of art against the Philistines. At the very least he resolved to make of his life, and its high style, an ornate decoration. Preoccupied as it was with the morbid and diseased, it afforded him material to spur his ruminations about disorder, early sorrow, death and suicide. The literature of decadence trafficked in exotic cults and rites. Just so: Harry would worship the sun, and practice bizarre rites in its name. The literature of decadence, leading as it did to such movements as Surrealism and Dada, made a virtue of inwardness. For the beginning writer, it must have been a relief to be liberated—in the name of an aesthetic principle—from the rigors of classical argument and composition, to be encouraged to record dreams as though they were works of art, bought cheap off the rack but admired for their perfect fit.

Six months after he quit the bank, Harry made an alphabetical list of words that had arrested or provoked him. He was building an inventory for his poems, and perhaps nothing better demonstrates the influence on his imagination of Baudelaire, Huysmans, Poe and Wilde: "absurd, bleak . . . chaos . . . desolate . . . disconsolate, disillusion, envenomed . . . entangled . . . fragrant, feudal, fragment, gnarled . . . grandeur . . . heraldic . . . illusion . . . idolatry . . . labyrinth . . . legend, lurid . . . mediaeval, mysterious, macabre, merciless, massacre, nostalgia . . . obsolete, orchid . . . primeval . . . perfume, pagan, phantom . . . peacock . . . preposterous . . . remote . . . ruin . . . sacred . . . Sun . . .

seer, sorceress . . . tempest, turbulent . . . unicorn . . . unchaste . . .
unchallenged, virgin, vampire . . . veil . . . yield. . . ."

On Baudelaire's birthday he sent imaginary black irises to the
genius of disease. And on a later April 9 (1925) he wrote him a sonnet,
touchingly vulnerable in its preposterous, *outré*, unmotivated gloom:

> *I think I understand you Baudelaire*
> *With all your strangeness and perverted ways*
> *You whose fierce hatred of dull working days*
> *Led you to seek your macabre vision there*
> *Where shrouded night came creeping to ensnare*
> *Your phantom-fevered brain, with subtle maze*
> *Of decomposèd loves, remorse, dismays*
> *And all the gnawing of a world's despair.*
>
> *Within my soul you've set your blackest flag*
> *And made my disillusioned heart your tomb,*
> *My mind which once was young and virginal*
> *Is now a swamp, a spleenfilled pregnant womb*
> *Of things abominable; things androgynal*
> *Flowers of Dissolution, Fleurs du Mal.*

The poem that inspired Harry's melancholy ditty is "Spleen IV,"
Baudelaire's apostrophe to disintegration and despair, taking as its
graphic central conceit the oppression of the poet's skull by his anguish, and the oppression of the earth itself by a low, dark and heavy
sky. The poem was much in favor among the decadents, and Arthur
Symons translated it. But it has best been done by Edna St. Vincent
Millay:

> *When the low, heavy sky weighs like the giant lid*
> *Of a great pot upon the spirit crushed by care,*
> *And from the whole horizon encircling us is shed*
> *A day blacker than night, and thicker with despair;*
>
> *When Earth becomes a dungeon, where the timid bat*
> *Called Confidence, against the damp and slippery walls*
> *Goes beating his blind wings, goes feebly bumping at*
> *The rotted, mouldy ceiling, and the plaster falls;*
>
> *When, dark and dropping straight, the long lines of the pain*
> *Like prison-bars outside the window cage us in;*
> *And silently, about the caught and helpless brain,*
> *We feel the spider walk, and test the web, and spin;*

Then all the bells at once ring out in furious clang,
Bombarding heaven with howling, horrible to hear,
Like lost and wandering souls, that whine in shrill harangue
Their obstinate complaints to an unlistening ear.

—And a long line of hearses, with neither dirge nor drums,
Begins to cross my soul. Weeping, with steps that lag,
Hope walks in chains; and Anguish, after long wars, becomes
Tyrant at last, and plants on me his inky flag.

It is no trick to imagine what effect "Spleen" had on Harry. He recognized its beauty, shining like a black pearl in a cup of dead-green absinthe. From the time he had accused the young matron Polly Peabody of having seduced him, he had been quick, even eager, to surrender his innocence, as Dorian Gray surrendered his to the demonology of Des Esseintes. If Anguish could plant its inky flag on Baudelaire's drooping head, then Baudelaire must set his "blackest flag" within Harry's soul, whose coordinates Harry truly believed he could locate.

The sonnet "Baudelaire" was written in 1925, and reprinted in 1927 in *Red Skeletons*, a collector's potpourri of decadent motifs and conceits, dedicated to its illustrator, Alastair, a languid, precious artist who dressed like Des Esseintes at his most fanciful, and drew delicate grotesqueries in the manner of Aubrey Beardsley. *Red Skeletons*, with epigraphs from Wilde and Baudelaire, the poems with titles like "Red Burial," "Black Sarcophagus," "Futility," "Gargoyles," "Lamentation" and "Black Idol" (a hymn to opium), was an act of craven idolatry. Harry soon enough recognized this, and bought up all the copies of *Red Skeletons* he had not sold or given away—eighty-four in number —and took them to Ermenonville, where he built a bonfire of eighty copies (around which the Crosbys danced a funeral jig) and shotgunned the rest till not a word was legible. Stout fellow, he finally realized that literary despair is as easily flaunted as is a black gardenia, but unless it has been earned it looks like the cheapest, most clownish of ornaments, nothing to be caught wearing in public. Baudelaire was an authentic master of renunciation and ruin: he was addicted to hashish, opium and alcohol, was psychotic, and died of tertiary syphilis. In contrast, Harry had life all his own way when he fell under the spell of the decadents, and was showing himself a mighty good time.

Excess was the only measure he knew. When he ate, he ate oysters, and when he drank, he drank champagne, and too much of both, yet he paid no price, laid on no fat and managed not to appear foolish. If he saw something he wished to have, he had it: "Went out this morning to buy silk pyjamas but came back with a 1st edition of Les Illuminations very rare as there were only 200 copies edited by Verlaine." Another day, going to look for zebra skins, he returned home with the skeleton of a girl wrapped in a yellow raincoat, her feet hitting the stairs of 19 rue de Lille as he carried her to his library, where he hung her from a bookcase: "And who was this woman, princess or harlot, actress or nun young or old pretty and passionate or ugly and numb?"

His seductive habits became legendary among his friends. If he noticed a girl who attracted him, he approached her, whatever his circumstances at the moment, or hers. He might be dining in a restaurant with Caresse and another couple, and suddenly his attention would deflect from them to someone else—a pretty girl, perhaps, at table with her husband. Witnesses testify that he was entirely capable of leaving his own table, going to a strange girl's and departing with her, without explanation or apology. At such times he was without guile or shame. He did not smirk or flatter. He was direct; he could afford to be, because he never sought the company of any girl he did not at that moment love, and any risk was worth the fulfillment of his love. He must have been rebuffed occasionally, but no one who witnessed his public seductions recollects an ugly scene resulting from his proposals. He gave the impression of decorous certitude, of a man bestowing rather than begging a prize. It would have been unthinkable to reproach him vulgarly, or to accuse him of vulgarity. There was never anything arch or coy in his manner:

> Saw a young girl crossing the Rue de Rivoli, the wind blowing her skirts up around her neck. Followed her across the Tuileries (a lean hungry greyhound walking after a heifer . . .) and over the bridge (there was a metallic aeroplane overhead flashing in the sun) and then I lost her and found her again in the Rue de Poitiers (Diane de Poitiers) and we had tea together in the Bois and oysters Chez Prunier and cocktails at the Piebald Horse and . . . she is the first girl I ever met who has eyes like mine and every time I see a new girl I think of [my father] and how he once said that there were plenty of fish in the sea plenty of birds in the sky (stirring of birds in my arms). . . .

Imagine Harry's mother and father. Having encouraged their son to renounce Polly Peabody and take up with multitudes of fish and birds, he first married her and *then* followed their advice. Six days after they met, the girl with his eyes was in Harry's bedroom, dressed in black, wearing a gold necklace and bracelet, and as she sat on his bed Harry told her how pretty she was, and when she left, "I looked up the word 'esculent' thinking that it might apply to her and in a way I suppose it does." Esculent means suitable for eating, and it was at about this time that Harry bumped into a distant but pretty American cousin near the Ritz. He was on his way to Morgan, Harjes to deposit Caresse's uninsured jewels in the sanctuary of a lockbox, but aborted his mission to take advantage of his lucky encounter—*carpe diem* was his watchword—and take the girl to drinks. Sometime later that day, having lost Caresse's jewels forever, he was putting the signature of his teeth upon the pretty neck of his angry and frightened kinswoman, who believes to this day that he was capable of killing her. Perhaps she should be forgiven for having devalued the purity of his intentions, for how could she have known that Harry had written in his notebook, shortly before he encountered her comely, esculent self, "Better that her neck should bear the traces of my loving teeth"? Better than what? One is afraid to ask.

There was much weird business in the air those days, and some of it drifted Harry's way, some ugly, satanic stories. An acquaintance won a million francs playing baccarat in Cannes and took his money to London, where he gave a party at which waiters, guests and a black orchestra all raped one another. (At such carnal institutions as the Four Arts Ball in Paris, patronized by Harry and Caresse, rape was not necessary.) It should be recorded in Harry's favor that apart from a light supping upon one lady's neck, he was never, till his bloody end, a man for cruelty or violence, physical or social. He instructed himself constantly to learn the arts of gentle love, and he pleased himself by pleasing those whom he loved. And when he tumbled into love with a new girl, he would not repudiate his previous mistresses. Nor, oddly, did they seem to feel jealousy toward their rivals—none, that is, till he took up with Josephine Rotch. He must have frightened more than one lover with his talk of suicide, but none fled from him. He recorded many of their love letters in his notebooks, and the following, slight but characteristic, indicates that his charms overcame his menace: "I think of you all the time," an unidentified girl wrote him. "I am so glad we have met and thank you. I will never forget you. I wonder what your philosophy of life is. I'm afraid it is rather wonderful and probably very dangerous. When I saw you you appealed to me right away."

When he discovered D. H. Lawrence, who later became his friend, Harry was awed, but not by everything he wrote. (He found *Lady*

Chatterley's Lover silly and salacious.) He noted that it had been said of Lawrence that "like a Roman voluptuary he would sacrifice a nation for a night of perfect love." Beside that extravagant claim, Harry penciled: "Who wouldn't who had any sense?" Like any seeker of sensation who manages to translate his most exotic fancies into acts, he was obliged to accelerate his desires as he satisfied them, to reach further and further for novelty.

Still, sometimes the act of imagining satisfied Harry, and stood surrogate for experience. So he might read about the extravagances of the corrupt Roman emperor Heliogabalus, and approve his megalomania and self-indulgence. The emperor would not agree to budge, even as a boy, without a procession of forty chariots. At his homosexual feasts the guests lay on silver beds and used the curly hair of boys as napkins. "Among the spectacles he gave in the amphitheater were naval displays on lakes of wine, the death of whole menageries of Egyptian beasts, and chariot races in which not only horses, but also stags, lions, tigers, dogs and even women figured; he himself had teams of naked women to draw him from place. . . ."

Harry was a hedonist with an income of not much more than twelve thousand dollars per year, who maintained servants (whose hair he would not have dreamt of trying to use as a napkin) and mistresses (who were of the social class that likes to pay its own way), who cabled his father from time to time to sell stock to bail him out, who sometimes meekly accepted scoldings from his father for the cables: "Two lecture letters from the family to reprimand me for extravagance. Cabled 'penitent.' " At other times, however, he chafed when he was bridled, as in an undated letter to his mother mailed sometime late in 1923:

> I was somewhat annoyed at your letter on extravagance and gambling. Just because I ask to have $1000 put to my account at the State St, why should it occasion all this furore? As I have explained more than once to you and Pa—I have invested in December 1922 and in January 1923 more than $5000—if not a good deal more—but not with any particular intention of keeping it invested. After all I could keep my securities here and have the company deposit my dividend cheques for me but I thought Pa liked looking after them. If he doesn't want to I shall see to them myself. We stayed at the Berkeley in London which was extravagant but it was the first time we had been away from Paris since February except for two days at Cubourg and we decided to have a fine time for three days rather than a fair time for ten days. That as you know is my theory on most subjects. Overdrawing the State St

was a mistake. I'm sorry but it doesn't seem very wicked although I do consider it a very bad habit.

And bad habit it certainly became, for Harry consistently overdrew his account not only at Boston's State Street Trust Co., but also at Morgan, Harjes. Both places indulged him, and the latter institution accustomed itself to honoring such of his checks as were delivered for collection written on napkins from the restaurant where he had dined, or on plates, or whatever came easily to hand. Harry did not like to carry a billfold.

Indeed, many of his notions regarding money were out of the way. He despised "filthy germ-ridden paper bills" and preferred to transact his business affairs with gold coins if cash was really necessary. He was generous with strangers as well as friends. One night at Prunier he noticed a lovely child, "with long innocent hair and softest eyes and young goldenness and we drove all over Paris trying to find a box of candy for her and we finally discovered an enormous one and I gave it to the vestiaire (pour Mademoiselle Charmante) and we were an hour late to the theatre and all through the performance (Revue Nègre) I kept thinking of her and what a contrast between Joséphine Baker and Mademoiselle Charmante." He lavished gifts upon many sorts and conditions of people. He bought a Morgan, Harjes teller, and his family, a shore holiday. The old lady from whom he bought violets for Caresse, and for his mother when she was visiting Paris, received from him a comfortable stool to sit upon, and warm mittens and a muffler to ward off the chill. The daughter of his bookbinder, ill-dressed by Harry's lights, was outfitted by him head to toe.

Several people have testified to his custom of paying more for a thing he bought than its listed price if he felt the object had been undervalued. He did this in no wasteful spirit, but from his own system of propriety, fixing merit and rewarding it. When he traveled, it was always first class, and he didn't hesitate to tell his mother, who proposed to take him with Caresse to Persia, what his expectations were: "Nor if we went to Persia would I promise you not to shock the missionaries (I have never liked missionaries) and I am sure I could never wear a top hat . . . and I would hate sleeping with Caresse under a net and I don't believe Narcisse would like it at all! . . . Besides, I think travelling is no fun unless deluxe—I had enough hardship in the war to last a lifetime. . . . I wish you and SVRC wouldn't worry so much about my morbidness. I have never been less morbid and as far as drinking last summer [1927] I drank about half as much as the summer before...."

Till the last year and a half of his life Harry was addicted to lists of every kind, especially statistical tables: how much he had spent, how many cold baths he had taken, how many drinks drunk or cigarettes smoked or books read or ladies kissed. One day in 1927 he calculated all the places he had stayed at one time or another in Paris: there were many hotels (the Crillon, Excelsior, Continental, Métropolitan, Meurice, Lutetia, Cambon, Goya, Hôtel du Palais d'Orsay, quite a few others) and several apartments. There was the Crosbys' first flat, on the Right Bank at 48 rue de Belles-Feuilles, and a tiny place on the Île Saint-Louis, overlooking Notre Dame and the Seine at the Quai d'Orléans, which they had taken on June 1, 1923. They would go to sleep listening to the cathedral's chimes, and Harry would sometimes paddle a canoe down the Seine as far as the Tuileries, then walk to Place Vendôme to work, and late in the afternoon sweat the boat back upstream. But the place was too small for Harry, Caresse, two children and servants, so in the autumn of 1923 they moved into the lavish apartment of Princess Marthe Bibesco, by birth Rumanian, by inclination Parisian, a woman of letters and friend of Walter Berry, who introduced his cousin to her. She let them have the flat at 71 rue du Faubourg St. Honoré till the spring of 1924 for fifty thousand francs (then about twenty-two hundred dollars). The bathroom was paneled in blue wood, and the Princess's bedroom had a mirrored wall, pearl-gray carpet, rose-colored wallpaper and pale green wall hangings. There was a small garden outside the ground-floor back entrance, and when the Crosbys moved in they brought with them "two maids and a cook, a governess, and a chauffeur."

In the spring, when Princess Bibesco returned to claim her flat, the entourage moved to a small *pavillon* at 29 rue Boulard, behind the Cimetière Montparnasse. There were only two family bedrooms, one pink and one green, and since Harry could not abide the little noise occasioned by the play of Billy and Polleen Peabody, and besides, wanted their room for a library, the children were exiled to a toolshed attached to a lean-to off the kitchen of the cottage. According to their mother, it was six feet by eight, the size of a small Pullman compartment. It was probably grander than that; in any case, the cottage was too cute and homey for Harry's taste, though from time to time Caresse displayed a modest domestic appetite for nest-building.

The family spent the summer of 1925 on the Normandy coast at Étretat in a deserted gun emplacement on a cliff that looked, in Caresse's phrase, "like a lump of sugar with curtains." Then, on September 8, they installed themselves at the Hôtel Goya, on the Faubourg Saint-Honoré, near Princess Bibesco's apartment: "There is a miraculous bathroom (black and gold)," Harry wrote, "and Spanish twin beds and an odor of richness and a balcony in the sun and we are high up and it is like being in a fortress." Harry gave the hotel three stars on his list of Paris residences, equaled only by the next and final entry, 19 rue de Lille, where they settled on November 27, 1925, and remained till the end. (Their wing of the building is now occupied by Max Ernst, a friend of Caresse, and his wife, Dorothea Tanning.) The building is in the Faubourg St. Germain, the Left Bank Paris of Walter Berry that opposed the Right Bank Paree of commerce and tourism where the Crosbys had till then spent so much of their time. Rue de Lille runs roughly parallel to the Seine and Boulevard St. Germain, and falls about midway between them. Number 19 has a courtyard, massive doors, sandstone columns and high windows. It is an eighteenth-century town house, austere in the balance of its exterior proportions, not worth a second glance, but within it was lavishly finished with hand-worked wood trim and cut-crystal light hangings, and in back there was a formal garden. The ceilings were high, the rooms large, and the Crosbys occupied all three floors of one wing.

Archibald MacLeish (to whom the Crosbys offered to lend 19 rue de Lille) recollects the place as "very comfortable, not grand or grandiose." But Harry and Caresse had a magic touch with every place they lived. There was a huge bathroom, with much inlaid wood and black and white tiles, with an open fireplace, and sometimes they and one couple or another from among their fellow free-thinking friends would bathe ensemble in the massive sunken marble tub. A Boston friend invited by Harry to 19 rue de Lille was shocked to be shown a concealed peephole through which he was invited to watch Caresse languishing in hot water and bubbles. She would have been amused to know that with the heat of embarrassed anger rather than prurient longing he renounced his host's invitation.

There was a formal drawing room that was seldom used, and Caresse's studio, and on the third floor Harry's huge library ran the length of the whole wing, with three windows opening onto a balcony overlooking the street. Harry called his library the Tour Grise, because of its gray walls, and he cluttered it with animal skins, spears, sea chests, ship models, and a skeleton, and with Saint Jerome's ever-present, staring skull to remind him of the finish line. There he worked, writing poems and polishing his journal, every morning and late every afternoon. Polly Peabody Drysdale remembers the ritual of the closing of the desk at about five or six every evening. When they were at home, Harry and Caresse ate dinner in bed, sitting surrounded by books, each wearing a gold necklace. Harry was just the man for bed: he liked to write as well as read there, and he and Caresse often entertained in their bedroom with a few half-moon tables set up according to the number of friends invited to stay for dinner. At eight, regardless of who was still in the room (which was decorated with bear and zebra-skin scatter rugs and portraits of each of them), Harry would costume himself in silk pajamas and a Magyar kimono embroidered with red and gold. At such times caviar and champagne were invariably served, and perhaps oysters or some American dish—a chowder or corn bread.

On more formal occasions the Crosbys entertained in a Sicilian dining room. They would receive in the salon before eating, and then retire to Harry's library for coffee and brandy after dinner. The whippet Narcisse would sit at table upon a cramoisy cushion, "very effective black against red," as Harry wrote his mother, continuing: "I shall do a Kitsa, that is describe what we had—first baccardi rum cocktails in small glasses, then clam consommé with whipped cream, then canard with dried oranges and mashed sweet potatoes, then a tomato cheese salad, finally marshmallows in a hot chocolate sauce. . . ." Sometimes the parties were less to Walter Berry's taste, and more to Dorian Gray's. A Boston friend of Caresse's and classmate from Rosemary Hall remembers cocktails at the Crosbys', where "everyone just fiddled around, as they always have. And when you left, you went down the stairs and facing you was a skeleton, and in its mouth, for a tongue, it had one of those French envelopes [a French letter, a rubber], with a wide border of black, about an inch wide, and that was your goodbye."

Horses were Harry's most time-consuming and costly indulgence. Less than three months after he married Caresse, he bought himself a bronze race horse, but wondered wistfully "when shall we be able to buy a real one?" Shortly before Thanksgiving, 1922, he lost two hundred dollars at the trotting races at Vincennes and "returned home in the subway downcast and discouraged. Resolved never to bet again." Had he only by then read *The Picture of Dorian Gray* he would have learned from Lord Henry Wotton that "good resolutions are useless attempts to interfere with scientific laws. Their origin is pure vanity. Their result is absolutely *nil*. . . ." Just so, because next day Harry "resolved to regain what we had lost. To Auteuil and in the big hurdle race plunged heavily on Abri who came from behind in the last few strides to win by a neck. Won three hundred dollars (qui ne risque rien ne gagne rien) and C is delighted. All night galloping horses whirled through my brain."

So the pattern was set: Harry would win, and resolve to win even bigger, lose and resolve to quit—but he never did. On April 1, 1923, calculating that he had won seven hundred dollars the month before on horse racing, he smugly listed the requirements for success at the track: "nerve, coolness when in adversity (which is the art of pulling down one's flag), a prearranged system, and a strong capital to work with. But the races are making me nervous and I am playing too high. Nor must I let racing interfere with books." When he gambled, he played always for the jackpot. He wasn't interested in the horse that played or showed. (Just as he believed he played best with blue chips, and at roulette went for the thirty-five-to-one shot, the single number.)

Three months after declaring the virtue of a prearranged system: "Calamity. Our race system on which we had banked such extravagant hopes crashed and we are poorer by two thousand dollars. Unpleasant awakening! What a bitter lesson! What a debacle. . . . Held with C a mock symbolic funeral by filling my magnificent grey derby (the one I wear at the races) with ordures from the kitchen and hurling it from our balcony into the Seine. Felt chastened and resolved to read the Bible Old and New Testament, from Alpha to Omega. Shall sell our etchings . . . and shall not gamble any more and shall not take any vacation." Within a week he was gambling, within two he and Caresse were on vacation. (But he did sell four etchings, one of which he later bought back, paying for it five times the amount which he received for the four he had sold.) Self-denial was not Harry's long suit, except that he did not spend much money on clothes for himself. ("Bought under-drawers, a remarkable event, but I have been wearing C's black lace pretties for a week.")

Harry was addicted not merely to gambling but to the elegant rites of horse racing. From February to December, excepting August, there was a race meeting every day within easy reach of Paris: at Chantilly (where the Prix du Jockey Club was run), or Longchamp (where the Grand Prix de Paris, the highest stake in Europe was run), or Auteuil, where they held steeplechases. And in August daily races were run at Deauville. Before the Sunday races near Paris it was customary to hold an elaborate brunch in town, and Harry and Caresse fell into the custom, consorting with such race-obsessed aristocrats as the Comte de

Civry, who tutored them in the etiquette and tricks of racing. On the Count's advice Harry won four hundred louis, more than twice his year's rent at the small house in Montparnasse, betting on Sir Gallahad at Saint-Cloud on April 15, 1924.

Also at the Count's urging, Harry in the spring of 1925 bought two race horses, Cataline and Dom Luco. He bought several more before he died, but one may fairly be said to represent them all: "Dom Luco runs in the sun, Dom Luco runs in the rain, but Dom Luco never wins." Many times Harry wished that Dom Luco would fall during a race and break his neck, so that his owner could collect a bit of insurance to defray his losses. But Dom Luco led a long and happy life; he was a prudent beast, protective of his health, careful where he stepped, content to finish twenty-second in a field of twenty-two, as he did one typical day at Longchamp.

Never mind, it was pleasurable to take part in the formal, elegant procedures of the track. The Count helped the Crosbys select their racing colors, purchased at Hermès: gray, royal rose and black. And in no time at all after buying their horses, they were deep into the kind of ritual he so cherished and required. On July 8, 1925, Harry was at Étretat and Caresse was at Prize Day at a boarding school outside Paris to which Billy Peabody had been exiled. Harry wrote her: "You must go out to see Catalina run—we have always had one of us when our colours came out and I feel it is a habit we should never break. . . . You would have adored this afternoon for I was bright and delicate in my white flannels and white sweater. I think Nubile likes me. Think of *us* at *her* age. . . . I hope Billy had a fine prize-day (you see how nice I am I am of course) I mean it Bunny for if you love your kids I at least like them and the little wretch you know I care for. . . ."

"The Little Wretch's" nursemaid, named Seline, known as Sea Lions, was another matter. Apart from caring for Polleen, it was her responsibility to place and collect Harry's bets when he was unable to go to the track. She began to neglect the child for the horses, her interest in which was enhanced by her cut of 5 percent of Harry's winnings. One day she claimed to have forgotten to bet Black Sun, who won, and Harry was out one hundred dollars. Convinced that she had conspired with the bookmaker, Harry fired her, and recollected his father's homily: "In all business as well as in all pleasure one should deal with the best people and go to the best places."

The day before moving into 19 rue de Lille, Harry lost five hundred dollars, wired home for a thousand, and reflected that "if it is awful to consider the follies we have done is it not a hundred times more awful to consider the follies we are going to do?" He made perfunctory attempts from time to time to find a rational motive for his addiction, linking it to his appreciation of the physical grace of a horse—or dog*—bred for speed, nervousness and arrogance, bred not only for fragile comeliness but for stamina. He himself continued to run, in cemeteries and forests, along beaches, wherever he happened to find himself when the mood was upon him. But he gambled because he loved risk and waste, because he believed, with Lord Henry Wotton, that "most people die of a sort of creeping common sense, and discover when it is too late that the only things one never regrets are one's mistakes."

His mother, fearful that her son would die from a want of common sense, rebuked him for his extravagance, but by 1927 he would no longer tug his forelock to her, or to anyone. He denied that he had gambled all his money away (in truth, he had not), and he reminded her that he gave a tenth of his income to charity. Still, since 1923 he had spent fourteen thousand dollars of his capital, in Boston a capital offense: "Pa has done everything for me financially in the management of my stocks and I always tell everyone that the wisest move in business I ever made was to get out of business altogether as my father looked after my things so well. . . . I have been extravagant I do not deny that but as far as that is concerned I am old enough to decide for myself. I believe I get a great deal for what I spend. Yes I dread scenes and particularly unnecessary ones that is why I did not consult you and Pa [about selling off some railroad shares]. Finances should be beneath discussion. . . ."

But just which finances Harry found beneath discussion were subject to his own peculiar standards of selectivity. In the spring of 1927 his father had cabled him that he would stake his son and daughter-in-law to five thousand dollars' worth of race horses. His expectations could abide the notion of a son in command of a racing stable far more easily than the notion of a son scribbling rhymes. However, something seemed to change his mind, and he decided he would rather the five thousand be spent on an automobile, so Harry wrote his mother: "I am

* The whippet Narcisse Noir, who won a good number of first prizes at dog shows in Paris, was also for a while the fastest dog in France. In late October of 1927 Harry wrote his mother that "Narcisse ran in the pouring rain Saturday and finished second in a field of six. He was much the fastest but stopped to bite an opponent. . . ." The sculptress Katherine Lane, who lived near Manchester on the North Shore, did the dog in a bronze bought by the Boston Museum of Fine Arts, and it was this piece that Harry went out of his way to see in exhibition his last day in New York.

afraid you have been influencing him. Well we don't want a car nor anything else except cash or a racehorse. Of course there is no reason he should give me anything. After all both of you have been tremendously generous so I hope you won't mind when I say like this that we are a little disappointed. What is your objection to a racehorse? It would be less dangerous than an automobile."

In the course of that year Harry bet only eighteen times, and came out about one hundred dollars ahead (less the thousands that he spent maintaining his own slow-footed stable); he was recklessly overdrawn during the year at both his banks, he owed a considerable sum to a bookie, and he was obliged to ask his father to sell another seventy shares of Union Pacific. By then he knew that Walter Berry would leave some money to him, and he had begun to bank on it and try to borrow from his father against it. In mid-July he wrote his mother that he and Caresse fancied that they would like to buy a boat for about two thousand dollars, or perhaps a car for twenty-five hundred, rather than another horse. (Absurdly, he suggested that a boat "would solve to a large extent the children problem," as though he would have tolerated in close quarters the children he could not abide in a very large town house.)

Six weeks later, Harry wrote home that he wanted a horse after all: "A racehorse is infinitely more glorious for the young." He wore his parents down, and in mid-November Stephen Crosby cabled him two thousand dollars to buy a horse. When Harry finally got around to picking one at Deauville nine months later, he bought a yearling called Sunstroke (at the suggestion of the Marquis de Saint Savian, a purchasing agent for the racing personage Lord Derby). The price was three thousand francs, not much more than one hundred dollars, and the Crosbys used the balance for a new car, a Voisin.

Harry finished 1928 ahead by seventeen hundred dollars, but in 1929 he went way down, almost three thousand, and by late summer of that year, after more than thirty consecutive losses, was growing irritated with himself: "Lost eleven thousand francs on a stupid horse called Sphinx. Terribly stupid of me and I am angry. My stakes are one thousand francs to win (this is the first time I have varied them for almost four years) and I should stick by them. Also lost five thousand at Baccara. This I didn't mind so much." The week before, he had enrolled in flying school. The regularity of clockwise, circular, earthbound, timebound track rituals had begun to bore him. He passed three thousand in losses one October afternoon at Auteuil, where he had gone with Pauline and Ernest Hemingway. Hemingway loved the races, but he had given them up because they cut into his work; later, in *A Moveable Feast*, he recalled quitting:

> It was hard work but at Auteuil it was beautiful to watch each day they raced when you could be there and see the honest races with the great horses, and you got to know the course as well as any place you had ever known. You knew many people finally, jockeys and trainers and owners and too many horses and too many things. . . . I stopped finally because it took too much time, I was getting too involved and I knew too much about what went on at Enghien and at the flat racing tracks too. When I stopped working on the races I was glad but it left an emptiness. By then I knew that everything good and bad left an emptiness when it stopped.

Harry filled his increasing emptiness with flying, and with friends, who were for a time a solace. And with booze and drugs. And with novelties and pretty girls and dangerous women. And with the worship of art, and the courtship of madness, and pagan rites. All led, by degrees, to emptiness. The emptiness was not sharp, like sudden hunger, or painful, like the loss of love. It was a want unsatisfied, evidently unsatisfiable. For a long time poetry seemed a way out of the prison of mortality. But only one indulgence failed to fail Harry, only one held his attention for good and all: the conjecture of his own death, his dream of killing himself, a dream within the reach of his whim.

10

"When, for whatever reason, men and women fail to transcend themselves by means of worship, good works and spiritual exercise, they are apt to resort to religion's chemical surrogates."

—Aldous Huxley, *The Doors of Perception*

If Harry was a sybarite, he was also in his outward appearance a fit and beguiling representative of young American manhood. His appetite in literature, true enough, ran to the school of decadence; his own theory of art, in part picked up secondhand and in part built piecemeal by himself, was a collage fabricated from the tailings of romanticism: art was to be worshiped through a worship of the self, and the self to be worshiped derived its godliness from genius, and genius was the product of obsession, madness and disease. Harry never vacillated in this belief, yet with a few notable exceptions he chose his friends for their boyishness (or girlishness) and health. He did not share with his friends, however close he might draw them to him, his aesthetic persuasions, so that those who first met him in Paris, who had no access to his manner before the war, were inclined to remark his gaiety, recklessness, loyalty, good looks, generosity and wit.

Such of his friends from Boston and St. Mark's who ran into Harry in Paris were of a different opinion. They found him intolerant of anything that gave off the merest whiff of righteous hometown morality. He impressed them as morbid, preoccupied by death, wasting in health and given excessively to drink. Harry used opium almost daily, and smoked intimidating amounts of it. Tote Fearing made his way to Paris every couple of years, and invariably would see his friend, but Harry suspected that his old chum did not much approve of him any more, and he was right. Fearing suspected that Harry used drugs, so Harry "tried to hide his life from me. He felt that I was Establishment, which I guess I was."

Harry would always agree to see old friends from Boston if they sought him out, but he would never extend himself to seek their company, and this considerably upset his mother and father. There were exceptions: he played the role of a sedate host on behalf of Gardner Monks and his wife, honeymooning in Paris. And he tried to tempt Ted Weeks to Paris, offering him and Mrs. Weeks the loan of 19 rue de Lille, and his affection for Stuart Kaiser never diminished during his lifetime. Kaiser had always had Harry's number, and after visiting Paris in 1924 he wrote him: "I know that you have suicide in the back of your head—although not for the present." Beside these words Harry wrote *Yes*. Kaiser had given him and Caresse an extravagant wedding present, a solid silver Paul Revere pitcher, "a beauty which must nearly have ruined him," he knew, for Kaiser was hard up, and he was moved by his friend's generosity. Even more was he impressed by his candor and his unwillingness to judge Harry by standards that were not Harry's.

One afternoon Harry invited a couple of Americans, sent to him by a Harvard friend named Ben Kittredge, to lunch: "One thought that every gentleman should knock down every negro he meets (and every negress? Knock up?) and the other considered love a form of indigestion. . . . Glad I am déraciné. Ubi bene, ubi patria." As Americans more and more found him a "queer" fellow, he more and more found America a queer place, and began to shun the company of his countrymen. It might be thought that he was merely exchanging one standard of social exclusion for another, but such was not the case. Certainly Harry was a snob, but his judgments about people were made case by case, and he never repudiated any friend who answered Harry's peculiar two-tiered requirement of himself—that he be outwardly merry and rash, and secretly serious unto death. He believed he could discern in others their hidden gravity and fixation, but he was often in error, and many times outward silliness merely concealed inward silliness.

Harry had explained to his mother, who persisted in sending childhood friends his way, that he and Caresse preferred to stay home at their work, and to avoid social obligations. ("If we are ever going to

amount to anything we must work and devote *all* our time to art.")
While it is true that he often cherished solitude, and that he sustained
his self-respect through the integrity of his work, he fled from the
company of his old friends only when they wearied or irked him.
Shortly before Christmas of 1924 Ben Kittredge—studying at Oxford
—showed up in town, ran Harry to ground, and talked him and Caresse
into making a party for dinner at Ciro's, together with a few of his
own friends, Gerald and Sara Murphy among them. Harry wrote his
mother about the occasion:

There was Kittredge "Le Bon Viveur" for he gloated on caviar and
other delicacies. He looks as if he had just stepped out of Pickwick
Papers pompous and very serious—always saying to me "What madness is this?"—no matter what I did. Then there was an effeminate
youth I didn't care much about. Men should have feminine traits but
should never be effeminate. And there was a beautiful boy I christened
The Virgin whom I tried to marry to Charlotte somebody or other
whom I called The Widow. I delight in giving people names. Then
there was a divorcée called Lucille—as a rule I love them, but she
was ignorant having only the words "I fancy" and the word "gorgeous"
to express herself with, and lacking the sparkle which usually accom-
panies charming divorcées. Mr and Mrs [Gerald] Murphy were with
us—he I liked a lot—very serious over trivialities and rather wise about
art and life. You know he paints. . . . His wife very sphinx-like but
knowing—particularly when she danced. And Caresse looking very
pretty and younger than ever. Everyone adores her—I most of all.
Then your son in a soft shirt as usual no hat or coat, rather vague. . . .
Here is the drift of my conversation during dinner with The Widow:
Harry: Charlotte, you are very defenceless, and I worry a great deal
about you.
Charlotte: That is very nice of you Harry. There is something so sweet
about you.
Harry: I love your dress. It achieves what it sets out to do. A girl with
hair of gold should always wear clothes of black. And your dress
with that expensive simplicity which is so very becoming. Are your
underthings also in black? But quite probably they are pink.
Charlotte: Do you like lavender, Mr Crosby?
Harry: That is a color I adore, Mrs Redway.
Charlotte: You are a very strange boy—it is strange I like you so much.
Harry: You were very charming that day we first met in the garden.
Do you remember, Charlotte? You reminded me of a flower girl
with your prettiness and your wistful eyes and your short skirts.
You seemed almost plaintive: so scented, so fragile.

Charlotte: It is so wonderful of you to say that, Harry. . . .

By this time the party had reached a somewhat advanced stage: Le Bon Viveur was pale and dignified and certainly quite intoxicated, the eyes of The Virgin were sparkling and his mouth was a pomegranate, The Widow was gay, Caresse soulful, the divorcée talkative, Mrs Murphy enigmatic, Mr Murphy more serious than ever—something to do with the painting of the insides of engines—as if engines had any insides, fish-face swallowing aspirin tablets for, poor dear, he felt cold—or drafty, as he expressed it, and I thinking of golden stars. . . .

Till 1926 the Crosbys' Paris guest books were full of the names of Boston and New York friends, but after that year three family names—Powel, de Geetere and Lymington—dominated the guest books and Harry's letters, diaries, notebooks and attention. On May 20, 1924, Ben Kittredge had been in Paris, and Harry had noted in his diary, "a Bohemian supper: Gretchen took a bath during the meal, C retired to bed, Croucher and Kittredge threw cream puffs out the window and I read the Paris-Sport. Everyone had a good time for everyone did what they wanted to do." Croucher was Howard Hare Powel, also called Pete, and Gretchen was his wife, and collectively they were known as the Crouchers because as a photographer he crouched to snap while Gretchen crouched over his shoulder to see what he saw. The only hard word Harry ever uttered about either of them was the impatient rebuke he issued in a letter to his mother in May of 1928 when he said that Powel, "if he wasn't so lazy, would be a better photographer than Man Ray." In fact, he respected Powel enormously, precisely because he did what he wanted to do, and no less.

Harry was impressed that, with almost no money, Powel, who had fled from the patrician expectations of his Rhode Island family, kept a cruising sailboat and an ancient Citroën, and managed to take life as it came to him, sweet and easy. Were he in America, Harry remarked, "he would be working like a dog selling bonds or in some bank and all à quoi bon?" Harry also admired Powel's languid wit and insouciance. One afternoon at a café some of Harry's friends were gossiping about a couple of counts—this count had never slept with his wife, and neither had that one. " 'What of it,' says Croucher, 'they have both slept with mine!' " Gretchen was from Texas, blue-eyed, and her blond hair was cut like Caresse's, in a Castle bob, short, with bangs. In Polly Peabody Drysdale's perhaps fallible recollection, the extremely close friendship between the Powels and Crosbys (and the de Geeteres) was sexually motivated. This is unlikely, although there is no reason to imagine that sexual intermissions did not from time to time interrupt their play. The two couples thought nothing of piling foursquare into a hotel bed, together with their dogs, Narcisse Noir and the Powels' white Great Pyrenees, Zulu. Gretchen Powel had a huge collection of jazz recordings, and excited Harry's interest in Bessie Smith, while Pete taught Harry to take photographs.

One night Harry consented to attend an A.D. Club dinner in Paris at Lapérouse, and smuggled Pete in under the title of the Duc de la Rochefoucauld (Armand de la Rochefoucauld was later a close friend of Caresse's), where he surprised the refined company by occupying himself with the taking of flash photos. On the record, at least, the association between the Crosbys and Powels was based on the unfettered pleasures they gave one another, on mutually entertaining mischief and simple gaiety. Harry found his friends "as free as birds," and relished their freedom because it enhanced his own, and by contrast to Pete Powel's indolence Harry's own regimen of reading and writing seemed like very industry.

For their part Harry seemed to be a joker, right up their alley—what a later generation might call a playboy. Occasionally he told them, with nonchalant resignation, that he would die very young, by his own schedule and hand. They discounted such announcements, called them "just literary." The two couples were addicted to larks and adventures. Once they drove through the country near Paris, stopping for food and drink only in towns of one syllable. On another occasion, August 22, 1927, Harry took a train to Brest to join Caresse and the Powels on the latter's newly purchased but antique sloop, the *Aphrodesia*. Their plan was to put the boat in operational trim, cross the wild Bay of Biscay to Spain and Portugal, then to sail down the Atlantic coast to Lisbon. But there were many bars along the docks of Brest and the boat leaked badly, was home to fleas, and didn't please the Crosbys at all. Harry did, however, like Brest, which was at the time a beautiful port. He hung out in the Bar de la Tempête, guzzling benedictines with Madame Suzanne, the bar lady, and musing on the information that their first destination was the Death Coast of Spain. While Caresse and the Powels outfitted the *Aphrodesia* with food and gear, Harry studied cryptography, puzzled together an elementary code of his own, and tried it out on his mother, to whom he wrote that he was homesick, and wished that their final port of call were Manchester rather than Lisbon: "You will be glad to hear today that I have really longed for the Shore and the Essex Links and the Essex Woods and the beach and The

Apple Trees especially if it is a day of fog I miss sleeping out on the sleeping porch and hearing the sound of the fog horn and today I am tired of the French and perhaps next spring or next summer we shall come back again. . . ."

Harry was growing a beard, soon began to tire of the Bar de la Tempête, and was increasingly dissatisfied with the sea-kindliness of the Powels' boat. A paid hand was brought aboard, but he complained about the fleas. The anchor chain parted and the mainsail tore; the bilges stank and the drinking water aboard was sour. Harry began to think about Huysmans' Des Esseintes, who started out one day in the rain from Paris to London, and on his way to the railroad station stopped at an English restaurant where he saw English men and women and ate roast beef and plum pudding: realizing that he had completed an imaginary journey to London more perfect, more English, than any actual journey, he returned home, satisfied.

So just eight days after arriving in Brest, Harry went home to Paris, taking along Caresse. He then wrote an imaginary log of their imaginary voyage (complete with a chaotic storm and his own death at sea), and was content to let the Powels sail on alone to Lisbon. The Powels did not reproach the Crosbys—people were expected to do what they pleased—and Harry appreciated that: "How understanding people are over here compared to people in America, everyone over here realizes that everyone must lead their own lives and not interfere with other people's lives. . . ." Pete Powel was apt to show up at the opera wearing tails and a pair of battered sneakers, and when he and Gretchen threw a party it was informal—as Harry said, "informal was no word for it!!!" Which meant that people wore what suited them, Caresse a golden tuxedo, Harry the severe and elegant suit that made him resemble a creature half bank president, half hangman. The Powels would serve strong punch and play loud music, and their parties ended when the last guest cried uncle, often a day and half after they began.

Frans and Mai de Geetere were accomplices in the liberated manners of the Powels and Crosbys. They had made their way to Paris from their hometown of Amsterdam on a barge, which they moored upstream from rue de Lille at the Pont Neuf. They were artists: she painted and he did a bit of everything—woodcuts, watercolors, miniatures. He had run away from home as a boy, painted murals on the walls of Dutch houses, worked in a madhouse. He and his wife had saved the money for their journey through canals to Paris by painting tulips on coal scuttles, which they then sold along the streets of Amsterdam. He was a couple of years older than Harry, tall, blond and slender, very intense, proud, with wild eyes. Mai was tiny, washed-out, timid, but with iron in her will.

Harry and Caresse first met the de Geeteres on March 15, 1927, through the agency of the Duchesse La Salle, who took them aboard the barge, *Le Vert-Galant*. Two days later Harry wrote his mother describing Mai's bright red velvet dress, gold necklace and gold bracelet, her pale skin and bobbed hair. "You would not have enjoyed their art for it is frightfully obscene, pornographic is the word, and then it was sacrilegious which I never care for. But the man has tremendous talent." (He had illustrated editions of Rimbaud, Verlaine and Baudelaire, which of course elevated him in Harry's esteem.) Harry never ceased to rail against censorship in any form, whether of books or of customs, but neither did he lose his contempt for pornography. (Sacrilege for him was in the eye of the beholder, for surely his own worship of the sun and of idols would qualify, by the standards of any Boston vestryman, as full-cry satanism.) He relished the erotic, but despised direct representation of sexuality.

Three weeks after they had first met, the Crosbys took dinner on the *Vert-Galant*, simple food cooked by Mai, and Harry considered the de Geeteres' servantless state notable enough to mention in print. The Crosbys were seduced by the gentle rocking of the barge, the lights flashing like exotic flowers on the river, and by Frans's muscular laughter. Later that night the two couples went to a six-day bicycle race. The Vélodrome was lit by arc lights, and the crowd was hysterical. At odd, surprising intervals pistols were fired to start new sprints, and loudspeakers made urgent unintelligible announcements, while prizes were bestowed with great solemnity on people for no evident reason. Harry loved it, the band blaring jazz, the popping of champagne corks, the click of bicycle wheels notching the persistent roar of a sweating, smoking crowd: "People standing on all the tables all the way round the track, actresses, royalty, jockeys, Jews, nouveau riches, scum of the earth. . . ."

He and Caresse began to see as much of the de Geeteres as of the Powels, and often all six would play together. Harry would paddle his new canoe, *Caresse*, upstream to the barge moored at the foot of the Île de la Cité at Quai du Vert Galant, and bask in the sun or sit below drying out after having been drenched by the Seine, wearing Frans's trousers and Mai's slippers, drinking brandy. At night after a party elsewhere the Crosbys would stop off at the barge on their way home and throw stones at it, and once, when no one answered, Caresse "took off one of her silk stockings I one of my silk socks and these we left hanging (two flowers rose and black) upon the knob of the lavoir door."

The "lavoir" was a public wash house on the embankment of the Seine where the de Geeteres cleaned their clothes. Themselves they scrubbed, kneeling face to face in a tin tub rigged beside the toilet room where Frans had hid when the barge crossed the Dutch frontier (he had no papers). Harry and Caresse came upon the couple bathing so primitively one afternoon, and afterwards the four went for a cheap meal at a café patronized by Mai and Frans: "And there was the smell of manure that had been sprinkled over the boxhedge and there was flour and water for soup and wretched fish (that I am sure had been living on sewerage) and weak beer . . . and the omelette had garlic in it." Harry was no bohemian. Still, he respected Frans's resourcefulness and virility, and liked to see him covered head to foot in tar, wearing a black wool lumberman's shirt, while he worked to close the seams of his leaky barge.

The de Geeteres fell into the custom of coming once a week to 19 rue de Lille to rub themselves down with expensive bath oils and to soak, drinking brandy, in the Crosbys' huge tub. By mid-May of 1927, just two months after the couples first met, Harry wrote his mother that he and Caresse went to the barge almost every day and that Frans and Mai were their best friends. "If it is possible for two people to be in love with two people then we are in love with them." Surely Frans was in love with Caresse, whom he courted avidly, to whom he sent a rose every day, according to Harry, who seemed flattered by his friend's attentions. The two men strengthened in their friendship, having in common a single object of love, and in the autumn of 1927 Harry wrote an essay on Frans's woodcut illustrations of Lautréamont's *Chants of Maldoror*, an hallucinatory prose-poem, remarkable for its cruelty and violence, which had had a measurable influence upon Baudelaire and Rimbaud:

The darkness of the forest where he was born, the sombre curriculum of the monks together with the rich darkness of ecclesiastical music, the spark of revolt kindled at the Academy of Brussels and whipped into a flame of hatred by the frescoes his father compelled him to paint in the neighboring churches, his first escape (if artists can be said to escape), the year of hunger whitewashing the walls of houses (le soleil contre le mur blanc) and, at nineteen, night duty as guardian in a maison de fous, these were, for M. Frans de Geetere, the foundation stones of that strange building men call the soul. In the madhouse he worked at his painting by day, and by night snatched unsettled hours of sleep, and in this environment developed those queer, abnormal faces that stare out at us from the pages of Maldoror. . . . And if "Lautréamont has liberated the imagination and dispelled our fear to enter into darkness" as Mr. Jolas so significantly remarked, M. de Geetere with a smoldering rage and fearlessness of creation followed the poet into darkness—"into the occult beyond" to quote Mr. Jolas again, "where new and demonic visions" (I am reminded of Beardsley and Redon and Alastair) "people our solitude."

Undiluted decadence here, what remained to be jousted for long after the Romantics had won their revolution. Harry next showed off de Geetere's illustrations and pointed approvingly to mad eyes and misshapen mouths, a dog baying at the moon, characters voluptuous and insane, "the defiled body of the young girl . . . (his art has the taste of death in it) . . . and there is the interesting study of legs (carbuncular legs) in the river scene where the suicide is stretched out upon the quays." It is fascinating that Harry discovered in de Geetere's peasant background so many elements in common with his own patrician history. Somber curriculum, ecclesiastical forms, revolt, hatred, escape into war as into a madhouse, a second escape—this one final—into art, an art turned weaponlike against the wardens of childhood.

For all their common taste for what was dark and enraged in themselves, Harry and Frans held fast to the youth that remained to them, perhaps from physical vanity but more likely because their instincts moved them toward stability and poise and salubrity. It required of them both an act of calculated will to promote their own decay, just as Harry calculated his own spontaneity. What would Baudelaire, Wilde and Beardsley have thought had they seen their disciples one May afternoon in 1928, on Jeanne d'Arc Day, enter a foot race of nine miles at Versailles? Harry wore his Harvard letter sweater, and after a few miles began searching for a taxi to carry him to the finish line, but Frans insisted that they see the thing through, and they did, Harry coming home seven hundred and thirty-seventh in a field of a thousand, Frans nine hundred and eighteenth.

The de Geeteres also shared Harry's enthusiasm for opium, and the two couples often smoked with a French submarine captain in his little house outside Melun, a suburb of Paris. One evening Harry smoked eleven pipes, which produced for him images he might have more easily experienced reading Coleridge—"slender chains of fire suns made of ice to break into fragments"—or looking at Beardsley—"naked

fire-girls with peacocks under their arms, panthers smothered in red."
The submarine captain kept him supplied with red tins of the sticky
drug, which Harry called "black idol," but it wasn't as though opium,
cocaine or hashish were difficult to come by in Paris. One of the most
popular drug bazaars was called The Hole in the Wall, a narrow bar
fronting the rue des Italiens with an exit into the sewers, a hangout for
opium peddlers and, according to Hemingway, for deserters during
and just after World War I. In such places hashish (which Harry
believed was a dangerous drug, unlike cocaine or opium) went for
about a dollar a joint—New York prices—to tourists, and five to the
dollar to such wised-up consumers as the Crosbys and de Geeteres.

The rich tradition connecting drugs with letters attracted Harry,
together with the illicit character of drug abuse and his partiality to
exotic states of consciousness. He had been reading Cocteau and Rimbaud on opium, and Archibald MacLeish believes that he smoked it
primarily as a literary venture: "This was a duty!" Surely Harry was a
man to proceed directly from an experience Rimbaud regarded as
metaphorical to its performance, and once having taken up the idea of
drugs he took up drugs for life.

One of the most deliciously comic scenes of debauchment in *The
Picture of Dorian Gray* transpires in an opium den, in which one of the
young men misled by Dorian is discovered friendless, destitute and
addicted. Harry couldn't wait to bring his own self to such melodramatic dissolution, and he noted with no little satisfaction the opinion of
the *Encyclopaedia Britannica*, whose thirteenth edition his mother had
sent him as a birthday gift, that opium smoking, carried to excess, was a
sign of moral imbecility exhibited by such wretches as were "often
addicted also to other forms of depravity. The effect in bad cases is to
cause . . . a degree of leanness so excessive as to make its victims appear
like living skeletons. All inclination for exertion becomes gradually lost,
business is neglected, and certain ruin to the smoker follows."

During the summer of 1924, while Caresse was on holiday in
America with her parents, Harry wrote her that "when you return we
must smoke opium together but I promise I won't attempt to without
you." Six months later, during a trip to North Africa, the Crosbys
bought four jars of the drug: "the best brand," Harry reassured himself, like any neophyte user, "and we have seen scorpions, Arab dances,
snake-charmers, little girls (eleven years old) for pleasure, and les
mangeurs de choses immondes." Polly Drysdale remembers that they
kept the opium, which looked to her like a pot of blackberry jam, in

her toy chest, and that prior to its appearance "there was a Verlaine jag with absinthe, so we had a great deal of absinthe around the flat." By the autumn of 1925 Harry and Caresse were going to Montmartre to mix "oysters and caviar, champagne and whiskey, cocaine and dancing." But opium was the drug of choice for Harry, and smoking it in his pipe became for him "almost a religious act, almost a prayer."

Opium (*pace* Coleridge and De Quincey) may be eaten, or, broken down into its alkaloid (morphine) or derivative (heroin), it may be injected. But for Harry the smoking was crucial because it was part of an exotic and Oriental tradition. To smoke opium required elegant paraphernalia and practiced skill: a bamboo dipper was used to remove a bit of the treacly opium, which was then twisted around the sharp end of the stick while the stuff was roasted, just so, over a lamp, till it resembled burnt wool. Too much flame and the opium was dried out, ruined; too little and it could not be smoked. At the exactly right moment the stuff was transferred from the dipper to the tiny bowl of a heated pipe, and inhaled three or four times. The preparation might occupy ten minutes, the smoking thirty seconds.

The early stages of opium abuse are characterized by vivid and exciting dreams, and Harry put a high price indeed on his dreams. Opium seemed as cheap a ticket as any both to Nirvana, beyond banal physical functions, and to Dionysian ecstasies—especially since it is one of the peculiar properties of opium that it can either still or excite, is either a stimulant or depressant, depending upon the psychology and physiology of the user at the time of use, upon the dose consumed and upon a full spectrum of environmental and spiritual variables. De Quincey describes his first experience of the narcotic in the 1821 version of his *Confessions of an English Opium Eater*:

> I was necessarily ignorant of the whole art and mystery of opium-taking: and, what I took, I took under every disadvantage. But I took it:—and in an hour, oh! heavens! what a revulsion! what an upheaving, from its lowest depths, of the inner spirit! what an apocalypse of the world within me! That my pains had vanished, was now a trifle in my eyes:—this negative effect was swallowed up in the abyss of divine enjoyment thus suddenly revealed. Here was a panacea . . . for all human woes: here was the secret of happiness, about which philosophers had disputed for so many ages, at once discovered: happiness might now be bought for a penny, and carried in the waistcoat pocket: portable ecstasies might be had corked up in a pint bottle: and peace of mind could be sent down in gallons by the mail coach.

Of course, De Quincey's acerbic irony had been provoked by a kind of hindsight-foresight, whereby the confessor knew very well what a high price in misery the novitiate in drug abuse would soon come to pay, and pay for the rest of his life. And he also knew what Harry could never afford to believe: that *Kubla Khan* had been conjured out of thin air not by opium but by Coleridge, a singular poet who had happened to use opium. De Quincey, again, on this crucial limitation: "If a man 'whose talk is of oxen,' should become an opium-eater, the probability is that (if he is not too dull to dream at all)—he will dream about oxen. . . ." Harry's dreams, recorded seriatum in *Shadows of the Sun* and in his unpublished journals, are of literary oxen, the claptrap of the School of Decadence, the trifles grasped by a fancy outreaching itself to achieve the fantastical. Any dozen of them are interchangeable; this is *Shadows of the Sun*, April 10 and 11, 1927:

> To the Chauve Souris to smoke opium and a perfect "ambiance"—a long facade of houses (each house a day) shortening and lengthening like an accordion with never a chasm or an abyss (thus do the days of the year lengthen and shorten) and there was a red exotic flower dressed like a girl stepping step by step through the dark forest of my soul step by step step by step and I could feel the silence but I could not see her face and when she had gone (step by step) there were red funnels vomiting sharp smokeplumes gold and cramoisy and grey and emerald into four high round suns which converged nearer and nearer until at last they collided into One Great Sun.
>
> And the bubbling sound of another pipe and another and another and the round contour of a breast and the touch of delicate fingers delicately gently snow upon snow and the metamorphose into oblivion beyond the beyond until the dreary awareness of a cold grey dawn and home to find a letter to say that in spring it would be wholesome to dive down into the depths of the black earth where all the flowers are aflaming still unsmitten and unbegun and all day across my soul red icebergs have been drifting like tombs across the Sun.

In her *Opium and the Romantic Imagination*, Alethea Hayter summarizes the most pervasive characteristics of the kind of opium user Harry Crosby was: a "restless mental curiosity about strange and novel mental experiences" and "a delight in secret rites and hidden fellowships, in being an initiate." The drug has other, more malign characteristics and consequences: pallor, languor, loss of appetite, sleeplessness, chills, night sweats, need. Samuel Putnam recalls the time he and Ezra Pound visited Jean Cocteau, then addicted to opium, and found him in bed beneath heaps of blankets, with an electric heater blasting at him while the temperature outside stood in the eighties. Ernest Hemingway recalled delivering a cold-cream jar filled with opium, at Pound's request, to Ralph Cheever Dunning, a poet who forgot to eat, who could only drink milk while he was smoking, whose wits had been addled by the juice of *Papaver somniferum*. Harry himself had ample evidence of friends who became "dangerously ill, the result of cocaine and protracted opium parties," and of another friend, "Y," "paler than I have ever seen her [reaching] out white hands like a child asking for its toy."

Opium made him careless and anxious, impaired his memory and digestion and concentration, but it never occurred to him to quit, or to consider quitting. He was not ignorant of addiction or its consequences. He tried hashish, adding it to opium and cocaine and passifloreine and brandy and absinthe and any odd thing that fell to hand. After all, a man under sentence of death has no fear of addiction, and Harry had long since sentenced himself, and moderation was unthinkable in such a circumstance. The only requirement he would allow to be thrust upon him was whatever was required to become a poet. He was in a rush, and dreams and ecstasies might propel him into art. The current felt overwhelming, and who knew where it led? To Coleridge, De Quincey, Baudelaire? With its hazards and cost, its erotic environment, its frenzies and mysteries, opium answered many of his needs. Best of all, to abuse it was to experience each time a miniature death, a liberation from need. It was to kill himself and survive his suicide.

In *The Passionate Years* Caresse wrote that she used it only once, then never again. Not so. Harry obliged her to smoke it with him, and one of his common reveries was of leading her into his own still void: "The stars burrowing under the hayricks the stars of my thoughts burrowing under the walls of your brain." Harry knew where he was going, and it became important to take Caresse, to take someone, along.

On the first night of 1928, Harry noted in *Shadows of the Sun* that he and Caresse had gone to "Git-le-Coeur to dine with Lord L . . . and Croucher appeared and then we all went down to the barge to smoke opium." Lord L was Gerard Vernon Wallop Lymington (pronounced *Limb*ington), the present and ninth Earl of Portsmouth. At the time he was twenty-nine, Harry's age, and his flat high up in the eaves of 1 rue Git-le-Coeur had been discovered for him by Caresse the year before. Later, he recalled that night with Harry and the Powels and de Geeteres in verse, "A Personal Poem for Harry":

> *. . . And the ghost of you with opium*
> *On the barge and that illusion there*
> *Of slow and muffled evil,*
> *Harnessed to the blacken'd stars*
> *And of our triad taxi journey*
> *With the Whores, who doped*
> *Behind their finger nails—*
> *The blazing joy in you that night!*

Lymington came from a boyhood and young manhood in England equivalent to Harry's own in Boston. He had studied at Winchester, then gone to war in 1916—first as a hospital orderly near the Front, then as a very young officer in the Life Guards. While Harry served his abbreviated sentence at Harvard, Lymington did likewise at Balliol College, Oxford. Lymington too had been scrupulously tutored by his family in the distinctions between ladies and whores; he too found the world as he saw it radically different from the world his tutors had described to him. He was restless, a wanderer, curious, in love with France and hospitable to Americans, some of whom he numbered among his kinsmen, and one of whom—a New Englander who died very young, a contemporary of Harry's—had been his closest friend.

Harry and Caresse bowled him right over. He fell half in love with Caresse the first time he saw her, and all the way soon thereafter. Harry dazzled him with his wit and power, his peculiarity, the fire he drew from life, his dreamy certitudes. He saw at once Harry's mix of foolishness, wickedness and sometime cruelty, but he discounted them as small enough prices to pay for his stimulations and bracing eccentricities. He took the flat to be near them, and kept it for the following three years as a hideout from his settled life as a farmer and political figure in England. In his memory, Paris's center during the late Twenties is fixed at 19 rue de Lille, where he would one day find André Gide and the next day a gunman, or Hart Crane, or models from the couturier Patou, or pirates and wastrels, bookies, whores, artists and photographers, or Archibald MacLeish, and where a party begun on Wednesday could persist into the weekend.

But for mischief, bad intentions and inventive self-indulgence no private party could equal the institution of the Four Arts Ball, a costume extravaganza staged every June by students of the arts in Paris, notorious for spectacular drunkenness and public fornication between stranger and stranger. The dances were restricted to male art students and as many women as wished to attend, but Harry and Caresse nevertheless went every year from 1923 till 1929, and brought along the Powels, the de Geeteres and Lymington. The Four Arts Ball marked the closing of the art academies for the summer and the climax of a year of study. Weeks before the orgy a masquerade motif was announced, though costumes consisted of not much more than body paint, a loincloth and an elaborate headdress. (Dress designers invariably smuggled in their scouts to steal ideas from the bizarre inventions.) It was understood by the police that anything except damage to people, and of course property, was permissible on Four Arts night. Attractive ladies allowed themselves to be kissed on the sidewalk by strangers got up to look like naked Roman senators; drivers permitted the hoods of their cars to be danced upon.

Jimmy the Barman (less well known by his formal name, James Charters) recollected in his memoirs, *This Must Be the Place*, that before the ball of 1927 a gang of students burst into Claridge's:

> The hotel was in a pandemonium as, half-naked, you must remember, we went screaming through the corridors, into the dining room, pulling the noses of the guests, snatching up their drinks, interrupting the dancing, even rushing upstairs to the bedrooms to open whatever doors were not locked and gaze upon the occupants in various states of dress or undress! You might think the hotel management would have objected, but they didn't, first because it was an accepted custom (and custom goes a long way in France), but perhaps more because we were backed up by a strong cordon of police.

The balls themselves, held in such huge halls as that at Luna Park at the Porte d'Auteuil, were attended by as many as three thousand men and women, the latter students and models and whores if French, and prominent ladies—slumming—if American or British. There was a parade of sorts to decide the most imaginative costume, and two orchestras played at opposite ends of the hall; people threw confetti and yelled at one another, and sweated, swore and roiled.

Harry's first ball was in 1923, and he returned from it drunk and naked in a taxi, having been removed from his Roman toga, his underdrawers and his money. The following year there were timbrels and dancing in the streets, and he talked his way in by saying he was painting a nude for the Prix de Rome. People beat on tom-toms, and danced past dawn, and the next day Harry, still under the influence of the ball, read erotic books. In 1925 he noted that he had "fed Ula the female monkey three gin fizzes and she ran up and down a rope ladder, and the Clever Girl was christened by a Russian Princess I should have liked to have violated and there were strawberry gin fizzes and drunken dancing and I was fortunate to get home."

So far he had been dabbling, but at the 1926 ball, Lymington's first, Harry set the tone of the following three full-throttle orgies. The motif was Incan, and he rubbed himself down with red ocher and wore a red loincloth and a necklace of three dead pigeons. But before the ball there was a supper party—if a champagne punch made from forty bottles of brut, and five each of whiskey, cointreau and gin, may be called supper—given in the library of 19 rue de Lille for eighty students and their girls. Lymington was there, and the Crouchers, and a Foreign Legionnaire, and Harry's lawyer. Caresse wore bare breasts and a turquoise wig, and at the ball won a prize of twenty-five bottles of champagne for the Crosbys' group by riding around the ballroom in the jaws of a papier-mâché dragon propelled through the Salle Wagram by a couple of dozen drunk students. Harry passed out and woke up next morning stinking of dead pigeons and sticky with paint, in bed with Lymington, Caresse, Lymington's girl (who was angry that he had not troubled to make love to her) and several others, newly met.

The following year Stephen Crosby was in approving attendance, caparisoned in an extraordinary Cambodian getup, with a toothbrush attached to his hat. Before the ball Harry, Caresse and Mai de Geetere enjoyed a bath together, then painted themselves green, together with Lymington and a girl for whom he and Harry shared an affection. That year Harry wore seven pigeons and carried ten live snakes in a sack—more and more was the only measure he valued—and he and Caresse gave a better party than last year's, for more people. The students clamored for GIN GIN GIN when the champagne punch ran out, and mobbed the Crosbys' maid—it was difficult to know which exactly of several things they wanted from her—and for an ugly moment Harry was afraid it had all gone too far. But he got the party under way to the ball at about ten o'clock, and as he wrote his mother two days later, by the standards of pandemonium it was a great success.

"Frans and Mai were with us and Croucher and Gretchen. At about one o'clock it was WILD men and women stark naked dancing people rushing to and fro. . . . From our loge I opened the sack and down dropped the ten serpents. Screams and shouts. Yet later in the evening I sat next to a plump girl who was suckling one of the serpents! Dear me! Somewhere about two o'clock came the costume contest and the Beauty Prize lovely nude models ivory-white against a black velvet curtain standing upon a dais. Deafening applause."

Lymington later had bad dreams of Harry's pigeons as though they were ghosts, and of the Four Arts Ball

> And of our friendship then
> And later your impetuous jealousy
> Of me, with C, when all the time
> I loved you both.

There was strain in chaos; for Harry liberty was singular, not to be shared, his own alone. Nevertheless, the next year he was at his post. In May he warmed up on the Bal Nègre and awoke next morning on the de Geeteres' barge fully dressed with a zebra skin pulled over his head. Caresse had three beaux with her, and would have had four had Lymington not been in England. He arrived June 29 for the Four Arts Ball, and 19 rue de Lille was, as Harry wrote his mother, "stripped like a destroyer for action—sackcloth over the walls and chairs and book-cases." The supper party was catered, like the one the year before, by Rumpelmayer, and was "as usual" riotous, with a brandy punch

> in the most enormous bowl and there were ladies and models and tarts and a stampeding up and down stairs . . . and at ten o'clock we rushed off . . . to the Salle Wagram and the costumes [Huns that year] were magnificent and there was the usual pounding and stampeding and a climbing up and down ladders and queer scenes in the corners (one plump girl lying naked on the floor while three men of red ochre made love to her et comment—a regular concours à la mort) and so home and to bed (many people in the house many people in bed but the best fun was painting girls' breasts (breasts by Crosby and Croucher) before the party.

Next morning Harry awoke to find six—not counting the dog Narcisse —in their bed, and a strange man wearing a pale blue undershirt sitting on the chaise longue playing the Gramophone, same song over and over, "Paris C'est une Blonde." The seven then helped one another scrub off their paint, and the bedroom and bathroom were like pigsties, and that was that for Harry, no more Four Arts Balls.

The following morning he and Caresse left by train for Venice, to get back their health, and Harry wrote his mother that "it really is too hectic and I think this will be our last 4 Arts. We are getting too old. . . ." Too old to dance, to old to run marathon races. But the truth was, it wasn't age that was wearing out his appetite; it was a reduction of novelty, the chief hazard of hedonism. Harry described his last Four Arts Ball as having consisted of the "usual" smearing on of paint, the "usual" gathering of crowds in the street, the "usual" dinner. For Harry, who lived for accelerating sensations, the first *usual* was a command to pack it in. Routine was worse than death.

11

"Harry has a great, great gift. He has a wonderful gift of carelessness."

—Ernest Hemingway, in conversation with Archibald MacLeish

It should not be assumed from his stunts and indulgences that Harry, posing as a poet, was merely a misfit, clown, or layabout. He wrote too much rather than too little, and wrote it too quickly, under too hot a fever. Between the time he quit Morgan, Harjes and his death six years later he published nine volumes of poems, tirades and dreams, plus the three volumes of *Shadows of the Sun*—many times polished—plus half a dozen book prefaces and literary essays. At the onset of this fervid literary animation, as excessive as any of his programs, he wrote his mother in the spring of 1924 that "I never realized until this year how appallingly ignorant I am. I have years of intensive reading ahead of me for I want to become erudite and a real intellectual and savant."

As innocent and wistful as his longing might seem, he acted on it precisely and compulsively, and thereupon set out on a course of self-instruction in classical and contemporary literature that remains, in its fanatical purpose and expense of energy, one of the most striking aspects of his history. An erratic young man, the prisoner of his various moods and impulses, a chronic violator of his self-laid laws and resolutions, often debilitated by drink and drugs, he nevertheless clung with astonishing fortitude and self-discipline to his late-begun education. To become a serious writer in the age of Eliot, Gide, Pound and Joyce was to assume an intimidating burden of cultural history and linguistic dexterity. It required learning as well as nerve to absorb the discrete particles that together composed what Eliot called *the tradition*, to rehearse their expression and to take one's own particular position within their mass.

Every weekday that he was in Paris he worked in his study from nine in the morning till lunchtime, then after lunch till late afternoon (when he would walk through the city alone, or rendezvous with a girl friend), then again after dinner, reading and writing. His determination to become "a real intellectual and savant" was touching and not a little sad in its origins, coming as it did from his desire to show *them* back home in Boston, and it is impossible not to smile condescendingly from time to time at such of his self-satisfactions as the following, written after he had spent some hours studying the *Encyclopaedia Britannica* (which he attacked, in accordance with his love of system, alphabetically, letting it lead him where it would): "I wonder how many children of the Ritz know who the Acoemeti were or what an Acrolith is or the meaning of the word Albedo." In the same entry, taken almost at random from his journals, he reminds himself to read (as later he did) Cicero's letters, Suetonius, Vasari's *Lives of the Painters*, Cellini's autobiography, Saint-Simon's memoirs, and Sir John Mandeville. He instructs himself as well to reread Keats and Plato: "in the sphere of poetry, the masters not the minstrels; in the sphere of philosophy, the seers not the savants." He also made a sensible inventory of books not to bother with, including "all argumentative books and all books that try to prove anything."

Harry was not much taken with novels, excepting the fiction of Flaubert, Proust, Balzac and Joyce, especially of Joyce, whom he idolized and whose syntactical reflexes he appropriated from *Ulysses* for crude reproduction in *Shadows of the Sun*. He much preferred English as a literary language to French, though he read as easily and frequently in the latter as in the former, using French translations of such third-language texts as Cellini's and Schopenhauer's if they were more readily available. Once he had begun a project like the fifty-volume set of *The Sacred Books of the East* he would invariably see it through to its end, just as he would read his way progressively through Shakespeare's works, or Marlowe's, and then exhaust every study he could find of Sufi mysticism, and follow this up with everything available by E. E. Cummings.

Reading and writing were for Harry—as for Kafka—a form of prayer. And perhaps because he was as literal as he was literary, he began to dwell on books as sacred artifacts as well as sacred processes. He noted in his journal that "books should be real things—they were so once when a man would give a fat field in exchange for a small manuscript." He was both intimidated and exhilarated by his realization that every age throws up only a few books able to stick to the ribs of the future, only a few works of literature—"news that stays news," in Pound's formulation. He never gave voice to his ambition to produce even one such enduring work, but it was his entire purpose, why he worked so hard to learn the trick of genius, why he transformed himself into what he perceived to be an artistic character.

Details mattered supremely; he understood that all art was detail, nothing more, so he studied paper and bindings and typography as he studied locutions, and began to thin out his library—huge even before the Walter Berry bequest—to narrow it to books of high value both as literature and as vessels of his worship. He was a tyrant in matters of form and sanctity, a disciple of such literary zealots as Baudelaire and Mallarmé, who set the products of fancy at a higher value not only than a fat field, but than life itself. A friend from Boston once remarked that he envied Crosby's "writing what you want to write," and Harry transcribed the statement with amazed disgust, adding, "Christ what a statement to make!" Of course one wrote what one wished, and caused it to be published. To be published, though, by whom? For Harry, in his zeal, to suffer the mail-watches and perfunctory rejections that make such a misery of the apprenticeship of most writers was unthinkable. Instead, beginning in 1925, he and Caresse followed the direct, self-serving procedure described in *The Passionate Years*: "We knew that some day we must see our poems in print—it did not occur to us to submit them to a publishing house—the simplest way to get a poem into a book was to print the book!"

Just so, and during 1925 they had two editions printed of Caresse's collected verse, *Crosses of Gold*, and one, limited to seventeen copies, of Harry's first effort, *Sonnets for Caresse*. The latter is an elegant artifact, tastefully designed and hand-printed by Herbert Clarke, an English typographer living in Paris; it was bound by G. Levitzky (who had also bound many of Walter Berry's most valued books) in turquoise Levant, stamped back and front with the Crosby crest in gold. Harry was surprised and pleased to learn how inexpensively books could be produced in Paris, where labor came cheap and a few dollars could buy many sheets of fine Japan or Holland paper and much excellent ink.

The happy confluence of a favorable exchange rate and the presence in Paris of a few wealthy aesthetes and many talented writers enabled a number of small presses to flourish. Nancy Cunard had her Hours Press, Robert McAlmon had Contact Editions, and William Bird the Three Mountains Press, but none of them enjoyed the prescience or exerted the influence of the Crosbys' Black Sun Press, begun in 1927 as a noncommercial outlet for their own work, extended briefly as a vanity publisher for other writers, and pursued in earnest as a showcase for writers as yet unknown or distrusted by commercial publishers, and as a nonprofit enterprise which produced deluxe editions of the work of celebrated writers. During the Twenties the Black Sun Press published books by Joyce, D. H. Lawrence, Crane, Pound, Proust, MacLeish and Kay Boyle.

Clearly the existence of such a press was beneficial to the Crosbys in many ways and for many reasons. It gave them an honest if not arduous job of work, a profession they could cite to lever grudging respect from their families. Further, it offered them immediate and easy access to literary personages they might otherwise never have met, and it gave their generous impulses an opportunity for dignified expression in that they could, as they often did, pay high prices for rights to books they could not hope to sell in adequate numbers to return their investment.

Robert McAlmon wrote in his memoir, *Being Geniuses Together*, that by 1926 it was "passionately the fashion to be an artist or a genius," and that in America and especially on the Continent "every second college boy, radical, or aspiring writer wished to start a magazine." Or, as he might have added of the Crosbys and himself, a publishing house. In France during that time the printer of choice was Monsieur Maurice Darantière, master printer of Dijon, whose father had set the works of Huysmans, and who himself set Joyce's *Ulysses* for Sylvia Beach's Shakespeare & Company edition, and Gertrude Stein's *Making of Americans* for McAlmon's Contact Edition. The Crosbys, however, found their own printer, Roger Lescaret, who worked a hand press in a tiny shop on the rue Cardinale, a narrow twisting street near St. Germain-des-Prés, off the rue de Furstenberg. M. Lescaret announced himself to be a *maître imprimeur*, but in fact till Harry and Caresse found him his press had produced mostly handbills and baptismal announcements. Like his street, like his shop, he was tiny and oddly designed, quick to bend, to bow, to laugh. He was cockeyed behind thick, ink-smeared spectacles, and randomly smutched. Odds and ends cluttered his shop, pages had been set out to dry on stair treads, his desk was piled topple-high with blank sheets.

Harry had a feeling about the man, a hunch that he would work willingly and well, and asked him to copy the typography and paper and ink of the Bodley Head edition of Donne's poems he'd brought along. Lescaret had never printed a book before, but he was eager to try his hand, did a perfect piece of work, and the enterprise was joined. At first it was called Éditions Narcisse (after the Crosbys' whippet), with a pool-gazing Narcissus—a splendid choice for a vanity press—in the colophon designed by Caresse. Five books, three by Harry or Caresse, one by Lord Lymington (which he paid to have published) and *The Fall of the House of Usher* were published under the Narcissus rubric. Then another was tried, "At the Sign of the Sundial," for Harry's *Chariot of the Sun*, but beginning with their next book, the first series of *Shadows of the Sun*, they took the name they kept.

The Black Sun Press had its offices upstairs in Lescaret's shop, 2 rue Cardinale, and there Harry and Caresse chose the spacings, margins and typeface for the printer's antique press, worked by a noisy pedal. Harry designed the bindings, boxes and ribbons in expensive materials —gold and red and gray and black—by Babout, whose work was then considered the state of the art. As time passed Harry alone came to select the titles the press would publish; Caresse would edit them, and usually perform the typographical design. The books of the Black Sun Press are clean, wonderfully easy and satisfying to read and touch, and even a dull poem takes some shine from its disposition on a page the Crosbys caused to have printed.

Great pains were taken in the selection of ink and of papers, usually handwoven. In sum, the effect of a Black Sun Press book is of elaborate care rather than wasteful expense, of delicacy rather than elaboration. Generally resentful of business obligations, Harry tended scrupulously to the most minute detail of his books. His journals are punctuated everywhere with reminders to himself to "tell Lescaret to be careful of not smudging" or to look up someone with a supply of a rare typeface. Soon enough the press attracted the attention of booksellers from London and New York, especially Harry Marks, almost next-door to New York's Gotham Book Mart at 21 West 47th Street. Marks recalled finding his way to the shop at 2 rue Cardinale one spring day and realizing "at a glance that here was something of vital importance to lovers of fine books." In his preface to a catalogue describing the Black Sun Press and its books, which he came to distribute in America, he described the confusion of the shop and the self-informed determination of the Crosbys: "In the mellow light the scene seemed like an etching by Rembrandt. . . . In this absorbing atmosphere, time seemed of little importance. Everything was done leisurely, with infinite care. . . . On proofs that lay about the shop I noticed the beautiful clarity of the type, the perfect spacing, the wide, elegant margins. . . . Then and there I made arrangements to handle the output of the Black Sun Press in America. No contracts were signed. The agreement made between the Crosbys and myself was above the usual routine of mere business. There was no thought of money involved in these transactions."

Perhaps, but Harry was thrilled when Marks (whose name, perhaps because it appeared on no contract, he consistently misspelt Marx) offered four thousand dollars for a huge stock of titles available in 1929. Marks did well for himself, selling them at prices from five dollars (*Sonnets for Caresse*) to one hundred and fifty (Laclos' *Liaisons Dangereuses*, fifteen copies in Japanese vellum, each containing a different original drawing by Alastair).

The Crosbys were introduced to Alastair—a pseudonym for the Baron Hans Henning von Voight, also called Hanaël—by the same Duchesse La Salle who first acquainted them with the de Geeteres. The occasion was Alastair's vernissage at the fashionable gallery and club, Fermé la Nuit, a place popularized by Jean Cocteau. The exhibition of drawings, death-struck and exotically cruel, busy with the standard paraphernalia of the school of decadence—dwarfs, suicides and tortured maidens and pederasts—opened February 4, 1927, and so excited Harry that he wrote his mother he "couldn't sleep all night."

Within five days he and Caresse had arranged an invitation to Alastair's flat at Versailles. There they talked further with the Bavarian baron (or perhaps Hungarian—the identity shifts from account to account), rumored to be the illegitimate son of an unnamed king, as peculiar as anyone Harry's most vividly surreal drug-dreams could command. His face was white as milk, and he had a hypnotist's eyes set theatrically deep beneath a skull that receded as though it had been operatically struck by its owner's hand just before he repeatedly swooned. Fainting was indeed one of Alastair's lesser stunts. He liked to wear a suit of silver lamé over a ruffled shirt, completing the costume with a flowing velvet cape which he wore in all weathers. Several decades after she met him Caresse recollected—for the benefit of collectors of Twenties lore at Brown University—their first private encounter: "He lived in a sort of Fall of the House of Usher house, you know, with bleak, hideous trees drooping around the doors and windows—we always suspected him of having them trimmed to look that way—and he had several blackamoors for servants. On the night when we came first to see him, a blackamoor ushered us into a room where there was a black piano with a single candle burning on it. Soon Alastair himself appeared in the doorway in a white satin suit; he bowed, did a flying split and slid across the polished floor to stop at my feet, where he looked up and said, 'Ah, Mrs. Crosby!' "

Now, *there's* artifice for you! He sang sad ballads with a high-pitched whine in several languages, accompanying himself on the piano, and brought Harry to his knees. Harry wrote his mother that he found the man fascinating, "exactly like what Shelley must have been—and the *only* person I have ever seen that expresses my idea of genius." Soon Alastair returned the Crosbys' visit, and at tea at 19 rue de Lille persuaded them to build the library fireplace up in faïence, and spoke quietly and with calculated shyness about art, how one must dive into a trance-state to create. He was frail, but as menacing as a gnome.

Very soon he was on a first-name basis with Harry, and explaining Harry's ambivalent feelings about Stephen Crosby: "It would be much more easy outwardly and superficially if your father was worse—badwilled and unkind." He appealed to his disciple's most vigorous instincts of the time by writing him that he had "played with the demons but they have not been able to destroy you." Alastair's judgments were honest and often sound, but he attracted Harry because of his eccentricities of costume and manner, and because he was a breathing, walking and talking precept struck from the fancy of Huysmans, Wilde and Beardsley. Before much time had passed, Harry amused himself with Alastair and displayed him to friends as he might a pet monkey, or a blackamoor tricked out in livery. In return, as he wrote his mother, he gave gifts to the artist, who "hasn't a sou" (despite servants in profusion, and much silk suiting), helped him as he helped the de Geteeres ("Vive les artistes!") and studied him.

Alastair very quickly realized what was expected of him by his young patron, and agreed to be shown off to Harry's mother in order to impress upon her the full liberation from convention of her only son. Harry brought her to Versailles for tea, and Alastair produced for the occasion an Oriental butler, incense, lilies, *Lieder* and much kissing of hands. "Be anything you imagine," he advised Harry, and rightly guessed that Mrs. Crosby thought him as quaint as any human specimen the *National Geographic* would ever display. As months passed, Alastair came to depend more on Harry than Harry on him: "I need a friend—no—I need you—because your demons do not frighten my angel and because I begin to know you better than you know yourself and because you are not only able to hold your own tongue but perhaps the tongue of others. . . . If you care for me tear up my messages. Please."

Perhaps Harry discovered in Alastair's attentions a sexual subtext, but he began to pull back from the "*only* person" whom he had ever seen who expressed his idea of genius. "Something in you is afraid of me," Alastair wrote Harry. "Why??? I know you ever so much better than you know me Harry. You do not even look at me—but the other way—I am sad that you did not tell me you disliked the . . . drawings. Other people told me. You wrote me other things. Why? It was unfriendly Harry and it hurt me." The fact is that Alastair is the only available measure of Harry's boundaries. He was over the line—too intense after all, too weird. Though only eleven years older than his friend, he seemed to drag death with him, and while death held no terror for Harry, Alastair's aura of disease, waste, lethargy and perversion did.

But Alastair was entirely off compass in his paranoid delusion that Harry disliked his work. In fact, Harry commissioned many drawings from him, illustrations that substantially helped bring Black Sun Press books to the literate world's attention. Alastair's first assignment was to illustrate with lurid drawings Harry's lurid verses in *Red Skeletons*, and then *éditions de luxe* of Poe's *Fall of the House of Usher*, Wilde's *Birthday of the Infanta*, and *Les Liaisons Dangereuses*. *The Fall of the House of Usher* was distributed in America by Ted Weeks, who soon sold out his allotment of two hundred and fifty copies priced at seven dollars and fifty cents. Weeks recalls that "I suggested an introduction by Arthur Symons, but I calculated that after we had paid Mr. Symons and the artist, and the import duty of fifteen percent of the list price, and the bookseller's discount, there would not be much left for jam."

Weeks was preoccupied with his work as an editor of *The Atlantic Monthly*, and Harry decided he could do better with Harry Marks than with his old friend, so their common enterprise was dissolved. While Harry negotiated with Marks, he asked his mother not to tell Weeks that he was considering a new American distributor for Black Sun Press books—a lack of candor that is notable because it was so rare. (Only once was Harry guilty of plain fraud, and it too was weaselry committed at 2 rue Cardinale. *Forty-seven Unpublished Letters from Marcel Proust to Walter Berry* was prepared for publication before Harry's death, with credit for the translation given to Caresse and to him. The French was actually translated by an English poet named Richard Thoma.)

Arthur Symons, the official theoretician of Decadence, found much to admire in Alastair's macabre illustrations of Poe's *Fall of the House of Usher*. He was seized by the artist's visualization of "doom and destruction, the malice of unnatural shapes and forms that float and exult in that atmosphere which is impregnated with horror, where one feels the pestilent vapour, dull and stagnant and sluggish, in the lurid tarn, where the vast battlements and the tall sinister trees stand stark against a bloodred sky. . . ." Harry himself wrote the foreword to *The Birthday of the Infanta*, which the Crosbys published primarily to provide an occasion for Alastair's interpretation of Wilde's tale. The short essay is evocative of—almost interchangeable with—his judgment of de Geetere's illustrations of *Les Chants de Maldoror*. He appreciated Alastair's "diabolic beauty," his artifice, originality, "capriciousness and extravagance," intricacy, "attention to detail, the delicate sense of balance." He reflected upon Alastair's art with a triad of modifiers— "Voluptual, Funebrial, Stabbed"—that could stand as the names of the three heroes of a comic allegory of decadent art; "infinitely secret and apart is the genius that has torn the heart from the black swan of beauty to offer it to some cool and mirror-like, infinitely delicate, infinitely secret sun which he has never chosen to unveil."

A bit of this kind of prose goes a long way, but finally, none too soon, Harry lost his taste for torn hearts and mutilated swans. There was a final unpleasantness with Alastair. Caresse abruptly demanded some drawings from him, and said she would send a car first thing in the morning to Versailles to fetch them. Alastair worked till dawn, the car never came, and he never forgave her: "Please do not act like that—I do not accept it from my friends. . . . I am grieved and must tell you so. I do not think there is ever any reason for acting unkindly." There were misunderstandings about money: Harry thought of himself as a generous benefactor; Alastair thought of himself as an ill-paid serf. It can be concluded that the Crosbys were more fortunate in their acquaintanceship with Alastair than was he with them.

Harry was not above suspecting people of trying to put him and his money to their own good use, and often enough his suspicions were justified—though never by Alastair. An instance was his association with a Russian sculptor of modest celebrity before the Revolution, Prince Trubetskoy, who patiently stalked Harry from one end of Paris to the other, pestering him to sit for a bust. One afternoon the Prince ran his quarry to earth at the Ritz, where Harry was eating lunch with an Italian count (whose name he never learned to pronounce or comprehend). Trubetskoy (whose own name and work have by now largely vanished from memory) insinuated himself into Harry's company in time to cadge a free brandy, and insisted that the three proceed at once to his atelier. Loath to offend, the Italian and Harry agreed, and presently found themselves in a garage in Neuilly:

> There were perhaps two hundred statues . . . and not one that was worth a damn. Of all the horrible bric-a-brac! He is a charming Prince but an impossible sculptor. And it is people like him . . . who get all renown while great artists like Alastair and MacLeish are almost unheard of. How banal, how stupid, how bourgeois, how disgusting the majority of humanity! Well we walked around and feebly murmured words of semi-praise, but I have never seen anything so entirely lacking in fire. . . . Everyone looked exactly alike. Bernard Shaw's face resembled the face of the young courtesan recumbent on a couch, Mussolini looked like Vanderbilt, Anatole France like Rodin. No wonder the latter sold the bust Trubetskoy did of him! And Trubetskoy to get even sold the Caryatid Rodin gave him! . . . There was even a statue of a young man at the wheel of an automobile! Ye gods, what I wonder would Bourdelle have said? Trubetskoy, as I had imagined, kept saying in front of everyone how wonderful I would be to model and what a wonderful full length statue he could do of me. . . . It was so obvious that . . . he had arranged for the nephew of J.P. Morgan to pose for some enormous sum. After failing with me he tried Caresse and finally in his desperation Narcisse. If he couldn't have the nephew of J.P. Morgan he wanted the wife of the nephew of J.P. Morgan and failing this the dog of the wife of the nephew of J.P. Morgan. Mon Dieu!

It wasn't because of money that Harry lost his enthusiasm for Alastair. Their falling-out was for Alastair caused by personal disappointment, and for Harry by a change of taste. While he continued to pay one dollar annually for his membership in the Edgar Allan Poe Society, to read and reread *The Picture of Dorian Gray*, to set a marble tablet on the Hôtel d'Alsace to commemorate the death there of Oscar Wilde, and drink a toast to him in absinthe, and to pay reflexive obeisance to the death-damp relics of art melodramatic and macabre, Harry was moving, reading his contemporaries, taking up a new position. This modernist persuasion was no less exclusive than what he was coming to reject, and far more demanding of technical skill, information and formal coherence. For Harry the exigencies of Flaubert and Joyce were suddenly more bracing than the affectations and easy effects of *Yellow Book* material. He had outgrown the attenuated Romanticism of the *fin de siècle*.

He had hung around in the Mauve Decade so long mostly because in his social and familial situation he found it useful to do battle against the straitened conventions of his childhood and hometown with an aesthetic program based upon principles of sensation and excess. It excited him to know that Bostonians despised the Decadents—and by association with them, himself—for their exhibitionistic irresponsibilities. Morse Peckham has summarized the movement called Aestheticism in language perfectly suited to Boston's judgment of the Parisian life of young Mr. Crosby, a life characterized by "relaxation of nerve, self-indulgence always hinting in the direction of sexual perversity, and often enough arriving there, remoteness, an unrealistic worship of art for its own sake, of a commitment to Aestheticism as a strategy for escape from a real world which these artists did not have the courage or manliness to face, an escape which often enough involved a return to the more sensate rituals and forms of religion, especially if they were anti-intellectual and mystic in the worst of the many senses of that word."

In his attitude and behavior Harry conformed to such an identi-kit dandy, but his aesthetic persuasions grew more complex the deeper he read. He never relinquished his devotion to Baudelaire, but during the last two years of his life that poet led him to Rimbaud and Eliot rather than to Wilde. Early in 1927 he ranked his favorite living poets thus: (1) T. S. Eliot, (2) Archibald MacLeish and (3) E. E. Cummings. He approved of Pound's work, and Gide's, and was instructed by Gertrude Stein. He learned to admire the hard-edged designs of the Imagists, and by 1928 the same Harry who had traveled out of his way to toss flowers on Shelley's grave in Rome was writing his mother that he had just eaten lunch at Alex Steinert's apartment and wished "he would do more modern things and not Shelley and Oscar Wilde songs."

Poor Shelley suffered also by Harry's comparison of his poetry with that of Archibald MacLeish. When *Streets in the Moon* was published in 1926, Harry read it and told a visiting Boston chum that he preferred MacLeish to Shelley, provoking his friend to chuck his tea, teacup and saucer through an open window of 19 rue de Lille. At the end of that year, during a Christmas ski holiday with Caresse and the children at Gstaad (where Billy Peabody was at school at Le Rosey), Harry met MacLeish for the first time. He and his wife Ada, a singer, had themselves come to Switzerland with their friend Ernest Hemingway, who was awaiting his divorce from his first wife so that he could marry his second.

Three days after Christmas the Crosbys spent the afternoon skiing (a new and novel divergence for the rich), and afterwards Harry joined Hemingway and MacLeish at a tiny bar to try the new wine:

> H the realist and M the dreamer. . . . And they both know Joyce and go to his readings. And they said he spent 1000 hours on the last chapter of Ulysses. . . . And they both think Cocteau is an ass and so do I and all three of us despise the English. And M said to read Anabase (Perse) and H said he wrote the story about the Wind Blows ["The Three-day Blow," collected in the book *In Our Time*, which Harry had recently read] (the best story in the book) in half an hour. And M is quieter but they both have charm—rare in anyone, especially in men— nowadays. And M said he read very little. And H had been to the cock-fighting in Seville. And we drank. And H could drink us under the table. And everyone wanted to pay for the wine. And M won (that is he paid.)

Back in Paris, Harry and Hemingway saw a fair amount of each other. They were together in Pamplona for the running of the bulls in July, 1927. Harry introduced Hemingway to lion tamers and clowns at a Spanish circus temporarily in Paris. (Harry was fascinated by lions and lion tamers, and big-game hunters. One of his early Paris friends had been a brutally racist lion hunter named Paul Rainey, who died at sea on his way to Africa in 1924, pitched overboard, his friends believed, by a black member of the ship's crew.) When Harry was with Hemingway, he usually drank too much, and after one particularly savage bout with him woke in disgust to notice that whenever he got drunk his hands got dirty. Hemingway introduced Harry to Goya's *Disasters of War*, and otherwise satisfied his appetite for the macabre by giving him a photograph of a man's arm that had been removed from the belly of a shark off Key West.

MacLeish, who was often in the party when Harry and Hemingway met, recollects Hemingway reading Harry's poems and observing that "he has a great, great gift. He has a wonderful gift of carelessness. He can be careless, just spill this stuff out." Not the least bit careless, MacLeish could nevertheless not have been better designed to win Harry's admiration. A Scot from a no-nonsense background in Illinois, he had been educated at Hotchkiss and Yale—where he had been a member of Skull and Bones—and at Harvard Law School, and had served with distinction as a captain in the field artillery on the French Front. In addition to shining within one of Boston's best law firms, MacLeish began to lecture at Harvard Law School as soon as he was graduated. He then threw over this career to write poetry—fine poems, taken seriously by serious men. By the time they met, MacLeish at thirty-four had five books to his name. Moreover, had Harry shared MacLeish's natural gifts, they were such poems as he himself would have written: poems of great virtuosity, yet composed under the influence of those poets, especially Eliot, from whom MacLeish was willing to take instruction.

The new friends continued to see each other frequently. The MacLeishes much admired 19 rue de Lille, and Harry offered it to them while he and Caresse were abroad on a planned holiday to Persia, where the MacLeishes had been and urged them to go. ("We shan't ask them for rent," Harry wrote his mother. "They are very hard up and I am only too glad if we can help them. Any man who can write Einstein should be looked after.") MacLeish's "Einstein" was a long poem, probably his most notable achievement to date, and entirely his own, and Harry proposed that the Black Sun Press print it in a deluxe edition, for which the Crosbys would pay two hundred dollars. MacLeish agreed, and one hundred fifty copies were printed and quickly sold: "Harry said it would be a handsome book," MacLeish recalls, and "it was that. This was quite a book to make for a man. Somebody, and I rather suspect it was Caresse, had taste. I know Harry had it too, but somebody *really* had it."

MacLeish thought of Harry as even younger than he in fact was, and their association was very much that of master and apprentice. Because Harry had plenty of money, frivolous friends, and all the time in the world (or so it seemed to MacLeish), it was difficult for the older man to take him seriously. MacLeish regarded himself as gaming for higher stakes than Harry: "At thirty-two I took my life apart to start writing my own verse. I found it very hard to be interested. That's why I didn't pay more attention. I should have paid more attention."

Like Walter Berry, MacLeish saw at once that Rimbaud, obsessed with dislocations of time, mind and memory, was the man to teach Harry what he wanted to learn. He tried to show Harry that Rimbaud was not merely a man who lived life on extreme terms, but that he was as well a radiant poet, that the writing and not the living was the main thing. Caresse found the MacLeishes to be "rather aloof and formal figures," not much beguiled by the Crosbys' custom of entertaining friends at dinner from their bed. Often Harry would encounter MacLeish walking, Harry "going like an express train," as he later wrote, MacLeish "controlled and collected (like a jockey holding his horse in)." Harry was fond of this conceit, and wrote of MacLeish "letting Eliot set the pace but feeling that MacLeish may perhaps have more in reserve." On another occasion he wrote again of MacLeish's self-control, of the poet as a jockey "holding in his horse until the straight-away where he lets him out to win." (After the final holocaust, should some new race mutate from the ruins and come to examine our culture and its artifacts, it may well conclude that our literature—like a hockey puck or a squash ball—was merely the device by which contests were decided, that poems were written to win something, the competition at Athens, patronage, a Pulitzer Prize; and that writers are truly prize fighters—as so many have testified—unable to fight well, or jockeys unable to ride. Harry was able to think of poetry as a tennis match, as well as a horse race, and recalled that as a boy he could improve his game only by playing with his betters, just as he could improve his verse only by reading his betters—Eliot and MacLeish.)

Harry took encouragement from MacLeish's first book of poems, *Tower of Ivory*, which he found—as he wrote his mother—"perfectly dreadful hardly a good thing in it." He realized that his master's mature work made his own *Red Skeletons* seem a poor and ragged thing, but later, like MacLeish, he'd pick up his pace; he knew it. MacLeish recalls being shown Harry's early poems, "manuscripts that seemed to me unmade beds. Too long and too diffuse and too careless."

But MacLeish liked Harry, and admired his energy and the youth he spilled so easily. Because of the success of *Einstein*, the Crosbys and MacLeish agreed to have the Black Sun Press publish the first edition of *New Found Land*, a book of fourteen new poems. In friendship and gratitude, MacLeish gave Harry for a Christmas gift in 1927 the manu-script of one of Harry's favorites—"No Lamp Has Ever Shown Us Where to Look"—and Harry was ecstatic, writing his mother that "someday it will be worth a thousand dollars." His excitement must have been enhanced by the final stanza of the early version MacLeish gave him, with lines that speak of

> *The staring and sand-buried eyes*
> *Of one long drowned, long dead, there stands*
> *Forever still upon unchanging skies*
> *The small, black circle of the sun.*

MacLeish explains that the reference to the black sun had nothing to do with Harry or his case: "My image was derived from an experience common to us all—the black disk that blinds the eyes for moments afterwards when we glimpse the sun." But the recipient of the manuscript used the lines perversely, as a provocation to persist in his death-dwelling, and to excite every morbid and extreme impulse he could dream up.

12

"It is a glimpse of chaos not reduced to order. But the chaos *alive*, not the chaos of matter. A glimpse of the living, untamed chaos."

—D. H. Lawrence, of Harry Crosby's poetry

Poets with free access to a printing press will write poems to keep it cranking out pages, and Harry Crosby's bibliographic chronology attests to his determination to save his printer from lassitude. *Sonnets for Caresse* was first published in the autumn of 1925, and a slightly revised edition appeared several months later. Yet another version was the first book produced at rue Cardinale by Roger Lescaret, and during that year, 1927, Harry also released *Red Skeletons*, made up mostly of sonnets from the previous three editions, together with ten new poems. Three books by him appeared in 1928: *Chariot of the Sun*; the first of three volumes of *Shadows of the Sun*; and another book of new poems, *Transit of Venus*. A book of tirades (*Mad Queen*), another volume of *Shadows of the Sun* and a book of dreams (*Sleeping Together*) were published by the Black Sun Press in 1929, and after Harry's death at the end of that year Caresse published two books from unrevised manuscripts completed during 1929: *Aphrodite in Flight*, a slim and slight manual of love based on principles of aeronautics, and *Torchbearer*, Harry's final book of poems, published in 1931 with an afterword by Ezra Pound.

More remarkable than its quantity is the development of his work:

during five working years Harry duplicated a century of complicated aesthetic transitions. If it is true that the literary topography of a certain age is best read in the contour maps left by its minor writers, Harry mapped the interior territories of several cultural epochs. His sonnets are conventional in form, and often in sentiment, and might have been written by a precocious Victorian schoolboy in imitation of Romantic poets under the influence of Elizabethan sonneteers. *Red Skeletons* is a decadent imitation of Baudelaire. *Chariot of the Sun* is a collection of symbolist verses, while *Transit of Venus* and *Mad Queen* are indebted to surrealism and to Dadaism. *Sleeping Together* is a post-Freudian exercise in the recovery of subconscious states, and *Torchbearer* traffics in automatic writing.

Yet for all the cultural baggage carried for a short time and then abandoned, for all the shopping-spree character of his cultural appropriations, Harry wrote few poems, if any, that are not marked by three preoccupations: that the poet is a holy man, a seer; that a metaphysical system governs the poet's days, and must be unriddled; that the poet owes himself a violent life and an early, explosive death. From the beginning he realized that as a poet come latterly to his calling, he would be obliged, were he to cut a place for himself, to short-cut his way to the upper elevations of fancy and expression he was pleased to think of as genius. Thus he tried to develop a personal, unique metaphysic, a symbolical system, a mythology.

But this followed *Sonnets for Caresse* and *Red Skeletons*. These two are work by an apprentice not yet impatient with his progress, a diligent student eager in the conventional way to develop formal and linguistic resources. Harry had come to the sonnet form by way of Caresse, who taught him how to make poems of fourteen lines, and to work variations on the arrangement of the lines. Caresse's own poems, mostly sonnets, appeared ten months before *Sonnets for Caresse* in 1925, under the title *Crosses of Gold*. And just as Harry took encouragement from Walter Berry, she took it from Walter Berry's friend and France's most distinguished (if not gifted) woman of letters, Anne, the Comtesse de Noailles. The Comtesse was a dazzling talker, intolerant of interruption and appreciative of idolatry, a chevaliere of the Legion of Honor, a poet and novelist, handsome, positive in her opinions. Caresse first called on her in November of 1925, and found her propped up on lace pillows in a huge bed. Between telephone conversations with the personages of Paris' *haut monde*, she counseled young Madame Crosby to study Shakespeare and Victor Hugo, and warned her that "to be really great one must be understood by everybody."

Thus instructed in what she might more easily have learned from a how-to-write handbook, and beguiled, Caresse left, observing as she departed many men awaiting their turn before the mighty lady, and a long line of limousines in the street outside.

Later Caresse and Anne de Noailles exchanged books of poems and a few visits, and several courteous, if perfunctory, notes of admiration for each other's work. Their superficial association was important to Caresse, and to Harry as well; as much as the young Crosbys might mean and seem to go their own way, with or without the endorsement of their parents and peers, they were as hungry for approbation as any apprentices. Harry wrote Caresse, when she was visiting her children in Switzerland, about Anne de Noailles' letter of appreciation for *Crosses of Gold* which had arrived in her absence, that it would encourage her as Berry had encouraged him: "These people count—as for the multitude whether they approve or disapprove makes really very little difference."

The title *Sonnets for Caresse* signifies a dedication rather than a subject. A few of the poems are about love, especially disappointed and betrayed love, but the collection is a potpourri of odds and ends on Harry's mind between the time of the war and the day of a given poem's conception. Mythological characters—Corydon, Daphne, Actaeon, Narcissus, Leda, Zorah and many more—are pressed into service, recruited from the pages of the Bible, Frazer's *Golden Bough* and the *Encyclopaedia Britannica*. A privileged childhood—dark with foreboding, of course—is recollected in two poems, "Toys of Time" and "Teatime." Blows are struck against the sexual conventions on which Harry was nurtured in "Lesbienne," a moist fancy, and "Corydon," in which the poet bravely inquires in the final clomping couplet: "Right or wrong, why seek we to discover,/Is not Love the counsel for the lover?" There is also some tourist color with gypsy dancing girls, and a few apostrophes to the glory of days past and forever gone, but the dominant note of Harry's early sonnets is sounded in the bass cleft, a lamentation, heavy as oatmeal, elegiac. There are an alarming number of references to the poet's early and violent death, to his terminal dose of suffering, to his suicide. The attitude suggests a calculated posture: the poet, too rare for this world, escapes first into imaginary realms, and finally into the undiscovered country itself from which no traveler returns. In these poems Harry has had the benefit of several guides: Poe and Baudelaire lead him a line at a time toward the underworld.

Harry was an apt pupil, and deadly serious most of the time. In such poems as "Narcisse Noir," in which "a silver blade stained red/

Glowed like a kiss beside the love-lost dead," he lunges for a pretty effect, but when he recites the horrors of his war, however much his voice might resemble the voices of hundreds of veterans, the sentiment, while banal, is sincerely held: "O unknown hero you have died in vain/To satisfy an emperor's lust for fame." A sterile childhood and the ruins of Western culture are held accountable for the poet's dread and anger. He smokes hashish to forget his misery, and dwells upon his misery to loot it for material appropriate to serious verse.

And nothing fuels his inspiration like the memory of neglected love. Enter Caresse. The poem is titled "Désaccord":

> My soul has suffered breaking on the wheel,
> Flogging with lead, and felt the twinging ache
> Of barbèd hooks and jagged points of steel,
> Peine forte et dure, slow burning at the stake,
> Blinding and branding, stripping on the rack,
> The cangue and kourbash and the torquèd screw,
> The boot and branks, and scourging on the back,
> The gallows and the gibbet. All for you.
>
> These tortures are as nothing to the pain
> That my soul suffers when you gaze at me
> With cold disdainful eyes. You do not deign
> To smile or talk or even set me free.
> Yet once you let me hold your perfumed hand
> And danced with me a stately saraband.

On the contrary. The plain and poetically useless fact was that when "Désaccord" was composed Caresse was a doting, love-struck wife. But what young poet has ever made his name from such a happy and regular situation? Harry's true purpose in "Désaccord" was to inventory the lexicon of exotic instruments of torture, a purpose born from writerly pep and curiosity rather than from dolor and dissension.

Harry's early work adds to a world of evidence that disease, weariness, pain and solitude are the safe subjects for a novice man of letters. He was vital; his manner was odd; his voice was oblique but arresting; he was an authentic revolutionary; people loved him and followed his lead. And not a whisper of his wit or singular charm, of his terrible energy, is detectable in his early poems. It seems that only the artist certain of what he has already made, able to behold the grave monuments he has raised, can liberate himself to commit such seemingly effortless works of reconciliation as Oedipus at Colonus, The Tempest or The Confessions of Felix Krull, works that discover as for the first time that art can be an antidote against death by laughing a little at it. Such acts of sublime play are accessible only to giants, of course, and moreover to giants at their full growth. Little poets while still sprigs never seem to choose to emulate such work: they sense how difficult it is, and try instead to ape their masters' more theatrical, noisy and mournful compositions.

Thus it was that Harry brought his increasing dexterity with the sonnet to its fullest expression in bald imitation of *fin de siècle* conceits and persuasions. *Red Skeletons*, illustrated by Alastair, is also dedicated to him, and displays introductory epigraphs from both Baudelaire and Wilde. Many verses from *Sonnets for Caresse* attend the same fancy dress ball costumed only in different hats. Thus "Désaccord" appears under the title "Temple de la Douleur," and "Into Forgetfulness" shows up wearing "Partout des Prunelles Flamboient." Locutions are fanciful, simple "flowers" in the sonnets changed to the awful "orchidaceous." Gargoyles and monsters abound, together with predacious beasts and seas magically aglow with phosphorescent algae. Chaos is much invoked and much admired; ditto murder and suicide. Madness is the state the poet longs to attain, and in his bizarre imagery he seems to be only a stop or two from the end of the line. "Necrophile," in which the speaker kills before he kisses his lover, is characteristic of the volume's preoccupations; it is also prophetic—or rather creates the kind of prophecy Harry bound himself willy-nilly to fulfill. Even more striking for the future it anticipates is "Lit de Mort":

> I shall not die within a mad man's cell
> Or in the city of unconquered pain
> Nor on the ocean in a cockle shell
> When mad March winds are blowing hurricane.
>
> I shall not die among the multitude
> Or as a martyr tortured at the stake,
> I shall not die in business servitude
> Nor as a soldier for my country's sake;
>
> But I shall die within my lady's arms
> And from her mouth drink down the purple wine
> And tremble at the touch of naked charms
> With silver fingers seeking to entwine.
>
> My dying words shall be a lover's sighs
> Beyond the last faint rhythm of her thighs.

What need, then, for a suicide note? *What* happened, if not exactly *why*, is proposed in the lines of these two poems—silly doggerel unless enacted, consequential stanzas by hindsight. There is a headlong recklessness to these verses, a forewarning of Harry's later manner. Familiar as he was with hard New England weather and the sea, he must have known that March is not the month of hurricanes; he must not have cared. He was too rushed, it seems, to paper over the infelicities of such locutions as "I shall strike with dreaded adder's hiss" and "I shall not die in business servitude." He was not so much making poetry in these lines as he was issuing an announcement: *Behold me, be warned, run for your life, I mean it, I mean what I say.* In the sonnet "Désespoir" he sensed and gave utterance to the peril in his extreme position: "It seems to him the world is upsidedown,/And he himself some half-bewildered clown/Whose fate it is to suffer and to die." Harry could risk almost anything save simple foolishness. He must have understood with perfect clarity that he could only redeem from clownish bewilderment such poems as he had chosen to write by an enactment of their convictions. As soon as he began to write, and to take himself seriously as a writer, he began to shut the lid on the box he had built for himself.

He sent many copies of *Sonnets for Caresse* and of *Red Skeletons* to his friends and kinsmen, and to writers he admired. The Boston *Herald*, whose managing editor was his brother-in-law Robert Choate, found much to admire in the former volume, and praised Harry's "splendid flights of imagination," declaring as well that his workmanship was "flawless." Perhaps Harry believed the reviewer, but probably he knew better. A review by F.B.B. in the Boston *Evening Transcript* (on which the Crosbys had no special influence other than their high social standing), dated February 12, 1927, was less effusive: "This is one of the most beautifully bound books we have ever had the happiness to possess. . . . Many of [these sonnets] are more or less meaningless—are just a collection of words which are poetic within their own syllables. Many, too, are often vergent upon the frankly sensual, striking the note which *The Captive* and other Lesbian literature is sounding of late. . . ."

On the one hand, this was confirmation for Harry that Boston was populated by cultural Yahoos, too dense to comprehend his language and too priggish to enjoy it. On the other, he was prepared enough to believe that his work was flawed; he was not a man to deceive himself. A critic he took more seriously was a distant cousin from Boston, Alice Gould, who had moved to Spain to complete groundbreaking scholarship on a life of Christopher Columbus. Harry had met her in Seville, and had been struck by her independent spirit and formidable erudition. She examined the character of his sonnets at length, and he copied her remarks verbatim into his working notebook. Her letter of 1926 is pedagogical, and not a little patronizing. She briefs the history and essential character of the sonnet, patiently explaining to her neophyte cousin that it was not invented for English rhymes, though Milton didn't do badly with it, but that Harry, lest he not know it, was unlikely to grow into Milton's boots. She then tickles him with faint praise:

> You seem to me to use the sonnet line naturally—to think in phrases of that length and structure, so that one never gets the feeling of an artificial form with arbitrary rules—a feeling given by very many writers, whom one wants to ticket with "Just see me write a sonnet." But while your phrases are sonnet-phrases, I do not think your ideas are sonnet ideas. I do not feel any tossing to and fro of an idea and finally reaching a conclusion—nor yet the other sonnet-fitting development of a parallel, a simile, a likeness in unlikeness between the two parts—I think that even the subjects on which you offer your ideas are not sonnet subjects. A picture in words is not to my thinking a sonnet-subject, nor yet is a statement or a single reflection. . . . Observation must come before explanation.—I claim it as an observed fact that as fourteen lines are the best length (in the long run), so fourteen lines of homogeneous length require that the ideas should be non-homogeneous. [The sonnet] must either stray forward by successive steps, considering each step, or march like Milton to a beating organ-time and bring up with a bang. . . .

For all her dogma, Miss Gould had a point. Harry's inclination, his habit of thought, ran entirely counter to the swing and balance with which sonneteers feel most comfortable. He never began at the beginning of things; he could not—and would not if he could—proceed from thesis to antithesis to synthesis. Rather, he grabbed at once for the synthesis, the illumination, the banging together of all odds and ends into a mystical system, a union. The constraints of rhyme within a tradition-hardened compositional form were not for him. For a time he must have hoped that the symbolical oddments of Decadence—art as worship, extreme situations, the macabre and profane used as principles —could be shuffled into a personal system appropriate to his inner vision. But this didn't work for him. He agreed with his cousin Alice's strictures about the form he had chosen, and on April Fools' Day, 1927, wrote his mother that he had abandoned Decadence:

> From the contents [of *Red Skeletons*] you can see that it will have literary effect if nothing more. And of course the Alastair drawings are extraordinary. . . . You will be glad to know that it is my swan-song to the decadent and that my next book Chariot of the Sun is to be the other extreme "and a sixth sect worshipped an image of the sun formed in the mind. Members of this last sect spent all their time meditating on the Sun, and were in the habit of branding circular representations of his disk on their foreheads, arms, and breasts . . ." Red Skeletons was almost inevitable what with the war and the tortures of courtship and my serious expedition into the Country of the Decadents, besides the less important reason to ennuyer les philistines whom as you know I have always despised.

So the sun was elected. He would stare into its explosive eye and resolve by its creative energy his illuminations, loop-the-loops of fancy, crazy quirks. The sun would contain everything. He had decided to pass beyond world-weariness and take up company with a band of mystics and seers: Blake, Van Gogh, Rimbaud, and once again his old friend Baudelaire—but Baudelaire come at anew, from a different angle, not as a splenetic scourge but as a maker of worlds unseen till revealed by him.

Harry was not unmindful that in reading his declaration of sun worship his mother would think him mad. He had learned long before then to connect neurosis and genius. Everything he had been reading and had heard in the air around him insisted on the connection. Where there was not madness, the fable went, there could not be genius. Madness came with the territory ruled by genius, and it also provided a shortcut to that territory. This was a principle not only of Decadent art but of Surrealism and Dada, and followed directly from Romantic postulates that the modernists otherwise pretended to abhor. Of course, the madness of a poem by Rimbaud or Baudelaire resides in the work rather than in the writer, and is contrived to allow a sympathetic but clinically sane reader access to mental states he has not experienced before. Baudelaire, as a critic has wonderfully remarked, was "crazy like a fox." No work requires more craft, cunning and guile than a simulation of insanity, and no work is easier to imitate and to botch. Moreover, the essential character of such work as Rimbaud's and Baudelaire's—fanatical, rigid, ritualistic, obsessive and compulsive—is so similar to the character of psychosis that unless the poet maintains exquisite control of his material and his means he is liable to infect himself with the very chaos that poetry, by identifying devils, is designed to dispel. Harry's dogma was high, but his control was loose. Like Icarus, of whom he wrote, he flew toward the sun till it melted his wings of wax, and plunged him down; unlike Icarus, however, he was forewarned by Icarus.

From his letters and poems it is evident that till 1925 Harry worshiped only two gods, the secular god of art and the sacred God whose lineaments resembled, however superficially, the God of his mother and school chums. But during 1925 Harry wrote a sonnet, called "Uncoffined," that became an essential part of his repertory till 1927, and is one of the few poems he considered crucial enough to require quoting in full in *Shadows of the Sun*, on the last day of the year in which it was composed:

> *How many things there are in my past life*
> *That I regret, how many misconceits*
> *How many hours of ill-considered strife*
> *And drunken-dreary days of full deceits?*
> *How many maids unzoned to me their charms*
> *While I persuaded them that love was truth,*
> *How many are the harlots in whose arms*
> *I've spent the shipwrecked night-times of my youth!*
> *And as I sought to find excuse I came*
> *Upon the fatal words of wise Voltaire:*
> *Tout est dangereux et tout est necessaire—*
> *They whirled like autumn leaves within my brain,*
> *Until I sought the Sun to disentomb*
> *This long-dead foetus from my strangled womb!*

If "Uncoffined" stands as a kind of testament of conversion, it is not easy to describe with any precision what it was to which Harry was converted. As an object of worship the sun is various and slippery, and in his rush toward a coherent system of belief and symbolic representation Harry confused unity with totality, so that he attempted to absorb within his belief every aspect and atom of the sun that man in his wisdom or silliness had ever found cause to venerate. The sun—all-seeing eye, blinding light, source of life, killer of Icarus and Phaëthon, masculine principle, creative principle, godhead and the eye of the godhead—is at once comprehensive and a paradigm of ambiguity.

To use its mythology and manifestations as material for literature or belief was to be drawn irrevocably into the sun's orbit, for the only way Harry could reconcile the paradoxes inherent in the sun was to worship it *in toto*. So he did, bringing to his worship a hotchpotch of Christian faith in an afterlife and pagan rituals, adding to his stew every scrap he could find left over from the Aztecs or Pharaohs, the Greeks or Romans, Goethe or D. H. Lawrence, Rimbaud or the tarot pack.

The sun figures as the nineteenth enigma of the tarot pack in an allegory in which the astral monarch dispenses light and heat, and a couple representing the Gemini—Harry's birth sign—bask in a wash of spiritual light. Purification, tribulation and showers of gold figure in the enigma, whose positive aspect is elevation of the spirit and illumination, and whose negative aspect is the vanity of spiritual aspirations incompatible with reality—Harry's own enigma, to be sure.

Historically the sun is also the symbol of choice for a worship of the heroic principle. Apollo was a favorite of Harry's (but so was Dionysus, Apollo's opposing principle in the cosmogony of Friedrich Nietzsche, whose ideas Harry also took to his bosom), especially the Apollo who dwells upon Mount Parnassus and from its prominence orders the muses to direct the pens of his favorite earthbound inklings. Moreover, for those artists more concerned with poetic symmetry than with mythological genealogy, Apollo displaces Helios as father of Phaëthon, who one day drove the Chariot of the Sun across the skies till his horses bolted when he met the Scorpion of the Zodiac, and an accident followed in which the earth caught fire, and Phaëthon, struck by the father of all gods with a thunderbolt, hurtled flaming downward. In paintings of the Renaissance, in particular of the Romantic era, Phaëthon is a kind of Prometheus, stealing fire and authority, shooting too high, aspiring to realms beyond his reach. The charioteer is the "self" of Jungian psychology who outruns the body (the chariot) drawn by the life force (horses). And the "Sun Chariot" is the Great Vehicle of esoteric Buddhism. Indeed, the chariot and charioteer are so pervasive that they figure in fables as various as Polish folk tales and the Vedic epic. The Chariot of Fire (the Sun Chariot) is the seventh enigma of the tarot pack, and when it bears a hero—whether it is called Phaëthon or Harry Crosby—it signifies a body sacrificed in the service of the soul.

In the same letter to his mother on April Fools' Day, 1927, Harry wrote: "I have already written seventeen poems for Chariot of the Sun which I hope to work on for the next seven years the way Baudelaire worked over his Fleurs du Mal. . . ." His sun-stroke was extreme; with the fit and fever upon him he produced another thirty-five poems in less than a year, and *Chariot of the Sun* was published in 1928. The titles of some of the verses give a sense of Harry's obsession: "Quatrains to the Sun," "Cinquains to the Sun," "Sun Rhapsody," "Angels of the Sun," "Sundrench and Sons," "Photoheliograph," "Sun-ghost," "Suns in Distress," "Young Sun," "Sunset, Sunrise," "Epitaph for the Sun," "Sun Testament" and "Proposed Titles for Sun-poems." If the rubrics suggest a fixation, imagine the verses! Some of them are hilariously innocent, as a first love letter might be. See "Sun Rhapsody's" inventory of metaphors:

> *The Sun! The Sun!*
> *a fish in the aquarium of sky*
> *or golden net to snare the butterfly*
> *of soul*
> > *or else the hole*
> *through which the stars have disappeared.*

In ancient theogenies, so recently studied by Harry, the hero whose manifestation was the sun is armed with heaven's weapon, the net (a web of stars) and binds up his victims—Harry among them—in it. In this poem the sun is also a "forest without trees . . . the roundness of her knees/great Hercules/and all the seas/and our soliloquies/ . . . a mother's womb/a child's balloon—/red burning tomb." As always, something chokes off the laugh; just as one half-expects to discover the sun likened to a half-penny bit, or called "the squash ball of the cosmos," that red burning tomb reminds the reader that Harry was no mere butt or Bottom, but the master of his convictions.

As usual, despite his recent illumination and the shove it had given his faltering poetic progress, Harry's verses in *Chariot of the Sun* are death-obsessed. "Dialogue with Dalmus" recalls nearly verbatim a conversation he'd had with the son of a French nobleman the previous December, in the child's nursery. Harry told him about Icarus:

Harry *and he flew nearer to the sun and all his wings were made of*
   wax and the sun melted the wax
Dalmas *what happened to him tell me what happened to him*
Harry *down and down—down down down—and he dropped down*
   into the sea—down down into the sea
Dalmas *then what? then nobody helped him? eh? tell me*
Harry *no nobody helped him after*
Dalmas *and he was drowned?*
Harry *yes he was drowned.*

The poem "Sunset" has a kind of drive of language missing heretofore from Harry's work—work which always, even in its silliest expressions, has the drive of sincerity, of fanaticism and stamina and courage. The poem taps a diction that for once seems truly to be Harry's. As the preposterous doggerel of "The Golden Gourd" does not:

> *What chance have snakes upon an asphalt road*
> *When giant limousines go sliding by,*
> *Or courtesans resolved to gratify*
> *The lust of lovers seeking new abode?*
>
> *I do not envy the unfriended toad*
> *Nor airships falling from a marble sky*
> *Nor mothers listening to their children cry*
> *What chance have blades of grass on being mowed?*
> *And yet the unmolested Sun rolls on . . .*

There is more, but more is not required to qualify this poem for consideration among the most comical ineptitudes in the language. Take your pick: shall it be "unfriended toad," the snakes rolled upon by "giant limousines," or those "blades of grass on being mowed"? But the point of breaking this sorry butterfly upon the wheel of quotation is to demonstrate the sun had truly struck Harry down, inspired him and blinded him, too. The sonnets have a kind of regularity of mediocrity, but with *Chariot of the Sun* Harry commenced to ride all over the sky in his work, occasionally attaining real achievement, more frequently sinking even lower.

D. H. Lawrence wrote an introduction to the volume, the best criticism of Harry's work by a literary personage, and the only one of four prefaces and notes (the others are by Stuart Gilbert, Ezra Pound and T. S. Eliot) not commissioned by Caresse after her husband's death. Lawrence writes of Harry's "whims, and fumblings, and effort, and nonsense, and echoes from other poets, these all go to make up the living chaos of a little book of real poetry."

The chaos is there, sure enough, both on the surface and below it, but "Photoheliograph" tries to blow away the mists in a concentrated graphic expression:

> *black   black   black   black   black*
> *black   black   black   black   black*
> *black   black   black   black   black*
> *black   black   black   black   black*

```
black   black   SUN   black   black
black   black   black   black   black
black   black   black   black   black
black   black   black   black   black
black   black   black   black   black
black   black   black   black   black
```

This black sun was no invention of Harry's, but the alchemist's *Sol niger*, prime matter, the unconscious in its unworked, base state. The black sun is at its nadir, hidden, and all is night. In the Rig-Veda the sun during its night crossing is at its most magical and portentous. It must and shall be resurrected, as Harry knew he should persist again, in and like the sun, beyond his own sun-fall. Here again, paradox and ambiguity: the sun that gave sea, soil, and life also stared down without pity at its creations and withered them, dried them out, burnt them. Or failed to shine, winking while life failed. Where the sun is, there also find the death principle, the chaos that reigned before light dispelled it, the chaos that Harry's life and work replicated in miniature.

Harry first read D. H. Lawrence as early as 1923, and pronounced "The Ladybird" perhaps "the best short story I have ever read." He copied a generous chunk of it into his journal, where it appears as one of the earliest entries in his working notebooks, and reprinted it in *Shadows of the Sun*:

To her softly. Now you are mine. In the dark you are mine. But in the day you are not mine, because I have no power in the day. In the night, in the dark, and in death, you are mine. And that is forever. No matter if I must leave you. In the dark you are mine. But in the day I cannot claim you. I have no power in the day and no place. So remember. When the darkness comes, I shall always be in the darkness of you.

Nothing can ever separate us, unless we betray one another. If you have to give yourself to your husband, do so, and obey him. If you are true to me, innerly, innerly true, he will not hurt us. He is generous, be generous to him. And never fail to believe in me. Because even on the other side of death, I shall be watching for you. And you will never leave me anymore, in the after-death. So don't be afraid in life. Don't be afraid. If you have to cry tears, cry them. But in your heart of hearts know that I shall come again, and that I have taken you forever.

It wasn't till 1928 that Harry again took up Lawrence, and again he was profoundly influenced. This time the work was *The Plumed Serpent*, Lawrence's symbol-ridden romance, set in Mexico, rife with pagan gods and ancient rituals of blood sacrifice. Harry read it during a trip begun in Paris on January 26, 1928, that took him and his mother and Caresse to the pyramids at Giza, along the Nile to Luxor and Abu Simbel, to Haifa, Sudan, Cairo, Jerusalem, Damascus, Beirut, Tripoli, Constantinople, Belgrade, Budapest, Vienna. Like Kate in *The Plumed Serpent*, Harry felt himself pulled toward the source, toward life-impulses centered in the sun. En route to Giza he read a bit of Gide, and André Breton's recently published and fashionably controversial *Manifeste du Surréalisme*, but once in Egypt he plunged into the spirit of the place and its mysteries, and began *The Plumed Serpent* on February 1. Two days later, while he knelt on a red mat placed in the bilges of a boat abreast of the Semiramis on the Nile, in dead of night, lit by stars and a lantern, a Hindu illegally tattooed a huge sun, six inches in diameter, on his back.

In some respects the trip was not a success for Harry. As a worshiper of the sun he was handicapped by an aversion to heat and to southern parts. Egyptian food did not agree with him, he loathed the English tourists he was forced among everywhere, and he hated to have things arranged for him. But there were consolations. He ate hashish with Caresse—they had only smoked it before, a less potent intoxication—and went to the Temple of Karnak, lit by a full silver moon, and there, to his delight, "experienced all the sensations of dying." At Heliopolis there were horse races, as there were at the great seat of sun worship, the Egyptian city called An. And at Luxor he was pleased to buy from a young beggar three mummified hands, black and stiff, each with a blue ring on the forefinger.

Caresse's account of the trip, comically romanticized in *The Passionate Years*, dovetails with Harry's on a few particulars. She recollects his sitting hour upon hour, cross-legged, on one boat or another plying the Nile, reading *The Plumed Serpent*. And her description of Luxor accords with his: a grand hotel, organized excursions to the tombs, donkey races organized by the hotel management and "nautch girls dancing in the secret recesses of small cafés." (Indeed, she and Harry gave a young girl a gold coin to dance for them naked, and she did, and beckoned them to come to bed with her, just as they had slept and made love with Zora, an eleven-year-old Tunisian girl, three years earlier in North Africa. This time they were content to pay the girl to arouse them, and to fashion, alone together, their own sexual adventure.) Caresse was offended by "the beggar women carrying babies whose sticky eyes were caked with flies, the guides with halitosis, and Moussa the magician with his bag of snakes, dust and dung and prattle and oaths. . . ."

Harry's account of the events of February 10, 1928, is more benign. He had watched Moussa draw with his songs scorpions from the walls and cobras from the fields—"Perhaps he held them up his sleeve (the way the magician gilly gilly gilly hid the chicklets up his sleeve)" —but he was intrigued by what he believed to be a true magician's chant, the chant of a man Lawrence would endorse. That evening, at sunset, he made a pilgrimage to the Temple of Luxor to watch the sun go down, and there found, cut deep into the temple's stone, a bold graffito: RIMBAUD! That his idol and inspiration—the genius of renunciations who had nonetheless written, in "Credo in Unam," an apostrophe to the sun, "the source of tenderness and life," had been there before him struck him as a gift of destiny rather than a cruel but pointed reminder that visionaries like Rimbaud travel alone. Harry could follow Rimbaud if he wished, dogging his trail into the desert, but he could never hope to walk abreast with him.

"*The Plumed Serpent* is the most inspiring novel I have read since The Enormous Room," Harry wrote. He quoted it everywhere during the trip, pressed it on Caresse and on his mother, and read aloud from its pages—"I without the Sun that is back of the sun am nothing"—and he was especially struck, but perhaps puzzled by "something about the arrows of the soul . . . and about the breaking of the cords of the world in order to be free in the other strength (the sunstrength)." One passage he loved: "Living I want to depart to where I am." He read and reread the novel, lingering with special love over the words that seemed aimed (arrowlike?) at his own soul, and like Lawrence, could not swear off that word, *soul.*

Time out to observe the fast, first day of Ramadan, and to celebrate the birthday of Schopenhauer—one of the theoreticians of suicide. Then back into Lawrence: "Say I am coming come Thou." Having read these words, Harry played ping-pong and tennis with his mother, raced donkeys, nodded at the English tourists. On leap year in Cairo he bought a gold ring—"The Sun-Ring!" is the complete entry for February 29—that he was told, and believed, had been stolen from the tomb of Tutankhamen. He thought the discovery of the ring was especially provident, that it was most assuredly a ring potent with good magic, and that because of finding it when he did ("on a day that comes only once every four years") he was forever free of the world his mother's presence reminded him of: "The tree of the past is chopped down with an axe of gold no branches no roots dragging me back and I am unchained to arrow into the Sun. . . ." Caresse also made much of the ring. She and Harry made a contract: it was their wedding band, and he was never, never to remove it. "It was in Tutankhamen's tomb for thousands of years before us," she wrote. "Unless fission unfuses gold, it will endure forever. The eternal circle, the letter 'O.'" (In conformity with his rites of sun worship, Harry made much of the letter O, the sun letter, and trained himself to form it backwards, clockwise, as the earth revolves about the sun.)

A curator later told Mrs. Crosby that a gold Byzantine sun-cup she had bought with Harry at his urging, another heisted treasure, was assuredly a fake, and regretted that the Museum of Fine Arts, Boston, could not accept it as a gift. The ring, too, seemed . . . suspect. Harry couldn't believe it. The ring and cup were his providential signs. How could they be counterfeit?

Even before he finished *The Plumed Serpent* Harry wrote Lawrence from Egypt to France, where Lawrence and his wife Frieda—the daughter of Baron von Richthofen—had come temporarily to rest during their wanderings. He sent Lawrence some of the poems to be included in *Chariot of the Sun*, for which he was thanked in a letter by return mail: "I am glad somebody reaches a finger towards the real Ra, and dip your hand in Osiris too, since you're there. It makes real poetry. I'm so glad when somebody waves a sunny hand towards me for once. And so thankful to catch a glimpse of a real poet in the real world: not a strummer on a suburban piano." Harry had praised *The Plumed Serpent* in his letter to Lawrence, telling him as he later told his diary that he liked the novel better than anything he had read since E. E. Cummings' book about the war. Lawrence reacted to the comparison with an edge of petulance: "What is *The Enormous Room*—and by whom and when? I never heard of it." Harry also offered a hundred dollars in twenty-dollar gold pieces, emblazoned with the eagle and the sun, for any sun-story that he might publish in a deluxe and limited edition.

The Crosbys returned to Paris on March 24, and in mid-April Lawrence wrote Harry again, offering to write an introduction to *Chariot of the Sun* in response to Harry's request, for which Harry paid him. A couple of weeks later, Lawrence also sent along the manuscript of his story *Sun*. Always before the story had been expurgated, and he was hopeful that at last it would be printed as written, as it soon was. The Black Sun Press set it in type upon receiving the manuscript, and Harry and Caresse leafed through samples of Holland Van Gelder paper. *Sun* was published in November of that year, and Harry sent two copies in gold boxes to Lawrence at his villa in Florence. He was always generous with Lawrence. He went to great pains to get gold for him, in accordance with his promise when he first solicited the manuscript. It was illegal to send gold out of the United States, and impossible to buy gold coins in France. Harry's hatred of paper money increased in proportion to his enthusiasm for the symbolic properties of gold in ancient rituals of sun worship, and he required a good number of gold coins. He wrote Ted Weeks and Stuart Kaiser, who secured them and sent them to Paris with a painter named James Sykes, called Bill, who smuggled twenty twenty-dollar gold pieces from Boston to Paris in the toes of his riding boots. No sooner had he arrived at 19 rue de Lille and emptied the contents of his boots on the Crosbys' rug than Harry was off to the Gare de l'Est to send the gold to Lawrence by the Rome Express. He had packed the coins in a hollowed-out book, together with a snuffbox that once belonged to the Queen of Naples, and he walked along the station platform with his valuable cargo till he saw what seemed to him an honest face looking out a sleeping-car window. He asked the man to mail the package from Florence. Is it a bomb? the man asked Harry. "No, it's gold for a poet." The Duke of Argyll then introduced himself, and took the package. (Later, a wagon-lit porter in Florence, in turn entrusted with the gift, tried to gouge the Lawrences for its safe delivery, and failed spectacularly to prize a single lira from their tight grip.)

Lawrence was grateful for Harry's generosity: "But *cari meiei*, it won't do. I am sure you're not Croesuses to that extent: and anyhow, what right have I to receive these things? For heaven's sake, you embarrass me! I hope to heaven you're quite, quite rich, for if you're not, I shall feel really bad about it. . . . Perhaps one day we can square it somehow. Meanwhile very many thanks—but in future I shall tell you the price of my pen to a centime, and not a button more." Indeed, Lawrence had no hestiation thereafter in discussing his price, to a centime several times sliced.

Lawrence's worship of the sun was more coherent and better focused than Harry's. For him the sun was the primal source, the locus of energy and creation. The sun could renew and transform. From his direct experiences in Mexico, and among the Indians of New Mexico, together with his use of the cerebrations of Sir James Frazer, Jung and Nietzsche, he had fashioned a doctrine of oppositions in which primal vitality and civilized self-denial were in perpetual conflict. "Start with the sun," he wrote at the conclusion of *Apocalypse*, his final book, "and the rest will slowly, slowly happen." It must have seemed to Harry, who had written in his notebook, "I am a tree whose roots are entangled in the sun," that he and Lawrence were traveling the same metaphysical track. Perhaps Lawrence tried to warn him that they were not when he wrote him, "I don't mind a chaos—though I'm fairly tidy by nature—if I feel sometimes the wind blows through the chaos."

Lawrence's introduction to *Chariot of the Sun*, which was also published in Allanah Harper's *Exchanges* in 1929 with the title "Chaos in Poetry," is a masterpiece of ambivalence. Certainly it was written in a spirit of friendly enthusiasm, and Lawrence had gone to considerable trouble to place it with a magazine as "a bit of an advertisement" for Harry. But he did not abdicate his critical sense merely to help a generous man he had never even met. He begins with five pages of ruminations on the history and contemporary state of poetry, in which he intelligently argues that in his fear of chaos man raised an umbrella to shield himself from it; that he was obliged from time to time to cut slits in this umbrella which concealed from him the pulses of the cosmos; that poets once could cut such slits, but that now the umbrella, with its simulacrum of the universe painted pretty on its underside, has too tough a membrane to be cut through. Hence, poets had begun to practice a nostalgia for chaos: "The desire for chaos is the breath of their poetry. The fear of chaos is in their parade of forms and technique. Poetry is made of words! they say. So they blow bubbles of sound an image which soon bursts with the breath of longing for chaos, which fills them."

Surely, as Harry read this for the first time, his heart must have dropped. Lawrence seemed to offer pity and contempt in equal measure for those who longed for chaos, and for those who fled it. And was not Harry, with his oxymoronically chaotic sun-system, doing both? Then, scanning the pages, well into the introduction, he must have paused at this, the point of the piece for him:

What, then, of *Chariot of the Sun*? It is a warlike and bronzy title, for a sheet of flimsies, almost too flimsy for real bubbles. But incongruity is man's recognition of chaos. If one had to judge these little poems for their magic of words, as one judges Paul Valéry, for example, they would look shabby. There is no obvious incantation of sweet noise; only too often, the music of one line deliberately kills the next, breathlessly staccato. There is no particular jewellery of epithet. And no handsome handling of images. Where deliberate imagery is used, it is perhaps a little clumsy. There is no colored thread of an idea; and no subtle ebbing of a theme into consciousness, no recognisable vision, new gleam of chaos let into a world of order. There is only a repetition of sun, sun, sun, not really as a glowing symbol, more as a bewilderment and a narcotic.

Not the kind of judgment a poet would pay another poet in gold coins to write. Nor the particular collection of sentiments a poet would choose to launch his new collection of poems. Lawrence rightly called attention to Harry's "confusing" symbols, and to the first line of the book's final poem ("sthhe fous on ssu eod"); Lawrence pronounced it "just nonsense." (He took it for an unpronounceable experiment with sound, whereas it is in fact a most uninteresting poem written in code, whose first line translates "Harry poet of the sun.") But he admitted that he could "bear a page of nonsense, just for a pause." He declared that the poem "néant" is a "a tissue of incongruity, in sound and sense. It means nothing, and it says nothing."

And yet: "and yet it has something to say." And now, for Harry, the good news, precisely the news he had come to hear: "It is a glimpse of chaos not reduced to order. But the chaos *alive*, not the chaos of matter. A glimpse of the living, untamed chaos." A straight shot from the sun, Lawrence might have added: "For the grand chaos is all alive. And everlasting. From it we draw our breath of life. If we shut ourselves off from it, we stifle." Lawrence continues, still damning particulars, but finding "a breath of true poetry" in the whole performance, and sunfall in its effect: "What does it matter if half the time a poet fails in his effort at expression! The failures make it real. . . . Failure is part of the living chaos."

It is so, as others have said. A poem may lack one thing, two things, three things, half a dozen. Some poems require only one thing to bring them to life. Many of Harry's have one thing: outrage, courage, nerve, futility—call it what you will, the element brings even the silliest of his poems stuttering awake to some semblance of life. Lawrence again: "Through it all runs the intrinsic naïvete without which no poetry can exist, even the most sophisticated." He is wrong, surely, to say that no poetry can exist without the innocent directness he writes of, but Harry's could not; it was the breath of life in those of his poems that live.

Lawrence contrasts the innocence he believed he had found in these verses to another kind of liberation sought by the young; he contrasts Harry's liberation into an ideal state to "merely negative 'freedom.' " He concludes by implying that Harry has escaped a sad fate: "to be young, and to feel you have every 'opportunity,' every 'freedom' to live, and yet not be able to live, because the responses have gone numb in the body and soul, this is the nemesis that is overtaking the young. It drives to madness." Lawrence did not seem to understand that Harry was driven to madness by yoked nemeses, by perfect freedom—given or grabbed—and by his fanatical fixation on the naïve principles of a vision of death in the sun.

Harry was thrilled with the introduction, despite its reservations, and he and Lawrence began to plan a meeting. But it was not till March, 1929, that they found themselves in the same place at the same time. On the fifteenth, Lawrence came to lunch at 19 rue de Lille, and Harry was stunned: "We disagreed on everything. I am a visionary I like to soar he is all engrossed in the body and in the mushroom quality of the earth and the body and in the complexities of psychology. He is indirect. I am direct. He admits of defeat. I do not. . . . Lawrence stayed until four attacking my visionary attitude but my fort withstood the bombardment and I marshalled my troops and sallied out to counter-attack. . . ." All of this to and fro of combat took time, so that, to his disappointment, Harry missed the opening of the flat races at Maisons Laffitte.

Lawrence had come to Paris to find a publisher for *Lady Chatterley's Lover*, which was being pirated in France and in America, where it was suppressed by customs as it had been banned in England. He commended it to Harry, telling him it was "a direct phallic book, i.e. the direct nocturnal connection of a man with the sun—the path of the dark sun." Harry read it and didn't like it at all, save for a single line about "fucking little jazz girls with small boy buttocks." Lawrence told Harry that he would be arrested because of *Lady Chatterley's Lover*, if he returned to England, which Harry found "too disgusting, but the book itself is so poor I have very little interest in its fate. Not like the Ladybird. Not like the Plumed Serpent." He instructed his mother not to read it, as though anything could have tempted her to. Yet while he found the novel salacious, he found Lawrence himself a prig. Lawrence was shocked when Harry sang the praises of the nip and the full bite as techniques of love-making.

Once again the Crosbys and the Lawrences tried lunch. Harry

played Bessie Smith's "Empty Bed Blues" on the phonograph, and Lawrence despised it; he played a recording of James Joyce reading from *Ulysses*, and Lawrence said of Harry's most revered idol, "Yes, I thought so, a preacher a Jesuit preacher who believes in the cross upsidedown." Earlier, Lawrence had told Harry that Joyce "bores me stiff—too terribly would-be and done-on-purpose, utterly without spontaneity or real life." Subsequent meetings became increasingly pugnacious affairs. (On first seeing Lawrence at a tea in Paris, Edmund Wilson found even his physical appearance to be aggressive. Wilson saw at once that having to fight for his life and art throughout his manhood, Lawrence had surrendered to "exaggerated self-assertion." On the particular occasion when Wilson met him, at a tea, Lawrence "suddenly became hysterical and burst out in childish rudeness and in a high-pitched screaming voice with something like: 'I'm not enjoying this! Why are we sitting here having tea? I don't want your tea! I don't want to be doing this.' ")

Presently, Lawrence quarreled with Caresse about money, feeling that a second story of his—*The Escaped Cock*—published by the Black Sun Press in the autumn of 1929 had been mismanaged by her. She had sold the entire printing to Harry Marks, and Lawrence, who stood to share the profits from the sale equally with the Crosbys, believed that she had sold too cheap. In February of 1930, just two weeks before he died of consumption, Lawrence acknowledged Caresse's check of about one thousand dollars by asking, "Did you sell the whole edition, *including the vellums*, for $2,250? If you did, you are not the good business woman I should expect you to be: and I resent bitterly these little few booksellers making all that money out of us." The final shot came from Frieda over the manuscript of *The Escaped Cock*, which Caresse was slow to return in the months immediately after Harry's death: "Are you only a business woman? With the usual tricks? No, my dear, Harry was different, he wasn't that kind—No! I won't give you another word of Lawrence's to print if I don't get the ms. of *The Escaped Cock*. Yours in disgust, Frieda."

A brotherhood in the sun, like a brotherhood in poetry, is not without risks. Perhaps such a brotherhood is not even possible, but exists only in the kinds of visions Lawrence argued against so violently with Harry. For Harry the vision was always so clear and noble, and inhabited by brothers and lovers, all perfectly united. Then breathing, hungry, troubled people intruded on the visions and botched them. There was no way to keep people from intruding on his visions, and only one way to escape them.

13

"He looked like a god. He didn't look like anybody on the street, or in restaurants, or anywhere. He was just different."

—Polleen Peabody, about her stepfather

Harry and Caresse went to Venice on the last day of June, 1928. They were both exhausted by their last Four Arts Ball, and Harry wanted to recuperate from the throat operation he'd had in Lausanne on June 10. Their plan was to relax, lie in the sun and forgo liquor for a few weeks. But Harry was agitated. In addition to his customary jumpiness, many of his excitements and fixations had intersected: he was writing constantly and desperately, and laboring to develop rites of sun worship, and he was dwelling deeper than ever in ruminations about his suicide. He had brought with him to Venice Nietzsche's *Thus Spake Zarathustra*, whose proposal that men of fire and iron might surpass themselves, become supermen contemptuous of Christianity's slave morality, of virtue, reason and happiness, could not have exercised a more malign influence upon Harry. He was especially arrested by Zarathustra's message "die at the right time," and he copied the passage into his journal, annotating it thus: "Die at the right time, so teacheth Zarathustra and again the direct 31-10-42. Clickety-click clickety-click the express train into Sun." ("31-10-42" is a reference to the date Harry and Caresse had selected for their twin suicide, October 31, 1942, the date when the earth and sun would be at the perihelion, their closest orbital proximity.) The next day he added another quotation from Zarathustra: "The voluntary death which cometh unto me because I want it." Immediately after the quotation, evidently without irony, he wrote that he hated museums because they are dead and "I like things that are Alive." (He had for the past week been studying Van Gogh, and especially his suicide.) And the following day he wrote: "I like the idea of a sun-death . . . from an aeroplane for when the body strikes the ground Bang, Twang flies the Arrow of Soul to and into the Sun For Eternity."

When not thus morbidly occupied, he ran along the beach, and he and Caresse swam at the Lido, ate well and went dancing. Though Zarathustra regarded love as a nuisance—a snare set up by the superman's enemy, biology—and woman as merely "the recreation of the warrior," Harry's entry for July 9, 1928, in *Shadows of the Sun* celebrates a woman he found fit for worship: "Enter the Youngest Princess of the Sun!" He even wrote about her to Lawrence—they had still to meet, and were not yet on a first-name footing—and Lawrence replied: "What luck to find a sun-maid! not a raisin but a real lass! *Americana Anche! proprio d'oro.*" The *Americana* was Josephine Noyes Rotch, descended from a distinguished family of Nantucket Quakers who first settled in Provincetown about 1690. Francis Rotch figured prominently in the Boston Tea Party, and later branches of the family were in the whaling trade in New Bedford as well as Nantucket. Josephine was the daughter of Arthur and Helen Ludington Rotch of 197 Commonwealth Avenue, Boston. She belonged to the Vincent Club and the Junior League, and was a graduate of Boston's Lee School before entering Bryn Mawr. She had quit college after two years, just a fortnight before she met Harry, because she planned to marry Albert Smith Bigelow, also of Boston. She had come to Europe to buy her trousseau.

Her friends called her Josie, but Harry knew her as the Fire Princess, or the Youngest Princess: she was twenty. His next book of poems after *Chariot of the Sun* he titled *Transit of Venus*, and she was his Venus. One of the poems is about her situation with the young man to whom she had promised herself:

> Her heart
> Is a number of things,
> Of whispered song
> Of comfort built with money

Of dead men's bones
Of necklaces and rings
Of faith
(he is fresh and funny
of good intentions
of good works
of goodly prospect
of grace force
    fascination youth)
Her heart is of marble
For defense
Of sweet days, of roses,
Of sweet indifference
When he proposes.

Josephine was dark and intense, and wore her hair according to the fashion of the day, in a tight helmet, just like Caresse's. Since the season of her coming-out in the winter of 1926–27, she had been known around Boston as fast, "a bad egg." One Boston lady who knew her called her swarthy, "with a good deal of sex appeal, as they say." To Tote Fearing, Josie was "very pretty, but not at all a sexy dish. Just a very pretty woman, and how nice that she enjoyed it." She was strong-willed and selfish, and she did not agonize much before deciding to become Harry's lover. They had only eight days together in Venice, and Caresse was about, but they used their limited time busily.

Harry made no effort to keep a secret of his liaison, though he did shroud it in such mystery as he felt appropriate to a coupling between a poet of the sun and a Fire Princess. He wasted no time telling his mother about his latest enthusiasm, writing her on July 24: "I am having an affair with a girl I met (not introduced) at the Lido. She is twenty and has charm and is called Josephine. I like girls when they are very young before they have any minds. She has made me like America very much and through her I have had many new points of view on the U.S. She sails tomorrow." A few days later he wrote his mother that he had been badly depressed when she left, and on the last day of July he even admitted to being homesick: "It is extraordinary that since we have lived in France, six years now, that Caresse has never had a touch of mal du pays—I cannot say the same." Josephine sent cables to Harry almost daily since they said goodbye, and on this same day she wired him a particularly urgent message from the *France*, at sea: DO NOT BE DEPRESSED. TAKE THE NEXT BOAT. YOU KNOW I LOVE YOU AND WANT YOU.

JOSEPHINE. Perhaps he liked the idea of taking the next boat, but nothing would tempt him to leave and lose Caresse.

By the third week of August, he was able to bring analysis to bear upon his passion, and wrote his mother that he had very recently written fifty-two poems for *Transit of Venus*: "Affairs I find stimulating and were it not for the Charming Josephine I would not have written them. She was mad and madness is very appealing especially to me who is mad. I suppose once in Boston she will marry and be very sage."

Like the poems in *Transit of Venus*, Harry and Josephine transacted their drama in short bursts, now self-consciously pacific, now furious, always elliptical. Neither the poems nor the lovers expressed *enjambement*, the French word for run-over lines in verse that translates "leg-over," and suggests transition. The poems, like Harry and Josephine's experiences together, are truncated: lines stick out busted like twigs after a storm, and fail to connect or to declare sense and sequence. The meaning of one poem in the collection is, however, transparently clear:

> *I wish to-night I were a cat*
> *That I might slink*
> *To where you sleep demurely*
> *(Sleeping above the brink of dream)*
> *And suck your breath*
> *Slowly and surely*
> *Into death.*

Harry jotted in his notebooks bizarre excerpts from their conversations together:

" 'I lie and I like it.' (to him [Bigelow] because of me)"
"The look in her eyes   Yes"
"you belong to me don't you   Yes"
"(burned scars with my black cigarette)"
"to brand her with teeth marks"
"with infinite care I ravish your eagerness"
"you must not talk about jumping into bed you must jump into bed"
"I'm as sick as a cat."
"I want to pounce on you."
" 'I bought a pack of cards today so I could send you my heart' (J)"

Harry composed an anagram:

J for Javelin
O for Orchid
S for Sun
E for Ecstasy
P for Panther
H for Harry
I for Innocence
N for Naked
E for Enchantress

And another, beside it, for himself:

H for Hawk
A for Aviator
R for Rapier
R for Rá
Y for Yes

Still, despite the fervor and foment, Josephine had not displaced all others from Harry's heart. Not at all. At the same time that he loved her he also loved—sometimes with more intensity, sometimes with less —Caresse, Constance Coolidge, Polia Chentoff and Bokhara, a desert boy come from Damascus to Jerusalem to beg, stowed away on a camel, wrapped up in a Bokhara rug. (Added to these, of course, were dozens of others, transients in his affections, ladies to whom he gave such names as the Girl in the Black Dress, or the Lady of the White Polo Coat.)

Bokhara seems to have been Harry's only partner in homoeroticism. They met on March 8, 1928, in Jerusalem, during the trip to Egypt and the Holy Land: "Bokhara the Temple-Boy and I fall in love with him (to hell with women). . . ." The following day, they sailed paper darts and dropped ink bombs from the balcony of Harry's hotel, and ate breakfast together. The next day the Crosbys were on the Sea of Galilee—"The Bokhara Sun over the Sea of my Heart"—and three days later in Beirut Harry tossed snowballs at the sun, dreaming of Bokhara.

Thereafter, whenever Harry listed the names of the many he loved, Bokhara was among them. In October, 1928, he composed within a sun and its rays a picture of the "fires in my heart." Bokhara was there (close to the brutal Arab homily: "A woman for necessity, a boy for pleasure, a goat for delight"). So also were these: *Mad Queen* (Josephine), *Cramoisy Queen* (Caresse), *Queen of Pekin* (Constance, Comtesse de Jumilhac), *Youngest Princess* (again Josephine), *Dark Princess* (Polia Chentoff). And another, the *Grey Princess*, whom Harry called Jacqueline, a most ephemeral figure, his favorite. In Harry's will he left five thousand dollars and his gold sun-cup to Jacqueline Crosby. There are references to her throughout his handwritten notebooks: Jacqueline, "a medieval princess"; Jacqueline, "Countess of Holland." He tattooed her name across his chest, and dreamt of throwing coins stamped with the name into the Seine. Once he dined with her in Paris at Chez Philippe and ordered two of everything he most enjoyed. In truth, he dined alone. Jacqueline never was—or rather, existed only in Harry's imagination, and in an etching by the Swedish artist Anders Zorn. Harry had once seen the etching in 1924, but had failed then to buy it, and despised himself almost immediately for his failure. Finally, on March 20, 1929: "the Zorn etching I have looked and looked for for so long arrived from London. It is Jacqueline the Grey Princess. Valkulla."

Caresse remembers her well: "I was only jealous of one rival, the imaginary 'Jacqueline,' the shepherdess of the Zorn etching Val Kulla (the one that looked like Harry); the others, The Lady of the Golden Horse, Helen of Troy, The Tigress, The Lady of the White Polo Coat, The Sorceress, Nubile, The Fire Princess, The Youngest Princess, all were substantial props to the poet's dream . . . thus I accepted them, all except the image of Jacqueline—she *was* the dream—the girl of infinite mystery . . . the everlasting shadow—no other loves were quite as true."

Polleen recollects Harry's magnetism: "I was absolutely in love with him. When he would talk to someone he was so focused on them, and his dynamic charm would be turned on you like a great beam of light, as in hypnotism, I suppose. It wasn't fake; it was true; that's why it was so powerful. There was never anything banal in his talk. Totally unexpected, unsettling, a virgin approach."

Harry had always taken a proprietary, if bemused, interest in his stepdaughter, whom he called "the Wretch," recording such of her "picturesque façon de parler" as "someotherbody" and "what part of us goes to heaven; is it our thinks?" He liked to take her to Sherry's for coffee milk shakes and to the Ritz for champagne cocktails—"The Wretch is very pretty in her white dress"—and to be driven around by his chauffeur with her seated in his lap.

Polleen remembers that Harry could invent a perfect world, and exclude from it everyone except himself and the girl he meant to charm. He would draw a tight curtain around the two of them, and make real their mutual dream. Harry once told her a story about a princess who spread gold coins among her subjects. His stepdaughter said she wished she could be such a princess. "But you are," he told her, and hired an open taxi to drive them—Polleen in her nightgown and pajamas—along the Champs Élysées, where the two of them threw coins to the people walking the sidewalks.

He could also be hard on her, impossibly exacting, almost brutal:

> He was very strict in things like putting books upside down in the bookshelf. I used to write poetry, naturally, like all children do, and I wrote this poem that I copied out of a book, and assumed that Harry would know it by heart. It was very famous, and I sent it to him—I used to send him all my poems—as a kind of joke. And he came storming down to the nursery, shaking with rage, and asked, "Did you really write this?" And I said "Yes," and he got more and more worked up and I got more and more frightened, and instead of saying, "Of course I didn't write it," I insisted it was my poem, and then he really went wild and dragged me to the cellar and locked me up, and I nearly went out of my mind. . . .

She recalls how rigidly he held to rituals: that he would touch various objects—his desk, the skulls he had stolen from the Catacombs—in a precise order as he began or finished work, and that he would never put on his left shoe before his right. "I was allowed up at the end of the afternoon's work, and he'd read me all this marvelous stuff. I read anything he liked: Joyce, Rimbaud. He used to read me things he'd written down that day, his dreams. And his sun-stuff: he had crosses tattooed on the bottoms of his feet, and I thought that would be terribly painful. I think for Harry that worshiping the sun was mostly important for the image it gave him of Harry worshiping the sun. He liked to watch himself do it."

To Polleen, taken to the Ritz or to Prunier or to the race track, "he looked like a god. He didn't look like anybody on the street, or in restaurants, or anywhere. He was just different." She also felt his fierce side, and he carried on with her about death. She calls him *farouche*, a word that faces north, south and east: it means wild and menacing, it means timid and coy; it means unsociable.

Harry used to tell her in detail about his lovers; he would read aloud to her Josephine's letters and laugh, probably because of the odd run-on passion of the Fire Princess, so extreme and quirky. Polleen was left with the impression that he didn't care all that much for Josephine, that he was flattered, yet "annoyed" and "bored" by her mad love. But Constance Coolidge, the Lady of the Golden Horse, the Queen of Pekin, was another matter. Polly remembers: "He had a terrific walk-out with her. They had a tremendous love affair. If he wanted to do something, he did it, and my mother had to lump it. Constance was marvelous-looking, and frightfully selfish. I'm fond of her, but she's one of the most selfish women I've ever known in my life. Mother was her friend always, but I think there was a slight resentment about this affair with her husband. Till mother died she saw Constance all the time, but I think she resented them not even hiding it."

And from her privileged position as Harry's confidante, how did she regard her mother's part in her stepfather's romantic life? "I felt then, as a kid, twelve when he died, that she didn't understand this man as *I* did. That I was much nearer to Harry's inner things than she was." Poor Caresse, brave Caresse. Every woman who knew Harry believed that his wife "didn't understand this man as *I* did"; every one believed that she herself was much "nearer to Harry's inner things" than Caresse was. Constance did indeed understand a great deal about Harry, but not everything. Born Constance Crowninshield Coolidge, the niece of Frank Crowninshield, editor of *Vanity Fair*, she had been married to and divorced from Ray Atherton. Atherton was a diplomat, and when he was at the United States embassy in China, Constance was known as the Queen of Pekin—"more," as Caresse justly remarked, "for her ability to dazzle than to rule." She was beautiful, dark, willful and daring. In China she had lived in a temple and raced Mongolian ponies. She cared not a fig what the world thought of her, so of course the world thought a great deal of and about her.

Harry found her in 1923; they were introduced by Caresse, who had met her at a luncheon for ladies: "She was perfection," Caresse writes. Excited by her rare find, Caresse invited Constance to a Sunday lunch before the races; Constance was addicted to horse racing and to games of all kinds, as long as they were risky. From then on, "The Lady of the Golden Horse was tangled in my hair."

After they had become lovers, Harry admitted to Constance that he had been "frightened" by her the first day they met; she was "very regal." But within days he wrote her that "I'm so glad you suggested a little less Mr. Crosby Mrs. Atherton—because Constance is the loveliest name I know." Soon they were in the thick of things together, Harry justifying his betrayal of Caresse by insisting that "one should follow every instinct no matter where" it leads, and telling Constance, as he had only the year before assured Caresse in his heartbroken letters to her, that she had "awakened everything that's beautiful in me. . . . God knows I've been an awful hound most of my life but if I ever had anything inside me that was pure and good you have inspired it."

Caresse learned about the couple's liaison, and in the autumn of 1923 left for London, declaring to Harry that "she doesn't want to see me until I love her more than anyone in the world. This is absolutely impossible." So Constance found the situation. Harry refused to leave his wife for her ("I must look after Polly and try to make her happy if I can and stick by her no matter what happens. I'm terribly fond of her and except for you love her more than anyone else in the world—but somehow Constance things will never be the same"), nor did Constance wish him to leave Polly. When finally she received a desperate letter from Caresse admitting that she had been made "very miserable" by her husband's affair with her friend, and that perhaps they "could all manage to be friends—I don't know, perhaps not," Constance wrote Harry that she would no longer see him, and that she was in fact in love with another man.

Harry was at once made desolate and furious by Constance's rejection of him, reacting much as he had when he could not utterly win Caresse during 1920 and 1921. He walked the banks of the Seine weeping, and wrote angry letters, full of injury: "Your letter was bar none the worst blow I have ever received. Nor dear did it seem fair. Once we promised never to part by letter. It is no way. . . . You are asking far too much. You say that Polly & I can be happy now. It is impossible as I told you. I wouldn't leave her under any circumstances nor as you say would you ever marry me—all that though isn't the point."

It was, though, the point exactly. Harry thrashed around, mooned through his final days at the bank, and in an episode that even Caresse would come to appreciate as high comedy bought Constance a gray German shepherd at a dog show. The dog was delivered with Harry's note advising that he "needs a bath & some food. . . . I hope he hasn't any fleas. He seems gentle—but he may be only stupid. . . . Don't hesitate to give him away if he's a bore. You can't hurt my feelings that way. I can never go back to Polly unless you see me. . . . I have been loyal and true to you—have faced Polly & told her the truth. Why can't you at least let me plead my case. A lover is defenseless. I have cried like a child. . . . If there were only a war I could go and escape. . . . I'll leave the hound here; throw him in the Seine if he's no good."

Instead she sent the animal to Polly Crosby, who also refused to accept it. Constance's rejection of Harry was not anything like as heartless or brutal as he made out. She had written with conspicuous affection and understanding: "There was something wonderful about your point of view and the way you look at things—which something in me responds to—a streak of our ancestors perhaps—anyhow I knew right away that it would be dangerous to see you very often. You are one of the most inspiring people I have ever met—like one of the knights come down the ages out of a fairy book—but life is not a fairy story anymore except in dreams. You will be in my life always—as something very beautiful that came and went suddenly like a rainbow between storms."

Harry was temporarily bitter, writing Constance that he believed "all three of us played our cards damn poorly: Polly became too upset, too excited, and rushed away too soon, you made a great mistake telling . . . friends about it, and you might have been far more gentle and . . . infinitely more understanding, I should have been much less youthful, much less passionate, and much less impulsive. I apologize. I'm really very sorry. I hope we'll all three become great friends—but I don't know." They soon became very close friends: Constance married Pierre, the Comte de Jumilhac, and Caresse returned to her original judgment that Constance was "the most attractive girl" she had "ever met." Harry and Constance together indulged their love of horses, gambling and opium.

An admirer of Constance has described her as "fortunate of face," but "unfortunate in husband." The Count's favorite wisdom, Harry reported, was "if you don't want to be a pigeon you must be a shark," and he was fond of saying that there was "no point in worrying about anything because nothing is ever worth worrying about." Constance said of her husband that he believed that "to think at all is a kind of laziness—one must act every second—once you begin to think you're lost." So after a few years of marriage Constance left the Count, but not her title; Harry and Harry's father were both firm in their advice that she retain her title: "My Uncle Jack Morgan once said to me," as Harry wrote her, " 'in life one must use all one's assets' and in your case this title is certainly an asset."

Constance's native Boston had a low opinion of the Comtesse de Jumilhac, a compound of Back Bay's outraged proprieties, and its envy and intimidation. Harry and Constance had bet each other five hundred dollars that the other would return to Boston first; Harry lost, and was told by a friend of his father's that "the only way for her to save her soul was for her to live within her income O Christ O Christ O Christ

O Christ." But Harry himself was concerned about her health and her finances. She was an even more enthusiastic user of opium than he. She exhausted herself going to the track every day (where she gambled recklessly—one of her horses once won a quarter of a million francs, but more frequently she lost), and going to parties and night clubs every night. She smoked excessively, and finally Harry gave her a pep talk by way of a letter mailed from Boston: he urged her to pay off her debts, to sell her jewels and her Hispano-Suiza, to move to less extravagant quarters than her flat at 41 Quai d'Orsay. "Harden your body. Attack and if you are beaten counter-attack and if you are beaten re-attack. And for Christ's sake attack don't sit and wait to be attacked."

Then, in the fall of 1927, Harry and Constance again became lovers. He was intrigued with her voice, "soft and pathetic . . . wistful," and with her eyes, and with her courage and intelligence. For her part, she found Harry "one of those inspired people who see things as they really are—and not just as they seem to be, dull and commonplace and of the earth." They exchanged luxurious gifts: Harry never failed to remember her birthday, January 4, and gave her paintings and books. She gave him a jade ring, and a gold belt with a gold clasp. He sent her a red leather-bound notebook, with a poem or quotation on every page, inscribed it "to Constance his Queen from Harry her Clown," and wrote on the last page, simply, "I love you."

In the spring of 1929, Constance and Harry quarreled at 19 rue de Lille. Incredibly, he kept a photograph of Josephine in his apartment, framed in silver, and Constance asked if the girl was Kitsa, so much did she resemble Harry. When he said she was not, that she was his girl friend, Constance criticized her hair style, and Harry left his apartment angry, taking the photograph with him. They loved each other too much to break off, however, and soon enough they were meeting again. On the anniversary of Davis Weld's death, always remembered, he took her to Prunier, and later, at her apartment, filled with Chinese treasures, she gave him a roulette wheel. He was distracted: "I keep thinking about the Sorceress."

Yes, yet another. In *Seduction and Betrayal* Elizabeth Hardwick has proposed that the seducer "at his work" is a clownish fellow, whatever grave injury his importunities might cause. Viewed from outside, reduced to dates and names and statistics, Harry's case is so exaggerated as to suggest slapstick, a Restoration comedy in which the horny fop runs so quickly from bed to bed that he loses sight of which lady he lies upon. It was ludicrous: less than a year after falling in love with Josephine, and while he was still in love with her and with Caresse and with

Constance and with Bokhara and with his idealized Jacqueline, the Sorceress was added to the string. Harry must have believed that he was only expressing his creative vigor in his outrageous excess of sensuality, and that by expressing this vigor in ways outlawed by society—and by the Society from which, *nota bene*, his mistresses came, one and all—he was demonstrating the majesty of the poet as law-defier, a law only unto himself.

Elizabeth Hardwick writes: "The seducer as a type, or as an archetype, hardly touches upon any of our deep feelings unless there is some exaggeration in him, something complicated and tangled and mysteriously compelling about a nature that has come to define itself through the mere fact of sex." Perhaps. Surely Harry did not define himself through sex, unless an idea of sex were spread to engross his death wish and his idea of himself as an artist. In which case sex, like the sun, would be too various to comprehend and too gross to see, save a bit at a time. Yet Harry did enkindle deep feelings. In part because of the wild recklessness of his affairs, his willingness to pay any price for them, his compulsion. And in part because he was an uncommon seducer. He persuaded women that he loved them as they had never been loved before simply because, strangely, he *did* deeply love them. For him each affair was hermetically sealed off from every other, so that on a single day he could dream about Josephine, visit Constance, make love to Caresse and fret about the Sorceress.

The wife of a classics scholar, the Sorceress was a woman who impressed herself on people. Her wedding had been a spectacular event in 1928, when she wore a medieval costume with a veil of gold falling from a towering headdress. The costume and setting, as reported by the society rag, *Town Topics*, "would have done credit to Hollywood." Now, seven months later, she and her husband had been sent by their friend Archibald MacLeish to meet Harry and Caresse. On June 17, 1929, they came to 19 rue de Lille: ". . . the intense impression as she arrived at the head of the stairs and came into the Enormous Room and we talk about Joyce and Cummings and Crane and Eliot and MacLeish and we drink cocktails and she is very pretty and very very physical and it seems as if all my life I have been waiting for her."

Harry's passionate affection for her was sometimes expressed on the very days when he yearned inconsolably for Josephine. He saw a great deal of her in August; an entry in his diary on August 8 is more physically direct than some others, but not atypical: "In the evening gin fizzes color of green and silver and the Sorceress girlish like a young actress feline as a puma she is even more feline and amorous by night and now we are together would that we might vanish together into sleep and . . ." She and her husband, by every account happily married then and later, left Paris on November 8: "It rains—a dark day until the Sorceress appears. . . . Yes Pucelle that witch that damned Sorceress. It was so terrible to have her go but I am damn happy for the word Yes is ringing in my ears and she has given me the letter A."

And there were others. There was Nubile, a young schoolgirl with a baby face and large breasts "and brown eyes like marbles" who excited Harry's fancy at Étretat. She was fourteen, and thought Rimbaud was an historian. Harry found her "naughty and charming," as he wrote to Caresse, who was in Paris. Nubile was a sport, innocent enough, nothing to trouble Caresse. Still, as Harry remarked years before turning his attention to the Wretch, "to corrupt the young is a temptation."

Polia Chentoff, however, troubled Caresse very much. The Crosbys met the tiny, dark Russian painter on November 7, 1927, at the most intense period of Harry's affair with Constance. They were both struck by her work at a huge opening that November night (next day, the critics agreed that it shone among the thousands of canvases in the Autumn Salon; one of her paintings won the salon's first prize), and Harry asked her to paint Caresse's portrait. They fell in love, and on November 13 Harry wrote his mother that Polia was "very beautiful and terribly serious about art she ran away from home when she was thirteen to paint and I think when she has painted Caresse that I'll get her to paint one of me—I adore being painted!" She told him gruesome stories about the Russian famine—that one month she and her family had eaten nothing but caviar, and the following month nothing but horses. And when an American missionary had come to their village from the Salvation Army to bring a little food and much faith, he was eaten, his boots too. A month after he met her, he told his mother that he loved Polia. Six months later, while he also had crushes on Constance and his cousin Nina de Polignac, and less than two months before he met Josephine, he wrote again that he loved Polia "more than all the Ninas and Constances put together." Sometimes when he took her to restaurants he would bump into Caresse and Manolo Ortíz, a painter and friend of Picasso whom Caresse had met the same night they met Polia.

"She has adorable feet," Harry had written his mother, "they keep pitter-pattering through my head," and he wrote a poem for her in *Chariot of the Sun*, or rather for her extremities, "Poem for the Feet of

Polia." Caresse had agreed with Harry's decision the night of the Autumn Salon to buy Polia's painting "First Communion" to hang in the dining room at their apartment, and had been pleased to commission a portrait from her. "But soon," as she remembered, "Polia became entirely Harry's as so many of our mutual enthusiasms did." Polia's portrait of him—the frontispiece to *Chariot of the Sun*—Caresse thought "strange and portentous." The painter/mistress had "made him so sort of languid."*

Caresse also took serial lovers. Late in 1927, Harry wrote his mother reminding her that it was once again November 22, his near-death day, the "metamorphose from boy into man" in 1917. The letter continues after an abrupt change of key:

> What a tea-party today! First Ortiz a young Spanish painter (we met him at the Comte Etienne de Beaumont's) then Zenoview who painted a picture we once bought and that hangs in the salon then Bunny Brooks who paints (from Boston) then Stanley Mortimer (who paints) then Alastair who appeared from nowhere all in black étrange almost like a shadow then La Dame Aux Perles (as Alastair calls Constance) and after the Comtesse arrived Madame La Marquise (Nina . . .)
> Caresse's boy friends are: The Comte Civry
> The Tartar Prince
> Ortiz
> Frans de Geetere
> Lord Lymington. . . .

Of the Tartar Prince nothing is now known save that Harry regarded him as "dangerous." The Count Ulric de Civry, who had introduced the Crosbys to the world of horse racing on the grand scale, is described by Caresse as looking like Santa Claus, "only noble and elegant as well." Manolo Ortiz, a Spanish gypsy with access to the upper strata of Paris salon society, received the most concentrated attention of any of Caresse's lovers, with the possible exception of Cord Meier, known to the Crosbys as the Aviator, a pilot wounded in the war, handsome

---

* In fact, she had made him sort of dead, and after Harry's suicide Caresse burned the oil, perhaps because, as she explained, she found it "metaphysically disturbing," but perhaps also because she remained jealous of her rival. As for Polia's portrait of herself, the poet St.-John Perse, whom Harry much admired, looked at it once in amazement, and said he had never seen the distaste of one woman for another so skillfully and subtly expressed.

and wealthy, a graceful dancer. (As Caresse notes in her recollection of the Aviator, Harry did not like to dance.) There was another, Bobby Fochin, and then, met in mid-May of 1928, the most important, Armand, Comte de la Rochefoucauld. The Crosbys met him at the Bal Nègre where, as Harry wrote his mother, "Caresse had *three* beaux Ortiz and Comte de Gamay and a *new* one . . . Armand. . . ."

Harry sounded cheerful enough about Caresse's goings and comings, but many entries in *Shadows of the Sun* describe violent fights over his wife's boyfriends. Caresse would come home and find Harry asleep from a surfeit of sherry cobblers, gin and love-making with someone or other, and then the next day be marched off to a clairvoyant that the Crosbys patronized, a gentleman named Baker, who would tell her that she must be faithful to Harry, that Harry liked "a girl whose first name began with a C that I AM a genius, but difficult to live with. . . ." As Caresse wrote, she "was becoming rather restless under the strain of Harry's search for clandestine fires, but he made me believe that my children balanced our account." She did only a little of what he did a lot of, but from time to time they strayed in harness, as when Harry and Caresse and two other couples would drive in three cars to the Bois de Boulogne, draw them up in a circle, lit headlights facing in, and mix and match. A friend of hers, who knew about these occasional pastoral orgies, said much later that she was not at all certain that Caresse's "sexual promiscuity was anything she herself wanted or enjoyed. It was one of the demands Harry made upon her, one of the complete reversals of everything she had been trained as a child, and a young girl, and a young married woman, to respect. She talked to me almost in guilt about these things, trying to make them funny, for her gallantry and humor were a part of her courage."

Though Harry never spoke ill of Caresse to anyone, he did, from time to time, put into the record of his notebooks musings about his married state. Many of these were merely aphoristic borrowings, such as this from *Chrome Yellow*: "Marriage is like a frog who jumps down a well; he gets plenty of water, but he can't get out." Others were more serious: "You have the desire to make me happy, but not the power, while I have the power to make you happy, but not the desire." Yet Harry knew better than anyone that they each had the desire and the power to make the other happy. Divorce was unthinkable, and long separations brought forth such letters from both as are usually sent only in the early weeks of love. (As it turned out, ironically enough, Harry's sister Kitsa decided in the autumn of 1929 to divorce her husband, Robert Choate, just as Harry had predicted to Caresse two years earlier: "And now the poor family will worry about her as they have worried and worry about me only she has caught up now in one fell swoop as I should like to catch up at the races.")

During a time in 1927 when Harry was aswarm with girl friends, he and Caresse decided that they'd like to be married again—to each other, of course—so much did they cherish the experience. Even Constance told Caresse that no one had ever approached her in Harry's affection: "He was so proud of you. He said you were so clever & modern—he was always telling me how old-fashioned I was—& he said you followed him and understood him in every step he took in life . . . no one else could have done it—no one else could have been so unselfish & true to him. . . . Everyone else failed him sooner or later in life except you. . . ." The others, Constance said, were mere "side issues."

Certainly Harry was indulged by Caresse, by Constance, by "the others." Kay Boyle, whom he met in the spring of 1928 and who was by no means one of his girl friends, believes she understands his attraction for women: "I think of the women who responded to him, and it seems to me now that their response to him was as much a part of their own problems as it was his need for them. He made each woman he approached believe that she alone was the answer to all his uncertainties. A veil seemed to hang between him and the sound of anyone's voice, the touch of anyone's hand. And I think these women believed that they alone could penetrate that veil."

Tests were essential to Harry, and he could not sustain love without posing them again and again. Constance was annoyed by his persistent trials of certification, his almost childish insistence that she—and Caresse, and Josephine, and the Sorceress—say yes, they would walk through the fire, yes, they would leave their husbands for him, yes, they would die with him.

Until Harry met Josephine, crazy and brave enough to face down any risk, only Caresse had passed all his tests. Even after he and Josephine so disastrously found each other, Caresse passed every test but one, and Josephine passed only that one—the last one—which for Harry became the only test that mattered. But there should be no doubt where his deepest passion rested. Early in their marriage, when he was first discovered wandering from bed to bed, he wrote Caresse from Paris to America: "O darling I may have caused you pain in the past but I love you so abjectly, so unreservedly, and with all that is noble and glorious in me that you must long since have forgiven me.

All the best in me is yours." He *knew* she had forgiven him, as she always would, and in his exhilarated acceptance of her forgiveness he added to his letter his curious, by now familiar, special signature: "I envy no one I scorn the world. And I am prepared for death."

But perhaps a truer test of the persistence of their almost theatrically passionate love is a look at their words to each other during 1929, after all their various love affairs had been begun, and while most of them were still under way. In January, Caresse, who was in London scouting manuscripts for the Black Sun Press, wrote Harry from Claridge's, quoting a line from one of their favorites among E. E. Cummings' poems: "London is no fun without you. I like my body '*only* when it is with your body—' [T. S.] Eliot is ill but hope he will recover soon—I am sure I could cure him, but he doesn't know that. . . . The moment we are apart my compass needle points strong and steady penetrating straight into your heart (true is the dial to the sun). There have been magnetic storms but always the needle has returned seeking its target in your center."

The two were so complexly intertwined that she had begun to write like him—the same idioms, same rhythms, same far-fetched conceits. So too were they tangled together, and once the net of their making had fallen on them, they never ceased winding its strands tighter. In March of 1929, Harry flew to London to buy Caresse a diamond necklace, a thirty-thousand-dollar gift, delivered there by Cartier. And in the summer of that year when she went off to Cannes with Manolo Ortiz he managed not to throw a temper tantrum, but instead seduced her back home: H MINUS C EQUALS O. H PLUS C EQUALS I. I COULD MEET YOUR TRAIN EARLY IN THE MORNING ANYWHERE DARLING. . . . I LOVE ONLY YOU. YOU ARE A DAMN FOOL IF YOU DONT REALIZE IT." He wrote her hot-blooded, coltish letters not commonly received by wives as they approach their seventh anniversary: "I have been feeling very physical. I hope you feel the same way. We don't make love enough. We must make love every day hereafter and more. . . . I wish we were making love together, kissing and kissing. I think we are absolutely and entirely made for each other. I know it. . . . I wish my head was right now between your legs. I love kissing you more than anything in the world. I am all strong and excited thinking about it I kiss you and kiss you and kiss you."

One rival especially stuck in Harry's craw. Armand de la Rochefoucauld—the current Duc de Doudeauville—was younger than Harry, short and sandy-haired, handsome, a carefree man about town.

His father was president of the Jockey Club, his mother was a Radzi-will, and from her brother he inherited in 1927 the Château d'Ermenon-ville. He was generous, knew everybody in Paris not afflicted by gravity or good sense, and was infatuated with Caresse. In the spring of 1928, that period shortly before Harry met Josephine, Armand invited Caresse and her husband to a party at Ermenonville, less than an hour's drive north of Paris, in the neighborhood of Chantilly and Senlis. Harry reluctantly accepted, and while his wife strolled through the grounds of the château with Armand and his brother Sosthenes, the Vicomte de la Rochefoucauld, and their guests—all in high spirits—he sulked and hid in the library reading *The Green Hat*. When they returned from their walk and were preparing for dinner, Harry abruptly insisted that Caresse leave with him at once. They had driven partway to Paris, when he felt remorse for his disagreeable behavior, and telephoned the château asking if he and Caresse might return. They might indeed, and during the trip back to Ermenonville Harry bought five revolvers, one for each of the male guests. Upon reaching the château, they entered the banquet room, and Harry solemnly presented the men with their pistols. There was a shocked silence even though they all knew, as Caresse put it, "of Harry's fantastic and embarrassing ways." Harry then invited any or all the men to shoot him for his rudeness. They frowned, they muttered, they looked away. Armand grinned, Armand laughed, they all laughed, and Harry had managed another coup de théâtre.

As far back as 1924, Harry had longed for a place where he might find healthful quiet, and some solitude. During July of that year, he wrote Caresse (in America with her mother) that "I have definitely decided that we must within the next year or two move out to the country where we can conserve our health and acquire serenity and work free of distractions as men like Michelangelo did. I hate the artificiality of modern city life. . . ." Having compounded the city's artifice with his own, having sought every kind of complicating dis-traction for the sake of novelty, he now, in 1928, decided that he was losing control of his life with Caresse, and that Something Must Be Done.

Hence, a couple of days after he met Josephine, Harry wrote his mother from Venice that he was recovering his health, which had degenerated during the previous several years. He wanted to find a place near Paris where he and Caresse could rest, and he could work. So no sooner had they returned to France than he wrote his mother telling her that he and Caresse had decided to buy a mill on the edge of the

Forest of Ermenonville, on grounds belonging to Armand de la Roche-foucauld. The Comte's proximity to Caresse created friction, but for the time being Harry was delighted with his decision to take a hide-away from Paris. "It will be nice for quiet," he wrote. It was no such thing; it was a madhouse.

14

"What is it I want?"

—Harry Crosby, on his last birthday

For extravagance, recklessness and impulsiveness, Armand de la Roche-foucauld was Harry's match. One afternoon in July, 1928, while he was showing Harry and Caresse around the nine thousand acres surrounding his château, the three happened upon an ancient and dilapidated mill, its wheel long gone, its courtyard between the stable and towered house grown to weed, the thatched roof of the stable ruined. Armand remarked that Jean-Jacques Rousseau had once lived in it, as well as the magician, mesmerist and alchemist Count Cagliostro. He was moving on to another point of interest when Harry asked if he might buy the place. Without more than a minute's hesitation, Armand agreed. The two men settled on a price, two hundred twenty-dollar gold pieces, and Harry at once wrote home asking his parents to sell some of his stock to pay for it and restore it, to buy furniture, install bathrooms and electricity, and repair the structures of both buildings.

By happy coincidence the letter crossed one from his mother telling him that Mr. Crosby had decided to buy a summer house for Harry and Caresse, preferably on the North Shore, but in France if they insisted. The Crosbys were eager to quiet down their son, and wished to seduce him away from the city at least for weekends and summer holidays. Of course Harry responded warmly to his father's offer, but insisted that he pay for half—"and even then it is an Enormous gift"—of the "Moulin du Soleil," as he had immediately named it.

All seemed well until Harry became entangled in that most potent characteristic of the French: their stubborn worship of real estate. On August 17, Harry received a visit from the Comte and Viscomte de la Rochefoucauld, bringing the sad and embarrassing news that "their mother the Duchesse de Doudeauville cried and cried when she heard they had sold the Moulin. She doesn't mind a bit renting it but she implored them not to sell it." So it was agreed that although Harry had paid in full for the mill, and papers had been signed, he and Caresse would instead rent it for five thousand francs per year—about two hundred dollars at the time—and retain the privilege at the end of each year for twenty years of deciding whether or not they wished to rent it again. They would also pay for all improvements. "Perhaps this way it will be just as well," Harry wrote his mother. "We were absolutely in the right but it would be disagreeable to row unnecessarily. But you can't beat the French in business affairs. They are dreadful." Two years later Caresse was obliged to beat back Armand and Sosthenes' lawyer, who wanted to increase the rent on the place, primarily because Harry in his enthusiasm for it had doubled his rent the previous year as a gesture of gratitude.

The Mill was worth every centime. It was situated at the border of a formal park, where a river came to its end. The grounds were verdant, and wild lilies of the valley filled the fields. On the trip up from Paris, Harry and Caresse passed in season fields gold with barley and wheat. The Mill was surrounded by evergreens, and in the forest at its edge lived deer and wild boar. The forest was oddly quiet—there were few birds thereabouts—and nearby was the mysterious Mer de Sable, a huge sea of gold sand that apparently had risen from the forest floor five centuries before. Poplars that turned bright gold in the fall stood near the mill and stable. The Crosbys had a swimming pool built, and fed it from the mill race. The sound of falling water was constant and reassuring. Harry had an oval track built, and upon this he and his guests raced donkeys just as he had at the hotel in Luxor. He had his own menagerie—a couple of race horses, cockatoos, a ferret, a cheetah, a macaw, a couple of whippets, two carrier pigeons, four donkeys, nine ducks (named One, Two, Three, Four, Five, Six, Seven, Eight, Nine) and a python. The stable was converted at ground level into a huge cobble-floored banquet hall, with a fieldstone fireplace. The hayloft was broken into ten bedrooms, small and simply furnished, each a different color. Above was an attic, its eaves almost at floor level.

Though standing room was limited here, it was snug around the fireplace, and beneath the eaves were cushioned benches covered in natural burlap where guests slouched or could lie down. The room was lit by candles, and there were zebra-skin rugs scattered on its floor. Meals for small parties—or, rarely, for Harry and Caresse alone—were served by Madame Henri, who with her husband had been hired as cook and caretaker, and installed in the tower.

Above the tower rooms was Harry's place of worship, where he went alone to take the sun and reflect upon its meaning. Many rituals were observed. Each morning and evening, in all weathers, he walked a mile into the forest to a signpost, at the Poteau de Perthe, a path intersection. He had carved a wooden sun at the sign's apex, and this he touched, and then said a prayer. In winter with his walking stick he might cut the Crosby cross in the snow, saying prayers as he did. Intoning his prayers from the Sun Tower, he would wear a silk robe that held symbolic significance for him, and the gold belt that Constance had given him. He would drink a ritual cup of wine from the counterfeit Byzantine vessel of gold he had persuaded his mother to buy, and at sunset he would fire a brass cannon brought to France from Manchester-by-the-Sea, where it had been used to start yacht races. And one of his first gestures upon assuming tenancy of the Mill was to install on its tower a marble headstone he had commissioned. With the highest elevation at the Mill, the spot received—back and front—the day's first and last rays, and was inscribed with the Crosby cross, the birth dates of Caresse and himself, and their death date, too: October 31, 1942.

Salvador Dali, a frequent visitor to the Mill, described a representative weekend there: "We ate in the horse stable, filled with tiger skins and stuffed parrots. There was a sensational library on the second floor and also an enormous quantity of champagne cooling, with sprigs of mint, in all the corners, and many friends, a mixture of surrealists and society people who came there because they sensed from afar that it was in this Moulin du Soleil that 'things were happening.' "

So that the Mill, meant to have been bucolic, was usually raucous, almost hysterical. One summer day in 1929, Harry recorded what the place was like. He had awakened hung over to find himself beneath a zebra skin, and walked alone to the sun-post in the forest, "a little battered from the riot of last night." Then he had taken a cold bath, and lay naked in the sun "listening to the shouts and cries in the court below where people were playing ping-pong and riding the donkeys or throwing arrowdarts at the target. More people for luncheon and more champagne and Maisie-Mouse standing on the ping-pong table while we played a match under the archway of her legs. . . . Then a fast drive to Chantilly Mortimer leading the way in his Chrysler and drinks at the Manor House . . . and so back to the Moulin. Hordes of people and a riot. . . ." Next day, the entry is a single, brave declaration: "New Every Morning."

More of the same every day—and everywhere, Harry might more accurately have written. On his birthday that same month people began to arrive again, the gang of painters and gamblers and idlers that Harry called generically "royalty," because Caresse had begun to busy herself collecting people with titles or, better yet, hopeless claims to thrones. As he listened from the tower to the people laughing below, he noticed that he was "bored and very restless. What is it I want? Who is it I want to sleep with? Why do I hate society? Thirty-one."

In his capacity as president of the Jockey Club, Armand's father would come down to the Mill to judge the races. The donkeys provided many amusements. Armand recalls the celebration of the mating of Castor with Sunrise, attended by much braying and the presence of Prince George of England, who bathed with a lady friend before joining the mob for a harem-scarem chase from the Mill to the château in a stagecoach pulled by Sosthenes' new Chrysler, but, Harry wrote, "not without twice crashing us into a tree and there was a great ringing of bells and a firing off of cannon from the top of the coach. . . ." Afterward the mob took dinner at the mill, with "Prince George signing GEORGE on the wall. . . ."

There was much signing of names. Douglas Fairbanks signed on the wall of the stable when he came to the Mill with Mary Pickford, who told people's fortunes. Fairbanks wore white spats and an "immaculate" overcoat, and in this costume he swung on a rope from the hayloft into the courtyard and back, amazing people, who applauded. The silliest incidents amazed them, and the most consequential made them, like Harry on his birthday, "bored and very restless." The Pickford-Fairbanks afternoon fell in October, a beautiful, still time at Ermenonville. Harry drove his Voisin to a nearby château "with the cut-out wide open. I nearly ran the car into the moat coming round the corner. . . ." Back at the mill, "I jumped into the swimming pool with all my clothes on. . . ." Why? It couldn't have amused him.

One night he knocked back a couple of bottles of champagne, and then danced and shouted and branded himself with coals hot from the fire before passing out beneath a zebra skin. His potential for violence was always evident, if usually controlled. Another day he shot a pheasant from his bathroom window. It seemed like a good idea at the time. He won two hundred dollars from Armand and Princess Indira playing baccarat: "After the game I bought from Armand . . . for one dollar the Queen of Hearts and when everyone had gone I burnt it in the fire symbol of her burning up in my heart and we all drank champagne the aviator was there and a literary critic from London . . . and as we were about to leave for Paris I found a magnum bottle in the corner that was still half full so for good luck I poured it over and rubbed it into my hair as I used to rub sand from the beach into my hair before going back to school only for another and a more sentimental reason that of preserving a few fold grains of that beach which in those days repre- sented all that I knew of happiness and love."

Sometimes Fairbanks and Pickford were not at the Mill, nor the Powels and de Geeteres, nor the Maharanee of Cooch Behar: "C and I were left alone together. What a relief!" A rare circumstance, and the date is worth recording: June 16, 1929, a few minutes after Max Ernst and Ortiz had left, together with "the usual raft of royalty." At such times the Crosbys would smoke a few pipes of opium together, to help sleep come, and read or write. Or perhaps Harry would absorb himself in a horse-race game of his invention, the Bedroom Stakes he called it, or sometimes the Frivolity Stakes.

Harry was beguiled by Armand, and perhaps it was for this reason that he reacted so violently to Caresse's affection for their neighbor and landlord. One day Harry stayed in Paris while Caresse went for the afternoon to the Mill. She had not returned by early morning, so he swallowed an opium pill, wrapped himself in a sweater and polo coat, and called a taxi to take him to Ermenonville. When he arrived at 3:00 A.M. and saw the Voisin, but no sign of his wife, he fired off the cannon. Presently, Caresse and Armand drove up together in Armand's car, "and I was so angry I said nothing and walked across the courtyard without saying a word and said to the chauffeur retournez à Paris and so drove back to Paris (it didn't seem a second no one on the road and the opium pill taking effect) and he let me down at the Pont Saint- Michel (time four a.m.) and I went down on the quays and curled up and fell asleep and when I woke up it was dawn. . . ."

They weathered that storm, and Harry spent the following after- noon with the Sorceress, drinking and lunching at the Ritz. But six weeks afterward they quarreled again about Armand, and Caresse started to jump out a window of 19 rue de Lille: "It happened so quickly that I hardly had time to be frightened but now three hours later I am really frightened I hope I don't dream about it." (For years he had suffered from nightmares, but now he dreamed only about his girls.) "Finally a miraculous coming together again and I guess I was jealous (I know damn well I was) and now we are wholly in love again." The following day he picked up a new girl at the races.

Harry was jaded that summer of 1929. He spent a day wandering around Paris, hunting for diversions: "I paid one franc to see a woman whose mother slept with an ourang-outang (she was covered with coarse hair and monstrous welts—she kept combing the hair on her legs with a red comb I was alone in the tent and felt very self-conscious) and another franc to see a liontamer insert his head between the jaws of a lion while a man beat on a drum and the crowd applauded. Quel metier!"

Then, in his passion for novelty, he decided—on August 1, 1929— to take leave of the earth, to learn to fly. "I do know how to fly in the final and real sense of the word that is in soul flights to the Sun but now I want to learn also in the Lindbergian sense of the word and I swear on my gold necklace . . . to add to my names of lunatic and lover and poet the name of aviator for as Shakespeare would say if he were alive these four names 'are of imagination all compact' and to-day I read in the White Devil what must be for me prophetic:

> *Of all deaths the violent death is best*
> *For from ourselves it steals ourselves so fast*
> *The pain once apprehended is quite past."*

Caresse increasingly passed her time in tears. She could not understand Harry any more. There was, for example, his curious affection for Goops. Gerhard W. Pohlman had transferred into Harry's ambulance section as a mechanic two days after the terror at Verdun, when Spud Spaulding had been wounded and Harry for a few minutes had imagined himself dead. No sooner had Goops, or Goopy, met Harry than he declared him the "greatest boy I have ever known." He was a rough, raffish character, ten years older than Harry, a chauffeur for New York Mayor Jimmy Walker before the war (while Walker was still a young hustler) and a wheel man for gangsters. There were rumors that Goops had killed a man, or several, and he took no pains to dispel such stories. He cleaned and tuned Harry's ambulance out of affection for him, and let the boy tease him. Tote Fearing recalls him as a congenital drunk, and a dangerous fellow. The lieutenant leading the section at Verdun was considered a coward by many of the men, and by all of them a damned fool, and one day Goops asked him to please put his thumb on a tire lug he was adjusting. He then hit the lieutenant's thumb as hard as he could with a lug wrench, broke it, apologized, and welcomed a new lieutenant into the section. Following the war, Goops described himself to Caresse: "You know I am very hot-headed and don't give a damn what I say when I am mad. It don't do me any good, but I'm not running for alderman, so to hell with them."

Pohlman returned to New York after the war, and worked as a mechanic, hotel night clerk, cabdriver, what have you. Harry had come to love him for his verve and reckless candor, and they corresponded. When he came home to marry Caresse, he took the time to look up his old friend and drink with him. In his turn, Goops gave the newlyweds a lottery ticket for a case of whiskey, and made Harry the beneficiary of his thousand-dollar U.S. Army life insurance policy, which he insisted be spent on strong drink, should he die before Harry. When Harry returned to America in the autumn of 1928, he again tracked Goops down and spent a drunken night with him. In the course of the evening Harry mentioned a wealthy cousin living in Baltimore, an old lady whose death was eagerly anticipated for the money it would provide. Goops offered to grease her way to heaven, and Harry asked how he would do it. Goops said he required only the lady's name and address, one hundred dollars and Harry's approval, and the job was as good as done. He proposed to poison her milk. Harry laughed, thinking it a joke, or perhaps *not* thinking it a joke, wrote his cousin's name and address on a scrap of paper, and forgot the matter.

Six months later Harry sent Goops one hundred dollars to buy a ticket to France. Goops mistook his benefactor's purpose, went immediately to Baltimore, hired an accomplice, and cased the old lady's apartment. They had problems, he wrote Harry some days later: ". . . it seems there had been a couple of robberys and there were plenty of cops about in the early hours." He had some good news, however: "Gossip has it that it won't be long now. All the time I was there, never left the house has bright's disease and belly trouble. . . . Shall leave again tomorrow night and try to get my brain working, which I do not believe possible after reading your mad queen. [Harry had sent him some of his verse.] That is a great brain softener. . . . I am so anxious to see you again, who are all I have in the world."

Harry decided that it was past time to call Goops off the case, and wired him to forget the murder and come to France. Which Goops did, after spending his passage money on whiskey. He worked his way across on the *Waukegan*, jumped ship in Belgium and sneaked into France on October 9, 1929. No sooner had he arrived in Paris than he drank two bottles of red wine and passed out at 19 rue de Lille. Caresse was not charmed by Harry's friend, and Polleen thought he "smelled like a badger, he never washed. I'm sure he slept under the bridges, and things like that. For some reason Harry thought he was engaging, and had him around." Harry offered him a job as a kind of watchman-foreman-court jester at the Mill, and Goops took it gladly.

Unbeknownst to Harry, one week after his arrival in France, Goops wrote his benefactor's father in Boston, whom he knew by virtue of a visit from Mr. Crosby after the war to thank Goops for having looked after his boy and his ambulance:

> . . . Am taking the liberty of writing you, to give my impressions. Since our first meeting twelve years ago [Harry and I] have always corresponded with each other, but I have always been interested to know just what [Harry] was doing. Since my arrival I have found out that he is not playing about, like the majority of Americans in Paris but really working hard. . . . Most Americans here, one can divide into three classes, The first have money and hit the bright lights, The seconde are bamboons who think they can write or paint, The third class are those who buy a Chateau, dream that they were well born, and have a lot of numskull foot-men, following them about, like Scotland Yard follows Crooks. Harry is different, he's all wrapped up in his literary work, not even stopping for lunch. . . . He plays as hard as he works, last Sunday had quite a large party here. At six in the morning he shot a Pheasant then played donkey Polo the rest of the morning. In the afternoon a large number of visitors arrived. There were more Barons and Vicomtes here than Mayflower descendants in Boston on a Holy Day. i.e. every days a holy day in Boston. . . . In all it was a distinguist Company, some of whose ancestors had been arrested for major crimes before Columbus'es crew signed articles. . . . I hope this letter will find you in the best of health, and I have never forgotten your visit to me at Romagne in 1921. I have had but few kindnesses done me in my life, and that is the outstanding one. I have taken a paternal interest in Harry since we first met at Belrupt, Verdun, and rest assured no harm will ever come to him if I can prevent it.

The letter was written from the Mill, on stationery bearing the Crosby cross. After Stephen Crosby had received it and digested it, he wrote his son, asking to be told what in the hell Harry thought he was doing with his life.

Harry was doing too much with his life: flying, drinking, praying, staring at the sun, abusing himself with drugs, mastering all three rings at the Mill, writing, writing every day. Busy, useful people were sometimes attracted to the Mill, and enjoyed it as a retreat rather than a carnival. On April 3, 1929, Harry entertained Frieda and D. H. Lawrence, who had come to be sculpted by Caresse, and Aldous Huxley. And on Easter Sunday, Lawrence read by the fire a story about the imaginary wanderings of Jesus after his resurrection, during which he met a priestess of Isis along the coast of Phoenicia, and they lived together, a missing link in the story of Christ. At once Harry begged to print *The Escaped Cock*—no one else dared—and for a short time there was harmony between the Crosbys and Lawrences because of the spell cast by the Mill. But noise undid it. One night Frieda sat alone in a corner, listening again and again to Bessie Smith's "Empty Bed Blues," which Lawrence so despised. Finally her husband erupted and smashed the record across Frieda's head. Harry immediately promised to replace the record, and to buy Frieda a phonograph to play it upon. So he did—and Lawrence never forgave the kindness.

Mai de Geetere sketched in watercolors several scenes from a weekend during that same April. One shows two donkeys, the cannon, the whippets, and Harry's camera pointed at the sun and at guests' bare crotches. Another shows Caresse gardening, and Harry playing donkey polo. Another shows Harry in bed, with sunken cheeks and crazy eyes, looking down and inward, close to tears or catatonia. This picture is captioned thus: "I can't give you anything but lo—v-e ba—b—y!! Dream awhile, scream a—while!!"

15

"I the Assassin chosen by the Mad Queen I the Murderer of
the World shall in my fury murder myself. I shall cut out my
heart take it into my joined hands and walk towards the Sun
without stopping until I fall down dead."

—Harry Crosby, "Assassin"

"Presently a rabbit flashed gray across the road, right under
our wheels. . . . Crosby stopped the car and we had to spend
a quarter of an hungry hour or more examining the road, and
edges of the forest which it ribboned, to discover the wounded
animal. The cruelty of leaving it to a lingering death was, to
Crosby, inconceivable."

—Stuart Gilbert, recollecting Harry Crosby

Transit of Venus—for Josephine—was Harry's third book published in 1928, and again (as with each of his books, coming in some
instances only a couple of months apart), he tried out the new forms
and ideas that he had developed or absorbed since writing his previous
book. He was whipsawed between his determination to construct,
symbol by symbol, a coherent personal cosmogony and his need—
much in the spirit of the day—to outrun fashion, to every morning
make himself and his work new. Thus the poem "Altazimuth," with its
"trigonometrical surveys," "chronometers" and "ultra-violet rays" is an
old-fashioned metaphysical poem yet brand-new for Harry, who had
never before tried to translate the unpoetic language of science into

poetry, and who had recently come upon John Donne for the first time.

If Harry may by now be said to have developed a style, it is one of ellipsis, arrest, stuttering hesitation and the diverted utterance. "Kiss," in part because it is brief and in part because the goal of its exclamation is there for the reader to comprehend, has both suspense and vitality: Will he reach it? the poem inquires, and races toward

> *This blessed fruit, this,*
> *This goodly red,*
> *This fire, this O, this*
> *This is the last of*
> *This kiss.*

Murder, suicide and a concentrated, deadly manner have dispelled the sun in most of these poems. The poet's voice is icy rather than frenzied, and every trace of the Decadent influence upon him has been expunged. The poet is found "shipwrecked," and "in the rain"; he is outcast and scorned. Harry, one of them, knows he has earned his letter: "we poets in our desire. . . ." Indeed, he was confirmed in this by a letter from Archibald MacLeish, responding warmly to these poems: "I think you have got hold of something valuable in *Transit of Venus*. I think also that the valuable thing you have got hold of (and this is almost always the case) is a by-product of the thing you were most after. To be precise I am not convinced that your device of the incompleted phrase is what you want. It gives you some good effects but it is very voulu. . . . On the other hand you hit upon a kind of true brevity in those and other poems. And that brevity is signed with your name." (The kind of coherent urgency Harry achieved in some of these poems cannot be counterfeited. Here is a man stammering because there is not time enough to finish what he must say, and the interruptions are both dramatic and movingly authentic.) MacLeish singles out half a dozen verses for high praise, calling one "a good poem . . . on any scale," writing of "the fine Shakespearean run" of another. He concludes: "I think you have learned the smell of your own flesh. I think you should be well satisfied. . . ." (Harry wrote in his notebook: "Praise from a man like MacLeish means something I should rather have a sincere word from him than a thousand and one laudatory effusions from the average critic for the average critic always reminds me of the man who said that he was never intensely excited (sexually) except when a spectator at a funeral.")

Since T. S. Eliot's funereal preface to *Transit of Venus* was not commissioned by Caresse till 1930, his equivocation might be explained by the principle *de mortuis nil nisi bonum*, or by Caresse's generosity. But no: Eliot was neither weepy for a dead man nor bought by a widow. It is unsettling to discover this most lucid of critics waffling and hedging: "I doubt whether we can ever understand the poetry of a contemporary, especially if we are engaged in writing ourselves." (This is simply not so.) Like Lawrence, Eliot many times clears his throat before closing with his subject: "When I first read some of his poems I concluded merely that he was a young man in a hurry." But Eliot distinguishes between a young man in a hurry to reach destinations others have reached before him—Harry chasing after Baudelaire, say, or Rimbaud—and a poet in a different sort of hurry. The Harry of *Transit of Venus*, Eliot writes, "was in a hurry, I think, because he was aware of a direction, and ignorant of the destination, only conscious that time was short and the terminus a long way off." Eliot admitted that he had no idea what Harry "was up to"; nor did he think he would appreciate it if he did know. But he admired Harry's vitality, and the risks he ran. "What I do like, in a serious sense, is the fact that Crosby was definitely going his own way, whether I like the way or not."

Mad Queen, Harry's first book of 1929, is a collection of tirades, some loose-footed verses and some prose poems. In them all, he is after speed and surprise; he tries to set off explosions, to shock and mortify, and, of course, to draw attention to himself. In a self-portrait called "Heliograph," a title he used for several different works, the narrator at first whines about his "standardized American childhood" passed on an oddly "sunless" desert, "flat and undisturbed."

> War and Violence. Catapults and Torches and the first stray thrusts of Sun into the Soul. Bombardments and Bordels. Heraldry and High Walls. Too rigid to crumple but not too strong to fracture. . . .

What a line! "Too rigid to crumple but not too strong to fracture." It is perhaps the single instance in which Harry perfectly understands himself. Rigid and fractured: Harry Crosby. Not bent, but cracked. Then:

> The Primitive Method of strengthening the soul by dropping red-hot sunstones into it. Rimbaud and Van Gogh. Counterattack. Turbulence. Chariot of the Sun.

The Mad Queen, The violent state of fusion. Her Sun tattooed on my
back. Multiplication of Madness. Anarchism. I lay Siege to the Sun. . . .

The most extended work in this volume is "Assassin," a sometimes
brutal, sometimes suicidal, sometimes visionary poem of more than a
hundred lines, with a prose introduction of several pages. The setting is
Constantinople on the "Seventeenth of the Month of Ramadan. It is
cold and late at night winter darkness with a cold hard wind hurricane-
ing across the Bosphorus." Harry was there. On the way home to Paris
from Egypt, the Crosbys had stopped over in Constantinople, primarily
to visit the United States ambassador, Harry's cousin, Joseph Clark
Grew. Ambassador Grew, a distinguished career officer in the Foreign
Service, was eighteen years older than Harry, athletic, tall, urbane, a bit
deaf, not in the least self-conscious. Two dispatches from wire services
in Turkey, clipped and saved by Harry, attest to his cousin's poise and
courage. One tells of his saving a couple from a burning automobile:
the other cries his praise for having jumped into the Bosphorus from a
ferryboat to rescue an ancient, veiled Turkish lady, who nevertheless
died.

Harry was intimidated by the Ambassador ("a gentleman in the
fullest sense of that distorted word, good-looking, intelligent, artistic
(he loves poetry and music and plays the piano). . . ."), and rather than
spend time with him he took Caresse to a whorehouse to watch a
couple make love: "I don't see how they did it the room was so damn
cold and they stark naked and for me at least it was a chaste spectacle
like two strong flowers curling and uncurling. . . ." On March 17, "the
Seventeenth of the Month of Ramadan," Harry implored a junior officer from the embassy to take him and Caresse outside the walls of the
city to watch Kurdish shepherds dance their wild, violent celebrations
in a huge tent. The Crosbys ate some hashish, and pressed it also upon
the young American. Then, while they watched the Kurds, and later
joined their dance, they all ate opium pills, and, back in the city,
washed down the adventure with a few bottles of champagne.

The following morning Harry was sick: "Seriously frightened and
there were colors exploding suns within suns and cataracts of gold and
I felt cold and trembled as if I had the ague and had a terrible time
getting dressed my brain in a maelstrom and a fear of falling forwards."
He looked up the antidotes for poison in a traveler's handbook, drank
cup after cup of strong coffee and begged Caresse not to let him pass
out. Then the young embassy officer's valet called to say that the
young man was seriously ill and couldn't be awakened. Harry thought

to go to the rescue of last night's friend, but instead instructed his valet "to administer hot stimulants and to keep him awake." Then the Crosbys left their suites at the Hotel Pera Palas and went to the embassy to say goodbye to the Ambassador, who provided his car to take them to the railroad station, "the Stars and Stripes crackling in the wind from the left front mud guard (a delicate attention in our honor). . . ."

Once on the Orient Express, Harry felt the sun boring deeper and deeper into the target on his back, "and everything was violent—a flock of birds became a flock of comets the telegraph poles were women burning at the stake the clickety click of the train going over the rails was the bursting of firecrackers. Suddenly a sharp severing of a cord 'the flash of what a tongue could never tell' the sudden touching of a match and my head cracked open and I explode into Sun." At that moment Harry experienced, probably for the first time, the madness he had courted for so long. It released him from something painful, and so he sought it again, never ceasing from then on to seek the "sharp severing of a cord."

"Assassin" is Harry's transformation of his experience in Constantinople into a vision of himself, and the vision is nihilistic and cruel. The work begins with a sharp-edged dreamlike exercise in the surreal, nonetheless grounded in the chronology and setting of Harry's night with the Kurdish shepherds. "We [others not identified; they rarely are in Harry's poems, since they are attendants upon his wishes rather than participants in his actions] are outside the walls. There is a feeling of emptiness like a night at the front during the War. A sharp turn over cobblestones the jarring of brakes and we are climbing out shivering into the wind. . . . We are standing before an enormous tent. A call and a sharp answer and a hand tearing open the flap as the wind tears out a strip of camouflage." The dancers dance, and the narrator eats hashish. There follows a second section in prose which dryly gives the derivation of the word "assassin" as the Arabic *hashshāshīn*, hashish eaters: Ismaili sectaries would intoxicate themselves with hashish in preparation for the ritual slaying of Christians at the time of the Holy Wars, and Harry explains that the drug induces megalomania in its most violent manifestation. "In this poem the Sun-Goddess, or Mad Queen as I shall call her, has replaced the Sheik and I am the Assassin she has chosen for her devices."

The poem begins:

> *The Mad Queen commands:*
> *Murder the sterility and hypocrisy of the world, destroy the weak*

and insignificant, do violence to the multitude in order that a new strong world shall arise to worship the Mad Queen, Goddess of the Sun.

After a couple of stanzas of place-setting, there then follows a section titled "Vision," which recovers the actual circumstances of Harry's morning-after in Constantinople:

> *I exchange eyes with the Mad Queen*
>
> > *the mirror crashes against my face and*
> *bursts into a thousand suns*
> > *all over the city flags crackle and bang*
> > *fog horns scream in the harbor*
> > *the wind hurricanes through the window*
> > *and I begin to dance the dance of the*
> *Kurd Shepherds . . .*
> > *I crash out through the*
> > *window, naked, widespread*
> > *upon a*
> > > *Heliosaurus*
> > *I uproot an obelisk and plunge*
> > *it into the ink-pot of the*
> *Black Sea*
> > *I write the word*
> > > *S U N*
> > *across the dreary palimpsest*
> > *of the world*
> > *I pour the contents of the*
> > *Red Sea down my throat*
> > *I erect catapults and*
> > *lay siege to the cities of the world*
> > *I scatter violent disorder*
> > *throughout the kingdoms of the world*
> > *I stone the people of the world*
> > *I stride over mountains*
> > *I pick up oceans like thin cards*
> > *and spin them into oblivion*
> > *I kick down walled cities*
> > *I hurl giant firebrands against governments*
> > *I thrust torches through the eyes of the law*
> > > *I annihilate museums*
> > > *I demolish libraries*
> > > *I oblivionize skyscrapers*
> > *I become hard as adamant*

Constance, Comtesse de Jumilhac ("the Lady of the Golden Horse"). *(With permission of André Magnus)*

Harry at The Apple Trees in his Bugatti, July, 1926.

Harry, with unidentified girl, at Four Arts Ball, Paris: "Two or three hours more and then Pandemonium begins. The house is stripped like a destroyer for action—sackcloth over the walls and chairs and bookcases and the champagne and brandy have arrived and the Rumpelmayer man has arrived and Lord L has arrived from England. It really is too hectic and I think this will be our last Four Arts. We are getting too old..." —Harry to his mother, June, 1928

Baron Hanäel de Voight ("Alastair"): "He lived in a sort of *Fall of the House of Usher* house, you know, with bleak, hideous trees drooping around the doors and windows—we always suspected him of having them trimmed to look that way ... On the night when we came first to see him, a blackamoor ushered us into a room where there was a black piano with a single candle burning on it. Soon Alastair himself appeared in the doorway in a white satin suit; he bowed, did a flying split and slid across the polished floor to stop at my feet, where he looked up and said, 'Ah Mrs. Crosby!'"
(With permission of the Morris Library, Southern Illinois University)

August, 1927, at Brest, aboard *Aphrodesiac* with Gretchen Powel (in cockpit between Caresse and Harry) and Pete (in stern). The boat leaked, and was hospitable to fleas. *(With permission of the Morris Library, Southern Illinois University)*

Henrietta Crosby, her son and Caresse at the Temple of Baalbek, winter of 1928.

Caresse, in Paris, spring of 1928.

Portrait of Harry Crosby, by Polia Chentoff, December, 1927: "One must be born and die in the same picture..." —Miss Chentoff, quoted by her subject. After Harry's death, Caresse burned this portrait, so deeply did it disturb her peace.

Caresse, drawn by a friend, Angeles Ortiz, 1928. (*With permission of the Morris Library, Southern Illinois University*)

Josephine Rotch Bigelow ("the Fire Princess").

"Jacqueline," Harry's mystery mistress, to whom he left a bequest from his estate. His deepest love. Harry bought the etching, "Valkulla," by Anders Zorn, from James Connell and Sons, Ltd., Old Bond Street, London, for £125. He had searched years for it till he tracked it down early in 1929, and gave it to Harvard upon his death. *(With permission of the Fogg Art Museum, Harvard University)* #M5047

Harry (note black flower) with Caresse, Narcisse Noir and sister Kitsa, on beach at Deauville when Kitsa announced her divorce from Robert Choate. *(With permission of the Morris Library, Southern Illinois University)*

Harry (in Walter Berry's coat) with Caresse and Clytoris, a mate for Narcisse Noir, at Le Bourget, 1928, following a cross-Channel flight. At the wheel of the Crosbys' Voisin is the last of their many chauffeurs, Auguste, like the others a heavy drinker, but unlike the others, amusing to Harry. *(With permission of the Morris Library, Southern Illinois University)*

Harry with Stephen V. R. Crosby, and a skull stolen from the Catacombs: Paris, 1928. *(With permission of Sylvia Choate Whitman)*

Le Moulin du Soleil from an etching of the eighteenth century, when Jean Jacques Rousseau was in residence. *(With permission of the Morris Library, Southern Illinois University)*

Harry at the Mill, with a raft of royalty and Caresse (on donkey at left) and Mai de Geetere (also on donkey).

Harry at the Mill with Kay Boyle, 1929. (*With permission of the Morris Library, Southern Illinois University*)

Harry, moments after his first solo flight, Armistice Day, 1929, Villacoublay. *(With permission of Stuart Kaiser)*

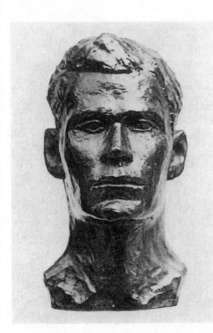

The head of Harry Crosby, sculpted by Caresse. From the frontispiece of her book *Poems for Harry Crosby*, published shortly after his death.

indurated in solid fire
rigid with hatred . . .
I am the harbinger of a
New Sun World
I bring the Seed of a
*   New Copulation*
I proclaim the Mad Queen

I stamp out vast empires
I crush palaces in my rigid
*   hands*
I harden my heart against
*   churches*

I blot out cemeteries
I feed the people with
stinging nettles
I resurrect madness
I thrust my naked sword
between the ribs of the world
I murder the world!

Admittedly it is not fitting to confuse a poem with a poet. A man performing a ritual does not expect his audience to deduce that his odd motions, habits and chants are natural to him—that they are other than a performance of which he is merely the premeditating and stylizing instrument. But "Assassin" is less a poem than a testament, and its art is almost overwhelmed by its pathology. Were it to end here, however, it would stand only as a perfect text for demons ancient and modern, a call to the perverse ecstasy of destruction, murder, backward sex and upside-down religion. But it does not end here:

I the Assassin chosen by the Mad Queen I the Murderer of the World shall in my fury murder myself. I shall cut out my heart take it into my joined hands and walk towards the Sun without stopping until I fall down dead.

A companion piece to "Assassin," titled "Sun-Death," is Harry's most explicit warning of his purpose. It begins with a catalogue of distinguished suicides: Diogenes, Socrates, Sappho, Brutus, Cassio, Cato, Dido, Cleopatra, Samson, Jesus (by Harry's reckoning self-martyred), Modigliani, Van Gogh, many more, among them the members of the Suicide Club, who drew lots each year in Paris to

decide whose turn had come to die. The prose piece harangues its
readers: "Go to Van Gogh, you sluggards, consider his ways and be
wise." The narrator quotes Nietzsche—"Die at the right time"—and
proceeds to describe the right time: "when your entire life, when your
soul and your body, your spirit and your senses are concentrated, are
reduced to a pin-point, the ultimate gold point, the point of finality,
irrevocable as the sun, sun-point, then is the time, and not until then,
and not after then (o horrors of anticlimax from which there is no
recovering) for us to penetrate into the cavern of the sombre Slave-
Girl of Death, to enjoy explosion with the sombre Slave-Girl of Death,
in order to be reborn, in order to become what you wish to become,
tree or flower or star or sun, or even dust and nothingness. . . ." This
violent end is a privilege denied "the majority . . . the stupid Philistines,
whose lives have always been a whimper, whose lives could never be
anything else but a whimper, whose lives must inevitably end with a
whimper, they who prefer senility, who prefer putrefaction of the
brain, who prefer hypocrisy, sterility, imbecility (do not confound with
madness) impotence, to the strength and fury of a Sun-Death dead
bodies and dead souls dumped unceremoniously into the world's la-
trine. . . ."

Had Harry Crosby walked the streets of Boston, or even Paris,
muttering his message or crying it aloud, he would have fallen under
the protective influence of the law. Had he declamed his judgment on
society and himself from a street corner soapbox, or delivered it from a
pulpit, society would have taken steps to protect itself from the menace
of his lunacy. Had he scribbled "Sun-Death" on sandwich boards, and
worn it, he would have been placed in society's custody. Had he repeated it to a state-appointed psychiatrist, he would have been certified
mad, just as he wished himself to be mad. But how the world honors
and indulges its poets! Even its self-certified poets: let the same threats
and tirades be set in type, and pathology becomes art. The poet, of
course, pays a price for the indulgence of society, for by permitting
him his free play of ideas, society treats his ideas as mere play. *He
doesn't mean it*, society says; *he's just being literary*. Harry meant it.

At a time when art was the chief secular religion, and multitudes
kissed the poet's hem, the little magazine *Transition*—where "Sun-
Death" first appeared beneath the title "Hail: Death!"—was a kind of
Holy Book. *Transition* was conceived, supported financially and edited
by Eugene Jolas, born in New Jersey of a French father and German
mother, and brought up in Lorraine. In his teens, he returned to the

United States and worked at menial jobs, finally settling as a newspaper reporter. He became equally fluent and articulate in English, German and French, and a devotee of the avant-garde in the arts of all Western nations, but particularly the experimental literature of America, Germany and France. With his tall and handsome wife Maria McDonald—from Kentucky, and trained as an opera singer—he returned to France as a reporter and became the city editor of the Paris edition of the Chicago *Tribune*. By living frugally and saving money, in the spring of 1927 he realized his dream of publishing a magazine of the arts. The first issue appeared in April and contained work by Gertrude Stein, Kay Boyle, Archibald MacLeish and, among others, André Gide, as well as James Joyce's *Work in Progress*, later to be titled *Finnegans Wake*. *Transition* appeared monthly for a year, then quarterly thereafter, a bulky magazine running to as many as three hundred pages. (With occasional interruptions, it lasted till 1938.) In its first year alone, contributors from seventeen countries were represented, reflecting Jolas' wide range of acquaintanceship and his ambition to help the arts cross national frontiers.

With a customary print run of three or four thousand, and many times as many readers, *Transition* printed work by Dylan Thomas, Samuel Beckett, Lawrence Durrell, Paul Bowles, Ernest Hemingway, Hart Crane, the French Surrealists, Italian Futurists, German Expressionists—seemingly everyone. It printed reproductions of the art of Paul Klee, Max Ernst, Man Ray, di Chirico and dozens more, and its covers were the creations of artists such as Marcel Duchamp, Pablo Picasso, Jean Arp and Joan Miró. Contributors were paid thirty francs per page, a bit more than a dollar, yet even this put a severe strain on the finances of the Jolases. To save money they moved to a rambling and run-down hunting lodge (later bought by Charles de Gaulle, who cherished and lived in it during the last years of his life) in Colombey-les-Deux-Églises, a village of fewer than one hundred people in the *département* of Haute-Marne. They rented it for one hundred and sixty dollars per year.

Caresse's unannounced visit in the company of Narcisse Noir to *Transition*'s offices at 40 rue Fabert was the first contact between the Crosbys and the Jolases.

Eugene Jolas had seen Harry's preface to Frans de Geetere's illustrations of *Les Chants de Maldoror*, and was eager to have a translation from him of some other work of Lautréamont, whose revolutionary literary program—like Rimbaud's and Baudelaire's—appealed to Jolas' rebellious impulses. At about this time, in the late autumn of 1927, Harry wrote Jolas with a generous offer: "I have inherited a little money, and if you approve, I would like to send you one hundred dollars (strictly anonymous) for you to send to the poet who in your judgment has written the best poem in the first twelve numbers of *Transition*. But for God's sake, don't make a prize out of it. Instead of going to some fathead organization, I should like this small amount to go to someone who will spend it on cocktails and books rather than on church sociables and lemonade. If you accept this, please forget it as quick as possible."

The two men soon met, and became friends. Jolas was a heavy drinker, but he was also stocky and powerful, and his energy was high. Modest in his own behalf, he was fanatically committed to the careers and reputations of the writers, especially Joyce, he believed belonged in *Transition*. Many of his friends remark what a good listener he was, and ideas, especially new ones, excited him passionately. He opened the pages of *Transition* to such an eclectic bunch—Futurists and Dadaists, Surrealists and Expressionists—that his own convictions might have been lost in the roil were it not for their urgency. He believed that language had atrophied and must be re-created, in the way that Joyce and, to a lesser degree, Stein were building a new vocabulary and syntax. He believed in the magic of dreams, that they were creations ("paramyths," he called them) of great value, messages from the subconscious. The strongest if not strangest of his faiths was in something he called "vertigralism" (a portmanteau word combining *vertical* and *grail*), "the intuitive reaching towards the above." The vertigralist "will participate in the collective consciousness of the universe" and will penetrate into the "world soul."

As though this were not sufficient attraction for Harry, who also believed in the power of his night words, who through powered flight and his worship of the sun was, he *knew*, "reaching towards the above," *Transition*'s associate editor was a novelist named Elliot Paul, born to a prominent Boston family, thumbing his nose at his hometown and its conventions. Once Paul told Jolas that "if I ever go back to Boston, it'll be on a steamer that will stop offshore to let down a raft from which I can jeer at that damned town." Harry showed Jolas and Paul his diary, and at once they wanted to print parts of it. At first he was reluctant, but Jolas—who wrote him that he was haunted by Harry's diary—pressed him, and he began to submit excerpts for publication in 1928. He also submitted many poems, always with an instruction to Jolas to destroy them if he didn't care for them, and to alter them as he wished should he choose to run them.

From late 1928 till his death, most issues of *Transition* had in them pieces by Harry. (Caresse made one contribution, and Pete Powel's photograph of a New York skyscraper was used as a cover; even Goops was commissioned to gather a lexicon of New York underworld slang for publication, a stillborn project.) Jolas was excited by the quality of Harry's writing, sending him frequent letters of encouragement, telling him how impressed Maria Jolas was with *Shadows of the Sun*, telling him what a great human document it was.

Later, he had reservations about Harry's procedures, and told him that he wrote his poems in too uniformly high a key, neglecting the soft pedal and battering unto death the theme of the sun, as well as exhausting images drawn from that theme. However much he might have wished that Harry move on to other facets of human existence, he nevertheless called upon him frequently for contributions. His encouragement was without bounds, and he wrote Harry again and again telling him how superbly he was smashing forward, how confidently he was conquering a unique place in literature, and not merely in the literature of his time, but in Anglo-Saxon literature of The Ages.

Jolas' praise must have unsettled Harry, and it certainly pricked him to write more, and to write quickly. He finished *Sleeping Together* in November of 1929 during, as he admitted in *Shadows of the Sun*, "three or four days but back of it are three or four years of hard work." It was written under the general influence of the Surrealists, whose exercises in the reproduction of dreams and the subconscious fascinated Harry. But an even more direct influence was Jolas, who looked to dreams for the fabulous and the magical, and who regarded them as mythic expressions of the mind akin to the legend and the ballad. *Sleeping Together* is raw material lifted, and left unrefined, from pedestrian dreams. Moreover, there are grounds for a suspicion that the dreams themselves were composed backwards, that Harry first read Freud and Jung, and then created conundrums for their theories to solve.

In addition to Jolas' enthusiasm, Harry had earned his gratitude. At the end of 1928, Harry paid for the printing of an entire issue, and also asked whether Jolas would let the Black Sun Press have something for publication. Accordingly, *Secession in Astropolis*, illustrative dreams and parables of Jolas' mythic theories, appeared the following year. Of Harry's financial generosity, Jolas wrote that he would never forget it, and that he wanted to be Harry's friend, a theme he sounded several times; once, in 1929, he wrote Harry that he would be obliged to fold *Transition* unless someone saved it, and Harry saved it. Two months later, Harry replaced Elliot Paul on the masthead.

It was no mere honorary title. Harry worked hard for the magazine, soliciting manuscripts, translating work from the French, and on one occasion helping to see James Joyce's exhausting proof through printing at the industrial town of Saint-Dizier, a few hours east by car from Paris. Stuart Gilbert, the friend and early explicator of James Joyce, and with Robert Sage and Matthew Josephson also an advisory editor of *Transition*, recalled a trip one summer day to the printer with Harry and his chauffeur, Auguste:

> . . . wraiths of night mist were creeping to blur the pale French roads. Crosby's chauffeur, a dreamer and an incurable collector of [speeding tickets], seemed unable to find his way; we were lost time and time again and Saint-Dizier seemed a mirage on a moonlit horizon. Yet there, we knew, *transition's* galley-pages were impatiently awaiting correction, and we were all rather cold and very hungry. Villages on the way seemed as dead as if the war had traversed them. Benighted peasants grunted misleading counsel. Crosby, seated beside the chauffeur, was content. To have lost the way—that was, I think, to him the best *hors d'oeuvre* for the belated dinner, still far away, the spice of the adventure. Any fool can find his way, a poet alone knows how to lose it. Our hostess had pressed on us a road-map when we were leaving. The writer of these lines—more shame to him!—insisted on stopping to examine the map (like "any fool") by the light of the headlamps. *We had brought the wrong map!* Harry Crosby laughed, like a mischievous child who has taken (as they say in France) the key of the fields and is playing truant. Presently a rabbit flashed grey across the road, right under our wheels. Despite demurs from ravenous materialists, Crosby stopped the car and we had to spend a quarter of an hungry hour or more examining the road, and the edges of the forest which it ribboned, to discover the wounded animal. The cruelty of leaving it to a lingering death was, to Crosby, inconceivable.

When Gilbert had first noticed Harry across the drawing room of a Paris apartment during a party, he was struck at once by his lithe and elegant poise, "but most of all, perhaps, by the curious remoteness of his gaze. . . . He seemed out of place, unseeing, as though his eyes, by some trick of long-sightedness or a queer Roentgen quality of their own, were watching some aerial pageant across the walls, out in the blue beyond. Such aloofness was almost disconcerting at first; 'a difficult man,' one thought, 'and perhaps an arrogant man'. . . . But, when one spoke to him, there was nothing aloof, nothing of arrogance, in Harry Crosby. An expert in the conversational *vol plané*, he could descend without the least gesture of condescension from his eyrie and talk lightheartedly of the latest recipe for cocktails and the dilative influence of limp Parisian ice on their gay Gordon hearts, or of his latest *trouvaille* in New York 'slanguage.' "

Maria Jolas was not attracted to Harry's chaos, but she discerned that his imbalance was "authentic." Caresse, she felt, was not as "genuine," and her responses were more "literary" than Harry's: "You don't call yourself by a name like that," Mrs. Jolas says of Caresse. "She did not interest me." Harry, though, was like an "eager child" in his touching desire "to be included in the writing world," and it would have been "an act of cruelty to slap him down." Besides, "he had talent."

Eugene Jolas, Maria recollects, who was six years older than Harry, treated him like a son or younger brother. He was thoughtful and gentle, sentimental even. Robert McAlmon lampooned Jolas cruelly in *Being Geniuses Together*, portraying him as having "flayed, tantalized, flagellated, and dreamed words all around the various bars of Paris. He had a 'soul,' and he was bewildered, and he sought a religion and an 'answer' in such a way as to make Margaret Anderson appear a cold and practical woman." (McAlmon's low opinion of him did not influence Jolas' high opinion of McAlmon's work, or his determination to publish it.) The portrait is distorted. For one thing, Jolas was a mischief-maker with a sense of fun. He delighted in outraging conventional American critics with the various manifestoes developed in *Transition*, and once wrote Harry that he had just set some more dynamite under their asses. In his unpublished autobiography, *Frontier-Man*, he gave as his literary and journalistic purpose the advertising of the irrational, and the outraging of pedants. He wished to invent new grammars and vocabularies, to bait the Babbitts with paradoxes, and to have fun, above all to have fun.

Perhaps the most notorious of *Transition*'s many and various programs was one called "the Revolution of the Word," which declared among other things that "the literary creator has the right to disintegrate the primal matter of words imposed on him by textbooks and dictionaries"; that "he has the right to use words of his own fashioning and to disregard existing grammatical and syntactical laws"; that "the writer expresses. He does not communicate. The plain reader be damned. (*Damn braces! Bless relaxes* . . . Blake.)"; and that "time is a tyranny to be abolished." The twelve-point manifesto was signed by

Kay Boyle, Caresse, Harry, Stuart Gilbert, Hart Crane, Elliot Paul, Eugene Jolas (twice: once under his name and once under his pen name, Theo Rutra), and several others. Later, Hart Crane told Malcolm Cowley that he was ashamed to have signed it, and was drunk when he did. Jolas himself later wrote that the manifesto, cooked up mostly by himself and by Harry, "was simply an aphoristic expression of my own convictions, an echo of my own concrete experiences," with the floating islands of three native languages, three lexicons, three syntaxes. Harry, however, swallowed "the Revolution of the Word" whole, without a grain of salt, and especially one article of his own devising: "Time is a tyranny to be abolished."

One of the most legendary episodes of the epoch took place on Saturday, June 19, 1926, the date of George Antheil's first performance of his *Ballet Mécanique* at the huge Théâtre des Champs-Élysées, Vladimir Golschmann conducting. Antheil was a very modernist composer indeed, and Ezra Pound's protégé, and among the audience were Pound, T. S. Eliot with the Princess Bassiano and the James Joyces, as well as Constantin Brancusi, Sergei Koussevitsky and a woman dressed in black who bowed in all directions as she took her seat. People whispered that she was a member of royalty; she was, in fact, Sylvia Beach's concierge. The ballet was scored for eight pianos, a player piano, percussion, xylophones, airplane propellers and machines of many kinds, all noisy, and as soon as the ruckus commenced so did a riot: cat-calling and cries of "thief" and "enough, enough!" mixed with applause; people throwing things. Fistfights broke out; and Ezra Pound's "voice was heard above the others'," as Sylvia Beach later recalled, "and someone said they saw him hanging head downward from the top gallery." The noise abruptly ceased as the airplane propellers began to spin, stirring a mighty wind in the hall and blowing the wig off a man seated beside Stuart Gilbert. Harry wrote in his diary afterwards that he had seen, had actually *seen*, James Joyce! "James Joyce, a black band over one eye, the greatest of them all. . . . And I would rather have seen Joyce than any man alive."

Harry had been studying *Ulysses*, using a first edition that he had bought the previous year for one hundred dollars, writing in his notebook Joyce's word coinages. He was determined to meet his idol, and in the spring of 1928 Hemingway introduced them briefly during an Ada MacLeish concert, but it was not till 1929 that Stuart Gilbert made an enduring introduction. Meanwhile, Harry's worship was boundless. He wrote his mother breathlessly that he had recently seen him "from a taxi. . . . He was walking slowly lost in thought (Work in Progress) absolutely unaware of the outside world. Almost a somnambulist." In nearly identical language he recorded the same stirring event in his diary, and added that the distant encounter had "worked in me the same emotion as when Lindbergh arrived. But what is the Atlantic to the Oceans Joyce has crossed?"

On March 4, 1929, Harry and Caresse were taken by Gilbert to Joyce's apartment in a cul-de-sac off the rue de Grenelle. They wanted a portion from *Work in Progress* for the Black Sun Press, and Joyce, having been favorably struck by the press's list, agreed to give them something. Harry presented him with a gift, the huge *Book of the Dead* from Walter Berry's library, and Joyce was almost childishly eager, as Harry put it, to have Picasso draw his portrait for the frontispiece of the Black Sun Press book, which was called *Tales Told of Shem and Shaun.* A month later, a contract was drawn up by Sylvia Beach, who had published *Ulysses* and had Joyce's power of attorney, calling for a payment of two thousand dollars for six hundred copies— one hundred of them signed—of a book containing three fragments already published by *Transition*: "The Mookse and the Gripes," "The Muddest Thick That Was Ever Heard Dump" and "The Ondt and the Gracehoper." Picasso refused Caresse's proposal that he do the portrait; he told her that he was not interested in James Joyce and, besides, never did work by commission. Brancusi, however, agreed to try something, and did a representative sketch, which Joyce liked and Harry and Caresse did not. Whereupon the artist substituted an abstraction, a maze of right angles. Joyce had hoped that Julian Huxley would write an introduction, but settled instead for C. K. Ogden, the creator of Basic English, whose interest in Joyce's linguistic experiments was extreme.

Harry was at the highest pitch of excitement to be working with Joyce, and the two got on well together. Joyce in his near-blindness (he was unable to move about his own apartment without stumbling into furniture) and Harry with his near-sightedness (he wore thick glasses in private, but would not be seen in them) shared an eye doctor who had recently died, and they talked of him, and of the Irish tenor Sullivan, whose singing Harry admired, provoking from Joyce some ballads in a high key. Joyce asked Harry to read aloud to him the fragments they would publish, and would then explain what the odd words and phrases meant. Harry confessed that the experience made him "realize how ignorant I am from the scholastic point of view and how sane a writer is Joyce." Joyce signed Harry's copy of *Ulysses,* and then insisted on tying it up in pink paper. Harry was struck by the conventional character and domestic quality of Joyce's apartment—brown-wallpapered, with a formal portrait of his father above the fireplace—and by his formal manners. The only suggestion in his demeanor of who he was came when Caresse asked him if he enjoyed his work, and he offered "a flash of triumph . . . the same flash of triumph when one bets high on a horse and sees him gallop past the winning-post a winner. . . ."

When Joyce came to 19 rue de Lille, he insisted that Narcisse be locked in a broom closet because he feared stumbling across him. Using an enormous electric light bulb to help him see, and a magnifying glass, he made seemingly endless revisions to his work, penciling so many changes on the galleys that Caresse said they came to look "like a bookie's score card." Harry took notes while Joyce revised, and later, as he helped his distinguished guest down the stairs, he asked him if he was superstitious.

"Why?" Joyce acked.

"Because you were walking under a skeleton."

He didn't mind the skeleton, Joyce said, but he was superstitious about deaf-mutes.

When the final revisions had been made, and Roger Lescaret was setting the book in type, he discovered to his horror that the last page contained only two lines, a printer's botch. He came to Caresse and asked whether Joyce might be prevailed upon to add eight or so lines, and she laughed in outrage, explaining that the greatest literary master of his age did not add words to fill to space like some hack newspaper reporter, and there was nothing to be done. Lescaret sadly pedaled away on his bike, but next day Caresse found him buoyant; eight lines had been found. Caresse asked him indignantly *where* they had been found, and Lescaret confessed that he had himself gone to Joyce and begged for them, and that Joyce, without a second thought, had added them.

Harry met Kay Boyle, who had been publishing stories and poems in *Transition*, when he went to buy a scarf for Caresse at the fabric shop of Raymond Duncan, the brother of Isadora Duncan. Miss Boyle and her daughter lived in Duncan's colony in Neuilly, and in exchange for a room at the villa, meals of goat cheese and yogurt, and about twelve dollars per month, worked as a salesclerk at his outlet on the rue du Faubourg St-Honoré. Harry was intrigued with her, a beautiful and intense girl, a worshiper of art, a dreamer, at once sharp and hard and bright and a throwback to the glorious days of Romanticism. He rushed home to tell Caresse about her, and later wrote his mother that the Black Sun Press would publish a collection of her short stories, her first published book: "I think she is the best girl writer since Jane Austen—I say this without exaggeration. . . ."

In turn, Harry began to show his work to Kay Boyle. In the fall of 1928, he showed her "Assassin," and while portions of it bored her— she didn't say why—she was impressed by the risks the poem took and by the sense that Harry possessed a "certainty of knowing *what* experiences he was willing to undergo." Then, in a spectacular misjudgment, she added, "Your particular politics of existence, being so much more consistent—and without complaint—than most, could save at least a generation from despair. If you haven't the time to do it for ours, wait a bit and do it for the Wretch's. . . ."

Kay Boyle was twenty-five when she and the Crosbys met. She had been married to a Frenchman from whom she separated, and was beginning to spend time with Laurence Vail, a hard-drinking writer, poet and pilot who had himself been married to Peggy Guggenheim, and was known as "the King of the Bohemians." Miss Boyle's poems and stories were preoccupied with disease, early sorrow and death, and just as Harry seemed a breathing embodiment of her sometimes morbid expressions, so did she in her own life adhere to her conception of the poetic manner—messy and soulful, contemptuous of the middle class, of money and conventions. She'd had a daughter by her first marriage, and it was in part on the child's behalf that she had entangled herself with Raymond Duncan's ménage.

When the Crosbys left town on a holiday, they let Miss Boyle have their Voisin and driver, and "every morning the long, black elegant car would call for me at the colony, and the chauffeur would open the car door and place a sable lap robe across my knees. . . ." The colony was becoming impossible for her. Raymond Duncan went up and down town wearing sandals and a white toga, preaching simplicity and purity, but it had become clear to Miss Boyle that he was fundamentally an entrepreneur, and a resourceful one, working his brethren at sweatshop wages. She decided to leave the colony, but her daughter was in effect its prisoner, since she had signed her over to its care and influence, so with the collaboration of Robert McAlmon she kidnapped her daughter and took her to the Mill. (Perhaps the kidnapping was actually necessary, but Miss Boyle herself repeats with some amusement McAlmon's judgment that she, "come hell or high water, had to romanticize every situation.")

Harry was distressed by the child's cries and whimpers. In any case, the stay at the Mill was not entirely a success. McAlmon thought Harry remote, found it "difficult to make any kind of contact," yet also felt his host was "too full of hero-worship (Rimbaud, Verlaine, Villon) and of ecstasies and ideas about experimenting with life in order to harvest all the sensations it has to offer."

Miss Boyle also has a vivid memory of that stay:

> There were too many people at Le Moulin that December afternoon. . . . Whenever I looked at [McAlmon] across the chaos of the great, wide room, where a fire burned in a raised fireplace vast enough to barbecue a steer in, he had the look of a bolting horse in his eye. It was almost always the case in Caresse's and Harry's gatherings: one had to hold onto a clear knowledge of what they were seeking and what they had relinquished, sacrificed even, in that search, in order to bypass the people who surrounded them. . . . But the struggle to keep close to Harry, and to isolate his fanatical purity of spirit in the welter that always pressed upon him, was not an easy thing, and sometimes one gave up in despair.

On the last night of 1928, during McAlmon's visit, the consequences of their style were almost a year off. Harry received a telegram from Josephine, and it excited him. He wrote that he would like to become a necromancer, that he would like to become a prophet of the sun, that he *was* a prophet of the sun. He concocted a potent drink for McAlmon that he guaranteed would send his guest into a poetic delirium, or to the hospital. McAlmon drank it: "It did no such thing." And afterwards, crossing the cobbled courtyard, to go to bed while guests rioted in the main room of the mill, McAlmon turned to Kay Boyle: " 'It's too damned depressing,' he said; 'so depressing that I can't even get drunk. They're wraiths, all of them. They aren't people. God knows what they've done with their realities.' "

16

"The years, after all, have a kind of emptiness when we spend too many of them on a foreign shore. We defer the reality of life, in such cases, until a future moment, when we shall again breathe our native air; but by and by, there are no future moments; or, if we do return, we find that the native air has lost its invigorating quality, and that life has shifted its reality to the spot where we have deemed ourselves only temporary residents. Thus, between two countries, we have none at all, or only that little space of either in which we finally lay down our discontented bones."

—Nathaniel Hawthorne

His realities were his adversaries, and Harry drove against them full bore, fueling his aggression with stimulations of higher and higher octane, burning out his life, refusing to settle for settled embers, drugging himself, multiplying his orgasms, testing death and the sun, reaching for an illumination, a poem or line or word or beat of silence. And in his extravagant disdain for his realities he found an accomplice, a poet sure enough, the real article, Hart Crane. A year Harry's junior, Hart Crane had been foretelling his self-destruction since he was a boy. It was indispensable to his program, a consuming ambition for himself as a poet that could be achieved, as he believed, only by spending himself into bankruptcy. Three years after they met, just before noon of a sunny April day in 1932, Crane jumped off the stern of the Ward Line's *Orizaba*, a day north of Havana and bound from Vera Cruz to

New York. The ship was stopped, life rings were thrown out, but the suicide was successful.

Like Harry, Crane believed that poetry was magic, and could be trapped only by recourse to magic, a black alchemy of self-induced exaltation. The trick, as both he and Harry knew, was not infinitely replicable, and as the poet and the trick became indivisible, when the trick failed the poet would vanish in its smoke. By January of 1929, when the two men were introduced by Eugene Jolas, their tricks had begun to fail for each of them. Crane, a homosexual and alcoholic, looked twenty years older than his age. His hair had gone gray, and he was obliged to roam further and hunt harder to bag the sailors whose temporary affections he cherished, and which seemed to deflate his self-regard. He had been precocious in all things. He left his Ohio home when he was seventeen to begin his career as a poet, and once in New York immediately succeeded in making a reputation with Allen Tate, Yvor Winters, Malcolm Cowley, Waldo Frank and Sherwood Anderson. But as he ripened, so did he spoil, quickly and luxuriously.

Crane's father, the inventor of the candy Life Saver, was a solid and respectable fellow, and thus an embarrassment to his son. His mother was a whining and possessive neurotic with a fixation on her only son. Because of his repudiation of his father, Crane was obliged to live on the charity of friends, and from odd jobs as an advertising copywriter. He was at the mercy of writing fellowships, and one of these— a grant of two thousand dollars from the banker and philanthropist Otto Kahn—had brought him to Europe, where he hoped to conclude his long poem *The Bridge*, begun several years earlier when his powers were at full flood.

Crane had been twelve days in Paris when he and Harry met at the Deux Magots. Harry took him and Jolas to Prunier for oysters and wine, and that night read "White Buildings" and was impressed. Four days later, he had Crane to lunch at 19 rue de Lille, and the poet and publisher agreed that for two hundred and fifty dollars the Black Sun Press would issue *The Bridge* as soon as it was finished. The same day, Crane sent a post card to a childhood friend: "Dinners, soirées, poets, erratic millionaires, painters, translations, lobsters, absinthe, music, promenades, oysters, sherry, aspirin, pictures, Sapphic heiresses, editors, books, sailors. *And how!*"

Harry invited him to use the Mill as a retreat where he might finish *The Bridge*. At first Crane merely drank too much, and made great noises as he played the record player at full volume, or shouted aloud his own verses and Marlowe's. Then, February 3, Harry reported on a "mob for luncheon—poets and painters and pederasts and lesbians and divorcées and Christ knows who. . . . Kay Boyle made fun of Hart Crane and he was angry and flung the American Caravan into the fire because it contained a story of Kay Boyle's (he forgot it had a poem of his in it) and there was a tempest of drinking and polo harra burra on the donkeys and an uproar and confusion so that it was difficult to do my work. . . ." Crane managed to seduce a count who was about to be married, and he wrote Malcolm Cowley about the situation:

> Have just returned from a weekend at Ermenonville . . . where an amazing millionaire by the name of Harry Crosby has fixed up an old mill (with stables and a stockade all about) and such a crowd as attended *is* remarkable. I'm invited to return at any time for any period to finish *The Bridge*, but I've an idea I shall soon wear off my novelty. . . . It takes a book to describe the Crosbys—but it has (I mean the connection) already led me to new atrocities—such as getting drunk yesterday and making violent love to nobility. As ——— was just about to marry, I couldn't do better, though all agree (including Kay Boyle and Laurence Vail) that I did my best.

Crane did not wear off his novelty, of course. Harry was dazzled by his mischief, just as Crane, something of a snob in matters of blood and money, was bewitched by Armand de la Rochefoucauld and his château's "marble halls and palace walls," by the Mill's frozen pond, busy with titled skaters, and by Harry's fondness for opium, which he tried but did not enjoy. But even after he had moved into the tower and furnished it to his taste with Harry and Caresse's personal furniture, even after he had enjoyed for a couple of weeks "all the service that millionaires are used to having" (he insisted on thinking of Harry, and describing him to friends, as "heir to all the Morgan-Harjes millions"), he could not cease fearing that at any moment Harry would chuck him out, during the coldest French winter in anyone's memory. Crosby, he wrote his friend Waldo Frank, "is highly erratic."

By contrast to his new friend, Harry was a pattern of stability. Crane was a pugnacious drunk, a furniture-breaker who, after passing through a preliminary dancing and singing stage, would smash a glass or two, and soon become, in Malcolm Cowley's fine phrase, "as morose as a chained bear in a Russian tavern." Then his voice would deepen to the pitch of a "foghorn far at sea," as Caresse recalled, and he would begin to abuse whoever came easily to hand. But never Harry; he was intimidated and pleased by Harry, and regarded him as a kinsman and fellow poet. And nothing Crane did managed to estrange Harry from him. "He is of the Sea as I am of the Sun," Harry wrote, describing Crane's poetic preoccupation and foretelling his death. Crane fought with shopkeepers up and down the streets of Ermenonville; Harry smiled. Crane invited a chimney sweep to share his bed in the white-rugged, white-walled, white-quilted guest room at 19 rue de Lille, and the fellow left his hand- and footprints on every surface, ruining the room; Harry and Caresse endured. Caresse found him "dynamite to handle," and when one night, during a return from the Mill to Paris with Constance Coolidge, he demanded that Auguste stop the Voisin so that he could piss at the headlights, she bit her lip and remembered what she had taught herself about the glories of the poet and the miseries of conventions and manners.

Crane held his belly when he laughed, and he laughed often. He was generous within the limits of his means, giving Caresse a necklace and Harry a pair of moccasins he had bought from a sailor. One day, he gave them both the manuscript copy of one of his finest poems, "O Carib Isle!," which Harry, with his fondness for rank, declared "one of the five best poems of our generation." Like most of Crane's verse, it is elliptical and inward, taking its life from a private symbolic system. Also, it is a poem about death, so that it is tempting, in regard to the surfaces of the two poets' work, to reach for similarities. But Crane, however elusive his conceits and however misbegotten his attempt, in *The Bridge*, to counteract what he perceived to be Eliot's nihilism in *The Waste Land*, was forever rooting for something substantial, a correspondence between dreams and their objective provocations. Whereas Harry's verse is truly rootless.

But upon reading "O Carib Isle!" and reacting to it, Harry celebrated Crane's own derangement of the senses, a calculated derangement they shared with Rimbaud, whom they both idolized. He wrote the author of "O Carib Isle!":—"Hart what thunder and fire for breakfast . . . someday when we are all dead they will be screaming and cutting each other's throats for the privilege of having it. . . . I am no critic but I know gold when I see it. You write from impulse and imagination not by rules—everyone should of course but they simply don't. . . . Well give 'em hell. . . ."

Finally, as Crane multiplied his disgraces at the Mill, insulting the servants and the postman, running up huge bills on the Crosbys' cuff, working on the seduction of the chauffeur, neglecting entirely the business he was born to do, the only excuse for his excess, Harry took measures. He stole Crane's hobnailed boots (at a stroke fettering the wandering minstrel and saving the abused floors of the Mill), and then his clothes. He brought him paper, a typewriter, a phonograph for the playing of the heavy-beated music by which Crane liked to compose his poems, and delivered to the room where his guest was pent up in the tower of the Mill a case of Cutty Sark. So Crane wrote some verses at last, a few stanzas to be added to the sum of *The Bridge*, but failed to finish the poem, as he had failed so many times before, and in March left for the South of France.

The next time Harry saw him was in court. On July 9, Kay Boyle sent him a note saying that Crane had been jailed at La Santé prison because of a bar fight at the Café Sélect in Montparnasse. Madame Sélect, the owner and cashier, was as contentious as her customer, and they had disputed his bar bill, which he refused to pay—or rather, with his odd French and wild gesticulations, seemed to refuse to pay it. She called for the police, and Crane fought with them till he was subdued, dragged by the heels down Boulevard Montparnasse, jailed and beaten. The literary community, French as well as American, protested violently, and Harry appeared at the Palais de Justice on July 10 to vouch for his friend's literary renown, if not for his good behavior: "Hart was magnificent. When the Judge announced that it had taken ten gendarmes to hold him (the dirty bastards, they dragged him three blocks by the feet) all the court burst into laughter. After ten minutes of questioning he was fined eight hundred francs and eight days in prison should he ever be arrested again. [He was also instructed by the magistrate to remain sober during the remainder of his stay in France, which, the court hoped, would be brief.] A letter from the Nouvelle Revue Française had a good deal to do with his liberation."

The police would not release Crane at once, so Harry went off to drink sherry cobblers in the sun for a while, got drunk, picked up a pretty American girl and took her to the Ritz. Finally, he and a couple of friends went to La Santé to take custody of Crane, but still they were obliged to wait, and they played checkers and drank beer with the guards for a couple of hours until "at last the prisoners began to come out, Hart the last one, unshaved hungry wild." Harry took him immediately across the street to fuel him with rum, then to the Chicago Inn for corn bread and poached eggs on toast, perhaps to remind his charge that there was another place, another shore, where he might make his mischief. One thing especially impressed Harry: "Hart said that the dirty skunks in the Santé wouldn't give him any paper to write poems on. The bastards."

Not that Crane, unable to write in the best of circumstances, would have put paper to any good use. But for Harry all crimes were pardonable in the name of art, every artist's call was immediately to be answered, and was Crane not an artist?

Two days after he was sprung from prison, Crane showed up at 19 rue de Lille "rather the worse for wear." He had been boozing and courting the night before in Montmartre, and appeared wearing bizarre stars and anchors pinned to his sweater, and commenced to read aloud from his poems, and then declared that "there was no greater poet than he. . . ." Harry thought it might be the right moment for a sea change, accompanied Crane to the White Star Line, and there bought him a ticket home.

A fundamental aspect of Hart Crane's aesthetic system, and of *The Bridge*, is an appropriation, for a modern mythology, of the machinery and mechanical fabrications of the twentieth century. The "Cape Hatteras" section of *The Bridge* attempts to yoke the poet-dreamer with internal combustion, so that man, in the clouds, perceives himself as an engine. More portentously, in the section called "The Tunnel," the airplane is imagined as the instrument to carry the poet to a death in glory.

It was no novelty to translate powered flight into a metaphor. In his various manifestoes, particularly that of 1909 published in French in *Le Figaro*, the Italian Filippo Tommaso Marinetti had rung the gong for Futurism with the thrust of the piston, the lift of wings:

We want to extol the love of danger, the habit of energy and valor. . . . We proclaim that the world's grandeur has been enriched by a new beauty: that of speed. The racing car, with its body adorned by huge pipes, with its exploding exhaust, the roaring motorcar, which seems to speed like a ball. . . . is more beautiful than the Winged Victory of Samothrace. . . . There is no beauty apart from conflict. There are no masterpieces without aggression. Poetry ought to be a cruel attack against unknown forces in order to compel them to humble themselves before man. . . . We want to extol war—the world's only hygiene— militarism, patriotism, the anarchists' destructive gesture, the glorious, death-giving ideas and—contempt for women. . . . We want to extinguish museums and libraries. . . . We will extol immense crowds, moved by work, pleasure or rebellion; the multicolored and polyphonic fits of revolutions in all modern capitals; the nightly vibrations of arsenals and shipyards beneath their powerful electric moons; the voracious railway stations devouring the steaming snakes; the factories, attached to the clouds by ropes of smoke . . . the gliding flight of airplanes whose propellers flow like the flutter of flags. . . .

Marinetti, who later became a Fascist, despised the pretty traditions of the art of the past, despised all things received, including syntactical systems and logic. He loathed elegance, and most of the customs and enthusiasms dearest to Harry. But in his celebration of destruction and of the machine—especially of the flying machine—Marinetti seduced Harry utterly. It is a long leap from the literature of Decadence to Futurism, and to the aesthetic descendants of Futurism: Dada and Surrealism. But Harry made it—and what's more, he lived out every inch of the metaphorical leap. It was not merely that he embraced a new program when he abandoned an old, but that he answered every appeal to his general worship of poetry, so long as the answer called for risk and sacrifice.

Flight was for Harry the perfect enactment of a metaphor. To fly—as to dream after the use of opium—was to experience poetry as well as to mine material for its fabrication.

As far back as the autumn of 1917, when he had lain on the hood of his ambulance in France and watched planes wink their guns and lights by night, then dart and fall, always droning in his dreams, Harry had longed to fly. Perhaps nothing that had happened to him at war, save his near-miss on November 22, had made so deep an impression on him as his witness of flight. Later, Walter Berry, who had been sent by the French government in 1905 to meet the Wright brothers, who had seen them fly and who returned to France "awed by the possibility of the 'strange futures beautiful and new' folded up within those clumsy wings," as Edith Wharton recalled, further fed Harry's curiosity and enthusiasm. But the climactic incident in his seduction was the arrival on May 21, 1927, of *The Spirit of St. Louis* at Le Bourget.

Harry, Caresse and Mr. Crosby (who had arrived that very day in Paris), together with the Powels, made their way through the crowds to catch a first sight of Charles Lindbergh's landing after the first transatlantic solo flight. As a member of the Aviation Club, Pete Powel wangled the group an admission to the field itself, and they arrived at 8:00 in the evening, when Lindbergh was reported two hundred miles off the coast of Ireland. A huge crowd pressed at the fence surrounding the field, and from sunset until night fell a French flier entertained everyone with alarming aerobatics. A roar would rise as searchlights picked up an approaching plane, but it was only a commerical flight from London, and then one from Strasbourg. Red and green rockets competed with the acetylene searchlights that hissed while the impatient crowd tried from time to time to amuse itself with songs. At 10:00 the night turned cold, and Harry nipped brandy from his flask with Gretchen and Pete Powel, while Mr. Crosby, jittery as ever, hurried with evident aimlessness from one part of the field to another.

And suddenly unmistakeably the sound of an aeroplane (dead silence) and then to our left a white flash against the black night (blackness) and another flash (like a shark darting through water). Then nothing. No sound. Suspense. And again a sound, this time somewhere off towards the right. And is it some belated plane or is it Lindbergh? Then sharp swift in the gold glare of the searchlights a small white hawk of a plane swoops hawk-like down and across the field—C'est lui Lindbergh, LINDBERGH! and there is pandemonium wild animals let loose and a stampede towards the plane and C and I hanging on to each other running people ahead running people all round us running and the crowd behind stampeding like buffalo and a pushing and a shoving and where is he where is he Lindbergh where is he and the extraordinary impression I had of hands thousands of hands weaving like maggots over the silver wings of the Spirit of Saint-Louis and it seems as if all the hands in the world are touching or trying to touch the new Christ and that the new Cross is the Plane and knives slash at the fuselage hands multiply hands everywhere scratching tearing and it is almost midnight when we begin the slow journey back to Paris. . . .

Harry was not one to be indifferent to the arrival of a "new Christ," nor to neglect the lessons of the experience. Just as there was in him a persistent willingness to worship heroes, so was there a persistent ambition to be worshiped. In his night thoughts he conjured up a vision of himself in pieces, torn apart by a mob, but it is difficult to say whether for him this was a nightmare or an erotic fantasy. (Certainly Lindbergh himself was, like his airplane, torn apart after his flight of thirty-three hours, a victim of hysterical adoration.) Caresse noticed that Lucky Lindy, boyish and tousled, looked almost like her husband's double.

He began to avail himself as often as possible of Imperial Airways' trans-Channel flights from Le Bourget to Croydon. By 1927, the service was carrying eighteen thousand passengers each year, close to schedule, and with rare mishaps. On a typical flight in January of 1929, on which he invited Hart Crane to join him (Crane liked to write poems about flight, but not to fly, and to Harry's puzzlement refused), the plane reached the breath-taking speed of one hundred miles per hour, at an altitude of one thousand feet. He strained to see below him a farmer plowing his field, who looked up at the plane in what seemed to Harry to be wonder, and he thought that "it must be fun to drop bombs." When the plane landed, he met Caresse, delivered to Croyden by Lord Lymington in a Rolls-Royce. She had with her a new whippet bitch, Clytoris, to serve Narcisse Noir, and the party, less Lymington, returned immediately to Le Bourget, "now over Dungeness and the Sun pours gold on the Silver Wings and the exhausts pour twin flames of fire and back of us I see a red hawk of an aeroplane hurtling through space in pursuit. . . ."

Harry started a scrapbook to be filled with clippings about flight, fliers, air races and air disasters. He was bewitched: "We are the first generation to get our feet off the ground we leave the ground we fly we soar we catapult into Sun while the engines roar ya-hoo ya-hoo ya-hoo ya-hoo and the wind hurricanes and we balance on the breast of the sky like a diamond on the breast of a woman. . . ." Under Eugene Jolas' spell he began to yearn to enact the jumbled aspirations of vertigralism, the ascendancy of spirit, neo-Romantic, that Jolas believed could counter the baser manifestations of Futurism and Surrealism. Harry began to test his spring: he was preparing to break free of the earth, and of gravity.

The decisive moment came in Deauville in August of 1929, when from the beach at noon Harry saw the foolhardy stunt pilot Détroyat fly upside down one hundred feet above the tide line, loop-the-loop as he climbed, spin and wag his wings. "As miraculous a Poem as I have ever seen," he decided, and "tomorrow I shall go to the flying field at Villacoublay and enter my name as a student pilot." And so he did, paying four hundred dollars for a course in pilot training. First he was subjected to a searching physical examination, which he passed despite the persistence, even after his tonsillectomy the year before, of a painful throat. He took his first flight with an instructor on August 20, and thereafter flew almost every day that the weather permitted. On their seventh wedding anniversary, he bought Caresse seven orchids, performed rites for and with her, and that afternoon flew—"Aviator Poet Lover All for the Cramoisy Queen."

In September, one of his fellow students, Raymond Delair, was killed when his plane crashed ten minutes after Harry had left the field. Like Delair, Harry had been practicing tailspins and had himself almost lost control, and now Caresse begged him to "take care" and not to "play with fire." But Harry wished to do just that, precisely, to invite his fiery finish, like Phaëthon's: "I do not want a funeral. I do not want to be buried in the ground. I want to be cremated. I want my ashes to be taken up in an airplane at sunrise and scattered to the four winds. . . . Purify me with fire. . . . Let there be no funeral marches or hymns unless it [*sic*] be the roar of the aeroplanes." On occasion, he dreamed of taking his Cramoisy Queen aloft, and plunging with her into the heart of Paris or New York.

By mid-September, Harry was flying as often as twice each day, and had become a close friend of his instructor, with whom he shared "the war, girl friends, love of adventure, detachment, drinking, misunderstandings with our families, attitude towards money, restlessness. . . ." The instructor, Detré, encouraged by his pupil, performed aerobatics over the field—to the envy of Harry's new friend, the Russian Prince Carageorgovitch, who was also learning to fly, who was also driven to the field by his chauffeur, a man who drank excessively as Harry's Auguste did. Harry began to dream of flying long cross-country voyages, just as "I used to run cross country many years ago at school. . . ." But, for all his recklessness with his own person, Detré was a cautious instructor, and he infuriated his pupil by refusing to let him solo till he believed he was ready.

The Crosbys were to sail home early in November, but on the fourth of that month, having invented excuses to his mother for his delay, Harry wrote in his diary that he would on no account leave till he had flown alone. Solo flight had become a fixation. On the ninth, he wrote that he had flown three times, "but I am not let loose. If I don't fly alone soon I shall go mad." He sat at the edge of the field that day, reading a love letter from Josephine Bigelow, while "Detré and Détroyat catapulted over us the wheels of their planes not half a foot over our heads and what a roar from the exhausts. But I did not fly alone to-day and I could almost cry with rage." Next day, he flew four times with Detré, and the day after, Armistice Day, on the eleventh minute past the eleventh hour of the eleventh day of the eleventh month, he was at last alone in the cockpit and free of the earth. In anticipation of this moment, D. H. Lawrence had written Caresse: "An aeroplane! Is Harry really tired of life?"

As Harry increasingly fell under the spell of modern machinery—of racing cars, airplanes and skyscrapers—so did his aesthetic ambitions and practices become more modernist. He took up photography in 1928, and by 1929 was using his camera frequently and to good effect. More often than not, the subjects he chose were the artifacts of technology. His impulse was invariably toward the abstract, but usually the object abstracted was an airplane engine, automobile exhaust pipe, bulldozer or crane. (*Transition* published several of his photographs, as did *Hound & Horn*, whose editors did not endorse his poetry.)

In a farcical instance during the autumn of 1929, Harry met Henri Cartier-Bresson, then twenty-one, at Le Bourget. The photographer had been placed under house arrest by the commandant of the air squadron to which he belonged for having been caught hunting without a license, but Harry persuaded the officer to release the young pilot into his protective custody for a couple of days at the Mill. Cartier-Bresson, then a student of Cubism, was at the point of abandoning his career as a painter to take up photography, and he and Harry shared talk about the possibilities of the captured image, which Cartier-Bresson translated metaphorically into what he called "the Decisive Moment." Harry, too, was obsessed by the Decisive Moment.

As Harry's admiration for the modern began to displace his worship of dead forms and customs—of the soft comforts of Decadence, of high European art—it was inevitable that his attention would turn toward home. For the machine, for speed, for brassy revolution, for noise, motion and progress, one looked to America. There is plenty of evidence that Harry's unquestioning preference for Europe and things European underwent a crushing deflation during 1929. "The End of Europe," one of the prose pieces in his final book, *Torchbearer*, attests to his disinfatuation:

> The shattered hull of a rowboat stuck in the sand a fire of driftwood a bottle of black wine black beetles the weird cry of sea-gulls lost in the heavy fog the sound of the tide creeping in over the wet sands the tomb-stone in the eel-grass behind the dunes.

He began to develop a deep and subtle prejudice against the French, born of his familiarity with Parisian society and culture. Harry was fluent in French, and could read it with ease and speed, but by 1929 he was writing of his "abhorrence" of that tongue, and noting that he had given away almost all his books in the language other than those by Perse and Rimbaud. The reasons are complex, and go some little distance toward explaining the gulf of ignorance and hostility that has divided French from American culture. Language, or more properly grammar, is the obstacle that blocks the path of anyone ambitious to fit within the skin of a cultivated Frenchman. English is a language in which literacy is achieved by the expression of a huge vocabulary, through the interstices of a loose and easy syntax. It is a language that prizes evolution and surprise, one that requires curiosity and diligence rather than the kind of compulsive analysis and repetition by rote that French children—to their later, greater glory—are obliged to suffer. In all languages the illiterate may be recognized by their ignorance of approved syntactical arrangements, but in English, once grammar has been absorbed, only vocabulary, and perhaps accent, distinguishes one speaker from his "inferior." Even in the written language, where accent is hidden, lexical gifts alone set degree between writer and writer, so long as the fundamentals of standard usage are honored.

But in the French language, grammar is a tyrant. It is monstrously difficult, and within its labyrinths are hidden all delicacy and sense, all meaning, all purpose, everything that Harry or any other writer would think of as literature. The grammar of literary French—as opposed to the language that Harry spoke at Walter Berry's teas—is not available for appropriation by an adult. It is the reward for a childhood nightmare in which the simple thread must first be unraveled from a tangle, and then again and again. French grammar is a reproach to any writer like Harry who comes late to a literary calling. Batter it as he might, it would not budge: French grammar was a wall of brass, and Harry, aspiring to the quality of Rimbaud, was enraged. Like most Frenchmen he was fluent enough to speak the language without embarrassment; like many Frenchmen he could have composed a perfectly passable article for a newspaper—but not for *Les Temps*, whose style was literary, as tightly wound as French verse, and whose writers came from the unassailable elite whose mark of class was its linguistic style. But Harry did not aspire to the condition of *many* Frenchmen, nor even to the condition of *most*. He wanted to write the kind of poetry he read and admired, and he could not write a line in the language that a French schoolchild in his third year at lycée could not have written more elegantly.

Harry knew this, and so his deepening commitment to language necessarily commanded a deepening commitment to one in which he had no such handicap. This in turn provoked a renewal of his curiosity about America. Accordingly, he and Caresse decided to spend the summer of 1926 abroad—at home. Their experience during that July and August, in New York, Boston and Nantucket, was mixed. Harry was attracted to America's vitality, but repelled by her vulgarity. He appreciated his father's indulgence when he was discovered once again to have overdrawn his account, but was impatient at his father's condescension. He was excited by the language of advertisements, but disgusted by the objects it described. Mostly he was cast down, bored and impatient to return to France. He found that he could not read or write in Manchester or Boston. He could not shut his ears to the persistence of his family's telephone, or to the "dreary voice of the singing kitchen maid." He was consoled by the Chinese Room at 95 Beacon Street, a room he believed that Baudelaire would have appreciated, a place where he yearned to smoke opium, and finally did. But nothing else in Boston pleased him, and he pronounced the city a "dreary place (dreary, drearier, dreariest) and entirely sunless."

Harry hated the filling stations, though not the automobiles they served, and the lurid billboards on the way out to Manchester from Boston (but not those in New York). He hated the community spirit his friends seemed to enjoy, and boosterism and self-satisfaction. "I hate the multitude," he wrote from Boston, with no little self-satisfaction. "Je suis royaliste and to hell with democracy where the gross comforts of the majority are obtained by the sacrifice of a cultured minority. And the telephone which rings all day . . . and I have been criticised for refusing to answer it. And all the life here is like this, broken up into ridiculous little ten minute scenes, wherein is no contemplation, no melancholy, no imaginativeness." (He was in error about the lack of melancholy: his father and mother were depressed and anxious about their son's rigidity and morbid preoccupations. There was sadness everywhere Harry stopped off that summer: the sadness of his friends —save for Ted Weeks, with whom he ran and relaxed at Singing Beach—of his family, and of his own uncertain self.)

The Crosbys went to Nantucket to visit Caresse's family, and stayed in Siasconset: "Mediocre to a degree. Frightening. Shrill voices of children, unsympatheticness, the horrid manners of Helen the cook. . . . after supper C and I and the mother-in-law to the cinema and it was disgusting, especially the audience, and there was rowdyism among the children (they hissed a picture of the parade of the French Mutilées) for whom this damned country seems to be run and how the place smelt, stank rather, of bananas and cococola and ice-cream. Resolved to become a Persian." He left America ahead of schedule by several days and as he had arrived, confirmed in his judgment of the "horrors of Boston and particularly of Boston virgins who are brought up among sexless surroundings, who wear canvas-drawers and flat-heeled shoes and tortoiseshell glasses and who, once they are married, bear a child punctually every nine months for five or six years and then retire to end their days at the Chilton Club. Christ what a narrow escape, far narrower than escaping the shells at Verdun."

Hence, as the following summer approached, Harry wrote his mother in the spring of 1927 that he and Caresse could not possibly return to America: it would be too unsettling. In anticipation of her protests, he added that while he knew his absence would be "hard" for her, she should set her mind upon "the mothers of the boys who were killed in the war or the friends of yours whose sons are at the ends of the world." But not six months later, in one of his stunning reversals of determination, he wrote her that he had not given up the idea of spending half of every year in America "if only I could find just the right place in the country." (He longed occasionally for a small farm near Annisquam, a stone farmhouse set above a flat stretch of sand and overlooking the sea. "The hell you say," he said of his longing.) This paradox was best expressed by Harry's anguished question—more a cry—uttered years earlier in a whorehouse in North Africa: "O God when shall we ever cast off the chains of New England."

So they returned in the fall of 1928, crossing during a full Atlantic gale. While plates crashed and broke in the dining salon, Harry wrote Constance, whose bed he had left the night before sailing with Caresse, that "to have affairs is mediocre and unstarlike and we mustn't have any more." He added that "I don't even care if I see this girl I liked last summer"—*Josephine*, as Constance wrote in the letter's margins—"I think instead I'll go to that City of Dreadful Night and be nice to my family so that I won't ever have to go to Boston again."

But no sooner had they arrived in Boston on November 18, the day after they landed, than Harry had a run-in with his parents, who were preparing to give a dinner for the Spanish Infanta and told Harry that he would not be welcome if he insisted upon wearing his black artificial flower. Of course, Harry refused not to wear it, and he and Caresse entrained the next day for New York. On November 24, they went to New Haven for The Game—where Harry saw Josephine, for whom he had in fact come home—and two days later the Crosbys attended the dinner for the Infanta at 95 Beacon Street, to which Harry wore his flower. Among the guests was a woman who boasted of having burned Caresse's poems in her fireplace because they had shocked her. Caresse was pleased and proud, but Harry began a tirade against censorship, one of his set pieces.

They went to the family Thanksgiving at the Grews, and Harry wrote Constance that he had been obliged to reinforce himself beforehand with "black idol": "It is so difficult to feign interest in long descriptions of my sister's children . . . conversations seem far off the way they do when one is sick." A younger cousin remembers the

Crosbys there, holding themselves apart, with their dog, Narcisse Noir, looking suitably bored.

A couple of days after Thanksgiving the Powels arrived, at Harry's invitation, from New York, but the Crosbys declined to invite their son's friends to stay at 95 Beacon Street, so Harry and Caresse refused to stay there without them. On leaving the house, the two couples hailed a passing fish wagon, a red wagon drawn by a stallion, and hired it to drive them past the Ritz to the Statler. Mr. Crosby, to whom Harry had suggested that the Powels and their dog share a room and bed with him and Caresse, was enraged, and drew the blinds at 95 Beacon on the scene. He had tried, he had let his son have his head in Paris, but Boston—damn it—was *his* town. Harry wasn't fair; he wouldn't budge an inch.

The friends slept four-abed at the Statler, listened to jazz on the radio earphones, and drank. Harry liked the jazz, and also a black review by The Blackbirds that he saw in Boston on the first day of December: "I would rather hear this sort of barbaric jazz than all the violin recitals in the world and what sting and fire this show had compared with the dreary musical shows in Europe." The same day he went across the Commons to the Boston *Herald*, at the invitation of his now ex-brother-in-law, Robert Choate, managing editor of the paper. He was awed by the huge presses, their noise and thrust and remorselessness: "In went the paper into the jaws of the dragon and when it was vomited forth it was all blackened with printed petertracks to turn our living eyes to stone." By now he was fascinated by size, listened for a driving beat, responded to hustle. Pistons and cornets were his instruments of choice, and New York—"a madhouse full of explosions"—was the place to find them.

He called a truce with his mother and father, the better to bid them goodbye, and took his wife and friends south to the madhouse. The New York prices amazed him: a couple of glasses of orange juice at Grand Central Station cost as much as a couple of bottles of champagne in Paris. He was stirred by the shrill whistles of policemen and of the tugboats in the Hudson, by the clang of metal against metal where skyscrapers were going up, by steam drills and jackhammers, by all the clamor of the Boom. And by Josephine, not yet married, here and there in his life in New York. But madness was his deepest pleasure, however it might come to him—"hard and violent" was best, as personified by the dredgers he so loved to watch as they "snout[ed] up whole streets like so many wild boars."

When Caresse left for France on December 7, Harry stayed behind: he was not yet finished with New York. He got drunk with William Carlos Williams, and then with E. E. Cummings, whom he met in a hotel lobby: "There were two hundred businessmen but we found him huddled up in the corner of a sofa his coat turned up about the ears his hat pulled down over his eyes. So does a poet stand apart from the flock a hawk among pigeons."

The Crosbys exchanged telegrams while Caresse was at sea, miserable, uncertain whether she had lost Harry for good. But he was equally miserable without her, and the day after she sailed he wished he had accompanied her. She was in truth his only constant, and on December 17, weeks before he had planned to leave, he sailed to France in his wife's wake. During the crossing, he felt as though his mainspring had wound down. Something once there was gone for good. So much he knew, without identifying what it was that he missed. On December 21, the shortest day of the year, he stood at the ship's rail: "The sun is flat and grey as slate. A pale winter Sun. Arctic. I understand this sea. I understand this Sun." Three days later he was home, and "Paris is dead. . . ."

Still Harry banged away at Boston, writing poems about it with names like "Scorn" and "Song of Hate." Perhaps his fullest treatment is one called "Target for Disgust":

> *I curse you Boston*
> *City of Hypocrisy*
> *City of Flatulence*
> *(with your constipated laws)*
> *Unclean City*
> *(with your atlantic monthlies*
> *and your approaching*
> *change of life)*
> *I curse you*
>
> *in the name of Aknaton I curse you*
> *in the name of Rimbaud I curse you*
> *in the name of Van Gogh I curse you*
>
> *your belly is a nest of worms*
> *your breasts tubercular*
> *you have a falling of the womb*
> *you are an ulcer on the*
> *face of the earth*
> *leprous*

hogs vomit when they approach you
    City of Stink-Stones
    City of Dead Semen
with your Longfellows and your Lowells

there is no Aphrodisiac can revive you
    it is too late
there is no Phallus can stir
    you to madness
    it is too late
too late for you to cleanse
yourself with Sun
    Aphelion

City of Tea Rooms
whose beverage is
the water of the Dead Sea
whose food is Salt Peter
    and the Juices of Cod
City of Invalids
City of Fetid Breath
walled in by shadow
    Sunless

your Libraries are clogged
    with Pamphlets and Tracts
but of Ulysses
    you have none
but of Gertrude Stein
    you have none
but of Maldorors
    you have none

your Churches are crowded
with Sabbatarians
but of Prophets
    you have none
but of Fanatics
    you have none
but of Sun-Gods
    you have none

you are an Abomination
    Unphallic City of Pulp
and I would rather defile a

> *dead body than uncover*
> *your nakedness*
> *and I would rather spill out*
> *my seed upon the ground*
> *than come near to you*
> *and I would rather dwell*
> *in the volcanoes of hell*
> *than dwell in your midst*
>
> *City of Swan-Boats*
> *City of Frog-Ponds*
> *you are an Abomination*
> *a perpetual sore*
> *a target for disgust*
> *and in the name of*
> *the Sun*
> *and the Moon*
> *and the Stars*
> *and in the name of Mad Queen*
> *I curse you*
> *Boston City of Hypocrisy.*

Such are the fruits of a hasty reading of *The Waste Land* by a poet driven to destroy rather than to subsume and mend. There is no authentic disgust in these lines, no driving tirade. Harry served up the poem in *Mad Queen* for no deeper purpose than the scandalization of Stephen and Henrietta Crosby*—and to that end it succeeded. Then, because they were henchmen together in what Harry called their "policy of revolution, of attack . . . of a tremendous campaign against the Philistines," Eugene Jolas printed the poem in *Transition*.

Maria Jolas refers to Harry's taste, manner and furnishings as "all that red velvet: it was just the sort of old-fashioned thing *Transition* tried to blow sky high." Both she and her husband believed that Harry was Boston's prisoner, that he refused to be set free, that he required his idea of that place to oblige him to forever shock it, asking of everything he did: "What would Boston say to *this*?" For the fall 1928 issue of *Transition*, Jolas asked a number of Americans living in Europe —Gertrude Stein, Robert McAlmon, George Antheil, Kay Boyle, Walter Lowenfels, Harold Salemson, Kathleen Cannell, Harry Crosby

---

* He asked his mother, though not his father, never to read *Mad Queen*, and she never did. But she heard about it.

and others—why they remained away from home,* and Harry wrote a poem (which he later reprinted in *Mad Queen*—waste not, want not—under the title "Enquête: Tumults and Chances") in which he enumerated his reasons for neglecting America on behalf of Europe. "Target for Disgust" renders "Enquête" more than a little redundant, but once again the thrust of Harry's attack is directed at America's impotence and caution. In Harry's America, even the stars were "all suffocated inside." He declares himself "an enemy of society" eager to hunt, in Europe, with fellow enemies. He declares his wish to be "in at the death of Europe," and says again, as so many times before, that he prefers "transitional orgasms to atlantic monthlies."

Harry wasted no opportunity to lampoon the magazine whose offices on Arlington Street were within sight of his father's front door, but neither did he surrender his efforts, all unavailing, to be published by *The Atlantic Monthly*. Other magazines shared opportunities to reject Harry's poems: *The Dial*, *The Saturday Review* (whereupon Mrs. Crosby was directed to cancel his subscription), *Harper's* and *Hound & Horn* (whose editor explained his lack of enthusiasm by his animosity to chaos, Harry's boon companion).

But Harry submitted poem upon poem to *The Atlantic Monthly*. (Gertrude Stein shared this compulsion: it took her thirty years to force her will upon the magazine, which finally, in 1933, took an excerpt from her *Autobiography of Alice B. Toklas*.) Harry's fixation was almost comical: it was as though having overturned his desk at Morgan, Harjes, he expected to be invited back as a partner. From 1925, and until he became a contributing editor of *Transition*, he and Caresse rained poems upon Ted Weeks and Ellery Sedgwick, the editor. Often the batches came only a couple of weeks apart. They all came back, as did *Shadows of the Sun*. Often Harry's borrowings—from Eliot, and especially from Joyce—tempered what little enthusiasm the editors might feel for the Boston outlaw's scribblings. Usually his poems were turned down flat, without comment, but a few came close. One rejection, dated October 25, 1927, and signed by The Atlantic Monthly

---

* Almost none of them represented themselves as exiles. Most of them regretted the lack of spirituality in their homeland, and seemed to enjoy the Frenchman's refusal to meddle in the affairs of strangers. Others lamented the new American technology, the country's "speed, noise, confusion and jazz." Some mentioned the availability of a decent living for an artist in Europe, but most refused to descend to matters as vulgar as the favorable rate of exchange between the dollar and the franc. Others wrote utter nonsense, the special nonsense that is licensed by a questionnaire.

Company, is representative. It reads, in part: "To us, the difficulty with the sonnet seems that the questions invited are such that it is hardly surprising no answer is given. And if we may put our own question, is the rhyme of the last line of 'Study for a Soul' permissible?" Harry submitted himself on fifteen occasions and in forty-four poems to this kind of condescension.

It is not recorded that he offered "Target for Disgust" to *The Atlantic Monthly*, but nothing in his behavior suggests that he would have hesitated to do so. He could not decide which he wanted more: to be published in Boston, or banned.

17

"I want a long straight road into the Sun and a car with the cut out wide open speeding a mile a minute into the Sun with a princess by my side."

—Harry Crosby

At thirty-one Harry was still far from middle age. People remarked his angularity, his strong, defined features and his energy. He was pallid, perhaps from opium abuse, but youthful after a fashion. Some years earlier he had been pleased when a painter told him that he had a beautifully shaped head, and the look of an old man with a young face, that he gave the appearance of having suffered. Certainly he did nothing to cultivate his boyishness, but he came naturally by a jaunty, eager walk, and fluttering, nervous hand movements. He had suffered a mild case of jaundice in his late twenties, and still complained about his throat, having it treated from time to time with "sharp knives and red-hot irons" and cocaine, but otherwise his health was excellent.

He was appreciated for the kind of witty self-deprecation he had learned from his Boston and school friends, an apparent refusal—among men only—to regard himself or his works with gravity. Among women he was different. He treated them, and his attentions to them, as the most consequential of affairs. As his comings and goings grew increasingly complicated, as he multiplied his commitments to people and their enterprises, his life assumed more and more a divided character, one aspect of it totally separated from another. So too he cultivated his natural love of secrets and mysteries—privileged information he was willing to share with only one other person, the other being any one of a crowd of women or fellow spirits—and this had devolved into a taste for deception, often practiced for no other reason than to deceive.

In his severe suits and black ties Harry cut a striking figure, but in no sense was he Carlyle's definition of a dandy, "a clothes-wearing man." In winter, people noticed his fur-lined greatcoat, an inheritance from Walter Berry, and his black *boutonnière*, and his gold belt with its gold buckle. But mostly they noticed his bare head, in its time such an extraordinary announcement of independence from convention that it inspired one of Harry's last published works, "Bareheaded," a single sentence of prose: "Hats are parasols, hats are *against* the Sun—we shall discard our hats we shall stand bareheaded on the top of the hill with the thunderbolt of the sun in our heads."

All his mature life Harry had battled against the reluctance of people from his kind of background to betray their enthusiasms, and Harry had retained to some degree a hesitation to thrust himself forward, to compel attention and a reply from the world. But he said what he felt, and didn't give a damn what people thought of him. Where matters of principle were concerned, he had raised candor to an aggressive pitch, refusing all compromise and temporization. He had become increasingly intolerant. His totem, he declared, was the wolf—lonely, hard, resourceful—and like the wolf, which resists domestication to the death, he said again and again that he was "never meant for a cage."

He loathed communities, and was as ready to declare himself an anarchist as a royalist, because either (provided in the latter case that one was among the royalty) afforded the maximum of personal liberty. Nothing infuriated him more than censorship, whether of books or of morals. "I hate America damning this out and damning that•out," he wrote his mother. "Well there is only one thing in the world that I 'damn out' and that is Puritanism. If it came to a choice I would rather be a degenerate any day."

How much Harry's heart was in his mischief is not easy to know. Certainly he delighted in offending his countrymen, and his delight was often childishly perverse. One night the Crosbys and Powels caroused through the night in the sleeping car of a train, finally provoking an outraged note from someone in a neighboring compartment: "If you have any consideration for anyone but yourselves—please be quiet. You are the type of Americans one is thoroughly ashamed of." The note was pasted, in a place of pride, on a full page of one of the Crosbys' gold-embossed leather scrapbooks. He dropped water bombs from hotel balconies, and deflated the pompous by mocking them.

Many people thought him an eccentric little boy; as a friend said, "There's that Harry again."

And like a little boy, he was full of good resolutions. Now he would resolve to eat a hearty breakfast of toast and cream of shredded wheat, following systematic exercises, a cold bath and a rubdown. The next day he would resolve to abjure from the use of certain words: *beautiful, wonderful, marvelous, rather, terrific* . . . On his thirtieth birthday, he wrote his mother that for a good many years he had regretted having been born, and that till recently he had believed that she and Stephen Crosby "owed me much for putting me into a world of dreadful night," but that now he was reconciled to life, was grateful to them for having given him its gift, and that he had drawn up ten laws for the government of his remaining days:

I To read four chapters of the Bible every day for the rest of my life
II To read a book every week for the rest of my life
III To continue to practice Rites . . . but to abolish superstitions
IV To never drink more than four drinks in any one period of twenty-four hours and to observe (the way SVRC does) one non-alcoholic month
V To be taciturn (best is to be silent rather than talkative)
VI To be unextravagant in everything except Books and Gifts for Caresse
VII To exercise every morning followed by a shave and a cold bath
VIII To be bright and delicate chaste and gentle with Caresse
IX To be an Ascetic rather than a Hedonist
X To worship with a chaste heart and soul and body the Sun

Within a week he had gambled extravagantly, drunk himself insensible, betrayed Caresse with two women, fought violently with her and forgone exercises. And within a month he had met Josephine and seduced her. With the passage of time his sun worship had grown curioser and curioser. He masturbated with the sun in sight and mind ("and tomorrow I will stand on the top of the hill with the rod of the Sun in my hand"), and called upon the sun to witness his graver acts, addressing it directly. He tricked himself out in a sun-worshiping cloak. He translated whole books of the Bible into a holy writ appropriate to his purposes, changing the names of God and the Holy Ghost to Sun. He declared again and again that he would labor to oblige his life to conform to a single narrow principle, the principle of the Sun, whatever it might be.

Harry had been struck by one of Paul Valéry's pronouncements—

that genius is a habit that can be acquired—and believed that he would acquire it from the sun. Valéry had also said, with an irony lost on Harry, that there were people abroad in the land who believed a metaphor to be a communication from heaven: "A metaphor is what occurs when one looks at things in a certain way, as getting dazzled is what occurs when one looks into a sun." Harry had worked up a mystical system so complicated that it managed to resist all explication—or to license any. But its center lay within him, as he understood one day, reading Schopenhauer, who advised that the "center of gravity (for me the Sun) should fall entirely and absolutely within oneself." As he gave away his books, so did he give away his ideas—and his choices—in a quixotic campaign of reduction. He sought "to reduce everything all literature to the word SUN but to do that the word SUN must be worth more than *all* the other words in the world. I believe this reduction is possible."

His friends indulged him as they might someone with a fixation on cats or numerology. They added to his collection of exotica as they might send porcelain bunnies to an enthusiast of miniature animals. For Harry's Christmas present in 1928 Mrs. Crosby selected a Solray ultraviolet sunshine machine—"a veritable Fountain of Sunlight," in the words of the company's prospectus. Stuart Kaiser fabricated an anagram from the letters of the names Harry and Caresse: *Ra's Rays Cheer.* From Cuba Ernest Hemingway sent a clipping from the New York *Times* magazine of July 7, 1929, reporting on modern rites of sun worship:

> Ra of the Egyptians and the cross-word puzzlers has become the god of débutantes and stenographers, bank clerks and the garment industry. . . . The cult in its purest form centers at Newport and Southampton, Coney Island and Long Beach. . . . Whatever the causes, the fact remains that the sun is definitely de riguer. It is the most fashionable of heavenly bodies. . . . The smartest girls come into town looking like figures molded in old Cordovan leather. . . . This new version of an old cult has its fanatics, its would-be martyrs, its metaphysicians who would make philosophic systems out of personal desires, and a new moral order out of the ancient human love of sun on bare skin. . . . It is told of the priests who sacrificed to the Mexican sun on the great pyramidal temples of Chichen Itza that, not content with giving up the outside of their bodies to be burned, they tore out their hearts, and offered them up, still beating, as a living sacrifice to the giver of life. . . . To the Dravidians of India the sun was as much of a malignant demon as it is to the man who tries to put a stiff collar around a sunburned neck. . . .

Harry was not amused, and in truth, while his friends might wink while his back was turned, none dared laugh outright at him. The possibility of that sacrifice, that arrow into the sun, that thrust through the membrane of life into the messy source of life, that suicide, was too apparent. "I must strive for an unbroken consistency and unity of aim all my life," Harry wrote in his journal, adding that "not failure but low aim is a crime." He resolved not to miss the Decisive Moment. One day the sun appeared at his window while he was writing verse, and he said that he would pray to it later, when he was done. But it began to rain, and rained all day, and the sun was gone: "Must not delay *ever* as regards the Sun." He was prompt thereafter and honored his self-appointments.

By late 1929, Harry had accumulated a formidable inventory of literary ambitions. He had plans for a novel, with dialogue "crisp and epigrammatic," whose heroine's life was to be "built upon the fact that once upon a time she had sold a bouquet of roses to the Queen of Roumania." Even less promising was his ambition, as he wrote Caresse, to write about the medieval city of Carcassonne "along the same general lines as Irving employed in writing the Alhambra. You know what a love I have for all that is feudal and medieval and here at last I have found the greatness of those ancient times embodied. . . ." He fiddled with his diary, intending to translate it into a cohesive autobiography, and perhaps to embellish it with fantasy. He planned to write a biography of Rimbaud. He considered a play based on Walter Berry's life.

He wanted to write an essay about Polia Chentoff and her work, and to extend into a book-length monograph the essay on sun dials he had written for his mother. Initially he had wished his diaries to be repressed until after his death, but soon after the Black Sun Press published the first of them in a strictly limited edition, not for sale, he showed them to the English publisher Jonathan Cape, who expressed a willingness to publish them. (Stephen Crosby's intercession following his son's death sabotaged the agreement between Cape and Caresse for a posthumous selection from *Shadows of the Sun*.) He resolved to learn shorthand, the better to record the fragments of conversation he liked to copy into his notebooks following a night on the town. Caresse suggested, and Harry promised himself to pursue, a book composed of letters he had received from Alastair, MacLeish, Berry, Weeks, Constance Coolidge, Goops, Stephen Crosby, Henrietta Crosby—and the phantom Jacqueline, together with his imaginary replies to her. He planned to edit Blake's proverbs, his own sun-thoughts, his own death-thoughts. In the latter part of 1929, he received the approval and attention of several American literary magazines: *Blues*, *Pagany* and *Morada* had all bought his poems. *The American Caravan* accepted a batch on December 11.

And he planned to buy an airplane, and embark on long cross-country flights, to fly like Icarus toward the sun, to fall like Icarus from the sky as from grace, like Icarus to plunge into legend. It did not occur to him, as it had earlier occurred to Breughel, and later to W. H. Auden, that Icarus had fallen unnoticed upon the unyielding crust of a busy world, and that his own return to Earth by gravity might make so small a splash. Such a fuss he hoped to make: "I want a long straight road into the Sun and a car with the cut out wide open speeding a mile a minute into the Sun with a princess by my side. . . ."

The day before Harry, Caresse and Constance sailed for New York on the *Mauretania*, the Crosbys had some people to tea at 19 rue de Lille: Ambassador Joseph Grew, Alex and Sylvia Steinert, the Crouchers, Goops and a few others. The next afternoon, November 16, several of these, together with Eugene Jolas, saw them off with a party on the railway platform in Paris. As soon as they boarded at Cherbourg, a telegram was delivered to Harry. The message was terse—YES —but to him not cryptic. It was signed by the Sorceress. Three days later, sitting with Constance in the smoking room during a storm—both at sea and with Caresse, who was sulking in her stateroom, jealous of Constance—and reading *Beating the Stock Market*, he was brought another radiogram.

"I guess this must be from my girl in Boston," he told Constance.

"Oh, Harry," she said, "I do hope you aren't going to get mixed up with that girl again. She's married, and you aren't really in love with her anyway."

"I love three people," he replied. "Caresse, you, and Josephine."

The next day he wrote a long letter to the Sorceress and told Constance that the principal reason he loved Josephine was that she loved him, and that she passed his tests of devotion. The following day, he wrote out a holograph copy of *Sleeping Together* for Caresse, as a token of his love. And the day after, November 22, the *Mauretania* docked in New York, "City of Arabian Nights."

The Crosbys took the Midnight Express to Boston—Aphelion, in Harry's judgment, in contrast to the Perihelion of New York—and were given the best guest room, at the back of 95 Beacon Street, overlooking the Charles River. Everyone was determined to make a success of the visit, but it began to come unstuck almost immediately. Harry preferred the Chinese room. He wanted to smoke opium there, gazing at the wallpaper with its motif of flying cranes and water lilies, its screens, its black-lacquered Chippendale with gilt patterns. Harry's parents bent to their son's whim, but they refused to let him use the room's old fireplace, or to permit Narcisse Noir to sleep on the bed.

The following day, Stephen Crosby's temper blew, and there was a bitter lecture, with recriminations, in the library. The subject was money. Mrs. Crosby had sent Harry and Caresse innumerable gifts and checks, offered to buy her son land, to take her son's family on holidays abroad or to bring them home. She had even insisted upon paying the school expenses of the Peabody children. Stephen Crosby had been at least equally lavish, now sending unbidden five hundred dollars, now a couple of thousand. During a trip to Paris in 1927, in a single day he had bought Harry shoes, socks, pajamas, a suit, an overcoat, a wine cellar, three paintings, a zebra skin and a polar bear rug. On the same day, he had also given his son and daughter-in-law a gift of cash, and had bought Caresse a dress. Still on the same day, he had fought with his son, who wrote his mother that Stephen Crosby "no more understands our mode of living than we his. But the fault I think is much more mine than his.* I have grown very temperamental and difficult." Now and then their mutual affection would overcome their antipathies, and Harry would suffer remorse ("what a disappointing son I have been"), or his father would, and they would embrace, drink a glass of brandy together, smash the glass for good luck and promise to try harder. But they never managed to glue themselves back together for long.

One or the other of Harry's parents were forever scolding him for his brutal invasions of the principal of his estate. He would cable home instructing his father to sell stock, which the senior Crosbys felt "wasn't right"; they would lecture him, and sometimes he would apologize and sometimes not. In 1926 he responded with a telegram signed PENITENT, and the following year he admitted to his mother, "I am a very naughty boy I am afraid." When Mr. Crosby received notice

* Compounding the disputations were some onerous estate taxes Mr. and Mrs. Crosby had been obliged to pay during 1927, and the pressures of a lawsuit brought against F. S. Mosely & Co., the firm of which Stephen Crosby was managing partner. The suit, for ten and a half million dollars, had been in litigation since 1923, and it was not till 1927 that a verdict against F. S. Mosely (and others) on behalf of the estate of George E. Willett was overturned by the Massachusetts Supreme Court, thus releasing Stephen Crosby and his firm from the prospect of bankruptcy.

from the State Street Trust Company in the summer of 1928 that his son had twice overdrawn his account, he managed to contain his anger and pony up the amount of the overdrafts, almost a thousand dollars. Then, in January of 1929, Harry instructed him to sell four thousand dollars of stock "to make up for certain past extravagances in New York," and he did so. And on July 19, 1929, after an expensive luncheon with the Sorceress, Harry cabled his father: PLEASE SELL TEN THOUSAND DOLLARS WORTH OF STOCK. WE HAVE DECIDED TO LEAD A MAD AND EXTRAVAGANT LIFE. Ten days later Harry received "three terrible letters from the family to damn us out for selling the stock with intimations that I need a guardian and that I am wicked and all gone to pieces and heaven knows what else. . . . there is only one action I can believe in and that is the action that leads me to eternity."

Moreover, he said as much to his parents:

Dearest Ma and Pa
The cable saying you were shocked and terribly hurt at our selling stock was I suppose perfectly logical (it is so difficult to understand other people's point of view) and I was afraid you would feel badly but everyone must *must* lead their own lives and what sometimes appears folly on the surface may be underneath wisdom. . . . Ma says she fears disaster "what is your life leading you to" I can say that it is arrowing me into the Finality and Fire of Sun by means of Catapults and Explosions Gold and Sorceresses and Tornados. . . . You feel it is wrong because I refuse to take the question of money seriously. If you really feel this way the simplest thing is to leave your money to Kitsa and to her children (as you already have done in a certain sense) who lead the lives you would have them lead. . . . If I wasted money gambling or sitting in bars drinking or entertaining chorus girls then I would be absolutely to blame but as it is I work and I am happy and *living* in the true sense of the word Alive Awake New Every Morning with the Arrow of my Soul pointing to Rá. . . . But I am really really sorry to feel that you both feel so hurt. I seem to have done so much in my life to make you unhappy but perhaps some day I shall have done a fine thing to make you happy.

What they wanted he couldn't give. Henrietta Crosby had once asked for it plainly, in a letter to Caresse, looking forward to a trip with her and with Harry: "I think we can have a most interesting time if [Harry] will just agree to help me by being more or less like other people. . . ." That wasn't going to happen, and by November of 1929, a couple of weeks before his death, they had all recognized this. Mr.

Crosby proclaimed endlessly that he had to think of what *they* think, here in Boston. Even in Paris, at the Four Arts Ball, he had to think of what *they* thought, back there in Boston. Harry didn't give a damn about his father's worries, or about bridge parties or buying and selling stock, his father's loves. He had the hard intolerance of the very young, and age had not tempered him. Sometimes he was cruel, as when he wrote his mother that he believed there could "never be a *real* intimacy between the older and the younger generation. The wall is half sex half war."

For their part, his parents had never learned to leave off lecturing their son about his clothes, about staying up too late, or about showing up five minutes late for lunch. They treated Harry, as unbending as a priest of sacrifice, like a school kid. Like his son, Stephen Crosby would turn sullen, dive into a black mood and then surface, ebullient, when he learned that Continental Can had risen a couple of points on the day's market. Mrs. Crosby recognized her husband's failings, and pleaded with Harry to be kind: "Dearest boy help Pa all you can he worries awfully . . . but I guess it's because he is tired and we are all getting older you know." Not Harry. He wouldn't grow older.

In the library of 95 Beacon Street, among the rich paraphernalia of their house, with its silver doorknobs, delicate fanlit entrance hall, family portraits, leather-bound books and down-filled cushions, the Crosbys lectured their son about the stock market. It was crashing. Economies must be practiced. Perhaps the staff in Paris could be reduced? Harry did not listen or care; the stock market was nothing to him, and he said as much. His mother was especially wounded. But nothing he ever did hurt her as much as his announcement that he did not wish to be buried in the plot she had bought and tended for him in a Manchester cemetery: "The thought of being encoffined there is as gloomy to me as the thought of that empty coffin in Escorial must be to the King of Spain. . . . I do not want to be buried in America—I want to be buried in France." So there was no hope, even beyond this life, of the reunion with her son she so longed for. Death was to have awarded the perfect intimacy, dignified and timeless. She had found the burial plot, a place beneath an American elm, and had nourished it, and written Harry about it, and finally showed it to him when he came home during the summer of 1926. Now he had repudiated it, and Manchester, and his country, and his family, and her.

The morning after Harry arrived at 95 Beacon, an envelope was hand-delivered to the Crosbys' butler. Josephine Rotch's letter was angry as well as longing. The Fire Princess was jealous of the Lady of the Golden Horse, and of Harry's Cramoisy Queen, but her principal purpose was to lay plans to meet. Harry and Josephine met that very afternoon, the Saturday of the Harvard-Yale game in Cambridge, and the following day she arranged, on the pretext of a visit by friends, to send her husband to her family's house on Commonwealth Avenue, so that he might study there in peace while she and Harry kept their own manner of peace together.

Albert Smith Bigelow was a first-year graduate student of architecture at Harvard. Five months before, on June 21, the day after his graduation from Harvard College, he and Josephine had been married at the Congregational Church in Old Lyme, Connecticut, where Miss Rotch's mother and grandmother had also been married. The couple's engagement had been announced the previous May, and was the provocation for a large advertisement in the Boston *Evening Transcript* on June 3, 1929, paid for by a firm of jewelers and silversmiths. The advertisement showed Miss Rotch, wearing a dark suit, a single strand of pearls and a serious face, and quoted her approving selection of some flat silver from the firm ("The Essex pattern is most attractive. . . . I'm delighted with it"). Explaining that Miss Rotch's wedding "is of great interest to Boston society," the ad was pleased to announce that "in preparing for her new rôle of hostess, the choice of her silver seemed among the most important of all decisions" to her.

The Friday of the marriage was also the day of Harvard-Yale boat races in nearby New London, and one of Bert Bigelow's ushers, Morris Brownell, rowed that day—after a noon wedding—on the varsity crew. The groom's other ushers included men with such surnames as Iselin, Ludington, Tiffany, Carnegie and Roosevelt, and his best man was his twin brother, Hugh, like Bert a celebrated Harvard hockey star. Albert Bigelow was twenty-three, and his bride twenty-one. The couple went to the West Coast on their honeymoon, and in Santa Barbara people gossiped about what a strange and wild girl Josephine seemed, and how disdainfully she treated her new husband. People were shocked—as they knew they were meant to be—by her words and erratic behavior.

For a couple of months after her wedding, Harry received no word from her, but he was patient: "She is mine—whether I hear from her or not has really very little importance." But on August 27 Stanley Mortimer brought with him to Paris a "pure gold letter from the Fire Princess." Mortimer and Harry had met several years earlier at St. Moritz, and since then had shared many adventures, sailing in Spain on a boat Mortimer had chartered, driving at high speeds in Mortimer's

Chrysler, buying jointly a useless race horse. Mortimer, a portrait painter dividing his time between New York and France, acted as a go-between for Josephine and Harry right to the end. Another convenient and helpful friend was Robert Choate, Harry's brother-in-law until his divorce from Kitsa. Choate figured prominently in the final liaisons between Harry and his Fire Princess, giving them the use of his house near Beacon Hill.

Albert Bigelow was busy with his studies and examinations, and would stay in Cambridge till well after dinner every night, so Harry and Josephine met day after day. Caresse didn't know, or didn't quite know everything. Tote Fearing knew, "and so did a lot of other people, as was usual in those cases; everyone knew about it but Bigelow." Harry had kept Josephine's photograph on display at 19 rue de Lille, and catalogued her letters to him in a book kept there, open to Caresse's investigation. Alex Steinert, present at the farewell party for the Crosbys on November 16, heard Caresse speak openly of Harry's girl in Boston: "She mentioned her name sadly, but not complainingly." However, Caresse later wrote: "I had no idea that during that visit Harry made foolish secret rendezvous. . . ."

Partial evidence bears out Caresse's further claim that they were happy together on that trip. They loved their room at the Savoy-Plaza, where they lay together and looked out at the Ritz Tower and the "amazing phallic skyscraper" of the Fuller Building. Harry's passion for her seemed as high as ever, but he was preoccupied. His affair with Josephine had about it a violence he had never before experienced so consistently with a woman. On November 29 she had written him complaining about the bruises he had inflicted on her arm, telling him that her husband had been alarmed by them and had tried to kiss them away when she told him she had been injured falling down. She wrote Harry that she was truly afraid of him for the first time.

Nevertheless, on December 2 she telephoned Harry to tell him she was coming to New York from Boston, and he realized that he had set in motion something not within his power to control. He described what they were like in his notebook: "It was madness, like cats in the night which howl, no longer knowing whether they are on earth or in hell or in paradise." And like cats in rut they fought as well as loved, loving and fighting alternately on the train out to Detroit. *Detroit!* What a setting for a poet to woo his Fire Princess; the city's principal appeal was its social neutrality—in such a desert Harry and Josephine might expect with some confidence to avoid recognition by people they knew. Robert Choate had preceded them there, and they checked into the Book-Cadillac on December 3, registering as Mr. and Mrs. Harry Crane in a twelve-dollar-a-day room on the twentieth floor. Most of their meals they took in bed, where they also smoked opium, made love and battled. They went to parties with Robert Choate, and to a speakeasy where they drank rum from teacups, not at all Harry's style. And when they weren't digging at each other, or making up, Harry scribbled lines in his notebook:

> Princess Yes
> The Little Yes Princess
> Little Animal
> Little Yes

Much of this can be found in *Shadows of the Sun* (in elliptical form), but one entry, that of their last day together in Detroit, December 5, appears as follows in the version which Caresse caused to have published: "Thank the Sun for Harry and Caresse." Harry had written no such thing. The manuscript from which the entries in *Shadows of the Sun* were taken tells another tale:

> Twelve hour sleep pillowed in silks and scented down when hushed awakenings are dear much refreshed oysters for breakfast J takes her bath luncheon at speakeasy J and I and Beamy [Choate] rum in teacups Mermaid book shop cash a cheque hot chocolate with J over the Bridge to Canada and back to the station she sees someone she knows and is upset . . . she cries many opium pills and all night we catapult through space J and I in each other's arms vision security happiness.

The entry for the following day, as published, corresponds precisely with the one in the journal: "New York J sick as a cat from the opium. 1 West 67th. I see C. I fight with J. I go to bed 2707 with C." One West 67th, the Hotel des Artistes, was Stanley Mortimer's address. (He later said that he had not realized Miss Rotch was married. Or perhaps some friends had told him that she was; he couldn't recall with any precision.)

On December 7, Mr. Crosby and Mrs. Bigelow said goodbye; she said, and he agreed, that she should go home to her husband. That night Hart Crane threw his wild send-off party for the Crosbys, who were to return to France a week later on the *Berengaria*. During the party, which persisted till dawn, Harry walked from Crane's Brooklyn apartment to a nearby speakeasy to fetch more gin. Margaret Robson, a friend of Crane's, went with him, listening to his tangled discourse about the "complicated splendors of love and death, and of a great love that should somehow be fulfilled in his own death."

That morning, Harry had invited Caresse, and would invite her again three mornings later, to jump from the twenty-seventh floor of the Savoy-Plaza with him. He had been watching, with a curious detachment, the sun die early each afternoon in their west-windowed room; in this northern winter it was young-looking, pale, and its fire seemed almost cool enough to touch. And Harry had been rewriting the Bible again lately, to elevate the Fire Princess to the station of a prophetess: "Josephine: and Harry said unto her if thou wilt go with me then I will go but if thou wilt not go with me then I will not go. And she said I will surely go with thee not withstanding the journey that thou takest."

Josephine did not go home to her husband, but joined one of her bridesmaids, Margaret Burgess, at her parents' Park Avenue apartment. On December 8, Harry relaxed in bed with his wife. The following day, Caresse received a telegram from one of her lovers in France, the Aviator, sent to her mother's Madison Avenue address: MISS YOU LOVE SICK. On the same day, December 9, a rambling document for Harry was delivered to the desk of the Savoy-Plaza. Written on the envelope that enclosed the message to her husband (a meandering poem of thirty-six lines) is, in Caresse's handwriting, her note of explanation, a wrenching complaint: "This letter Josephine brought to Harry at the Savoy Plaza the night before he died. She had not left town as she had promised to do."

The poem is an inventory of those objects and impulses which Josephine believed that she shared with her lover. It is explicitly sensual, and invokes their mutual love of orchids, caviar, champagne, the number 13 and the color black. It declares that they share a belief in the final act of Van Gogh, that together they worship the sun as a god, and that a child, Pamela, belongs to them. Its concluding line is unambiguous: "Death is *our* marriage."

Two days earlier, the day she had promised to return home, Josephine had sent Harry a telegram: I LOVE YOU I LOVE YOU I LOVE YOU. A day later he wrote in his notebook another message meant for publication which Caresse suppressed: "One is not in love unless one desires to die with one's beloved." Harry was in love with Caresse, and with the Sorceress (whose own YES he carried with him in his billfold), and with Constance. On December 9, he telephoned Constance and begged her to join him for dinner. She could not. He was also in love with Josephine. She seemed to be the one; she was prepared for the test.

Harry was also prepared. A year earlier, he had bought an automatic, had the sun engraved on its side and was carrying it. "I never take second helpings," he had written. And: "It is better to be too soon than too late." "One must submit to the consequences of a principle which one has established oneself." The locution is perhaps a shade formal for the occasion, for the execution of its declaration, but there it is, plain enough.

On December 10, Harry took Caresse to look at an exhibition of the sculpture of Katherine Lane, an artist from the North Shore whose bronze of Narcisse Noir was on loan from the Boston Museum of Fine Arts. Afterwards he kissed Caresse goodbye, first removing his eyeglasses. (He would not kiss any girl wearing his eyeglasses.) Caresse left him to meet Mrs. Crosby and go with her to Uncle Jack's for tea; Harry promised to meet them there before dinner and the theater with Hart Crane.

Harry ate lunch, went to Stanley Mortimer's studio and met Josephine there, where they had many times met before. The three of them exchanged pleasantries, joked and teased, and then Mortimer left, to give them some time alone together.

18

CROSBY POEMS CLEW IN DUAL DEATH: Passion Verses
Secret Reading of Slain Bride
—New York *Daily News*

CROSBY DIED FOR A THRILL, SAYS PARIS, JEERING "PACT"
—Chicago *Tribune*

POET SLEW SOCIETY SWEETHEART, NO SUICIDE PACT
—*Daily Mirror*

"A vote of confidence in the cosmos."
—Ezra Pound, on the same subject

Hart Crane told Henrietta Crosby that her son was dead, and told Caresse that her husband had shot himself and a girl. He had sat through that painful dinner with the two ladies and with Margaret Robson, while they all wondered what had become of Harry, and tried not to guess. As they were at the point of leaving the Caviar restaurant, Mortimer called with the news that his studio seemed to have been, well, *bolted*, from the inside, and that no one answered his knock. Perhaps Harry was asleep?

Crane took the ladies to the Lyceum theater, and left his seat number at the box office, together with word that he might receive a message. It came during the first act. Mortimer's door had been breached with an ax, he told Crane above a ruckus of excited cries at his end of the telephone. The police had been sent for. It was all over.

Caresse and her mother-in-law returned to the Savoy-Plaza to help each other and to mourn. Crane took Margaret Robson to the Hotel des Artistes: "I remember," she said, "there were policemen there, and everyone wanted to go up but we weren't allowed to. And I remember seeing the dial, showing the floors, going up and stopping on the ninth. Like a movie sequence, you know, of a detective story." Before the night was over, a dozen detectives, perhaps drawn by the prominence of the dead couple, had been assigned to the case. But there wasn't much for them to investigate in such hermetically sealed circumstances, and it soon became clear that what little could be learned of what had happened between Stanley Mortimer's leave-taking of his apartment at 4:15 that afternoon and his return six hours later would come from medical investigation rather than conventional detection.

At the scene of death, Deputy Chief Inspector Mulrooney announced to reporters that murder most foul had been committed, followed by suicide. Dr. Charles Norris, Chief Medical Examiner, disputed the Inspector's conclusion and offered his judgment, based on the disposition of the bodies, that a suicide contract had been executed. Then a post-mortem examination was conducted by Deputy Chief Medical Examiner Thomas Gonzalez, who characterized the case as one of homicide and suicide. Reporters quoted Gonzalez as having said that he inferred homicide from the position of the bodies, "and the expression of smiling expectancy on the dead face of the beautiful young wife, indicating that she had gone to her rendezvous expecting a caress, not deadly bullets." But Dr. Gonzalez also announced that rigor mortis had set in when the two were discovered, suggesting that they had been dead since 2:00 P.M., two hours before Mortimer exchanged banter with them. Dr. Norris, his superior, did not budge from his judgment of a suicide pact, nor from his conviction that Josephine had died a considerable while before Harry.

Caresse begged Archibald MacLeish to maintain a death watch over Harry's corpse at the morgue of Bellevue Hospital, and he agreed. (Stanley Mortimer was in seclusion.) She and Harry had promised each other a death watch, just as they had promised each other a death together unless the moment were snatched from one of them prematurely, but she wasn't up to the execution of her oath. MacLeish had no reverence for the Crosbys' mortuary practices: "This was part of Harry's phony mysticism." So the poet Harry admired more than any alive, other than Eliot, saw him out: "As I sat there looking at his corpse, seating myself where I wouldn't have to see the horrible hole in back of his ear, I kept saying to him: you poor, damned, dumb bastard.

He was the most literary man I ever met, despite the fact that he'd not yet become what you'd call a Writer. I never met anyone who was so imbued with literature; he was drowned in it. I think I'm close to deciding literature is the one thing never to be taken seriously. (I take *poetry* seriously.) Harry took it literally. That's what made me so damned mad at him."

As soon as word reached Boston, Albert Bigelow, together with his twin brother and wife's parents, tried to charter an airplane to fly them to New York, but no pilot would agree to make the trip that night, so they did not arrive until the following day. Bigelow, who had never met Harry but had heard Josephine speak of him casually once or twice, was certain what had happened: "This man lured her to his apartment and murdered her. I don't believe in any suicide pact no matter what the police or anybody else says, and I believe my wife to be the victim of a mad poet who turned murderer because he could not have the woman he wanted—and who was true to me." He told another newspaper: "We were happily married, and she continually told me how devoted she was to me." Yet another quoted him as saying, "I don't understand it. It is a terrible nightmare. I loved her and thought and believed she loved me." His judgment squared with the recorded opinion of her friends, one of whom assured reporters that "a clandestine affair was a contradiction of her whole personality."

The previous week Josephine had told her husband that she would be visiting friends on Philadelphia's Main Line; instead she was in Detroit. Her telegram to Harry of November 18—I AM IMPATIENT . . . —was in his pocket (as was A's YES), and was released by the police to the press, where much was made of it. Nevertheless, Albert Bigelow stoutly refused to budge from his belief that his wife's sturdy honor had caused her death, that she had died because she would not "listen to his love pleas." Bigelow demanded that the police pursue their investigation in order to restore to his dead wife her good name. (He was spurred also by his knowledge that in cases of ritual suicide the Episcopal Church refuses to consecrate the dead, so he finally temporized a bit, conceding the possibility of her temporary insanity. In the event, she was buried in Old Lyme, where they had been married six months earlier, and the service was held in the same Congregational church.)

The shooting of his wife by the man she had betrayed him with must have been painful enough, but Bigelow's torture was prolonged by three days of front-page copy that was lurid even by New York tabloid standards of the day. Josephine was represented as a "restless

Junior League bride of . . . a Harvard campus idol." She was a "frustrated lover of the exotic Crosby" and she and her enamorato "met for a last bitter-sweet rendezvous" during which they were "joined in death as they never would be in life." Her husband, "scion of one of Boston's best families . . . cried from the depths of his despair. . . ." The *Daily Mirror* judged the event "an erotic epic of twisted lives, illicit love and hearts in exile." The *Daily News*, informing its readers of Harry's wish to be scattered across France rather than America, concluded that this was for the best in that "he will be far removed from . . . the six months' bride of another, who [*sic*] sleeps in a Puritan graveyard [*sic*] at Old Lyme, Conn., a last resting place in keeping with her life up to the time she wilted under the spell of Crosby's torrid verse." In another edition, the *Daily Mirror* citing Dr. Gonzalez's analysis of the alcoholic content in the dead couple's brains (yielding an efficient of "plus-one" for him and "plus-two" for her), concluded that "Jo-Jo Bigelow" had been not quite, but almost, "dead drunk." But perhaps no run of prose inspired by what all routinely labeled "the Tragedy" equals in plain vulgarity a paragraph from the New York *Telegram*'s front page on the day after the shooting: "In the morgue's sooty anteroom, where daily weeping culls and drabs of the town seek news of missing kinfolk, the cousins of Mrs. Bigelow waited to identify her slim, well-nurtured body. Characters out of the social register seldom step into the grisly old Bellevue Morgue on private business."

By contrast, the Boston papers remained introspective. Robert Choate's Boston *Herald* printed not one word about the event save for a paid announcement, set in agate measure, of Mrs. Bigelow's burial. The *Globe* played the story low and inside, and the *Evening Transcript*, noting in its story's second sentence that "the bodies were fully clothed," gave the pedigrees of all, noting especially that Mortimer was "a member of the most exclusive clubs in New York." The Boston *Post* ran its story on page 12, by its headline and subhead putting as much distance as possible between Harry, Josephine and their hometown: MAN AND GIRL DEAD BY PISTOL: Suicide Pact Evident in New York Tragedy. The Associated Press story relied on Stanley Mortimer's account:

> Mortimer, who had known Crosby for years, told police he was not well acquainted with the woman. He identified her, but said he understood she had been married less than nine months ago.
>
> "Harry and his friend called on me about 3 o'clock this afternoon," Mortimer told police. "I excused myself an hour later, took a walk and

visited some acquaintances. The entrance to my apartment is from the ninth floor into the gallery. I knocked for some time, thought they might have decided to leave, and asked the management to let me in. No one could find a key.

"The manager finally broke in the door with an ax and we found the bodies in the first bedroom on the gallery. I am not sure Miss Roche [*sic*] had married, but I recall hearing friends talking about it recently. I don't remember who they said she had married. We searched the apartment thoroughly. They had left no notes."

Predictably, the newspapers were careless about the facts of the case, which interested them only for its short-term advantages. Thus Harry was said by one story to have been Josephine's "sweetheart" five years and more. Another, confused by the ballistics of the case, decided that Harry must have been left-handed. The New York *World* gave Harry's age as thirty-five, his residence as New York, and Josephine's name variously as Roche and Mrs. Herbert Bigelow. The international edition of the *Herald Tribune* said that Henrietta Crosby was the widow of Stephen and that at Harvard, Harry, not yet thirty, had "distinguished himself as an athlete and a student," perhaps confusing him with the man he had caused such misery.

Some of the newspaper errors may be traced to Stanley Mortimer's account. Abashed to find himself broadcast in the public prints as a "complacent friend," and a kind of pander, he decided to invest himself with a casual manner and memory. He told the *Daily News* that he knew Josephine as "Miss Rotch," and the *Sun* that he knew her as "Mrs. Rotch." He was particularly reticent with the New York *World*, to whom he described Harry as a poet, "but when or where his poems were published Mortimer could not say." He went on to report that in borrowing the key to his studio Harry "did not explain what use he wanted to make of the rooms, and was not accompanied by Mrs. Bigelow. The couple entered the apartment during his absence. . . ." Later, after the superintendent had knocked the door off its hinges, and the two men had entered the dark apartment, Mortimer had called out: " 'Crosby, old man, where are you?' There was no answer." Mortimer added that he "knew nothing of [Harry's] family connections or of his acquaintance with Mrs. Bigelow."

To the *Daily Mirror* the next day, Mortimer was more forthcoming:

"Crosby was an old friend of mine. I have often loaned him my studio for—well—I suspected that he wanted to entertain women friends there. I knew Mrs. Bigelow slightly but not by that name. Harry always called her Miss Rotch in my presence. When he popped in about noon Tuesday with Miss Rotch I knew he was going to ask me to leave. The two of them went up to the balcony. I was at my easel downstairs painting. They leaned over the balcony rail and kidded me. Crosby gave me a signal and I got on my street clothes and went out."

He told substantially the same story to the New York *Herald Tribune*, but brought Harry to the Hotel des Artistes an hour later, and for the first time mentioned alcohol, saying that on his arrival Harry "showed the effects of liquor" and that between the time of his guests' arrival and his departure they drank, without his assistance, the best part of a quart of whiskey. (The autopsy was not consistent with Mortimer's judgment that Harry "showed the effects of liquor.")

None of the discrepancies would much matter (save for what they revealed of Harry's effect on the old friend whose indulgence he repaid with a mighty mess) were it not for the mystery created by uncertainties of chronology and motive. Simply: When did Harry arrive? When did he shoot Josephine? When did he shoot himself? Was he drunk? The answer to the last question is almost certainly *no*. The accumulated evidence points to an arrival at the Hotel des Artistes shortly after 1:30. In the judgment of Dr. Charles Norris, it is probable that Harry shot Josephine, with her consent, at about 5:00, just as he was due at J. P. Morgan's for tea, and that he shot himself a couple of hours later. But the chronology remains uncertain, and for this reason gave license at the time to a tantalizing rumor that was never confirmed, probably because it was not accurate. It appeared the day after the killings in the *Daily News* and elsewhere: "The poet, detectives believe, had gone home for a last farewell to his wife before returning to Mortimer's apartment to end his life. Employees at the Savoy-Plaza, where Crosby and his wife were registered with his mother . . . saw Crosby and his wife leave about seven p.m."

Night city editors like a bit of mystery in their suicide stories, of course. The Crosby-Bigelow slaughter was not precisely what such editors would have ordered, had they had their wish. It was all questions, no answers. It was too literary. It was kinky, but not sexy. And there was no note to wrap it all up. The rhythm of such stories is commonly punchy, the epilogue brief. If the suicide, because of the prominence of the characters, commands attention, there is a frenzied question: WHY? The headline MOTIVE SOUGHT is obligatory. A single follow-up then reflects on the "tragedy" and explains it: debt, disappointed love, depression, alcohol, terminal illness. It almost has to be one of these, and the note tells which. Harry simply had decided that it was time to die. But even if he had left a note saying so, or something like it, even if he had scribbled something about never taking second helpings, or that he liked to leave the table before he was full, the newspapers—and most of his friends—would not have believed him. (Newsmen and the police were not alone in their surprise at the want of a note. Malcolm Cowley told Archibald MacLeish that he found it astonishing that someone as articulate—or at the least voluble—as Harry, with hours to spend between the moment he knew he must kill himself and the moment he killed himself, put not a single word about himself or his act into a final record.)

The newspapers—and those friends—looked for motives. They picked through his poetry, and found clues, spelled *clews* by the Chicago *Tribune*, which printed an irreverent piece datelined Paris that tells a few home truths about why the killing came about:

CROSBY DIED FOR A THRILL, SAYS PARIS, JEERING "PACT"

Old Friends Laugh at Idea of Love Suicide

As a writer and publisher and a wealthy, amusing fellow besides, Crosby just about set the pace for the whole crowd of expatriates, who credit him with having "lived more fully than any man of his generation." None of his fast-moving crowd believe Crosby committed suicide for love, and are sure he sought death just to see what it was like. . . .

Other reports offered other, less brutally direct motives: temporary insanity . . . shell shock during the war . . . "some melancholy, some impulse" . . . disillusionment . . . morbid sensuality . . . expatriation . . . modern letters . . . his association with *Transition*—"in which the band of exiles express their sometimes half-mad thoughts on love and life." It was left to the *Daily Mirror* to indulge in a bigoted outburst of exasperated ignorance: "Crosby's effete mind had often dwelt on thoughts of death and suicide. He was of the school of morbid poets. His large-eyed morose face indicated his temperament. The police, examining his remains, discovered a significant fact. He had dyed his hair a becoming bronze red."

His "remains" revealed nothing of the sort. They were taken by the mortician Charles Schroeder from Bellevue Morgue to the Fresh Pond Crematory in Queens on December 12; there they were burned, and then returned to Caresse, who had them placed in a silver urn. It is uncertain what became of them thereafter. One report had it that she removed them to the Mill, but this was presently denied by Pete Powel, who explained to the press that the Mill did not belong to the Crosbys, and that the ashes had been scattered "over New York City from an airplane, in compliance with a wish made by him several years ago." (It had indeed once been his wish to be scattered through the skies above New York. And the French, as mentioned earlier, were intolerant of people who haphazardly scattered the remains of their friends just any old place in French territory.)

On December 14, only five days after the slaughter, Harry and Josephine disappeared from the newspapers, which had had enough of their insoluble puzzle. The story of Josephine's burial in her family plot at Old Lyme's Duck River Cemetery was pushed off page 6 of the *Daily News* by a report that "J. Pierpont Morgan recently bought his first painting, 'Apollo and Marsyas,' by Tintoretto for a sum in excess of $100,000, it was learned yesterday. His late father, founder of the Morgan millions, spent more than $300,000,000 acquiring one of the world's richest art collections."

Caresse was haunted by a police report regarding Harry's sun ring, the gold band they had bought together in Cairo, a ring said to have been stolen from the tomb of Tutankhamen. Later, a museum curator said the ring was a fake, but no matter: Harry had promised her never to remove it. The police said they had found it on the floor of Mortimer's bedroom, crushed under foot. Here, then, is a lie from *The Passionate Years* that Caresse might be forgiven: "It was on his finger when he died and now it is on mine."

So now it was the turn of friends to reflect on why he'd done it, why he'd truly done what he had always promised he would do. Hart Crane, less than three years shy of his own self-slaughter, told Katherine Anne Porter that what Harry had done was "imaginative, the act of a poet." D. H. Lawrence, months away from his death by consumption, laid Harry's suicide, oddly, at Mammon's feet and, less oddly, at art's: "Too much money—and *transition surréalisme*." His contempt in tight check, Lawrence wrote Caresse that Harry had had a true gift "if only he hadn't tried to disintegrate himself so! This disintegrating spirit, and the tangled sound of it, makes my soul weary to death. . . . The doctor came from England, & said I must be in bed for two months, & do *nothing*, & see no people—absolute rest. Oh dear!—and Harry was really so well, physically. And my nerves are so healthy, but my chest lets me down. So there we are. Life and death in all of us. . . . It was too dreadful a blow—and it was wrong."

These responses, even Lawrence's, were surely invited by Harry. He anticipated—indeed, insisted—that his act be read as a literary work, whether or not it was regarded as manqué. Eugene Jolas' telling a Paris reporter that Harry's "Hail: Death" was astonishing and frightening," and that had he lived, its author would have been a famous poet within five years—this was the sort of return Harry had expected. He would have been appalled that in some quarters, and most particularly the Latin Quarter, his suicide was regarded as a kind of practical joke.

Constance Coolidge blamed Josephine, "that poor demented girl." It was Josephine who "inspired him with that mad idea. . . . When he called me up the night before . . . he seemed to be full of enthusiasm. He said 'New York is marvelous, I like it even better this time than before. I'm going to stay here a long time.'" In Constance's judgment, Harry would do "*anything* on a dare. . . . She put the idea in his head & he could not back out—it was something like that. He never would back out of anything it would be a point of honor."

Constance's reading of Harry's act is flawed only by her insistence that he was in his impulsiveness merely a little boy, pure but naughty, who never grew up. He was not that. He was snared not by impulsiveness but by an excess of calculation.

Archibald MacLeish, on the other hand, recognized another aspect in Harry's character: "This whole thing caught up with Harry; he'd built it up, the black sun, a philosophy with edges of demonology in it; he peddled it to an awful lot of girls. This one, apparently, took it seriously. Then he was faced with a situation from which there was no escape whatever. He couldn't walk out of that place alive." MacLeish believed that Harry did not love Josephine then, and probably never had—that she was, in effect, a metaphor like Jacqueline. Gretchen Powel, who ate lunch with Harry the day he shot himself, agreed, and said that he was annoyed that Josephine had not left New York as she had promised, but continued to pester him, and had even threatened to kill herself in the lobby of the Savoy-Plaza if he didn't agree to see her again that day. The details of the story are not likely, but its burden— that Harry was not infatuated—is. Mrs. Powel remembers that he talked a great deal about suicide, but said that his talk was "just literary." For Harry, of course, the locution "just literary" would have been oxymoronic.

Polleen also misread the seriousness, or rather the consequence, of Harry's intentions: "He said he'd finish himself off when he was thirty-five or forty, I can't remember which. . . . I don't think my mother believed him, but I'm sure she'd say she did. I'm sure he had no intention of doing it at all; I'm sure it was a mistake, that the joke turned back on him."

He had meant to do it; it was no mistake; it was not a joke. If anything of Harry Crosby commands respect, perhaps even awe, it was the unswerving character of his intention. He killed himself not from weariness or despair, but from conviction, and however irrational, or even ignoble, this conviction may have been, he held fast to it as to a principle. He killed himself on behalf of the idea of killing himself.

Because it was an idea Harry did not share with his mother and father, they—heroic, both of them, in their mutilation—were obliged, not unlike the press, to search for some exterior reason. Or rather unreason, for they chose to fabricate an excuse based on their son's madness. In fact, in the aftermath of the suicide it seemed as though Stephen Crosby would himself come apart. Ted Weeks called on the family at 95 Beacon Street as soon as he heard the news. Mrs. Crosby had returned to France with Caresse, December 13, on the *Berengaria*, but Stephen Crosby, desolate, weeping, met him on the steps. He was holding one of Harry's miniature books from the Black Sun Press, showing how delicate and subtle it was, trying to speak, sobbing, inarticulate. He never wholly recovered from the crime his son had committed against them all, and as late as 1952, when *The Passionate Years* was published, a friend sped to 95 Beacon with the news that the book had been reviewed in the Boston papers so that Henrietta Crosby could intercept and hide them from her husband. (That good lady wrote Caresse that she was obliged to read the book in bed, late at night, "so that Steve won't catch me at it.") Yet in the immediate aftermath the family pulled together and acted with grace. (The community of which the Crosbys, Rotches and Bigelows were a part responded with an expression of perhaps limited delicacy: *Town Topics* of December 19 reported that the "announcement in Boston that the Assembly has been cancelled for this winter brought about a lot of chatter and, while it was officially announced that it was postponed until next season because of the absence of two of the committee, Mrs. Bayard Warren being in Aiken and Mrs. Edward Bigelow being in mourning, the consensus of opinion seems to be that the stock market crash is responsible.") Mr. and Mrs. Crosby assured Caresse that they would assume responsibility for her welfare, and would continue to educate her children and help out with the Black Sun Press. They begged her only to economize as best she could, and to try to live within an allowance of five thousand dollars a year, a generous sum in those depressed days.

Pursuing their decorums from beyond the grave, Harry made further trouble for the family by the instrument of a last will and testament so scandalous that a judge of the Massachusetts court, in probating Harry's estate, agreed—thanks to some prodding by friends of the Crosbys—to close the proceedings to the public, and to maintain the privacy of the document. Harry had had the will drawn first on April 2, 1929, then had destroyed it and had a new version created, according to his odd wishes, on August 19. To Caresse he left one hundred thousand dollars outright, together with the entire sum eventually due him from Walter Berry and the gold sun-ring that had been crushed underfoot in Mortimer's studio. To the imaginary Jacqueline Crosby he left his very real gold sun-cup. He left twenty-five thousand dollars and a pearl pin to Josephine, called in the will "Mrs. Albert Bigelow," and a gold necklace, together with another twenty-five thousand, to "Mrs. Charles Walker." Also ten thousand dollars, together with some gold and porcelain horses, to "Constance Comtesse de Jumilhac." There were bequests to girl friends whose husbands' names appeared with their own. He left his books to Harvard College (which did not want them), and instructed that *Shadows of the Sun* be published at the expense of his estate, together with special Harvard editions of the the *Rubáiyát* and of Rimbaud's works. He left money for a prize for poets, another for aviators, and his war medals to his father.

The will was never honored, as it was decided that, for the purposes of the Commonwealth of Massachusetts, it had not been properly witnessed or dated. Mr. and Mrs. Crosby regarded it as evidence of their son's sad mental instability. Stephen Crosby consulted a psychiatrist, who advised him that without question Harry had been a victim of shell shock during the war, and that in such cases "the sex complex is very over-developed." Mrs. Crosby also relayed to Caresse the information that her husband had been assured that "it was bound to get worse as time went on so that comforted Steve for no one could want any one we loved to go to pieces & I felt that was happening, but no one realizes better than I do that you & Harry had a very rare life together & I, like you, like to think of the beautiful side of it and what you meant to each other. I still keep feeling that letters may come from Harry, such a habit had it become to watch for them."

There was, of course, more mercy than medicine in the psychiatrist's diagnosis, but mercy was a quality deserved by his battered mother and father. Eight months to the day after Harry's death, Mrs. Crosby wrote Caresse to thank her for a presentation copy of *Poems for Harry Crosby*; her letter is a masterpiece of decency and sympathy and, because of its sanity, a tribute to her son:

> Dearest Caresse,
>
> I was awfully pleased to get the book in memory of Harry and I like so many of the poems and they make him still more living if that can be for he lives with me, in me, every hour of every day. You may not understand what I mean but he has so much influenced my life and I can scarcely read a book or see a picture but it comes over me how he would have liked or disliked it. I realize so much his quick and keen perception, I who lumber along like a slow old farm horse, he who shot by like Narcisse on the run and was there waiting to receive me or to help me to arrive. And if it is thus to me, what must it be to you? More and more do I marvel at how advanced for his years he was. . . .
>
> I shall do all I can for you & K[itsa] so long as I have it to do with. And we must be thankful that it's not like many who haven't enough to eat a large part of the time. . . . Goodnight dearest girl. I wish we lived nearer together for you always help me & I should like to feel that I sometimes might help you.

Tributes to Harry Crosby were plentiful. Some were offered from conviction, most were the usual—chock-a-block with rhetorical flourishes, firm in their assurance that the world would not look upon such a young man's like again. Spud Spaulding, whose life Harry had helped save at Verdun, wrote Caresse two days after the suicide that he had "never felt so terribly in all my life. If it hadn't been for Harry I wouldn't be here today. I loved him for what he did for me. . . . I have suffered a lot of losses lately, Polly, but this is the first time I've cried my eyes out since I was a kid and about all I can seem to say is 'I'm sorry and heartbroken—it just doesn't seem right.'" He meant it.

At first there was a rush to inflate the value of Harry's work. Writing for the Winter 1930 issue of the literary magazine *Morada*—the "Harry Crosby Number"—Norman MacLeod, introducing Harry and a few of his poems, wrote that Crosby's was "undoubtedly one of the most beautiful, and at the same time seethingly denunciatory voices of the time. . . . Crosby was another Rimbaud, but a more engaging literary personality." Writing for *The Rebel Poet*, Jack Conroy went the distance: "a rare and delicate spirit," he called Harry, whom he had not met, "his clear eyes unblinded by wealth, his Muse untarnished by the fool's gold of commercialism, we shall not look on his like again: salve atque vale, H.C., ego moriturus te saluto." For the occasion of

Transition's Harry Crosby memorial issue even Kay Boyle, whose rigor and scarab-hard glitter had so engaged Harry's admiration, gushed: "to be living now, to be living, alive and full of the thing, to believe in the sun, the moon, or the stars, or in whatever is your belief, and to write of these things with an alertness sharp as a blade and as relentless, is a challenge that is the solemn privilege of the young. In any generation there are but few grave enough to acknowledge this responsibility. In ours, Harry Crosby stands singularly alone. . . . He wrote his poems and wrote his diary in words that never faltered in their pursuit of his own amenable soul. . . . There was no one who ever lived more consistently in the thing that was happening then. And with that the courage to meet whatever he had chosen, with no consistency except the consistency of his own choice, and always the courage to match it. His heart was open like a door, so open that there was a crowd getting into it."

A couple of years later, in an unpublished introduction to a commercial edition of *Shadows of the Sun*, Kay Boyle had moved one hundred and eighty degrees in regard to Harry's relationship with the present tense, and with his contemporaries: "Yet Crosby was in no sense a modern," she wrote, with enviable certitude, "having no place, no interest, no taste for experiment in modern life." Similarly, she changed course on the subject of Harry's heart, previously wide open: in the revised version he took the sun as a symbolic shield to protect himself against "all that assaulted him" (Boston, his education, his "position in the bank") and "above all, against people. . . . His soul rejected them, they dismayed and bewildered him. . . . People were the enemy; his intimates were such things as 'a superb collection of old keys, illuminated manuscripts, stained glass windows . . . old book bindings, the sixteenth century bed.' "

Today, once again restored to her toughness, Miss Boyle judges Harry to have been "a very cruel and heartlessly self-centered man" who victimized his wife. Caresse* she recollects as "too uncertain of herself, too lost to be able to sort it all out. She existed, with her wonderfully human responses and inexhaustible energy, in the nightmare Harry lived in—a terrible, terrible hell of his own making." The

* *My Next Bride*, Kay Boyle's novel about Harry, was published in 1934 and dedicated to Caresse with an introductory epigraph from Laurence Vail: "Knife will be my next bride." In it a young lady much like Miss Boyle is subjected to the generosities and eccentricities of a would-be painter, Antony Lister, who has too much money for his own good and kills himself in New York. The fictional headline reads: PROMINENT YOUNG CLUB MAN CUTS VEINS IN FATHER'S OFFICE . . . WALL STREET LOSSES RUMORED."

hell was characterized by a fixation on money, money "needed with a kind of wild hunger" for hand-tooled leather notebooks with blank pages, probably never to be written in, and for the extravagant devices and entertainments of his circus at the Mill. For this Harry, unrecognizable as Miss Boyle's previous Harrys, all values had gone off course; he was a man for whom the spendthrift Dolly sisters (whom Harry once watched lose a quarter of a million dollars apiece at Deauville) "were as important as Joyce or Brancusi." In the current estimation, "the sadness, as well as the lack of beauty, in Harry's story makes it seem a succession of failures to the final moment."

It is appropriate that most of those who thought deeply about Harry's act were themselves poets, and many wrote poems about him and his suicide. Ironically, many of these poems attack him viciously, or make mock of him. But not Hart Crane's "To the Cloud Juggler," written for *Transition* in Harry's memory, nor Archibald MacLeish's "Cinema of a Man," more about what Harry represents than about who he was. E. E. Cummings' collection *W* [Viva], contains a cruel poem, titled "IX," about two characters, "y" and "z." The former is a "WELL KNOWN ATHLETE'S BRIDE" and the latter is "an intrafairy of floating/ultrawrists who . . . SHOT AND KILLED her . . . & HIM/self in the hoe tell days are/teased . . ." So:

> *2 boston*
> *Dolls;found*
> *with*
> *Holes in each other*
>
> *'s lullaby and*
> *other lulla wise by UnBroken*
> *LULLAlullabyBY*
>
>   *the She-in-him with*
> *the He-in-her(&*
>
> *both all hopped*
>   *up)prettily*
> *then which did*
> *lie*
> *Down,honestly*
>
> *now who go(BANG(BANG*

Three decades later, and in a similarly playful spirit, William Jay Smith wrote "*Petits Chevaux*: The Twenties":

> *Harry Crosby one day launched the Bedroom Stakes—*
> *Frivolity out in front, Fidelity overtaken by Concubine.*
> *The play was fast, the bets were high. Who lost? Who won?*
> *Green baize drank the tilting shadows of the sun,*
> *And death left the players' goblets brimming with blood-red wine.*

Not at all the effect Harry had wished and planned for. Where was gravity? Where was the weight of his act, its exemplary burden? Was it no more than this, then, a bloody joke? At least John Wheelwright was closer to Harry's own judgment of the matter when he called the suicide Harry's "best poem." And Wheelwright's "To Wise Men on the Death of a Fool," printed in *Hound & Horn*, certainly was *serious*, but where was his awe, or even his admiration or surprise? Wheelwright used the suicide to excoriate Boston as well as to lampoon Harry, an economical, perhaps pinch-fist use of an act that had been calculated to inspire a poet's benediction:

> *Wise men, when Crosby died, looked on each other*
> *And saw musicians, who did not mistake*
> *The catgut of their instruments for heart strings*
> *Withered by necessary, if regretful, Life.*
>
> *—Wise men, presented in self-portraiture—*
> *Presume to hold your scales, like Rhadamanthus;*
> *And weigh yourselves and Crosby; your own scales*
> *(After due vacillations of the dart)*
> *Will rest, to show your reassured eyes*
> *A pound of lead outweigh a pound of feathers.*
> *Crosby, in feathers, danced through a sealed house*
> *Which he unsealed, whose Idol's cerements,*
> *In ever-lessening spirals, he unwrapped*
> *With helian desire to grasp the Sun.*
>
> *And saw no sun, but saw the uncovered skull;*
> *Shuddered upon a sharp and fleshless mouth;*
> *And then, to warm his covered skeleton*
> *Fired his borrowed feathers. A night bird*
> *He blazed in plumes of smoke before the crowd.*
>
> *A traveler once wrote home from Africa:*
> *"I saw the fowl. But the time was out of season.*

It was only a chick. And when young, the Phoenix
Is no more astounding than a barn-yard cock."

Hierophants, turned neophytes, adore
This worshipper of Faithfulness in wolves,
Wisdom in doves and Gentleness in snakes.
Let not New England join, from whence he sprung,
Towards which he looked, too eager to amaze,
And wondered, "What may Boston say about me
"Now"; and dying, exulted, wondering "What
Can they now say?" State Street, maintain your silence.
His mad impiety is holier than your sane
Infidel doubt; but, you sane infidels
You wise men, named in Crosby's diary,
Whose words are linked with his words, be discreet
And please the financiers, who have exacted
Murder and suicide with Investment Council.

Let men made easy by his death keep silent
Resenting Crosby's life, and Crosby's death
Resenting. Poetry has saints. He was not of them.
His death was his best poem, and Crosby, dead
Shall live in history, like the marauders
Infatuate of new-found luxuries
Who fired the scrolls of Alexandria
To warm the waters of the public baths . . .

This did not nourish Caresse, nor satisfy her estimation of her late husband's place in the world, so she took pains to put Harry in as favorable a light as she could. No sooner was he burned, and she back in France, than she began to write poems to his memory and his ghost. *Poems for Harry Crosby* does not transcend as literature her limited gifts, but it does express anger, puzzlement, hot love and defiance, sentiments beyond the artifice of grief and memorial convention. She tackles head-on Josephine's mystifying reference to "our child" Pamela in the poem in which she announced to Harry that their marriage by death was at hand. In *Shadows of the Sun* Harry once referred to the possibility of a child by them both, but gave it no name. Caresse seems to have some inkling of the matter in her poem called by the name Josephine gave the child:

> *Pamela—does she live stillborn to you?*
> *Pamela has existed once is true,*
> *No Sorceress or Princess ever knew*

> *Pamela as I knew*
> *And if I die recount the scars—*
> Pamela—You.

She also directly addresses the suicide and its commissioner, "you have hurt us most," and its fruit, "debris."

Caresse commissioned an introduction from Stuart Gilbert, who had already contributed to the Harry Crosby memorial issue of *Transition*. He agreed to write one if her book was "dignified," but he refused to let her use the introduction if she persisted in her plan to title the book *Poems for Harry by Caresse*, arguing that "a title composed of two pet names is out of keeping with my preface, will make it look absurd and incongruous. Can one imagine Robert Browning's wife entitling a book of her poems: *Poems for Bob, by Bessie?*" Wisely, Caresse surrendered, and Gilbert puffed some hot air into her husband's reputation, if not into hers:

> Living near Harry Crosby was like the experience of an equatorial springtime, when the tyrant Sun, lord of life and death, strikes dazzling down, summoning from the four horizons storm-clouds and thunder and cyclone, when the scorched soil quakes and crumbles and life is fevered almost to frenzy, in strained expectancy of the monsoon. Like Rimbaud . . . Harry Crosby seemed to radiate a restless energy, an impulse to live dangerously, a menace of *insolation*. It was, indeed, the very excess of that life-force which proved his undoing. The sun rays, 'motive force of all life,' are also dispensers of death, shafts of that Apollo whose name itself . . . derived from that most tragic of Greek verbs ἀπόλλυμι; destroyer.

Now, that was more like it, and so Caresse began to busy herself arranging for the systematic posthumous publication of Harry's complete works. She was not alone in her enthusiasm. Hart Crane fueled her conviction that her husband's poetry merited wide distribution, and strangers, sending condolence, added apostrophes. Hugh Hanley, the treasurer of Rebel Poets ("an Internationale of Song"), confusing Harry's rebellion against the Morgan interests with a red fist extended on behalf of the Workers, advised Caresse as he offered her honorary membership in the brotherhood that "those of us who so deeply admired the work of Mr. Crosby have entered upon a campaign to perpetuate his work. I am personally of the honest opinion that no greater poet has yet been produced in this twentieth century. . . ."

Caresse gathered together the poetry and commissioned prefaces from T. S. Eliot (*Transit of Venus*) and Ezra Pound (*Torchbearer*). She had already in hand Lawrence's words about *Chariot of the Sun*, and used Stuart Gilbert's memorial remarks from *Transition* in *Sleeping Together*. (Harry had never met Pound, though he had once sent him a friendly post card from Haifa, during the 1928 trip with his mother. Soon thereafter he and Caresse had journeyed to Rapallo for a meeting with Pound, but from the railroad station the town appeared to be so bleak that they went on to Pisa.)

Pound had been familiar with Harry's work before the suicide, and the poems in *Torchbearer* have the usual preoccupations: suicide, fever, madness, scorn ("mort aux bourgeois") and sun worship. Most are displayed as prose, and give off a sense of haste that is less sloppy than driven. Pound echoes many of Lawrence's and Eliot's sentiments: Harry's work is chaotic and poorly crafted, but it has some magic. "There is an antithesis," Pound wrote, "between artist and illuminatus." Though Harry was no artist: "Crosby's life was a religious manifestation. His death was, if you like, a comprehensible emotional act, that is to say if you separate five minutes from all conditioning circumstance and refuse to consider anything Crosby has ever written. A death from excess vitality. A vote of confidence in the cosmos." He found in Harry a "natural ally who wd. probably never join one in any particular enterprise."

Caresse persisted in her efforts to perpetuate him. In the immediate aftermath of the suicide, Goops Pohlman had stayed on at the Mill, trying to help out. He wrote Billy Peabody (who had heard of his stepfather's death from Lord Lymington, while the boy was at Cheam) a couple of months later, spurring him on to manhood, giving advice ("always judge a man by Harry's standards; he was the greatest boy I have ever known") and letting drop the news that Caresse planned to learn how to fly, then to buy a Moth, then to fly across the Atlantic— and with Goops! "Harry meant to do this and she wishes to follow his wishes to the last detail. Please don't think that she won't do it."

Polleen was shattered by the news of Harry's suicide, and from that time forward never felt what she might have wished to feel about her mother. She recollects her now as a "beautiful widow: she took to widow's weeds, and looked too pretty for any words. She had great scores of gentlemen in rows deep on the doorstep, and she had an absolute ball." Caresse did indeed take a succession of lovers after Harry's death, but this was hardly out of keeping with his own customs. In fact, she suffered a remorse that was, if anything, excessive under the circumstances, about her appetite for men other than her dead husband, and wrote Constance Coolidge to ask whether she thought it wrong of her to keep intimate company with men; did it corrupt the memory of Harry? (Of course not, Constance told her. Have anyone who suits you, whomever might please you. Just don't aim too low.)

Caresse also plugged away at *Shadows of the Sun*, printing the volumes herself in accordance with Harry's expressed wish, and despite the scandal they would feed. She knew that whatever claim he might have to the literary world's attention probably rested with them. Jonathan Cape offered a generous contract until, in the spring of 1930, he learned of Stephen Crosby's objection to their publication, and withdrew his offer. Then an American publisher, the MacAuley Company, expressed interest in them to Hart Crane, but again nothing came of the venture. As late as 1965, Cyril Connolly contracted with Caresse and an English publisher to bring out a condensed version of *Shadows of the Sun*, with his introduction and Caresse's annotations, and in 1967 she was begging him to get on with the work, "please, please." But he never found the time. Harry's shot was not heard round the world, nor did its bang reverberate beyond the merest instant.

Afterword

"There exists an obvious fact that seems utterly moral: namely, that a man is always a prey to his truths. Once he has admitted them, he cannot free himself from them. One has to pay something."

—Albert Camus, *The Myth of Sisyphus*

If no exemplary legend has been fabricated from Harry Crosby's works and days, it is not the fault of Malcolm Cowley. Cowley met Harry briefly at Hart Crane's party, and after the suicide he borrowed *Shadows of the Sun* from Archibald MacLeish with a view to writing something or other about its author. But it wasn't till five years later, after Crane's suicide, that Harry's story became the concluding and summarizing section of *Exile's Return*.* Cowley's thesis in this most important book about the literary life of the Twenties is, first of all, that there *is* such a collection of discrete beings that can be lumped in what he calls a "generation," and second, that in the life and character of Harry Crosby can be found most of the circumstances and elements representative of what he uneasily calls, *pace* Stein and Hemingway, the Lost Generation. These are: service abroad in the Ambulance Corps, exile in Paris, a fanatic devotion to art, a repudiation of received social conventions, an insistence upon personal quirks and convictions

* At first Caresse was furious that Cowley used excerpts from the diaries without her permission, but later the two were reconciled and he helped her with *The Passionate Years*.

to the point of madness and beyond, and a final demoralization. For Cowley, Harry's life "had the quality of a logical structure. His suicide was the last term of a syllogism. . . ."

In a note accompanying the revision of *Exile's Return* twenty years after its original publication, Cowley explains that he chose Harry as a subject because he could not bring himself to write about Hart Crane's suicide. (Shortly before Crane jumped into the sea, Cowley's estranged wife, Peggy, became his first heterosexual love; he and Peggy planned to marry, and she was with him on the voyage out from Havana.) Perhaps because he did not know Harry well, and had selected him as a stand-in, Cowley conceived of him as a figure of mathematical purity, the "term of a syllogism," a proof.

In Cowley's thesis, much depends on one's willingness to assume that there is such an odd creature as a literary generation—to accept Faulkner, Frost, Pound, Hemingway, MacLeish and Crane as belonging together in ways that go beyond their common dedication to the execution of their various talents. More important, it also depends on an attractive and far-fetched assumption about Harry's suicide: that it was a second rather than first death. To Cowley's fascination, Ernest Hemingway had written about his own injury at the Italian front when as an ambulance driver during World War I he was wounded in the leg by an Austrian trench mortar: "I died then. I felt my soul or something coming right out of my body like you'd pull a silk handkerchief out of a pocket by one corner. It flew all around and then came back and went in again and I wasn't dead any more." Cowley, committed to establishing a connection between one representative figure and another—between Hemingway, say, and Crosby—extrapolates from one war catastrophe to another, from Italy to Verdun, November 22, 1917: "Harry died in those endless moments when he was waiting for the road to be cleared. In his heart he felt that he belonged with his good friends Aaron Davis Weld and Oliver Ames, Jr., both killed in action. Bodily he survived, and with a keener appetite for pleasure, but only to find that something was dead inside him. . . ."

What had in fact died, as it died with so many other children who had come to that war, was Harry's innocence. It is true that he set his innocence at a remarkably high price, and that the day he almost died (quite a different matter, he was happy to note, than truly dying) marked him forever. But there was a calculated character to his observance of his near-death day, as there was also for his reverent memorials to Weld and Ames, not at all his "good friends." He knew, that is, what he meant to feel about their deaths. What he meant to feel was a *post facto* justification of what had for him become a logical proposition: he would have neither the time nor the manner of his death chosen for him; he would die when he was ready, when he wished to die. To decide this was bracing and liberating: it had something to do with the conquest of fear, much to do with Verdun—where the choice was almost snatched from him—and nothing whatever to do with Cowley's thesis that an age went out with the last days of 1929, and that "Harry Crosby, dead, had thus become a symbol of change."

It is possible to *use* Harry's life and suicide as hooks on which to hang the customs and failures of a putative literary generation, but it is not possible to *explain* his life, much less his suicide, by them. Cowley writes that as time passed "Harry was remembered again by others. His death, which had seemed an act of isolated and crazy violence, began to symbolize the decay from within and the suicide of a whole order with which he had been identified." If Harry was remembered—and he wasn't remembered by many—it was thanks to Cowley's narrative, which gracefully tells a remarkable story. The story is remarkable not for its illustration of general principles or its symbolic burden, but for its isolation, its lonely singularity. However, because an act is isolated—personal, if you will (and what, if not suicide, may be called personal?)—is not to conclude that it was "crazy." Harry knew what he was doing, and did what he wished.

Harry's first thoughts of suicide must have come to him during the war. He had learned in France to subdue his terror and saw at first hand that death, as he had been taught by funeral-loving Boston and a pious mother, was both an occasion for celebration and a reunion with one's kinsmen already dead. As a child Harry believed in a life after death, and as a man of thirty-one, about to shoot Josephine and himself, he believed in a life after death—moreover, a better life than any earth could afford. Nothing else can explain his joyous anticipation of his death with Caresse. As far back as 1921, before the Lost Generation or a modern work of literature was known to him, he invited that death, self-imposed, for her and for himself. Nothing could be more astonishingly natural or boyish than the sentence dropped in the midst of a forty-page letter of love to Caresse: "If by any chance I should die or be killed (I promise you never to kill myself unless you die or unless I kill us both together) I hope you'll end your life and come to me right away so we can be together as One in Heaven."

He was at Harvard when he wrote that but he meant it, and meant to live by it. Three years later, he reminded Caresse that he was ready to die with her at any time; she needed only to say the word (the word that Josephine doubtless said, just the precise *yes*).

As time passed, the squalor of Verdun could be recollected by Harry only by calculated effort, and death took on a more formal, more elegant aspect as he saw Berry into a world to come, a world he himself welcomed. Along the way, from time to time, something would steel his conviction: he was deeply impressed upon reading in *The Picture of Dorian Gray* that "youth is the only thing worth having. When I find that I am growing old, I shall kill myself." The promise is conventional, but to Harry it must have been persuasive. He must have imagined himself in middle age, losing his looks and his charm and his hold on the beautiful women whose devotion he invited and returned. What would his old age have been? He might have imagined himself a Polonius of doomsayers, the club bore, wearing a silver whistle around his neck, an old geezer clucking and shaking his head over the good old days when he had sown his wild oats and damn near killed himself.

Suicide must have seemed a way, the only way, to authenticate his seriousness and his stature. Harry had noted with approval the opinion of William James that when a man takes his own life "the fact consecrates him forever. Inferior to ourselves in this way or that, if yet we cling to life, and he is able to 'fling it away like a flower' as caring nothing for it, we account him in the deepest way our born superior."

On November 8, 1925, Harry—by God knows what persuasion—obliged Caresse to enter with him into a contract, which they signed together and which he thereafter carried with him always, as a man with an exotic blood type might carry with him a card in case of an accident so that he does not bleed to death before a companionable blood type is found. Written in ink on note paper bearing the Crosby cross, the contract is titled "Burial Instructions of Harry and Caresse Crosby," and calls for their cremation together, followed by their burial together, beneath a "strong, simple gravestone wrought of white marble." It offers detailed instructions for the inscription on the stone, and specifies burial in the Cimetière de l'Abbaye de Longchamp if possible, and at Manchester-by-the-Sea if not. The intention is simply stated: "Having sworn a sacred pledge to die together which pledge we believe to be beautiful and true in sight of God. . . ."

The Crosbys had found the cemetery during a walk in the Bois de Boulogne at the close of 1923, and Harry had seen at once that it was "a *real* burying place." Thereafter he visited the boneyard compulsively, became friendly with the groundskeepers, selected a headstone and had it delivered to the cemetery. But while all this transpired he began to write yet another instruction in his diary, and on odd scraps of papers and on his calling cards and in the margins of books, and this also he carried in his billfold:

> Instructions to be carried out at our death:
> We desire to be cremated together
> We desire that our ashes be mingled together
> We desire that our ashes be taken up in an aeroplane at Sunrise and scattered over New York.

This too was signed with both their names, but he had signed it for her. He was so beside himself with the idea of the disposition of their bodies that he could not decide which he most desired, the burial near the Bois or an ash fall over New York, the dive down or the flight up.

Similarly, Harry was torn at first between methods of self-slaughter, and could not fix for himself a satisfactory death-date. In 1924, he thought he might kill himself at the Cimetière de l'Abbaye de Longchamp, in a gesture noble in its economy. But how? He collected methods and cases like a connoisseur. During Harry's years in Paris there were many notorious suicides. There was the dandy Jacques Vaché, known for his epigrams, who had been outraged while fighting for France at the Front that the means and time of his death might not be within his power to control, and who decided then to kill himself and did so, poisoning himself and two unsuspecting friends. And there was Jacques Rigaut, who said that "suicide is a vocation," and who shot himself a couple of weeks before Harry: a "theoretic suicide" it was called, committed on behalf of Dada. Willy Seabrook had tried cannibalism, it was said, knew of a bistro where they served human flesh, but settled finally for suicide. The painter Jules Pascin, a friend of Kay Boyle, hanged himself after writing a note in blood upon his chest. René Crevel, who wrote about gassing a fictional character to death, gassed himself to death.

Harry clipped news stories about suicides, about a woman who swallowed needles till she died and about a man who had caused himself to be locked up in a cage for thirty minutes with lions, to whom he read his verses (the lions were pacific, or paralyzed with ennui). Visiting Vesuvius, Harry decided that suicide in the actual crater would not be possible, for one would be maimed before reaching the rim. In 1924 he settled on laudanum, a gentle death, and four years later, buying with his mother the gold sun-cup in Damascus, he still thought that he and Caresse might drink poison from it.

It never entered his mind to die alone, and he instructed himself and Caresse in the custom of certain Hindu wives who throw themselves on their husbands' funeral pyres. He noted with appreciation the case of a female lion who had pined away and died in the London zoo when her mate had died before her. Harry wished "to have influence strong enough to lead a band of followers into the Sun-Death." Solitary suicide was no good by his lights: it might be misread as a vulgar symptom, the final convulsion of a man suffering terminal depression or anxiety or failure. To convert another to one's faith: that was the point. To validate one's faith and enact it: to love dying and die loving. He had tried to persuade Constance to his singular conviction, writing her a letter of love that declared "you will never leave me anymore in the after-death. So don't be afraid in life. Don't be afraid. If you have to cry tears, cry them. But in your heart of hearts know that I shall come again, and that I have taken you forever." Constance would not go: at the back of a book he had given her she wrote in red that "Harry committed suicide with a girl in Boston. He wanted to commit suicide with me—but I refused."

At the end of 1928 Harry had picked the means of his death with Caresse, and the date: "The most simple Sun-Death is from an aeroplane over forest (31-10-42) down down down down Bang! the body is dead—up up up up Bang!!!! the Soul explodes into the Bed of Sun." Still, a pistol was always a serious rival to the plunging airplane: it was easily available, conveniently employed and it made a loud bang. He had a fixation on Eliot's catch line from "The Hollow Men" about whimpers and bangs, and since he refused to be remembered as a hollow man, and inclined to take metaphors literally, in the end he settled for his little Belgian automatic, with the sun engraved upon it.

It should not be imagined, however, that in his vacillation about the means he would use to kill himself he was in any way tormented, or fundamentally irresolute. He enjoyed the quandry, and his writing is at its most exuberant when he is recording the history of suicide, the physiology of suicide, the rationalization for suicide, and when he is quoting Montaigne on suicide, Nietzsche, Schopenhauer, Freud, Burton, Voltaire, anyone who shared his passion, his hobby.

He talked it over with friends he respected, not as though he were sharing with them a sordid confidence but as though he were offering wonderful news about some unexpected bounty that had come his way. MacLeish "knew of his central commitment to dying while one was in the full of life, of choosing his own death. My impression was that it was all good fun, good décor, but not to be taken seriously. My own conviction was that he wasn't serious about it, till I found out the hard way that he was deadly serious about it."

It can be said that Harry was at his most healthy, at his least morbid, when he studied his forthcoming death. "Death: the hand that opens the door to our cage the home we instinctively fly to." He seized for himself a great adventure, created for himself a cosmos, and abandoned it in his own good time.

Postscript

Caresse remained in France till the mid-Thirties, continuing the work of the Black Sun Press, and establishing Crosby Continental Editions, a paperback publishing company, years ahead of its time, that printed work by Hemingway, Faulkner, Dorothy Parker and many other luminaries. She met a handsome Westerner, Selbert Young, sixteen years her junior, who never learned to spell her name accurately: to him she was Carress. They were married in Virginia, in March of 1937, and bought Hampton Manor there, a plantation fallen to ruin, but designed by Thomas Jefferson. They had as their guests Salvador Dali, Henry Miller, Max Ernst, Stuart Kaiser, and as many of the old Mill crowd as found their way to America. Bert Young was a drunk, and a nasty one. Caresse was obliged to keep the services of a full-time carpenter to mend by day the damage that her husband had done by night, and she divorced him during World War II and moved to Washington, where she opened an art gallery on G Place N.W. Later, she established an expensive mixed-media magazine called *Portfolio*, which went through several issues, all well reviewed. She continued her friendship with Kay Boyle, and enormously enlarged her circle to include such friends as Kenneth Rexroth, Allen Ginsberg, and Anaïs Nin. Her correspondence on file at Southern Illinois University is huge: the Ezra Pound folder alone contains enough material for a monograph by someone interested in that kind of thing.

She bought a castle in Roccasinibalda, fifty-five miles north of Rome, near Rieti, a huge hilltop fortress that carried with it the honorific *Principessa*, which she enjoyed. After the war she converted it into an artists' colony, and became active in such causes as Women Against War and Citizens of the World, of which she was founder and president. In her latter capacity, she was euchred by Archbishop Makarios into buying a mountaintop in Cyprus for a world meeting center, after she was barred from Greece, where she had bought another mountaintop for a like purpose in Delphi. She remained to the end ebullient, an odd mixture of shrewdness and goofiness, courageous in the extreme, and proud. While she labored to finish *The Passionate Years*, she corresponded with Malcolm Cowley, who advised her, properly, to confirm her facts and dig deeper into the motives and purposes of her actions and Harry's. She replied in exasperation, with as astute a sketch of her character as can be made: "As for ideas underlying the actions of the 20s, I haven't the foggiest notion. As you say, I am not introspective, not do I ever judge motives, only actions. I am 100% extrovert (or was); if I had been otherwise I doubt it I could have weathered the 20's. I don't suppose I ever have a thought unrelated to action—and I can't describe our ideas, only what we did." She died at seventy-eight, in Rome, on January 24, 1970.

Caresse and her daughter did not get along well. Polleen despised Bert Young, and would not tolerate his company, and there were quarrels about money. Caresse was never a generous mother, and as years passed she came increasingly to envy and compete with her daughter— who has herself been three times married: to the Comte de Mun, to the Honorable John North and to Stephen Drysdale. She divides her time between London and Ibiza, and plans to write an account of her recollections of her chaotic yet bracing childhood.

Polly's brother William was a student at the Lennox School after Harry's death (G. Gardner Monks was his headmaster there). He was graduated from Williams College, and was active in World War II. He married a French lady, and died in 1955 as the result of a gas leak in their Paris apartment.

Albert Bigelow remarried in 1931, and became a painter and architect. In 1958, he was arrested for sailing his boat, *The Golden Rule*, into a nuclear test area, and for this protest spent sixty days in a Honolulu jail. (The law by which he was convicted was later ruled to be unconstitutional.) In 1961, he was an Alabama Freedom Rider, and his bus was bombed and burned in Anniston. He lives in Marion, Massachusetts.

Harry's sister Katherine, his only sibling, remarried after her divorce from Robert Choate, and in 1959 killed herself by gunshot. One of her two daughters jumped to her death from the Golden Gate Bridge. As facts, these have no meaning; they explain nothing; their resonance is metaphorical. I do not believe that the death wish, if such a drive even exists at some base level of instinct, can be genetically imprinted. I do believe in the power of suggestion: Harry's decision may have struck these two ladies, in their desperation, as exemplary.

But I kneel before such speculations. Nine days after I interviewed Gretchen Powel, grilling her particularly about Harry's suicide, she was dead from stomach cancer. Such was her forbearance that I was not conscious of her pain. And because I did not know what had brought her to Washington, D.C., from France, I did not know what pain my questions must have caused her. I was attempting, with her help, to understand Harry Crosby, to puzzle out why he pulled the trigger on himself and on Josephine, almost half a century ago. "He didn't," was Gretchen Powel's reply: "He couldn't have." I protested, and she shook her head. No: I was quite wrong, she *knew* I was *quite* wrong. Harry *talked* of suicide, of course. But he would never choose to die. Why would anyone choose to die?

Minor Lives

"It's interesting—things that are interesting interest me." In *Black Sun*, I judged Harry Crosby's mother's declaration to be "scatterbrained." Now I'm not so sure. Shortly before the publication of that book in 1976, I heard from a writer to whom I had sent a complimentary copy. He was generous with praise, but closed with a question friends and reviewers have asked many times since: "Why Crosby?" He even essayed, in a friendly way, to answer it: "Probably he was all that was left over."

The gunshots had briefly inspired flamboyant publicity; the grisly theater of murder/suicide played the tabloids for a few days, and then citizens turned their attentions elsewhere. Crosby's widow fueled, without much success, the legend of her husband; Malcolm Cowley brought Crosby onstage to drop the curtain on *Exile's Return*. But otherwise Harry Crosby—his life, work and death—endured in the world's memory as a mere footnote to the cultural history of Americans in Paris in the Twenties.

I learned about Crosby from Cowley's narrative fifteen years before I began to write about him. Simply: his story stuck in my mind. I searched libraries for more about Crosby, and something by him. I found his poems in rare-book rooms, and didn't like them. As little as I liked them, however, there was something about their badness—energy, will, a breathtaking ignorance of literary conceit—that also stuck in my mind. I found his journals, *Shadows of the Sun*, and was struck by their consistent, even obsessive, vision: Crosby lived every minute as though it were his last. He was reckless, indifferent to consequence. He was not brave; a brave man overcomes fear. He was fearless. He announced again and again, from the time he was twenty-two, that he would kill himself, choose his own means and moment to leave the table before he was full. He was a phenomenon, not exemplary. Cancer might be regarded as exemplary, while a lightning strike is phenomenal. Crosby was like a lightning strike, and he interested me.

The reviews of *Black Sun* were mostly magnanimous, but the reviewer for *Time* magazine justly observed that since I regarded Crosby as "unique, he was not a proper symbol of anything." From this simple enough declaration, the reviewer extrapolated a question: "What then is the point of inflating an interesting footnote to the dimensions of a sizable book? The answer, certainly, is gossip." *The New Republic*, having judged *Black Sun* "an elegant book," concluded in the same sentence that it was a "pointless and disappointing one. Geoffrey Wolff doesn't claim anything for Harry Crosby; he knows . . . that his life was neither Art nor artful." Christopher Lehmann-Haupt, in *The New York Times*, felt cheated: "In the end, we are somewhat disappointed. One is not especially uplifted to have enjoyed a three-ring circus of scandal and antisocial behavior. . . . And though Mr. Wolff skillfully dismantles Malcolm Cowley's thesis that Harry Crosby's life and death were paradigmatic of the so-called Lost Generation . . . he doesn't offer much by way of explanation to replace it." When the book appeared in England it was reviewed by prominent people in prominent media at considerable length. After detailing the scandalous, glamorous and sensational character of Crosby's life and death, the reviewer would typically ask: Who could care about such a man? Who would *write* about such a man?

(During my senior year as an undergraduate, a pal and I sat in the dark, day after spring day, watching *American Bandstand.* Outside it was warm and sunny, and we sat watching with the windows shut and the curtains drawn. One afternoon I said to my friend, "Good God, what a way to put in hours!" I was speaking of course of the rock 'n' rollers. I felt my friend look at the back of my neck. He said, "Yeah.")

So why Harry Crosby? *It's interesting—things that are interesting interest me*. It seemed to me in 1971 when I began working on this biography that any story that had stuck to my memory for fifteen years was trying to tell me something. Too, there was an unexplained mystery about his suicide: Why did he kill himself, healthy, wealthy, happily married, in love and loved back, young? Why didn't he leave a note? Did he murder the woman he shot, or did she choose to die with him?

I did not know the answers to any of these questions and was eager to find them out.

I understood when I began that I would not introduce to the world a great lost poet, or even a good one. I knew also that I was distrustful of theses, that everything in my experience ran counter to the generalizing impulse. I hoped, when I was done with Crosby, to understand a man, not to have unriddled the secret of Man. I hoped also to bring news, as the word *news* is kin to *novel*. I had written three novels when I began *Black Sun*, and had an affection for the novelist's control of his world, the sense of a world poised to be made up whole and shaped. I believed when I began *Black Sun* that such control was Crosby's principle ambition, and the most consequential fact of his life: he sought to make himself over and up. He determined to translate himself from a Boston banker into a Great Poet by the agency of Genius. Genius he calculated to attain by the agency of Madness. He was purely without a sense of metaphor, so that he willynilly enacted rather than imagined his progress from Harvard boy to surrealist. He *did* what gifted poets write. Thus, for him, suicide was neither an idea nor a figure of speech; it was a bullet in his head.

Harry Crosby was the willing prisoner of his announcement that he would control his end, die when and as he chose. The biographer is, of course, the prisoner of his subject's facts. For a biographer like myself, more responsive to narrative design than to archival duty, the facts of certain kinds of lives are impediments. Let's pretend for a moment that *minor* and *major* accurately describe a distinction between human beings and their works: what kind of book can be written of a man or woman who has written major poems and lived a minor (would this modifier suggest *uneventful? serene? within the law? with moderate use of alcohol and non-prescription drugs?*) life, or died a minor death (*not in war, or in the fiery crash of an automobile, or if in a fiery crash not while driving an Italian or German roadster whose top could be lowered, or by gunshot?*). Surely, in such an instance, the subject's work is what matters. The subject has subsumed and shaped in work the mess of life. In Crosby's case his life stood as so much material, so much documented material, and I was left with what seemed to me the enviable task of making something from it. Harry Crosby walked the earth thinking of himself as a major poet in the making. He looked forward to the judgment of posterity, and made that judgment easily accessible by saving every scrap of paper that memorialized his vagrant scribbles. But however lunatic his calculated instruction book for readers better to understand him, when he shot himself he left no note, wisely apprehending that whatever paltry and infelicitous message such a note gave the world would be the last word the world would take from him. By not leaving a note, by leaving everything else—letters, notebooks, variants of poems, diaries, receipts, guest books, photographs, scrapbooks, report cards, passports—he seemed to invite such a history as I tried to write, such a collaboration.

Black Sun is indeed gossip, insofar as gossip is narrative. Some gossip is unsubstantiated, and some gossip is true. The gossip in *Black Sun* is substantiated hearsay. Like any biographer, I have passed along other people's mail, trafficked in rumor, eavesdropped on the conversations Crosby recorded in his notebooks, pried into school and college transcripts, gossiped with his surviving friends and relatives about him. I did this not because I labored under the delusion that Crosby was exemplary of good poets (or even bad poets, though I might have made a case for the symptoms he shared with other bad poets of his age). I never thought of him as standing for Harvard or Boston or Paris or the Twenties or exiles or philanderers or gamblers or ambulance drivers. I was from the beginning less drawn to his superficial similarities with his fellow men than to his elemental differences. I assumed those differences and left it to readers, whom I cannot pretend to know with such intimacy as I know Crosby and myself, to discover likenesses between Crosby's case and their own.

W. H. Auden's pugnacious essay about autobiography, "Hic et Ille," addresses the question of the unique case, the hermetic life. Midway through a progression of aphorisms, Auden's temper snaps: "Literary confessors are contemptible, like beggars who exhibit their sores for money, but not so contemptible as the public that buys their books." Calming himself somewhat, he quotes Cesare Pavese, putting him in italics: *"One ceases to be a child when one realizes that telling one's trouble does not make it any better."* (Pavese, like Crosby, ceased to breathe when he ceased telling his trouble; their suicides were not their last, best pieces of work, they were evidence that there was no work left in them.) Auden's case against the literature of the single personality, the kind of story that *Black Sun* means to be, builds to this heartfelt dogma: "Our sufferings and weaknesses, in so far as they are personal, *our* sufferings, *our* weaknesses, are of no literary interest whatsoever. They are only interesting in so far as we can see them as typical of the human condition. A suffering, a weakness, which cannot be expressed as an aphorism should not be mentioned."

Now, here's a surface to press against! I freely confess that I never calculated Crosby's confessions, as I articulated them, to incline toward the aphoristic, to build toward some generalizing trope, some "thesis" such as Lehmann-Haupt of the *Times* yearned to have in place of Malcolm Cowley's. It has been my experience as a reader that a strategy of connection and generalization is bound to fail. In fiction it produces flat characters, types whose accessories and quirks are designed only to reinforce conventional wisdom. As artless as the aphoristic impulse may be in fiction, in biography it is inhumane, filing the burred edges, the *interesting* burred edges, from a subject in order to fit him smoothly to the shape of other characters of his "type," to slip him like a greased key into the lock of received expectation. And in autobiography the impulse to generalize the writer's personal case is an unpardonable presumption: I cannot presume to know what experiences I share with you. If we share none, I can be certain you will find little of interest in my history, but I cannot design *my* history to satisfy my notion of *your* deepest yearnings.

These questions are not concluded in the purity of a vacuum, of course. Empirical data condition the biographer's apprehensions. When I told people in conversation about Harry Crosby—what he did rather than what he stood for—people seemed interested. As morally repugnant as this may be, it seems that his suicide authenticated his life. It is awful to watch someone with good eyesight and all his senses on full alert walk with gravity and determination toward the edge of a precipice, and keep going. Had Crosby stopped at the edge, peered down, turned around and died in bed at eighty, I would not have written a book about him. I'm troubled by this fact; it is ghoulish, but I don't pretend not to understand it. My preoccupation, for better or worse, was with narrative, and without Crosby's suicide his narrative would have been shapeless, pointless.

I run counter in this assertion to the conventions of biography. The authentic biographer is above all a writer who receives facts and bravely accommodates them. If the biographer's subject writes a great book or passes a great law at the age of twenty-four, and thereafter lives a life of dwindling vision and intensity, dying at ninety-four, following ten years of senility, well, there you are, that's life, that's death. Crosby gave me a pretty arc, a life lived flat out, a death chosen as a fitting climax. Because he calculated his death's effects, I was left to judge the act's aesthetic value as well as its moral horror, and welcomed the occasion to pipe up about something that interests me deeply. Harry Crosby noted with approval the opinion of William James that when a man takes his own life "the fact consecrates him forever. Inferior to ourselves in this way or that, if yet we cling to life, and he is able to 'fling it away like a flower' as caring nothing for it, we account him in the deepest way our born superior."

That is, the question of suicide is interesting. Camus said, and I agreed when I embarked on this book, that there is no question more interesting. And because Crosby's was uncomplicated by bad health, alcoholism, unrequited love, unpaid bills, old age or a disappointing Christmas, his suicide seemed on the face of it worth thinking and writing about.

Critics have distinguished between the Romantic and Augustan conventions in biography and autobiography. The Augustan impulse is exemplary (though not, probably, as Auden would have understood the term): it is a memoir in two boxed volumes by a statesman, or a biography of a major author. It inclines toward the archival, the archaeological. Joseph Blotner's *Faulkner: A Biography* (1974) is such an Augustan labor. William Gass has called this a "massive Egyptian work... not so much a monument to a supremely gifted writer as it is the great man's grave itself, down which the biographer's piously gathered data drops like sheltering dirt...." Gass has imagined the subject of such biography, a fellow named Feaster, whom he addresses, warning what the future will make of him: "It would mount in a museum your high school ring, wonder at your watch, your St. Christopher medal; and then your body, from dental crown and crew cut to appendix scar and circumcision, would become, as all enduring human matter does, abstract and general; you would not be a member any longer, but a species, a measure like the meter bar in Paris."

The Romantic convention celebrates the member rather than the species, investigates the particular case. It is fundamentally autobiographical, and for better or worse my own work—I confess!—has tended toward it. During the editing process of *Black Sun*, about a man who died eight years before I was born, I was told many times, too many times, that my book had "too much Geoffrey Wolff in it." To the extent that the biographer's voice derails *his* narrative, or bullies his subject into submission, the biographer has botched his work. But to deny biography the signature of a style, the sound of a single voice rather than the crowd noise of the species Biographer, seems perverse, artless and servile.

Leon Edel has written that the art of biography "lies in the telling; and the telling must be of such a nature as to leave the material unaltered." I'm not certain that any telling can leave material unaltered; point of view alters data, dogma deforms it, and putative objectivity (the absence of a point of view) confuses it. The best the biographer can hope for is what Lytton Strachey demanded of himself, that he ". . . lay bare the facts of his case, as he understands them."

Where are the facts of a "minor" case to come from? To ask this question in 2003 would be risible. Google them, fool! Nexis the details and Bob's your uncle! In the dark ages of 1971 one pretended to be a sleuth. Expecting to learn about Crosby in Paris, among his surviving contemporaries, I took my case to France, and enjoyed France, but I learned nothing there about the man I had promised my publisher I would write about. I returned to America chastened, and anxious. A book titled *American Literary Manuscripts* listing major holdings of letters and manuscripts by our libraries directed me to the New York Public Library, which in fact had no Crosby papers, and to Brown University, which did. At Brown were some letters and photographs, and many volumes of notebooks, the raw material from which *Shadows of the Sun* was formed.

At Brown I learned that huge numbers of papers belonging to Crosby's widow Caresse had been purchased by Southern Illinois University in Carbondale, and these I was allowed to examine during several week-long visits. Here were letters to Crosby from D. H. Lawrence, James Joyce, Archibald MacLeish, lady friends, his parents and relatives. Here were notebooks in which Crosby recorded in close detail the most intimate aspects of his life. By checking his notebook entries against letters to his wife and mother and father, I soon learned that he was a reliable truth-teller; I could trust him. I also realized that his short life was so amply documented that it left little to surmise, save the ruling question of his life: his death.

I resolved to take advantage of this documentation to the fullest, weaving the raw facts of his history through my text as artfully as I knew how, using the dialogue he had so thoughtfully preserved. I had no wish to be accused of having "novelized" my biography, and I knew that without supporting apparatus to identify the sources of the data I presented, I would not, should not, be taken on faith. Whenever a bit is taken from here and another bit from there, sometimes in violation of chronology, the synthesis is partial, even tendentious, and I wanted my readers to have access to the exact parts that comprise *Black Sun*'s whole, calling for generous citation. I chose to place notes at the back of the book to free my narrative of cluttering justifications and attributions.

The following passage from page 278 of *Black Sun* gives a sense of the kind of narrative synthesis biography might employ. Here, for the sake of illustration, I identify with intrusive footnotes where the scraps came from:

> The day before Harry, Caresse and Constance sailed for New York on the *Mauretania*, the Crosbys had some people to tea at 19 rue de Lille: Ambassador Joseph Grew, Alex and Sylvia Steinert, the Crouchers, Goops and a few others.[1] The next afternoon, November 16, several of these, together with Eugene Jolas, saw them off with a party on the railway platform in Paris.[2] As soon as they boarded at Cherbourg, a telegram was delivered to Harry. The message was terse—YES—but to him not cryptic. It was signed by the Sorceress.[3] Three days later, sitting with Constance in the smoking room during a storm[4]—both at sea and with Caresse, who was sulking in her stateroom, jealous of Constance[5]—and reading *Beating the Stock Market*,[6] he was brought another radiogram.
>
> "I guess this must be from my girl in Boston," he told Constance.
>
> "Oh, Harry," she said, "I do hope you aren't going to get mixed up with that girl again. She's married, and you aren't really in love with her anyway."
>
> "I love three people," he replied. "Caresse, you, and Josephine."[7]

1. The names of the Crosbys' visitors, and the fact that there was such a party, came from a guest book among papers at Southern Illinois University.
2. I know that Eugene Jolas said goodbye to the Crosbys from his unpublished memoir, which his widow let me read in Paris.
3. The telegram from "the Sorceress" is among Crosby's papers, at Brown University, and I surmise that it was delivered in person to Harry by an instruction on the envelope: "Deliver to stateroom."
4. That there was a violent storm during their passage I learned from New York newspapers on microfilm in the annex of the New York Public Library.
5. That Caresse sulked, jealous, in her stateroom while Crosby passed time with Constance, I learned from *Shadows of the Sun*.
6. That Crosby was reading *Beating the Stock Market* during the afternoon this second telegram was delivered I learned from his meticulously annotated reading record, among his papers at Southern Illinois University.
7. The conversation between Harry and Constance was duplicated in a letter from Constance to Caresse following Harry's suicide.

In addition to twenty-eight pages of notes, an annotated bibliography and a chronology (which liberated me to move back and forth through the text in time, following where topics rather than the calendar led), I included an index, so that readers could locate the "major" figures who intersected my minor subject. I interviewed as many people as I could find (and would talk with me), but not until I had soaked myself in Crosby's documents. More than forty years had passed since his death, and the people I interviewed were called upon to reach back in memory more than half a century. A few had astounding recall: Edward Weeks and Archibald MacLeish could attach episodes to dates accurate within a tolerance of a week or two. But for the most part the utility of these interviews was to observe in which ways memory had altered Crosby into a figure of legend or derision, to watch the critical faculty seep through the compost pile of all those years. Finally, when I caught myself giving rather than taking information, when I spent more time telling Crosby's friends and kinsmen what they *really* knew about him than asking what they knew, it was time to go home and begin writing.

The book I wrote after *Black Sun*, titled *The Duke of Deception*, is . . . what? Biography, sort of. Autobiography, I guess. On its account I stopped asking questions and began writing, not because I finally knew all I could know, but because there was so little really to know. That book is about my father—Arthur "Duke" Wolff—a "minor" subject if ever there was one, but a major father to me. He is remembered, and not fondly, by hornswoggled bankers, unpaid merchants, and police and prison officers of the four quadrants of the United States. And by me. He died before my children met him, and the book I have written about him, and my childhood with him, is for them.

Like *Black Sun*, *The Duke of Deception* begins with its subject's end. These are minor characters, after all, and to begin with their beginnings, with births, would beg much of a reader's patience. More important, I don't like books that tease, and I have tried to tell stories whose suspense is of character rather than episode: *Here's what Harry Crosby did; let me try to show why.*

What Crosby said he'd do he did, exactly, which is why he interests me. What my father said he had done, he had not done. I grew up in a family in which much was suggested and little was explained, in which misapprehensions were exploited, lovingly manured. My father was a Jew, and said he was not. My father said he was a Groton and Yale and Skull & Bones man, and he was not. My father said he had inherited a huge fortune, but he did not. Everything that mattered most to me I learned late, and in a rush. And that is how I learned that my father would not live forever.

When I turned twenty-one my father gave me a heavy gold signet ring that he said had been in our family many years. In fact, the ring had been fabricated according to his design in Hollywood and had never been paid for. Beneath lions rampant on a field of fleurs-de-lis is a motto, engraved backwards to come out right on a red wax seal. It says NULLA VESTIGIUM RETORSIT, and my father told me this means *don't look back*. In fact it means, if it means anything, *not a trace left behind.*

Well, I'm left behind, and my sons and my elder son's son are left behind. And the only way I knew to deal with that intractable fact was to write about it, to write about my father for my sons. I have been writing about him since I began to write, at first in anger. By the time I began *The Duke of Deception* the anger seemed mostly to have dissipated. My father left many victims, and for a long time I numbered myself among them. I was ashamed of him, and detested the lies he had told me, especially the lie he had told most insistently, that only "truth can set us free, that the only way we could confirm our love for each other was to tell each other the truth."

I decided, when my father died, that only my attempt to tell the truth could convey to my children the experience of having been my father's son, and that it was important that they have a record of that experience. I was mindful, and am more mindful now, that the truth, as it is regarded by scientists and philosophers, is beyond my reach. I was nurtured by lies about my history, and some of these can never be unraveled. Memory is selective, and the iron principle of life as well as narrative is the partiality of point of view.

I knew as little about the facts of my father's history when I began as I had known of the facts of Harry Crosby's, and when I was finished I had fewer facts about him than about Crosby. I began with the conviction that lives can be revealed only by their enactments, a conviction deepened by my experience of Harry Crosby. I would not put my father on the couch, pretend to fathom his motives. I would instead reveal his comings and goings, his doings. As I could not with Crosby, I would try to give the sense of him, how he filled space in a room, the key and range and timbre of his speech, his smell of leather and tobacco and silver polish.

I knew by now, having anatomized Harry Crosby's will to change himself from one kind of character to another, that a mask is often more interesting than the "authentic" character it disguises, and I felt prepared to give my father his givens, to judge them as I had tried to judge Crosby's suicide, aesthetically as well as morally. In plain words, I was less interested in what my father *was*, in whether he was in fact a Skull & Bones man, than in what he wished people to believe he was.

Given my interest, how can I concern myself with the world's judgment of major and minor subjects? Surely we know enough to realize that celebrity cannot enhance an autobiographer's claim to a reader's attention. In the kind of book it has been my ambition to write, the work itself stands as the writer's bid for a place in the world, as the writer's subject's bid for a place in the world. If I have done my work well someone will say, reading it, *I wish I had known that Duke*, by which the reader will mean not that he would have liked to have met a Skull & Bones man, but that he would have liked to hear my father lie about being a Skull & Bones man.

Narrative demands calculation and proportion, and the critical faculty that drives any comely narrative insists that character—if it is to connect, if it has the hope of connecting—be born into the narrative as into the world, selfish, but not alone. Character in narrative is interesting only in relation to other characters in narrative. The ubiquitous "I" may in fact be a solipsist, but his effect on others must be registered, and the effect on him of others, too. Children think of themselves as alone in the world. At least I did; narrative restored my case to its deeper reality, a process of strophe and antistrophe, commerce, community, a family, the annihilation of such modifying titles as "major" and "minor."

William Gass has located the peril at the heart of autobiography, and it is only a more extreme instance of the tunnel vision of biography, the insane sense that one alone counts: "The lively force and narcissistic drama of one's situation, like a passion or a toothache for which the world shuts shop, so only one's wound is open, only one's pain is beating, easily leads to the conviction that the rush of lust through the loins, the ache, the ear which won't stop ringing, are universal conditions of consciousness. . . ."

So, with Auden, one hopes that one's case will touch others. But how to connect? Not by calculation, I think, not by the assumption that in the pain of my toothache, or my father's, or Harry Crosby's, or more recently John O'Hara's, I have discovered a "universal condition of consciousness." One may merely know that no character is unaccompanied and hope that a singular story, as every honest story is singular, will in the magic way of some things apply, connect, resonate, touch a major chord.

Chronology

1892 *(Apr. 20):* Birth date of Mary Phelps Jacob (Caresse Crosby) in New York City.

1898 *(June 4):* Birth date of Henry Grew Crosby in Boston.

1911 *(Sept.):* Harry Crosby enters St. Mark's School.

1915 *(Jan.):* Mary Jacob and Richard Rogers Peabody are married by Rev. Endicott Peabody.

1916 *(Feb. 4):* Birth date of William Jacob Peabody.

1917 *(Apr. 6):* The United States declares war against Germany.
(June): Harry Crosby graduates from St. Mark's.
(July 6): Harry sails for France aboard the *Espagne*; arrives July 19.
(Aug. 8): Harry, as a volunteer in the American Field Service Ambulance Corps, carries his first wounded soldier, at the Somme.
(Aug. 12): Birth date of Polly ("Polleen") Peabody.
(Sept. 21): Harry enlists as a private in the U.S. Army; returns to ambulance section.
(Nov. 3): Harry arrives at Verdun with Section 29, attached to 120th French Division.
(Nov. 22): Harry's friend Way Spaulding is injured by a shell burst ten yards away from Harry's ambulance, which is totally destroyed: "I thank God with all my heart for saving me."

1918 *(Aug. 23–25):* The Battle of the Orme; Harry's section carries more than two thousand wounded, and is cited in the field.
(Nov. 11): Armistice is signed between Allies and Germany.

1919 *(Mar. 1):* "Oh Boy!!!!!! won the Croix de Guerre. Thank God."
(Apr. 1): "AMERICA!"

(*Apr. 6:*) Harry Crosby returns to Boston, and matriculates at Harvard College.

1920 (*July 4*): Harry meets Mary ("Polly") Peabody in Boston.

(*July 20*) After attending church in Manchester-by-the-Sea, Harry and Polly spend the night together.

(*Aug.*): Harry visits World War I battlefields with his Harvard roommate, Francis Lothrop.

1921 (*May*): Harry Crosby threatens suicide if he cannot marry Polly.

(*June*): Polly begins formal separation from Richard Peabody.

(*June*): Harry receives his War Degree from Harvard College.

(*July*): Harry begins work with the Shawmut National Bank in Boston; Polly has moved to New York City.

(*Dec.*): Richard Peabody, following six-month separation from his wife, offers divorce.

1922 (*Jan. 1*): First entry in *Shadows of the Sun*.

(*Feb.*): Polly and Richard Peabody are divorced.

(*Mar. 14*): Harry Crosby, following a six-day bender, resigns from the Shawmut National Bank.

(*May 1*): Harry moves to Paris to work for Morgan, Harjes & Co.; Polly has preceded him there.

(*July 22*): Polly, angry and jealous, leaves France for America.

(*Aug. 30*): Harry proposes to Polly by telegram and sails the following day, aboard the *Aquitania*, for New York.

(*Sept. 9*): Harry and Polly are married in the chapel of the Municipal Building in New York City; they return to France forty-eight hours later aboard the *Aquitania*.

1923 (*June 1*): Harry and Polly Crosby take apartment overlooking the Seine at Quai d'Orléans, on the Île Saint-Louis.

(*Sept. 7*): The Crosbys move to the apartment of Princess Marthe Bibesco, in the Faubourg St. Germain.

(*Nov.*): The Crosbys first meet Harry's cousin Walter Van Rensselaer Berry, who advises Harry to give up banking.

(*Dec. 31*): Harry quits Morgan, Harjes & Co.

(During 1923, Harry fell in love with Constance Coolidge.)

1924 (*Jan.*): The Crosbys travel through northern Italy; Henrietta Crosby visits them in Paris.

(*Feb.*): Mrs. Crosby takes her son and daughter-in-law for a skiing holiday to St. Moritz, where Harry first meets Stanley Mortimer.

(*May*): Stephen Crosby visits Paris and takes Harry and Polly on holiday to Vienna.

(*June 14*): Harry buys his first race horse.

(*Oct. 16*): Harry and Polly discover the Cimetière de l'Abbaye de

Longchamp: "Perhaps it is here I shall kill myself."

(Dec.): The Crosbys change Polly's name to Caresse.

1925 *(Jan.):* Harry and Caresse Crosby travel through North Africa; Harry for the first time uses opium, and has crosses tattooed on the soles of his feet.

(Mar.): Harry travels through Spain with his mother.

(Apr.): Harry buys two race horses.

(July): The Crosbys take a house at Étretat, on the cost of Normandy, where Harry meets "Nubile," fourteen years old.

(Nov. 17): The Crosbys move to 19 rue de Lille, their address thereafter in Paris.

(During 1925, Caresse Crosby's *Crosses of Gold* was first published, and Harry's *Sonnets for Caresse.*)

1926 *(Feb., Mar.):* Henrietta Crosby visits her son and daughter-in-law in in Paris.

(Mar. 28): Harry and Caresse buy the whippet Narcisse Noir.

(June 19): The performance of George Anthiel's *Ballet Mécanique.*

(June 30): The Crosbys sail for America, returning to Paris Aug. 31.

(Dec. 28): Skiing at Gstaad, the Crosbys meet Ernest Hemingway and Archibald MacLeish.

(During 1926, a revised version of *Sonnets for Caresse* was published.)

1927 *(Feb. 4):* The Crosbys meet Baron Hanäel von Voight ("Alastair") at an exhibition of his drawings.

(Mar. 10): The Willett Case, brought against Stephen Crosby's investment firm, is finally settled, and the defendants acquitted.

(Mar. 15): Harry and Caresse first meet Frans and Mai de Geetere at the salon of the Duchesse La Salle, who also introduced them to Alastair.

(Apr.): The Black Sun Press is founded by the Crosbys, under the name Éditions Narcisse, at 2 rue Cardinale, Roger Lescaret: Master Printer.

(Apr.): The first issue of *Transition* appears.

(May 20): Stephen Crosby arrives in Paris, and the following day goes with Harry and Caresse to Le Bourget to see the arrival of Charles Lindbergh's "Spirit of St. Louis."

(July): Stanley Mortimer and Harry charter a fishing boat at Biarritz, and journey with difficulty to Spain, where they join Ernest Hemingway at Pamplona.

(July 18): Harry instructs his father to sell seventy shares of Union Pacific, learns he is to be Walter Berry's residual legatee.

(Aug. 22): The Crosbys spend eight days in Brest with Pete and Gretchen Powel, preparing to cruise along the Death Coast of Spain; the cruise is aborted.

(Sept. 16): Harry learns he contracted jaundice in Brest.

(Oct. 12): Walter Berry dies at sixty-eight.

(Oct. 17): In charge of Berry's funeral, Harry writes his mother: "Thank Christ I am not a Christian . . . never, *never, never* must have a funeral."

(Nov. 14): The ashes of Walter Berry are buried at the manor of Harry's cousin Nina Crosby, the Marquise de Polignac: "There was a dinner of twenty all royalty except us and then a motor race."

(Dec. 2): Polia Chentoff, whom the Crosbys met the previous month, completes Harry's portrait; he announces that he is in love with her.

(During 1927, Harry Crosby's *Red Skeletons* was published, together with Caresse's *Painted Shores* and *The Stranger*.)

1928 *(Jan. 26):* Harry and Caresse Crosby, together with Mrs. Crosby, leave on trip to Egypt, Jerusalem, Turkey and Yugoslavia, returning Mar. 24.

(Feb. 10): Harry discovers Rimbaud's name cut into the stone of the Temple of Luxor.

(Mar. 8): Harry meets Bokhara in Jerusalem.

(Apr.) Harry meets Kay Boyle in Paris shop.

(May 8): Harry receives the Walter Berry library—eight thousand rare books.

(May 22): The Crosbys first meet the Comte Armand de la Rochefoucauld.

(June 11): Harry has a throat operation in Lausanne.

(June 30): The Crosbys travel to Venice to recuperate from their last Four Arts Ball, returning to Paris July 24.

(July 9): Harry meets Josephine Rotch at the Lido.

(July 24): Harry writes his mother that he and Caresse have secured a twenty-year lease on the Mill at Ermenonville, an hour from Paris.

(July 25): Josephine Rotch sails for America.

(Aug. 31): Harry meets Jonathan Cape, who expresses high enthusiasm for *Shadows of the Sun*, which he wishes to publish.

(Nov. 7): Caresse sails for America on the *Majestic*; Harry follows three days later on the *Berengaria*.

(Dec. 7): Caresse returns to France, after visiting Boston and New York with Harry, on *Majestic*; Harry remains behind, returning to Paris on Christmas Eve.

(Dec. 28): Harry writes his mother that he "feels let down by Paris after New York," and wishes to have ten thousand dollars' worth of his stock put in Caresse's name.

(During 1928, Harry Crosby began to appear regularly in *Transition*; also published during that year were his books *Shadows of the Sun, Chariot of the Sun* and *Transit of Venus*, as well as Caresse's *Impossible Melodies*.)

1929 (*Jan. 19*): Harry Crosby, through Eugene Jolas, meets Hart Crane, and agrees to publish *The Bridge*, as yet unfinished.

(*Mar. 4*): The Crosbys visit James and Nora Joyce to discuss details for a Black Sun Press edition of Joyce's *Work in Progress*.

(*Mar. 9*): Harry burns eighty copies of *Red Skeletons*, after first shotgunning them, at the Mill.

(*Mar. 15*): Harry meets for the first time D. H. Lawrence, with whom he has corresponded for more than a year; they argue violently about everything they discuss.

(*June*): Harry appears on the masthead of *Transition* as a contributing editor.

(*June 17*): Harry meets "the Sorceress" at 19 rue de Lille.

(*June 21*): Josephine Rotch and Albert Bigelow are married in Old Lyme, Connecticut.

(*June 23*): Hart Crane is jailed after a bar fight; Harry helps arrange his release, and buys him passage home to New York.

(*Aug. 13*): Harry secures a student pilot's license.

(*Oct. 9*): Goopy Pohlman arrives from America to serve Harry as bodyguard, wheelman, and bad influence.

(*Nov. 11*): Harry completes his first solo flight.

(*Nov. 16*): With Caresse and Constance, the Comtesse de Jumilhac, Harry sails for New York aboard the *Mauretania*; receives telegram from the Sorceress—YES, signed A.

(*Nov. 18*): Harry receives radiogram from Josephine—IMPATIENT.

(*Nov. 22*): The Crosbys dock in New York, and travel with Constance to Boston.

(*Nov. 23*): Harry visits Josephine before the Harvard-Yale game.

(*Nov. 25*): Caresse checks into the Savoy-Plaza Hotel in New York, and Harry joins her there three days later.

(*Dec. 3–5*): Harry and Josephine stay at the Hotel Book-Cadillac in Detroit, registered under the names Mr. and Mrs. Harry Crane.

(*Dec. 7*): Hart Crane, in Brooklyn, throws a going-away party for the Crosbys; in attendance are E. E. Cummings, William Carlos Williams, Walker Evans, Malcolm Cowley, Matthew Josephson and a crew of drunk sailors.

(*Dec. 10*): Harry is meant to meet his wife and mother for tea at J. P. Morgan's, and then go to dinner and the theater with them and Hart Crane; he fails to appear, and it is learned that he has shot and killed Josephine Bigelow and himself at Stanley Mortimer's studio.

(*Dec. 12*): Harry is cremated.

(*Dec. 13*): Caresse and Harry's mother sail for France aboard the *Berengaria*.

(During 1929, the following of Harry Crosby's books appeared: *Mad Queen*, *Shadows of the Sun—Series Two*, *The Sun* and *Sleeping Together*.)

1931   Richard Rogers Peabody dies.

1937   *(Mar. 24):* Caresse Crosby and Selbert Young, twenty-six, are married in Richmond, Virginia.

1955   *(Jan. 25):* William Peabody dies in Paris in an accident caused by a leaking gas oven.

1957   *(Aug.):* Henrietta Crosby dies.

1959   *(Jan. 3):* Stephen Van Rensselaer Crosby dies.

1970   *(Jan. 24):* Caresse Crosby, divorced from Selbert Young, dies.

Notes

The numbers to the left of each citation refer to the pages of the text in which the relevant passages appear. Each passage is identified by the key word(s) with which it begins, followed by an ellipsis and the passage's final word(s). In the case of multiple passages, closely linked in the text and from a single source, the last word(s) of the final passage end the citation. I have used shortened titles in these notes, but all sources are identified in full in the bibliography. From time to time, I identify the library where an unusually rare periodical was finally run to ground. Unless otherwise identified, letters are unpublished. Interviews were conducted by the author.

The following abbreviations are employed:

BSP:	The Black Sun Press
BU:	The Harris Collection, John Hay Library, Brown University
CC:	Caresse Crosby
	(These initials apply as well to her name by her first marriage—Polly Peabody—and to her maiden name—Mary Jacob)
GW:	Geoffrey Wolff
HC:	Henry Grew Crosby
SIU:	The Black Sun Press Archives, Morris Library, Southern Illinois University
SOTS:	*Shadows of the Sun*

The nature and scope of collections of Crosby material in various libraries are treated in the bibliography. In a very few instances, I was given information about Harry Crosby, his family and his friends with the understanding that I would not disclose my informant's name. I have honored such requests; mercifully, they were rare, affecting fewer than half a dozen quotations.

—G.W.

Page   CHAPTER I

4   "When he . . . out": Stanley Mortimer, quoted by New York *Daily Mirror*, December 13, 1929, p. 4.
4   PLEASE . . . LIFE: HC to Stephen Crosby, July 19, 1929. SIU
5   "For the poet . . . seriously": Holograph copy, HC to Stephen and Henrietta Crosby, July 23, 1929. SIU
5   "Why . . . bills": *SOTS* (June 16, 1928).
6   "I have . . . apart": HC, "In Search of the Young Wizard," *Sleeping Together*.
6   "and kill . . . Dear": HC to CC, June 2, 1921. SIU
7   "strange . . . people": Constance, Comtesse de Jumilhac, to CC, January 26, 1930. SIU
7   "You will . . . you": CC to HC, November 25, 1929. SIU
8   " 'Let . . . shone' ": Malcolm Cowley, interview, May 19, 1971, New York City.
9   "She just . . . didn't": Clark Grew, interview, November 7, 1972, Southborough, Mass.
10 "yellow . . . letter A": Police report, quoted by New York *World*, December 11, 1929, p. 1.
10 CABLE . . . IMPATIENT: Josephine Rotch Bigelow to HC, November 19, 1929. SIU
10 "He was . . . wonderful-looking": Archibald MacLeish, interview, April 21, 1973, Conway, Mass.
11 "passing fancy": Elizabeth Beal Hinds, interview, December 19, 1972, Manchester, Mass.
11 "Harry . . . reluctantly": Gretchen Powel, interview, April 25, 1973, Washington, D.C.
11 "Mr. Crosby . . . America": Paris *Herald Tribune*, December 12, 1929, p. 1.
11 CROSBY . . . "aunt": New York *Daily News*, December 12, 1929, p. 3.
12 "*Within . . . abominable*": HC, "Baudelaire," *Sonnets for Caresse*.
12 "Profoundly . . . adventure": New York *Daily Mirror*, December 13, 1929, p. 3.
12 "*the hand . . . amiss*": HC, unpublished notebook. SIU

CHAPTER 2

16 "quite . . . Harvard": Esther Grew Parker, telephone interview, December 21, 1972, Sherborn, Mass.
16 "he had . . . history": Elizabeth Beal Hinds, interview, December 19, 1972, Manchester, Mass.

Page

16   "lightest . . . Harvard": Rev. G. Gardner Monks, interview, December 18, 1972, Boston, Mass.

16   "lived on it": Elizabeth Beal Hinds, interview, December 19, 1972, Manchester, Mass.

16   "he used . . . death": Ruth Ammi Cutter, interview, December 20, 1972, Cambridge, Mass.

17   "I was . . . do": Rev. G. Gardner Monks, interview, December 18, 1972, Boston, Mass.

17   "It's interesting . . . me." Henrietta Crosby, quoted by HC, unpublished notebook #2. BU

17   "He cast . . . impossible": *SOTS* (June 1, 1924).

17   "Be careful . . . chemise": HC to Henrietta Crosby, December 23, 1927. SIU

18   "She looks . . . pretty": *Ibid.*, September 7, 1928. SIU

18   "He had . . . happy": Esther Grew Parker, telephone interview, December 19, 1972, Sherborn, Mass.

18   "Steve . . . era": James Grew, telephone interview, December 18, 1972, Andover, Mass.

19   "*There's no . . . seven*": HC to Henrietta Crosby, *War Letters* (July 11, 1918).

20   "Don't think . . . advice": *Ibid.* (September 4, 1918).

20–21   "Boston . . . usher": Lucius Beebe, *Boston and the Boston Legend*, p. 37.

21   "I ponder . . . life": HC, unpublished notebook #3. BU

23   "Do you . . . hand": HC to Henrietta Crosby, *War Letters* (September 10, 1917).

24   "So for . . . school": *SOTS* (September 15, 1929).

CHAPTER 3

25   "singularly . . . Church": *St. Mark's School Catalogue: 1917–1918*, p. 1.

25–26   "distinction . . . in": Albert Emerson Benson, *History of Saint Mark's School*, p. 236.

26   "Some . . . wealth": *Ibid.*, p. 205.

26–27   "I suppose . . . socialism": *The Vindex*, Fall, 1914.

27–28   "*Sunday . . . Corsair*": Fragment of HC's school diary. SIU

28   "Dear Ma . . . cut": HC to Henrietta Crosby, February 20, 1912. SIU

29   "The heroes . . . football": George Richmond Fearing to GW, November 29, 1972.

29   "Running . . . esteemed": Rev. G. Gardner Monks, interview, December 18, 1972, Boston, Mass.

29   "He was . . . shine": Richardson Dilworth to GW, December 6, 1972.

29   "an amusing . . . homework": Porter R. Chandler to GW, January 16, 1972.

Page
29   "As the head . . . do": *SOTS* (March 27, 1923).
29   "I was . . . house": Rev. G. Gardner Monks, interview, December 18, 1972, Boston, Mass.
29–30 "Needless . . . mile": Rev. G. Gardner Monks to GW, December 3, 1972.
30   "in keeping . . . intensely": Rev. G. Gardner Monks, interview, December 18, 1972, Boston, Mass.
30   "squeezed . . . today": George Richmond Fearing, interview, January 24, 1973, Santa Barbara, Cal.
31   "home . . . remember": HC to Henrietta Crosby, February 1, 1927. SIU
31   "he never . . . him": Richardson Dilworth to GW, December 6, 1972.
31   "He hates . . . alone": Recorded by HC, unpublished notebook #1. BU
31   "That's damn . . . work": HC to Katherine Crosby, *War Letters* (September 18, 1917).
33   "a heavy . . . sand": HC, *The Vindex*, 1917.
34   "On rereading . . . morons": HC to Henrietta Crosby, April 1, 1924. SIU
35   "Gifts . . . equipment": A. Piatt Andrew to *The Vindex*, 1916.
36   "from prison to prison": HC, unpublished notebook #5. BU
37   "not to . . . cherry": Edward Weeks, *My Green Age*, p. 44.
37   "Why should I": Quoted by Stuart Kaiser, unpublished war diary (July 12, 1917).
38   "Scudder of Yale": *Ibid.*

CHAPTER 4

40   "a blue . . . gold": HC to "Dear Family," *War Letters* (July 19, 1917).
41   "He also . . . 'Boches' ": *Ibid.*
41   "I must . . . 'Militaire' ": *Ibid.*
42–43 "He delighted . . . dared": Rev. G. Gardner Monks, interview, December 18, 1972, Boston, Mass.
43   "Did I . . . violin": HC to Katherine Crosby, *War Letters* (July, 27, 1917).
43n   "a boy . . . made": HC, unpublished notebook. SIU
44   "It was . . . way": George Richmond Fearing to Edward Weeks, October, 1972.
44   "I can . . . here": HC to Henrietta Crosby, *War Letters* (August 19, 1917).
44   "The wooden . . . 'temple' ": *Ibid.* (August 16, 1917).
45   "in the most . . . pan": Stuart Kaiser, unpublished war diary (October 2, 1917).
45–46 "First . . . 'there' ": HC to Henrietta Crosby, *War Letters* (August 30, 1917).

Page

46   "Over here . . . known": HC to Stephen Crosby, *War Letters* (August 2, 1917).

47   "You were . . . nights": Edward Weeks, interview, November 6, 1972, Boston, Mass.

47   "Then they . . . to them": HC to Stephen Crosby, *War Letters* (October 14, 1917).

48   "I saw . . . here": HC to Henrietta Crosby, *War Letters* (October 2, 1917).

49   "way off . . . sun": *Ibid.* (August 19, 1917).

49   "I got . . . off": *Ibid.* (September 8, 1917).

50   "who had . . . join": Edward Weeks, *My Green Age*, p. 55.

50   "Fearing . . . Oh-well": Stuart Kaiser, unpublished war diary (September 21, 1917).

50   "I was . . . escaped": This autobiographical fragment has been taken from a mutilated copy of a book of thirty-two pages, printed and bound in France, titled *Diary*. The only copy I have seen (or heard of) is in the possession of Harry Crosby's cousin, Elizabeth Beal Hinds, who let me read it but cannot remember exactly how she came by it. Its first two chapters, presumably about Harry's childhood and St. Mark's experiences, had been ripped violently out of the delicate volume. The stilted rhetoric of *Diary*, nothing like as articulate as his later work, suggests that this may be the first book Harry caused to have printed. It is not, however, dated.

50   "Is War . . . parties": HC to Henrietta Crosby, *War Letters* (September 27, 1917).

50   "We hadn't . . . else": George Richmond Fearing, interview, January 24, 1973, Santa Barbara, Cal.

51   "they ought . . . game": HC to Henrietta Crosby, *War Letters* (September 29, 1917).

51   "lounge . . . Bay": *Ibid.* (October 6, 1917).

51–52   "Here we . . . history": HC to Stephen Crosby, *War Letters* (November 3, 1917).

52   "almost . . . seat": Stuart Kaiser, unpublished war diary (November 8, 1917).

52   "In a dream . . . me": John Dos Passos, *The Fourteenth Chronicle*, p. 232.

52   "pure . . . do": George Richmond Fearing, interview, January 24, 1973, Santa Barbara, Cal.

52   "They have . . . coming": Stuart Kaiser, unpublished war diary (November 12, 1917).

52–53   "We were . . . grim": Edward Weeks, interview, November 6, 1972, Boston, Mass.

53   "we carried . . . States": HC to Katherine Crosby, *War Letters* (November 11, 1917).

53   "Ten years . . . forget": HC to Henrietta Crosby, November 22, 1917. SIU

Page
53–54 "There was . . . car": HC to Katherine Crosby, *War Letters* (November 23, 1917).

54 "he was . . . Spaulding": Stuart Kaiser, unpublished war diary (November 23, 1917).

54 "nervous . . . miracle": Edward Weeks, interview, November 6, 1972, Boston, Mass.

54 "God . . . life": HC, *Diary* (see above note for p. 50).

54–55 "God . . . again": HC to Katherine Crosby, *War Letters* (November 23, 1917).

55 "As long . . . Harvard": Edward Weeks, interview, December 22, 1972, Boston, Mass.

56 "You were . . . sarsparilla": HC to Henrietta Crosby, *War Letters* (July 5, 1918).

56 "What you . . . dancing": *Ibid.* (October 2, 1917).

56 "Them were . . . forward": HC to Katherine Crosby, *War Letters* (September 26, 1917).

56–57 "if I . . . today": HC to Henrietta Crosby, *War Letters* (October 8, 1917).

57 "You and Pa . . . anywhere": *Ibid.* (September 19, 1917).

57 "Have you . . . hell": HC to Stephen Crosby, *War Letters* (December 2, 1917).

57–58 SOCIETY . . . "today": Undated newspaper clipping pasted in scrapbook belonging to HC and CC. SIU

58 "Now . . . it": HC to Henrietta Crosby, *War Letters* (July 18, 1918).

58–59 "Water . . . oysters": HC, unpublished notebook #3. BU

59 "Death's . . . magnet": HC to Henrietta Crosby, *War Letters* (November 18, 1917).

59–60 "It is . . . YES": HC, unpublished notebook #4. BU

60 "it may . . . St. Mark's": Albert Emerson Benson, *History of St. Mark's School*, p. 211.

60–61 "magnificent . . . *at last*": Albert Emerson Benson et al., *Saint Mark's School in the War Against Germany*.

61 "We, his family . . . returned": George Weld to GW, December 6, 1973.

61 "very low beings, morally": HC to Henrietta Crosby, *War Letters* (December 17, 1917).

61–62 "They don't . . . trivialities": *Ibid.* (November 10, 1917).

62 "the French . . . tremendous": *Ibid.* (November 5, 1917).

62 "God . . . before": HC to Stephen Crosby, *War Letters* (November 6, 1917).

62 "coveted . . . skill": *Ibid.* (September 8, 1917).

62 "I'd give . . . it": *Ibid.* (November 7, 1917).

63 "Wish . . . one": HC to Henrietta Crosby, *War Letters* (October 6, 1918).

63 "disdaining . . . zones": The full citation to Section 641 reads, "Dédaignant le danger, sans souci de la fatigue, a poursuivi sans

Page

71 "dubious . . . years": Cleveland Amory, *The Proper Bostonians*, p. 300.

71 "Harry's . . . trouble": Edward Weeks, *My Green Age*, p. 107.

71–72 TEN HILL . . . "fall": Harvard *Crimson*, undated 1919 clipping pasted in scrapbook belonging to HC and CC. SIU

72 "went on . . . with": Edward Weeks, *My Green Age*, p. 107.

73 "who always . . . Wow": Stuart Kaiser, unpublished war diary (December 24, 1917).

73 "you needn't . . . water-wagon": HC to Henrietta Crosby, *War Letters* (August 29, 1918).

73 "I'm still . . . resolution": *Ibid*. (October 18, 1918).

73 "I came . . . live": George Richmond Fearing, interview, January 24, 1973, Santa Barbara, Cal.

73 "He was . . . blazes": Rev. G. Gardner Monks to GW, December 3, 1972.

73 "there were . . . inches": Helenka Adamowski Pantaleoni to GW, October 17, 1974.

73 "shell-shocked": J. Brooks Fenno to GW, November 22, 1973.

74 "subtle . . . extraordinary": HC, *Diary* (see above note for p. 50).

74 "when his . . . character": George S. Weld to GW, December 6, 1973.

74 "war . . . accentuated": Rev. G. Gardner Monks, interview, December 18, 1972, Boston, Mass.

74 "incapable . . . speech": Henry S. Morgan to GW, January 24, 1973.

74 "His energy . . . touching": William Ellery Sedgwick, obituary notice in *Class of 1922: Fourth Report*. Harvard University Archives

75 "people . . . alleys": HC, unpublished notebook #2. BU

75 "charming . . . family": Lawrence Terry to GW, November 25, 1972.

CHAPTER 6

76 "Harry . . . ruthless": CC, *The Passionate Years*, p. 95. (Page references are to the soft-cover edition, published by Southern Illinois University Press in 1968.)

76 "to know . . . experience": *Ibid*., p. 94.

77 "Church . . . Polly": HC, from pages torn from *Line-a-Day* diary. SIU

77 "ride . . . cotillions": CC, *Passionate Years*, p. 14.

77 "I grew . . . existed." *Ibid*.

78 "What I . . . pass": *Ibid*., p. 63.

78 "a part . . . horses": *Ibid*., p. 37.

78 "If ever . . . changed": Adelaide Chatfield-Taylor Sohier, telephone interview, December 20, 1972, Manchester, Mass.

79 "I said . . . yes": CC, *Passionate Years*, p. 65.

Page
80 "My nest egg . . . Dick": *Ibid.*, p. 76.
80 "unsensationally": *Ibid.*, p. 79.
81 "My love . . . sunrise": *Ibid.*, p. 112.
81 "I don't . . . to": HC to CC, August 6, 1920. SIU
81 "said . . . chippies": George Richmond Fearing, interview, January 24, 1973, Santa Barbara, Cal.
81 "Paris . . . of": HC to Henrietta Crosby, *War Letters* (September 23, 1972).
82 "We are . . . discontent": *Letters of Elizabeth Cabot* (privately printed), 1905.
83 "many . . . vice": Mrs. John Farrar, *The Young Lady's Friend.*
83 "for the family's sake": HC to CC, June 2, 1921. SIU
83 "I'm in . . . you": *Ibid.*, October 13, 1920.
83–84 "I promise . . . life": *Ibid.*, Christmas, 1921.
84 "if worse . . . Heaven": *Ibid.*, June 2, 1921.
84 "I still . . . beautiful": *Ibid.*, undated (1921).
84 "an evangelistic aura": CC, *Passionate Years*, p. 68.
84–85 "*Thank You . . . Amen*": HC to CC, January, 1921. SIU
85 "As I . . . God": *Ibid.*, June 2, 1921.
85 "melancholy . . . life": Quoted by Cleveland Amory, *The Proper Bostonians*, p. 249.
85 "I'm very . . . me": HC to CC, August 1, 1922. SIU
85–86 "I was . . . reached": *Ibid.*, March, 1922.
86 "I'm so . . . mine": *Ibid.*, August 7, 1922.
86 "You'll probably . . . nights": *Ibid.*, June 2, 1921.
86 "Today . . . it": *SOTS* (February 7, 1922).
86 "and dear . . . have": HC to CC, undated (probably late May, 1921). SIU
87 "She married . . . down": George Richmond Fearing, interview, January 24, 1973, Santa Barbara, Cal.
87 "Pray God . . . up": CC, *Passionate Years*, p. 111.
87–88 "the entire . . . worked": *Ibid.*, pp. 90, 91.
88 "As an unhappy . . . her": Emily Post, *Etiquette*, p. 509.
88 "unheard of . . . Episcopalians": George Richmond Fearing to GW, November 29, 1972.
88 "The fellows . . . middle aged": John Dos Passos, *The Fourteenth Chronicle*, p. 91.
89 "Bostonians . . . Bostonians": *SOTS* (October 19, 1923).
89 "To hell . . . busy-bodies": HC to CC, June 2, 1921. SIU
89 "my old man . . . already": *Ibid.*, May, 1921.
89 "You couldn't . . . disappointed": Elizabeth Beal Hinds, interview, December 19, 1972.
90 "I haven't . . . did": Richard Rogers Peabody to CC, January, 1922. SIU
90–91 "overwhelmingly . . . words": Quoted by Sidney Hyman, *The Lives of William Benton.*
91 "I am . . . bank": HC to CC, September 16, 1921. SIU

Page
91 "where there . . . waitresses": *Ibid.*, Christmas, 1921.
91 "Can't you . . . Heaven": *Ibid.*, September 16, 1921.
91 "Don't worry . . . it": *Ibid.*, December, 1921.
91 "loathed . . . kid": Edward Weeks, *My Green Age*, p. 131.
91 "Boozed . . . exhausted": *SOTS* (January 4, 1922).
92 "You're my religion . . . protection": HC to CC, August 6, 1920. SIU
92 "You never . . . alone": *Ibid.*, September, 1921.
92 "I think . . . N.Y.": *Ibid.*, Christmas, 1921.
92 "except when . . . alone": *Ibid.*, June 2, 1921.
93 "You mustn't . . . circumstances": *Ibid.*, undated (early summer, 1921).
93 "How are . . . unloosened": *Ibid.*, July, 1921.
93 "You are . . . cheap": *Ibid.*, October, 1921.
93 "Remember . . . want": *Ibid.*, June 2, 1921.
94 "The financial . . . enough": *Ibid.*, September, 1921.
94 "I hate . . . régime": *Ibid.*, August 7, 1922.
94 "We'll never . . . Boston": *Ibid.*, June 2, 1921.
94 "*March 8th* . . . Bank": *SOTS* (March 8–14, 1922).
95 "I saw . . . vicissitudes": HC to CC, March 22, 1922. SIU
95 "one of . . . future": *SOTS* (March 21, 22, 1922).
95 "It looks . . . complication": Undated clipping from *Town Topics* (April or May, 1922), pasted in scrapbook belonging to HC and CC. SIU

CHAPTER 7

96 "when you . . .": HC to CC, March, 1922. SIU
97 "tossed . . . London": *SOTS* (May 1, 1922).
97 "dropped . . . nest": CC, *Passionate Years*, p. 108. (Caresse writes that she and Harry flew immediately to Venice. Harry's personnel file, his diary, and their letters contradict her: they went by train to Venice a month later.)
97 "at a salary . . . time": Details of Harry's record at Morgan, Harjes come from his personnel file, #599, provided by the Morgan Guaranty Trust Company.
97 "And how . . . Waste Land": *SOTS* (May 24, 1922).
98 "Boston . . . hyena-matron": CC, *Passionate Years*, pp. 108, 109.
98 "Why did . . . withdrawn": *SOTS* (July 22, 1922).
98 "Another closed . . . unafraid": *Ibid.* (August 12, 1922).
98 "most unbalanced . . . square": *Ibid.* (July 31, 1922).
98 "I am . . . dignified": HC to CC, August 7, 1922. SIU
99 "*Pour* . . . race": *SOTS* (August 9, 1922).
99 "elaborate . . . advanced": *Ibid.* (August 15, 1922).
99 "Masked Marvel . . . squares": *Ibid.* (August 22, 1922).
99 "1/To behave . . . happens": SIU

Page

99   "Wilder . . . say": *SOTS* (August 18, 1922).

99   "can't . . . longer": *Ibid.* (August 30, 1922).

99   BUNNY . . . HARRY: HC to CC, August 30, 1922. SIU

100   "a crowd . . . away": *SOTS* (September 5, 1922).

100   "hair . . . eaten": *Ibid.* (September 6, 1922).

100   "Felt . . . collapse": *Ibid.* (September 9, 1972).

100–101   "Nevermore . . . Gethsemane": CC, *Passionate Years*, p. 110.

101   "Am I": *SOTS* (September 21, 1922).

101   "the fox's . . . trapped": *Ibid.* (January 27, 1922).

101   "don't pamper . . . me": HC to CC, June 2, 1921. SIU

101   "our infants": *Ibid.*, August 7, 1922.

101   "We'll take . . . down": *Ibid.*, September 20, 1921.

102–103   If you . . . drunkard": Undated, unidentified clipping. SIU

103   "Dearest . . . long": Richard Rogers Peabody to CC, March 19, 1927. SIU

103   "I was . . . madness": Polly Peabody Drysdale, interview, May 25, 1973, London.

104   "strive . . . life": HC, unpublished notebook #2. BU

104   "a *real* burying place": *SOTS* (December 18, 1923).

104   "It is . . . late": HC, unpublished notebook #4. BU

104   "disheartening . . . bed": *SOTS* (January 4, 1924).

105   "in a sordid . . . Princess's": *Ibid.* (November 27, 1923).

105   "In view . . . persons": Clipping pasted in scrapbook belonging to HC and CC. SIU

105–106   "How natural . . . bells": *SOTS* (November 4, 1923).

106   "When I . . . them": HC, unpublished notebook #2. BU

106   "You only . . . confessions": *Ibid.*

106–107   "in 1922 . . . mine": CC, unpublished memoir. SIU

107   "there is . . . harem": HC, unpublished notebook. SIU

107   "As for . . . double L": *SOTS* (April 1, 1923).

107   "*fantaisiste distingué*": Morgan, Harjes personnel file (see above note for p. 97).

107   "occupy . . . do": *SOTS* (March 27, 1923).

107   "fed up . . . arguments": *Ibid.* (January 24, 1923).

107–108   "After the age . . . Jesus Christ": HC, unpublished notebook #4. BU

108   "to defecate . . . morning": *Ibid.*, #2.

108   "a dismal . . . cynicism": *SOTS* (May 22, 1923).

108–109   "Uncle Jack . . . me": HC to Stephen Crosby, November 3, 1923. SIU

110   "Nude . . . away": HC to Henrietta Crosby, November 15, 1923. SIU

110   "Oh that . . . book": *SOTS* (August 3, 1924).

111   "veree bad": HC to CC, October, 1921. SIU

111   "perhaps . . . read": *SOTS* (December 7, 1923).

111   "I'm thrilled . . . himself": HC to Henrietta Crosby, November 15, 1923. SIU

Page

123   "It doesn't . . . WVRB": HC, unpublished notebook #4. BU

124   " 'The Englishman . . . Sun' ": *SOTS* (April 17, 1926).

124   "in the dining . . . 'd'acclimations' ": *Ibid.* (June 17, 1926).

125   "like a delta . . . sarcophagus": CC, *Passionate Years*, p. 135.

125   "going . . . locomotives": *SOTS* (January 2, 1925).

125   "the books . . . books": *Ibid.* (December 10, 1924).

125   "Good . . . up": *Ibid.* (April 19, 1925).

125   "make . . . typography": *Ibid.* (May 10, 1927).

125   "Why not . . . not": CC, *Passionate Years*, p. 144.

126   "I have . . . creditable": HC to Henrietta Crosby, December 12, 1924. SIU

126   "from this . . . bareheaded": *SOTS* (April 17, 1926).

126–127   "At my death . . . come": Codicil to Walter Berry's will. SIU

127   "When I . . . hurt": HC to Henrietta Crosby, August, 1927. SIU

127   "Poor . . . example": *Ibid.*, October 14, 1927.

127   "in his lugubrious dress suit": *SOTS* (October 14, 1927).

127–128   "voice . . . dead": *Ibid.* (October 17, 1927).

128   "never . . . funeral": HC, unpublished notebook #5. BU

128   "The master . . . inside": *SOTS* (October 17, 1927).

128   "Under . . . winds": Handwritten on card bearing Crosby cross. SIU

129   "What . . . care": Olivia Coolidge, *Edith Wharton: 1862–1937*, p. 204.

129–130   "she is . . . leave": HC to Henrietta Crosby, October 14, 1927. SIU

130   "if you . . . possible": *Ibid.*, October 18, 1927.

130   "I wonder . . . them": *Ibid.*, October 24, 1927.

130   "Women . . . say": *Ibid.*, October 25, 1927.

130   "seeing . . . me": Edith Wharton to Alice Garrett, quoted by Louis Auchincloss, *Edith Wharton: A Woman in Her Time*, p. 161.

131   "inexperienced and unmanageable": Edith Wharton to Gaillard Lapsley, quoted by R. W. B. Lewis, letter to GW, August 22, 1974.

131   "and not . . . sort": HC to Henrietta Crosby, November 18, 1927. SIU

131   "Walter's . . . cad": Edith Wharton to John Hugh Smith, November 23, 1927, quoted by R. W. B. Lewis, letter to GW, August 22, 1974.

131   "an exceedingly cold letter": HC to Henrietta Crosby, December 6, 1927. SIU

131   "Books . . . Dead": *SOTS* (May 4, 1928).

132   "grab act": CC, *Passionate Years*, p. 221.

132   "I loved . . . down": CC to George Leinwall, June 25, 1969. SIU

CHAPTER 9

133   "There were . . . brain": Oscar Wilde, *The Picture of Dorian Gray*, pp. 304, 305.

Page
134 " 'The mutilation . . . unlawful' ": Oscar Wilde, quoted by HC, unpublished notebooks #3, #4. BU
134 "Would I . . . courage": *SOTS* (October 16, 1926).
135 "to corrupt . . . temptation": *Ibid.* (July 5, 1925).
135 " 'The only' . . . applause": *Ibid.* (July 19, 1925).
135 "The sun . . . Wilde": *Ibid.* (July 21, 1925).
135 "You and I . . . all": Oscar Wilde, *The Picture of Dorian Gray*, p. 385.
135 "One's innocence . . . morals": *SOTS* (October 11, 1923).
136 "sturdy . . . one": *Ibid.* (August 25, 1923).
136 "the one . . . parties": Oscar Wilde, *The Picture of Dorian Gray*, p. 143.
136 "If you . . . it": *Ibid.*, p. 223.
137 "I should . . . Caresse": HC to Henrietta Crosby, September 28, 1928. SIU
137 "no one . . . only 14": CC to Malcolm Cowley, November 19, 1949.
137 "against . . . unbalanced": *SOTS* (November 4, 1923).
137 "shadow . . . man": *Ibid.* (April 15, 1928).
137 "We were . . . waiting": CC, *Passionate Years*, p. 155.
137 "I worship . . . brings": HC to CC, July 2, 1924. SIU
138 "By our background . . . envied": CC, *Passionate Years*, p. 134.
138–139 "absurd . . . yield": *SOTS* (June 15, 1924).
139 "*I think . . . Mal*": *Ibid.* (April 9, 1925) (see also *Red Skeletons*).
139–140 "*When the low . . . flag*": "Spleen IV," from Edna St. Vincent Millay's translation of *Les Fleurs du Mal*.
141 "Went . . . Verlaine": *SOTS* (November 15, 1925).
141 "And who . . . numb": *Ibid.* (April 6, 1928).
141 "Saw . . . arms": *Ibid.* (September 5, 1927).
142 "I looked . . . does": *Ibid.* (September 11, 1927).
142 "Better . . . teeth": HC, unpublished notebook #2. BU
142 "I think . . . away": *Ibid.*
143 "like . . . sense": HC, unpublished notebook #1. BU
143 "Among . . . place": *SOTS* (August 25, 1928).
143 "Two lecture . . . 'penitent' ": *Ibid.* (January 16, 1926).
144 "filthy . . . bills": *Ibid.* (June 16, 1928).
144 "with long . . . Charmante": *Ibid.* (November 7, 1925).
144–145 "Nor if we . . . before": HC to Henrietta Crosby, September 9, 1927. SIU
145 "two maids . . . chauffeur": *SOTS* (September 7, 1923).
146 "like a lump . . . curtains": CC, *Passionate Years*, p. 130.
146 "There is . . . fortress": *SOTS* (September 8, 1925).
146 "very . . . grandiose": Archibald MacLeish, interview, April 21, 1973, Conway, Mass.
147 "very . . . sauce": HC to Henrietta Crosby, January 7, 1927. SIU
147 "everyone . . . goodbye": Adelaide Chatfield-Taylor Sohier, telephone interview, December 20, 1972, Manchester, Mass.
147 "when shall . . . one": *SOTS* (November 15, 1922).

Page
147   "returned . . . again": *Ibid.* (November 24, 1922).
147   "good . . . *nil*": Oscar Wilde, *The Picture of Dorian Gray*, p. 203.
148   "resolved . . . brain": *SOTS* (November 25, 1922).
148   "nerve . . . books": *Ibid.* (April 1, 1923).
148   "Calamity . . . vacation": *Ibid.* (July 10, 1923).
148   "Bought . . . week": *Ibid.* (April 8, 1924).
149   "Dom Luco . . . wins": *Ibid.* (November 4, 1925).
149   "You must . . . for": HC to CC, July 8, 1925. SIU
149   "In all . . . places": *SOTS* (April 30, 1925).
149–150   "if it . . . do": *Ibid.* (October 27, 1925).
150   "most people . . . mistakes": Oscar Wilde, *The Picture of Dorian Gray*, p. 185.
150n   "Narcisse . . . opponent": *SOTS* (October 24, 1927).
150   "Pa . . . discussion": HC to Henrietta Crosby, August 8, 1927. SIU
150–151   "I am . . . automobile": *Ibid.*, April 12, 1927.
151   "would solve . . . problem": *Ibid.*, July 18, 1927.
151   "A racehorse . . . young": *Ibid.*, October 7, 1927.
151   "Lost . . . much": *SOTS* (August 17, 1929).
152   "It was . . . stopped": Ernest Hemingway, *A Moveable Feast*, p. 62.

CHAPTER 10

154   "tried . . . was": George Richmond Fearing, interview, January 24, 1973, Santa Barbara, Cal.
154   "I know . . . present": Stuart Kaiser, quoted by HC, unpublished notebook #5. BU
154   "a beauty . . . him": HC to CC, July, 1926. SIU
154   "One thought . . . patria": *SOTS* (November 24, 1924).
154–155   "If we . . . art": HC to Henrietta Crosby, April 4, 1924. SIU
155–156   "There was . . . stars": *Ibid.*, December 20, 1924.
156   "a Bohemian . . . do": *SOTS* (May 20, 1924).
156   "if he . . . Man Ray": HC to Henrietta Crosby, May 25, 1928. SIU
156   "he would . . . bon": *Ibid.*, August 15, 1927.
156   " 'What of . . . mine' ": HC, unpublished notebook #5. BU
157   "as free as birds": HC to Henrietta Crosby, June 30, 1927. SIU
157   "just literary": Howard Hare Powell, interview, April 25, 1973, Washington, D.C.
157–158   "You will . . . again": HC to Henrietta Crosby, August, 1927. SIU
158   "How understanding . . . lives": *SOTS* (August 30, 1927).
158   "informal . . . it": HC to Henrietta Crosby, March 26, 1927. SIU
159   "You would . . . talent": *Ibid.*, March 17, 1927.
159   "People . . . earth": *Ibid.*, April 8, 1927.
159–160   "took . . . door": *SOTS* (April 23, 1927).
160   "And there . . . in it": *Ibid.* (June 22, 1927).
160   "If it . . . them": HC to Henrietta Crosby, May 17, 1927. SIU
160–161   "The darkness . . . quays": HC, "The de Geetere Maldoror," an unpublished typescript of four pages. BU

Page

161–162 "slender . . . red": *SOTS* (October 17, 1928).

162 "This was a duty": Archibald MacLeish, interview, April 21, 1973, Conway, Mass.

162 "often . . . follows": *Encyclopaedia Britannica* (thirteenth edition), volume 20, p. 137.

162 "when you . . . you": HC to CC, July 1, 1924. SIU

162 "the best . . . immondes": *SOTS* (January 10, 1925).

163 "there was . . . flat": Polly Peabody Drysdale, interview, May 25, 1973, London.

163 "oysters . . . dancing": *SOTS* (September 17, 1925).

163 "almost . . . prayer": *Ibid.* (November 22, 1925).

163 "I was . . . coach": Thomas De Quincey, *Confessions of an English Opium Eater*, pp. 72, 73.

164 "If a man . . . oxen": *Ibid.*, p. 33.

164 "restless . . . initiate": Alethea Hayter, *Opium and the Romantic Imagination*.

165 "dangerously . . . parties": HC to CC, July 21, 1926. SIU

165 "paler . . . toy": *SOTS* (October 31, 1926).

165 "The stars . . . brain": HC, unpublished notebook #4. BU

165 "Git-le-Coeur . . . opium": *SOTS* (January 1, 1928).

166 "*And the ghost . . . night*": Gerard Lymington, Earl of Portsmouth, "A Personal Poem for Harry," chapter headnote in unpublished memoir, holograph ms. SIU

167 "The hotel . . . police": James Charters, *This Must Be the Place*, p. 46.

167–168 "fed . . . home": *SOTS* (June 13, 1925).

168 "Frans . . . applause": HC to Henrietta Crosby, June 12, 1927. SIU

169 "And of our . . . both": Gerard Lymington, Earl of Portsmouth, "A Personal Poem for Harry" (see above note for p. 166).

169 "stripped . . . party": HC to Henrietta Crosby, June 29, 1928. SIU

169 "it really . . . old": *Ibid.*, dated "Day of Four Arts Ball."

CHAPTER 11

171 "I never . . . savant": HC to Henrietta Crosby, April 1, 1924. SIU

172 "I wonder . . . anything": *SOTS* (September 21, 1926).

173 "books . . . manuscript": HC, unpublished notebook #5. BU

173 "writing . . . make": HC, unpublished notebook #2. BU

173 "We knew . . . book": CC, *Passionate Years*, p. 156.

174 "passionately . . . magazine": Robert McAlmon, *Being Geniuses Together*, p. 282.

175 "tell . . . smudging": HC, unpublished notebook #2. BU

175–176 "at a glance . . . transactions": Harry Marks, *The Black Sun Press: 1930*, privately printed catalogue. Sylvia Beach Collection, Princeton University

176 "couldn't . . . night": HC to Henrietta Crosby, February 5, 1927. SIU

Page

176–177   "He lived . . . 'Mrs. Crosby' ": CC, quoted by Jane Baltzell, "The Answer Was Always Yes!" *Brunonia*, New Year's Issue, 1955, p. 7. BU

177   "exactly . . . genius": HC to Henrietta Crosby, February 11, 1927. SIU

177   "It would . . . unkind": Baron Hans Henning von Voight ("Alastair") to HC, May 26, 1927. SIU

177   "played . . . you": *Ibid.*, March 17, 1927.

177   "hasn't a sou": HC to Henrietta Crosby, June 3, 1927. SIU

177   "Vive les artistes": *Ibid.*, May 17, 1927.

177   "Be anything you imagine": Alastair to HC, May 26, 1927. SIU

177–178   "I need . . . Please": *Ibid.*, September 5, 1927.

178   "Something . . . me": *Ibid.*, April 30, 1928.

178   "I suggested . . . jam": Edward Weeks, *My Green Age*, p. 244.

179   "doom . . . sky": Arthur Symons, introduction to *The Fall of the House of Usher*, p. xii.

179   "diabolic . . . unveil": HC, foreword to *Birthday of the Infanta*, pp. i–iii.

179   "Please . . . unkindly": Alastair to CC, undated (probably early 1929). SIU

180   "There were . . . Dieu": HC to Henrietta Crosby, April 22, 1927. SIU

181   "relaxation . . . word": Morse Peckham, *The Triumph of Romanticism*, p. 303.

181   "he would . . . songs": HC to Henrietta Crosby, October 2, 1928. SIU

182   "H the realist . . . paid": *SOTS* (December 28, 1926).

182   "he has . . . out": Ernest Hemingway, quoted by Archibald MacLeish, interview, April 21, 1973, Conway, Mass.

183   "We shan't . . . after": HC to Henrietta Crosby, September 22, 1927. SIU

183   "Harry . . . attention": Archibald MacLeish, interview, April 21, 1973, Conway, Mass.

183   "rather aloof and formal figures": CC, "How It Began," an introduction to *A Bibliography of the Black Sun Press*.

184   "going . . . in": *SOTS* (December 9, 1927).

184   "letting . . . reserve": HC, unpublished notebook #2. BU

184   "holding . . . win": HC, unpublished notebook #4. BU

184   "perfectly . . . it": HC to Henrietta Crosby, undated (early 1928). SIU

184   "manuscripts . . . careless": Archibald MacLeish, interview, April 21, 1973, Conway, Mass.

184   "someday . . . dollars": HC to Henrietta Crosby, undated (early 1928). SIU

184   "*The staring . . . sun*": Archibald MacLeish, presentation ms. SIU

185   "My image . . . sun": Archibald MacLeish to GW, March 6, 1976.

187   "to be . . . everybody": *SOTS* (November 30, 1925).

188   "These people . . . difference": HC to CC, December 22, 1925. SIU

191   "splendid . . . flawless": undated clipping from *Boston Herald* pasted into scrapbook belonging to HC and CC. SIU

192   "You seem . . . bang": Alice Gould to HC, copied by HC, unpublished notebook #2. BU

193   "crazy like a fox": Morse Peckham, *The Triumph of Romanticism*, p. 98.

198   "the best . . . read": *SOTS* (December 7, 1923).

198   "To her . . . forever": D. H. Lawrence, quoted by HC, *SOTS* (December 7, 1923).

199   "experienced . . . dying": *SOTS* (February 7, 1928).

199–200   "nautch . . . oaths": CC, *Passionate Years*, p. 201.

200   "perhaps . . . sleeve": *SOTS* (February 10, 1928).

200   "*The Plumed Serpent* . . . Room": *Ibid.*

200   "I without . . . sunstrength": *Ibid.* (February 11, 1928).

201   "on a day . . . Sun": *Ibid.* (March 1, 1928).

201   "It was . . . 'O' ": CC, *Passionate Years*, p. 206.

201   "I am . . . it": D. H. Lawrence to HC, February 26, 1928. SIU

202   "No . . . poet": CC, *Passionate Years*, p. 230 (see also *SOTS* [March 29, 1928]).

202   "*But cari* . . . more": D. H. Lawrence to HC, May 26, 1928, *The Letters of D. H. Lawrence*, p. 743.

203   "I am . . . sun": HC, unpublished notebook #2. BU

203   "I don't . . . chaos": D. H. Lawrence to HC, undated (1928), *The Letters of D. H. Lawrence*, p. 744.

203   "a bit of an advertisement": D. H. Lawrence to HC, April 29, 1928, *The Letters of D. H. Lawrence*, p. 739.

204   "Harry . . . sun": Victor Reed, "Reading a 'Sound Poem' by Harry Crosby," *English Language Notes*, volume VI, #3, pp. 192–96.

205   "We disagreed . . . counter-attack": *SOTS* (March 15, 1929).

205   "a direct . . . sun": D. H. Lawrence to HC, August, 1928 (received August 19). SIU

205   "fucking . . . buttocks": D. H. Lawrence, quoted by HC, *SOTS* (August 19, 1928).

205   "too disgusting . . . Serpent": *SOTS* (March 30, 1929).

206   "Yes . . . upsidedown": D. H. Lawrence, quoted by HC, *SOTS* (March 29, 1929).

206   "bores . . . life": D. H. Lawrence to HC, September 6, 1928, *The Letters of D. H. Lawrence*, p. 758.

206   "exaggerated . . . 'this' ": Edmund Wilson, *The Twenties*, p. 149.

206   "Did you . . . us": D. H. Lawrence to CC, February, 1930. SIU

206   "Are you . . . Frieda": Frieda von Richtofen Lawrence to CC, undated (1930). SIU

207   "Die . . . Sun": *SOTS* (July 6, 1928).

208   "The voluntary . . . Alive": *Ibid.* (July 7, 1928).

208   "I like . . . Eternity": *Ibid.* (July 8, 1928).

208   "What luck . . . *d'oro*": D. H. Lawrence to HC, undated (July, 1928), *The Letters of D. H. Lawrence*, p. 755.

208–209   "*Her heart . . . proposes*": HC, "Coeur de Jeune Femme," *Transit of Venus*.

209   "very . . . it": George Richmond Fearing, interview, January 24, 1973, Santa Barbara, Cal.

209   "I am . . . tomorrow": HC to Henrietta Crosby, July 24, 1928. SIU

209   "It is . . . same": *Ibid.*, July 31, 1928.

210   "Affairs . . . sage": *Ibid.*, August 21, 1928.

210   "*I wish . . . death*": "You Would Not Scream," *Transit of Venus*.

210–211   "'I lie' . . . "Yes": HC, and quoted by HC, unpublished notebook #6. BU

211   "Bokhara . . . women": *SOTS* (March 8, 1928).

211   "The Bokhara . . . Heart": *Ibid.* (March 9, 1928).

211–212   "fires . . . delight": HC, unpublished notebook #5. BU

212   "a medieval . . . Holland": HC, unpublished notebook #2. BU

212   "the Zorn . . . Valkulla": *SOTS* (March 20, 1929).

212   "I was . . . true": CC, *Passionate Years*, pp. 256, 257.

212   "I was . . . approach": Polly Peabody Drysdale, interview, May 25, 1973, London.

212   "picturesque . . . thinks": *SOTS* (August 28, 1924).

212   "The Wretch . . . dress": *Ibid.* (October 9, 1929).

213   "But you are": Polly Peabody Drysdale, interview, May 25, 1973, London.

213   "He was . . . mind": *Ibid.*

213   "I was . . . different": *Ibid.*

214   "annoyed . . . was": *Ibid.*

214   "more . . . heir": CC, *Passionate Years*, pp. 122, 123.

214   "frightened . . . regal": HC to Constance Atherton, undated (1923).

214   "I'm so . . . know": *Ibid.*

214–215   "one should . . . it": *Ibid.*

215   "she doesn't . . . same": *Ibid.*, October, 1923.

215   "very . . . not": CC to Constance Atherton, October, 1923.

215   "Your letter . . . point": HC to Constance Atherton, November, 1923.

215   "needs . . . good": *Ibid.*

216   "There was . . . storms": Constance, Comtesse de Jumilhac, quoted by HC, unpublished notebook #2. BU

216   "all three . . . know": HC to Constance Atherton, December, 1923.

216   "the most . . . met": HC to Constance, Comtesse de Jumilhac, April, 1927.

Page

216 "if you . . . shark": Comte de Jumilhac, quoted by HC, unpublished notebook. SIU

216 "no point . . . lost": Constance, Comtesse de Jumilhac, to HC, July, 1927.

216 "My Uncle Jack . . . asset": HC to Constance, Comtesse de Jumilhac, November, 1928.

216–217 "the only . . . Christ": *SOTS* (December 3, 1928).

217 "Harden . . . attached": HC to Constance, Comtesse de Jumilhac, November, 1928.

217 "soft . . . wistful": *Ibid.*, undated (1923).

217 "one of . . . earth": Constance Atherton, quoted by HC, notebook #2. BU

217 "to Constance . . . you": Undated red leather notebook, gift from Harry to Constance.

217 "I keep . . . Sorceress": *SOTS* (October 11, 1929).

218 "The seducer . . . sex": Elizabeth Hardwick, *Seduction and Betrayal,* p. 177.

218 "would have . . . Hollywood": *Town Topics,* January 10, 1929, p. 11. On file at Library of Congress

218 "the intense . . . her": *SOTS* (June 17, 1929).

218–219 "In the evening . . . sleep and": *Ibid.* (August 8, 1929).

219 "It rains . . . letter A": *Ibid.* (November 8, 1929).

219 "and brown . . . marbles": *Ibid.* (July 2, 1925).

219 "naughty and charming": HC to CC, July, 1925. SIU

219 "to corrupt . . . temptation": *SOTS* (July 5, 1925).

219 "very . . . painted": HC to Henrietta Crosby, November 13, 1927. SIU

219 "more than . . . together": *Ibid.*, May 19, 1928.

219 "She has . . . head": *Ibid.*, December 2, 1927.

220 "But soon . . . portentous": CC, *Passionate Years,* pp. 283, 284.

220 "made him . . . languid": CC, taped interview with Ralph Bushee. SIU

220 "dangerous": HC to Henrietta Crosby, August 16, 1927. SIU

220 "only noble . . . well": CC, *Passionate Years,* p. 183.

220n "metaphysically disturbing": *Ibid.*, p. 284.

221 "Caresse . . . Armand": HC to Henrietta Crosby, May 22, 1928. SIU

221 "a girl . . . with": *SOTS* (March 13, 1929).

221 "was becoming . . . account": CC, *Passionate Years,* pp. 235, 236.

221 "sexual . . . courage": Kay Boyle to GW, January 23, 1973.

221 "Marriage . . . desire": HC, unpublished notebook #2. BU

222 "And now . . . races": *SOTS* (September 27, 1929).

222 "He was . . . others": Constance, Comtesse de Jumilhac, to CC, January 26, 1930. SIU

222 "I think . . . veil": Kay Boyle to GW, January 23, 1973.

222–223 "O darling . . . death": HC to CC, July 2, 1924. SIU

223 "London . . . center": CC to HC, January 22, 1929. SIU

Page

223 H MINUS . . . IT: HC to CC, July 16, 1929. SIU
223 "I have . . . you": *Ibid.*, June 25, 1929.
224 "of Harry's . . . ways": CC, *Passionate Years*, p. 175.
224 "I have . . . life": HC to CC, July 1, 1924. SIU
225 "It will . . . quiet": HC to Henrietta Crosby, July 24, 1928. SIU

CHAPTER 14

227 "and even . . . gift": HC to Henrietta Crosby, August 3, 1928. SIU
227 "their mother . . . dreadful": *Ibid.*, August 17, 1928.
228 "We ate . . . happening": Salvador Dali, quoted by *Newsweek*, January 15, 1945.
228–229 "a little . . . riot": *SOTS* (June 9, 1929).
229 "New Every Morning": *Ibid.* (June 10, 1929).
229 "bored . . . Thirty-one": *Ibid.* (June 4, 1929).
229 "not without . . . wall": *Ibid.* (May 19, 1929).
229 "with the cut-out . . . on": *Ibid.* (October 13, 1929).
230 "After the game . . . love": *Ibid.* (September 15, 1929).
230 "C and I . . . royalty": *Ibid.* (June 16, 1929).
230 "and I . . . dawn": *Ibid.* (August 9, 1929).
230–231 "It happened . . . again": *Ibid.* (September 24, 1929).
231 "I paid . . . metier": HC, unpublished notebook. SIU
231 "I do . . . *past*": *SOTS* (August 1, 1929).
231 "greatest . . . known": Gerhard Pohlman to William Peabody, undated (February, 1930). SIU
232 "You know . . . them": Gerhard Pohlman to CC, April 6, 1930. SIU
232 "it seems . . . world": *Ibid.*, May 13, 1929.
233 "smelled . . . around": Polly Peabody Drysdale, interview, May 25, 1973, London.
233 "Am taking . . . it": Gerhard Pohlman to Stephen Crosby, October 16, 1929. SIU
234 "I can't . . . a — while": Sketchbook. SIU

CHAPTER 15

236 "I think . . . satisfied": Archibald MacLeish to HC, April 22, 1929. SIU
236 "Praise . . . funeral": *SOTS* (May 5, 1929).
238 "a gentleman . . . piano": *Ibid.* (March 16, 1928).
238 "I don't . . . uncurling": *Ibid.* (March 15, 1928).
238–239 "Seriously . . . cord": *Ibid.* (March 19, 1928).
244 "I have . . . possible": Quoted by Eugene Jolas, "Harry Crosby and *Transition*," *Transition* #19–20, June, 1930, p. 228.
245 "three or four . . . work": *SOTS* (November 2, 1929).
246 "wraiths . . . inconceivable": Stuart Gilbert, "Harry Crosby: A Personal Note," *Transition* #19–20, June, 1930, p. 225.
246–247 "but most . . . 'slanguage' ": *Ibid.*

Page

247   "authentic . . . talent": Maria Jolas, interview, May 29, 1973, Paris.

247   "flayed . . . woman": Robert McAlmon, *Being Geniuses Together*, pp. 283, 284.

247   "the literary . . . abolished": "The Revolution of the Word," *Transition* #16–17, June, 1929.

248   "voice . . . gallery": Sylvia Beach, *Shakespeare and Company*, p. 124.

248   "James Joyce . . . alive": *SOTS* (June 19, 1926).

248–249   "from a taxi . . . somnambulist": HC to Henrietta Crosby, September 30, 1927. SIU

249   "worked . . . crossed": *SOTS* (September 29, 1927).

249–250   "realize . . . winner": *Ibid.* (March 27, 1929).

250   "like . . . card": CC, *Passionate Years*, p. 196.

250   "Why . . . skeleton": James Joyce, quoted by HC, unpublished notebook. SIU

251   "I think . . . exaggeration": HC to Henrietta Crosby, October 12, 1928. SIU

251   "certainty . . . Wretch's": Kay Boyle to HC, undated (1928): SIU

251   "the King of the Bohemians": Matthew Josephson, *Life Among the Surrealists*, p. 86.

251   "every . . . knees": Kay Boyle, *Being Geniuses Together*, p. 363.

251   "come . . . situation": Robert McAlmon, quoted by Kay Boyle, *ibid.*, p. 373.

252   "difficult . . . offer": Robert McAlmon, *ibid.*, p. 348.

252   "There were . . . despair": Kay Boyle, *ibid.*, pp. 366, 367.

252   "It did . . . thing": Robert McAlmon, *ibid.*, p. 348.

252   " 'It's too . . . realities' ": Robert McAlmon, quoted by Kay Boyle, *ibid.*, p. 368.

CHAPTER 16

254   "Dinners . . . *how*": Hart Crane to Samuel Loveman, *The Letters of Hart Crane*, p. 333.

255   "mob . . . work": *SOTS* (February 3, 1929).

255   "Have just . . . best": Hart Crane to Malcolm Cowley, February 4, 1929, *The Letters of Hart Crane*, p. 335.

255   "marble . . . walls": Hart Crane, quoted by John Unterecker, *Voyager: A Life of Hart Crane*, p. 584.

255   "all . . . having": Hart Crane to Waldo Frank, February 7, 1929, *The Letters of Hart Crane*, p. 336.

255   "heir . . . millions": Hart Crane, quoted by John Unterecker, *Voyager: A Life of Hart Crane*, p. 584.

255   "is highly erratic": Hart Crane to Waldo Frank, February 7, 1929, *The Letters of Hart Crane*, p. 336.

255   "as morose . . . tavern": Malcolm Cowley, *A Second Flowering*, p. 209.

255   "foghorn . . . sea": CC, *Passionate Years*, p. 237.

Page
256 "He is ... Sun": *SOTS* (January 25, 1929).
256 "dynamite to handle": CC, *Passionate Years*, p. 241.
256 "one of ... generation": *SOTS* (February 6, 1929).
256 "Hart . . . hell": HC to Hart Crane, March 1, 1929. Columbia University
257 "Hart ... bastards": *SOTS* (July 10, 1929).
258 "rather ... than he": *Ibid.* (July 12, 1929).
258–259 "We want . . . flags": F. T. Marinetti, quoted by Wiktor Woroszylski, *The Life of Mayakovsky*, p. 39, translated by Boleslaw Taborski. (Another translation of Marinetti's manifestoes may be found in Eugene Weber's *Paths to the Present*.)
259 "awed ... wings": Edith Wharton, *A Backward Glance*, p. 319.
260 "And suddenly ... Paris": *SOTS* (May 21, 1927).
261 "it must ... pursuit": *Ibid.* (January 24, 1929).
261 "We are ... woman": *Ibid.* (March 1, 1929).
261 "As miraculous ... pilot": *Ibid.* (August 11, 1929).
261 "Aviator ... Queen": *Ibid.* (September 9, 1929).
261 "take ... fire": CC to HC, quoted by HC, unpublished notebook. SIU
262 "I do not ... aeroplanes": *SOTS* (September 6, 1929).
262 "the war ... restlessness": HC, unpublished notebook. SIU
262 "I used ... school": *SOTS* (September 13, 1929).
262 "but I ... rage": *Ibid.* (November 9, 1929).
262 "An aeroplane . . . life": D. H. Lawrence to CC, November 1, 1929. SIU
263 CC's version of the brief friendship (cf. *The Passionate Years*, pp. 253, 254) is utterly fanciful. HC did not give Cartier-Bresson his first camera, nor did he introduce him to photography.
263 "abhorrence": HC, unpublished notebook #6 (dated "3-7-29"). BU
265 "dreary voice ... maid": *SOTS* (July 26, 1926).
265 "dreary place ... sunless": *Ibid.* (July 16, 1926).
265 "I hate ... imaginativeness": *Ibid.* (July 25, 1926).
265 "Mediocre ... Persian": *Ibid.* (July 31, 1926).
265 "horrors ... Verdun": *Ibid.* (January 28, 1924).
266 "hard ... world": HC to Henrietta Crosby, April 29, 1927. SIU
266 "if only ... country": *Ibid.*, September 6, 1927.
266 "The hell you say": *SOTS* (July 21, 1924).
266 "O God ... New England": *Ibid.* (January 9, 1925).
266 "To have . . . again": HC to Constance, Comtesse de Jumilhac, aboard the *Berengaria*, November, 1928.
266 "It is ... sick": *Ibid.*, November 29, 1928.
267 "I would ... stone": *SOTS* (December 1, 1928).
267 "a madhouse ... explosions": *Ibid.* (December 4, 1928).
267 "hard ... boars": *Ibid.* (December 12, 1928).
268 "There were ... pigeons": *Ibid.* (December 7, 1928).
268 "The sun ... Sun": *Ibid.* (December 21, 1928).

Page

268   "Paris is dead": *Ibid.* (December 24, 1928).

270   "policy . . . Philistines": *Ibid.* (April 3, 1929).

270   "all that . . . *this*": Maria Jolas, interview, May 29, 1973, Paris.

271   "all suffocated . . . monthlies": Leigh Hoffman, *Transition* #14, Fall, 1928, p. 114.

271n "speed . . . jazz": *Ibid.*, p. 101.

272   "To us . . . permissible": The Atlantic Monthly Company to HC, October 25, 1927. *Atlantic Monthly* files

CHAPTER 17

273   "sharp . . . irons": SOTS (June 18, 1928; see also October 18, 1929).

274   "never . . . cage": *Ibid.* (February 4, 1924).

274   "I hate . . . day": HC to Henrietta Crosby, April 5, 1927. SIU

275   "There's that Harry again": Adelaide Chatfield-Taylor Sohier, telephone interview, December 20, 1972, Manchester, Mass.

275   "owed . . . Sun": HC to Henrietta Crosby, June 4, 1928. SIU (See also SOTS, same date.)

275   "and tomorrow . . . hand": SOTS (July 7, 1924).

276   "A metaphor . . . sun": Paul Valéry, quoted by Edmund Wilson, *Axel's Castle*, p. 70.

276   "center . . . oneself": HC, unpublished notebook #4. BU (See also SOTS [June 29, 1927].)

276   "to reduce . . . possible": *Ibid.*

276   "a veritable . . . Sunlight": HC to Henrietta Crosby, September 11, 1928. SIU

276   "Ra . . . neck": Mildred Adams, "Modern Worshippers of That Old God, the Sun," New York *Times Magazine*, July 7, 1929.

277   "I must . . . crime": HC, unpublished notebook #2. BU

277   "Must not . . . Sun": HC, unpublished notebook #4. BU

277   "crisp . . . Roumania": HC, unpublished notebook #2. BU

277   "along . . . embodied": HC to CC, March 31, 1925. SIU

278   "I want . . . side": SOTS (October 8, 1928).

278   "I guess . . . Josephine": Constance, Comtesse de Jumilhac, to CC, January 26, 1930. SIU

278   "City of Arabian Nights": SOTS (November 22, 1929).

279   "no more . . . difficile": HC to Henrietta Crosby, May 31, 1927.

279   "what . . . been": SOTS (May 14, 1923).

279   "wasn't right": Henrietta Crosby to CC, January 9, 1930. SIU

279   "I am . . . afraid": HC to Henrietta Crosby, August 2, 1927. SIU

280   "to make . . . New York": SOTS (January 11, 1929).

280   PLEASE . . . LIFE: HC to Stephen Crosby, July 19, 1929. SIU

280   "three terrible . . . else": SOTS (July 29, 1929).

280   "there is . . . eternity": *Ibid.* (July 22, 1929).

280   "Dearest Ma . . . happy": HC to Henrietta and Stephen Crosby, July 23, 1929, holograph copy of draft of letter. SIU

Page

280 "I think . . . people": Henrietta Crosby to CC, September 11, 1927. SIU

281 "never be . . . war": HC to Henrietta Crosby, September 22, 1927. SIU

281 "Dearest . . . know": Henrietta Crosby to HC, transcribed by HC into unpublished notebook. SIU

281 "The thought . . . France": HC to Henrietta Crosby, May 11, 1927. SIU

282 "The Essex . . . decisions": Boston *Evening Transcript*, June 3, 1929, p. 9. Boston Public Library

282 "She is . . . importance": *SOTS* (October 19, 1929).

282 "pure . . . Princess": *Ibid.* (August 27, 1929).

283 "and so . . . Bigelow": George Richmond Fearing, interview, January 24, 1973, Santa Barbara, Cal.

283 "She mentioned . . . complainingly": Alexander Steinert, interview, February 9, 1973, New York City.

283 "I had . . . rendezvous": CC, *Passionate Years*, p. 256.

283 "amazing phallic skyscraper": CC to HC, November 25, 1929. SIU

283 "It was . . . paradise": HC, unpublished notebook. SIU

284 "Princess . . . Yes": HC, dated "November 29, 1929," unpublished notebook. SIU

284 "Twelve hour . . . happiness": HC, typescript for *SOTS* paginated 1–5 and dated November 12–December 7. I infer that HC's holograph diary entries were typed at CC's direction, and then altered by her for publication in *SOTS*. This entry is dated "December 5" on the typescript.

284 "New York . . . with C": *Ibid.*, December 6, 1929 (see also *SOTS*, same date).

285 "complicated . . . death": Margaret Robson, quoted by Hugh Ford, *Published in Paris*, pp. 209, 210.

285 "Josephine . . . takest": HC, unpublished "Bible Notes." BU

285 MISS YOU LOVE SICK: Cord Meier to CC (addressed to "Caresse Crosby Jacob," c/o CC's mother, 680 Madison Avenue), December 9, 1929. SIU

285 "This letter . . . do": CC, on envelope enclosing Josephine Rotch Bigelow poem.

285 "Death . . . marriage": Josephine Rotch Bigelow to HC, December 9, 1929. SIU

285 "One is . . . beloved": HC, unpublished notebook. SIU

286 "I never . . . helpings": HC, unpublished notebook. SIU

286 "It is . . . late": HC, unpublished notebook #3. BU

286 "One must . . . oneself": HC, unpublished notebook. SIU

Page   CHAPTER 18

288   "I remember . . . story": Margaret Robson, quoted by John
      Unterecker, *Voyager*, p. 610.
288   "and the expression . . . bullets": New York *Daily Mirror*, Decem-
      ber 13, 1929, p. 4.
288   "this was . . . mysticism": Archibald MacLeish, interview, April
      21, 1973, Conway, Mass.
288–289 "As I . . . him": *Ibid.*
289   "This man . . . me": New York *Daily News*, December 12, 1929,
      p. 4.
289   "We were . . . to me": Albert Bigelow, quoted by New York
      Daily News, December 12, 1929, p. 4.
289   "This man . . . loved me": Albert Bigelow, quoted by New York
      World, December 12, p. 1.
289   "a clandestine . . . personality": New York *Daily News*, Decem-
      ber 12, 1929, p. 4.
289   "listen . . . pleas": Indirect quotation of Albert Bigelow, New
      York *Daily News*, December 13, 1929, p. 3.
289–290 "restless . . . Crosby": New York *Telegram*, December 11, 1929,
      p. 1.
290   "met . . . despair": New York *Sun*, December 11, 1929, p. 1.
290   "an erotic . . . exile": New York *Daily Mirror*, December 13, 1929,
      p. 4.
290   "he will . . . verse": New York *Daily News*, December 14, 1929,
      p. 6.
290   "plus-one . . . drunk": New York *Daily Mirror*, December 12,
      1929, back page.
290   "In the morgue's . . . business": New York *Telegram*, December
      11, 1929, p. 1.
290   "the bodies . . . New York": Boston *Evening Transcript*, Decem-
      ber 11, 1929, p. 1.
290–291 MAN . . . "notes": Boston *Post*, December 11, 1929, p. 12.
291   "distinguished . . . student": Paris *Herald Tribune*, December 12,
      1929, p. 3.
291   "complacent friend": New York *Daily News*, December 11, 1929,
      p. 6.
291   "Miss Rotch": *Ibid.*
291   "Mrs. Rotch": New York *Sun*, December 11, 1929, p. 31.
291   "But when . . . Mrs. Bigelow": New York *World*, December 11,
      1929, p. 1.
291–292 " 'Crosby . . . out' ": New York *Daily Mirror*, December 13, 1929,
      p. 4.
292   "showed . . . liquor": New York *Herald Tribune*, December 12,
      1929, p. 5.
292   "The poet . . . seven p.m.": New York *Daily News*, December 11,
      1929, p. 6.

Page

293   CROSBY . . . "like": Chicago *Tribune*, December 13, 1929, p. 4.

293   "some melancholy, some impulse": New York *World*, December 12, 1929, p. 1.

293   "in which . . . red": New York *Daily Mirror*, December 11, 1929, back page.

294   "over . . . ago": Newspaper clipping, without date or other identification. SIU

294   "J. Pierpont Morgan . . . collections": New York *Daily News*, December 14, 1929, p. 6.

294   "It was . . . mine": CC, *Passionate Years*, p. 206.

294   "imaginative . . . poet": Hart Crane, quoted by Philip Horton, *Hart Crane*, p. 287.

294   "Too much . . . *surréalisme*": D. H. Lawrence, quoted by George Wickes, *Americans in Paris*, p. 185.

294   "if only . . . wrong": D. H. Lawrence to CC, January 30, 1930. SIU

295   "astonishing and frightening": Chicago *Tribune* (datelined Paris), December 12, 1929.

295   "that poor demented girl": Constance, Comtesse de Jumilhac, to CC, December 12, 1929. SIU

295   "inspired . . . 'time' ": *Ibid.*, January 26, 1930.

295   "*anything* . . . honor": *Ibid.*, December 12, 1929.

295   "This whole . . . alive": Archibald MacLeish, interview, April 21, 1973, Conway, Mass.

295   "just literary": Gretchen Powel, interview, April 25, 1973, Washington, D.C.

295–296   "He said . . . him": Polly Peabody Drysdale, interview, May 25, 1973, London.

296   "so that . . . it": Henrietta Crosby to CC, November 20, 1952. SIU

296   "announcement . . . responsible": *Town Topics*, volume CII, #23, December 19, 1929, p. 6. Library of Congress

297   "Mrs. Albert Bigelow . . . Jumilhac": HC, last will and testament. BU

297   "the sex . . . them": Henrietta Crosby to CC, January 14, 1930. SIU

298   "Dearest . . . you": *Ibid.*, August 10, 1930.

298   "never . . . 'right' ": Way Spaulding to CC, December 12, 1929. SIU

298   "undoubtedly . . . personality": Norman McLeod, "Comment," *The Morada*, #2, Winter, 1930. New York Public Library

298   "a rare . . . saluto": Jack Conroy, "Harry Crosby: In Memoriam," *The Rebel Poet*, volume I, #1, January, 1931. New York Public Library

299   "to be . . . it": Kay Boyle, "Homage to Harry Crosby," *Transition* #19–20, June, 1930, pp. 221, 222.

299   "Yet Crosby . . . 'bed' ": Kay Boyle, "Harry Crosby and His Diary," unpublished preface. SIU

299–300   "a very cruel . . . moment": Kay Boyle to GW, January 23, 1973.

Page

300 "WELL KNOWN . . . *BANG*": E. E. Cummings, "IX," *Poems: 1923–1954*, pp. 228, 229.

301 "*Harry* . . . *wine*": William Jay Smith, "*Petits Chevaux*: The Twenties," *The New Republic*, February 9, 1963.

301–302 "*Wise* . . . *baths*": John Brooks Wheelwright, "Wise Men on the Death of a Fool," *Hound & Horn*, Spring, 1931, pp. 401, 402.

302–303 "*Pamela* . . . You": CC, "Pamela," *Poems for Harry Crosby.*

303 "dignified . . . *Bessie*": Stuart Gilbert to CC, May 14, 1931. SIU

303 "Living . . . destroyer": Stuart Gilbert, introduction to *Poems for Harry Crosby.*

303 "those . . . century": Hugh Hanley to CC, January 13, 1930. BU

304 "There is . . . enterprise": Ezra Pound, note to HC's *Torchbearer.*

304 "always . . . it": Gerhard Pohlman to William Peabody, February 20, 1930. SIU

304 "beautiful . . . ball": Polly Peabody Drysdale, interview, May 25, 1973, London.

305 "please, please": CC to Cyril Connolly, June 12, 1967, carbon copy. SIU

AFTERWORD

307 "had . . . syllogism": Malcolm Cowley, *Exile's Return*, pp. 248.

307 "I died . . . more": Ernest Hemingway, quoted by Malcolm Cowley, *A Second Flowering*, p. 224.

307 "Harry . . . him": Malcolm Cowley, *Exile's Return*, p. 250.

308 "Harry . . . change": *Ibid.*, p. 288.

308 "Harry . . . identified": *Ibid.*, p. 284.

308 "If . . . Heaven": HC to CC, June 2, 1921. SIU

309 "youth . . . myself": Oscar Wilde, *The Picture of Dorian Gray*, p. 169.

309 "Burial . . . God": HC, written on card carried in his billfold. SIU

309 "a *real* burying place": *SOTS* (December 18, 1923).

310 "Instructions . . . New York": Among HC's personal effects. SIU

310 "suicide is a vocation": Cesare Pavese, quoted by A. Alvarez, *The Savage God*, p. 231.

310 "theoretic suicide": Samuel Putnam, *Paris Was Our Mistress*, p. 238.

311 "to have . . . Sun-Death": *SOTS* (September 4, 1928).

311 "you will . . . forever": HC to Constance, Comtesse de Jumilhac, November, 1928.

311 "The most . . . Sun": *SOTS* (December 22, 1928).

311–312 "knew . . . it": Archibald MacLeish, interview, April 21, 1973, Conway, Mass.

312 "Death . . . to": HC, unpublished notebook. SIU

POSTSCRIPT

314 "As for . . . did": CC to Malcolm Cowley, November 19, 1949.

Bibliography

The principal sources of information about Harry Crosby, his family, friends and work, are documentary. The recollections of his friends come from a great distance in time—more than half a century for his college classmates and comrades at war—and tend to cluster about his most extraordinary characteristics: his bizarre costume, his excesses, his wildness. They do, however, put flesh on the bones of those documents that have made it possible to read the man's anatomy.

The documents themselves are extraordinary, numerous, well-preserved and accessible. Caresse appreciated their value; moreover, she recognized their value as a collection, and hence resisted, with a single exception, the temptation to sell letters and manuscripts piecemeal. Because she saved so much that touched not only Harry's life with her, but his life before he met her, there are few holes in his history. She even saved Josephine Rotch Bigelow's final love letters to Harry, together with Josephine's decision in verse to die with him as she did. (These particular letters were casually slipped inside Harry Crosby's billfold, which was in turn kept in a cigar box, and I stumbled upon them quite by accident among some as yet uncatalogued Black Sun Press papers at Southern Illinois University.)

The most important collection of Crosby material is at Morris Library, Southern Illinois University. Harry T. Moore, a close friend to Caresse for many years and a professor of English there, persuaded her to sell her Black Sun Press Archives to the university in 1963. Then, in 1971, after Caresse's death, her estate sold another lot to the same university. Together they comprise a huge mass of letters, books, manuscripts, scrapbooks, photographs and memorabilia. Most of the papers and objects concern Caresse's activities following Harry's death, but those from 1929 and earlier make a full record of the life and times of a busy and sociable poet and publisher. Of principal value to this volume are Harry's letters to Caresse and to his mother (the latter mostly from 1927 and 1928, bound), his letters to and from Alastair, D. H. Lawrence, Hart Crane, Archibald MacLeish, Kay Boyle, Walter Berry (there is also a Berry Collection at Morris Library), James Joyce and Eugene Jolas. In addition, the Black Sun Press Archives contain crucial unpublished notebooks, newspaper clippings and manuscripts, as well as an almost comprehensive collection of books published by the Black Sun Press.

It would not have been possible to write this book using only the resources of Southern Illinois University, but it might have been possible to write it using only their resources and those of Brown University. Since 1955, the Harris Collection of John Hay Library at Brown has had ten volumes of Harry's holograph notebooks. Much of the material from these bound notebooks, of approximately two hundred and fifty pages each, found its way into *Shadows of the Sun*, but much more did not. In these notebooks (the first six volumes of which are given over to general matters, the seventh and eighth to Bible notes, the ninth to sun notes, the last to encyclopedia notes) may be found love letters written to Harry and transcribed, a running record of his likes and dislikes, an inventory of books read (together with his opinion of them) and occasional financial summaries. In common with Southern Illinois University, Brown University has a large collection of books published by the Black Sun Press, and also an album of photographs taken of Harry (and by him) during World War I. These, and many other items of interest to Crosby scholars, were gifts from Caresse in 1955, on the occasion of an exhibit at Brown of Black Sun Press books.

For a brief time during the late Fifties and early Sixties, Caresse considered making a bequest of Black Sun Press papers to the Library of Congress, which put a great many of them on microfilm. There would be no reason to use this microfilmed material in preference to primary sources at Brown and Southern Illinois University; however, the Library of Congress is a useful repository of otherwise unavailable periodicals, such as early issues of *Town & Country* and of *Town Topics*.

The New York Public Library is listed in the book *American Literary Manuscripts* as having a large collection of Harry Crosby letters and manuscripts. It has none, but its annex contains the fullest microfilm collection of New York City newspapers—invaluable to a reconstruction of Harry Crosby's death, and its immediate aftermath. The Boston Public Library is likewise useful for its microfilm collection of Boston newspapers.

Harvard University's Houghton Library has a good collection of Black Sun Press books, together with a couple of letters from the Comtesse de Noailles to Harry and Caresse.

The Beinecke Rare Book and Manuscript Library at Yale has photographs of Walter Berry, a brief correspondence between the Crosbys and Ezra Pound (Caresse's voluminous correspondence, post–World War II, with Pound is at Southern Illinois University) and letters from *Hound & Horn* to Harry.

Princeton University's Firestone Library has in its Sylvia Beach Collection a few notes from her to Caresse, and vice versa.

The Humanities Research Center of the University of Texas has six letters from D. H. Lawrence to Harry, together with fifty-five books from Walter Berry's library which contain Harry's marginalia.

The relentless wheels of diploma mills grind exceedingly fine, but as far as I know no one has used the magnificent Black Sun Press collections at Southern Illinois University or at Brown as the foundation of a dissertation, doctoral or otherwise. Till now, to discover Harry Crosby a reader either discovered Malcolm Cowley, or *Shadows of the Sun*, or read of another character in *The Passionate Years* who had assumed Harry Crosby's name.

The bibliography is divided into three sections: the published work of Harry Crosby (of which by far the most crucial to me were the three series of *Shadows of the Sun*, and *War Letters*); work, published and unpublished, in whole or in significant part, concerning Harry Crosby; and books of more general utility.

I: THE PUBLISHED WORKS OF HARRY CROSBY
(listed chronologically)

These books are rare, though not impossible to find. Most of the libraries I have mentioned above have most of them in their collections. It is difficult to know with certainty how many copies were printed of each title. The consensus is that forty-four copies were printed of the various series of *Shadows of the Sun*, yet I have myself seen that many. I was offered the three-volume diary several years ago for two thousand dollars; the price seemed steep then, and still does.

Anthology. Dijon: Maurice Darantière, 1924. (Harry Crosby's favorite poems, printed for his personal use)
Sonnets for Caresse. Paris: Herbert Clarke, 1925.

———, second edition. Paris: Herbert Clarke, 1926.

———, third edition. Paris: Albert Messein, 1926.

———, fourth edition. Paris: Éditions Narcisse, 1927. (The first book printed for the Crosbys by Roger Lescaret)

Red Skeletons. Illustrated by Alastair. Paris: Éditions Narcisse, 1927.

Chariot of the Sun, first edition. Paris: At the Sign of the Sundial, 1928.

Shadows of the Sun. Paris: Black Sun Press, 1928. (The first book to bear the imprint of the Black Sun Press)

Transit of Venus, first edition. Paris: Black Sun Press, 1928.

———, second edition. Paris: Black Sun Press, 1929.

Mad Queen. Paris: Black Sun Press, 1929.

Shadows of the Sun—Series Two. Paris: Black Sun Press, 1929.

The Sun. Paris: Black Sun Press, 1929. (A miniature book: 2.5 x 1.9 cm)

Sleeping Together. Paris: Black Sun Press, 1929.

Shadows of the Sun—Series Three. Paris: Black Sun Press, 1930.

Aphrodite in Flight; Being Some Observations on the Aerodynamics of Love. Paris: Black Sun Press, 1930.

Collected Poems of Harry Crosby (four volumes, boxed):

    Chariot of the Sun. Introduction by D. H. Lawrence. Paris: Black Sun Press, 1931.

    Transit of Venus. Preface by T. S. Eliot. Paris: Black Sun Press, 1931.

    Sleeping Together. Introduction by Stuart Gilbert. Paris: Black Sun Press, 1931.

    Torchbearer. Notes by Ezra Pound. Paris: Black Sun Press, 1931.

War Letters. Preface by Henrietta M. Crosby. Paris: Black Sun Press, 1932.

II. ARTICLES AND BOOKS IN WHOLE OR GREAT PART ABOUT HARRY CROSBY

Baltzell, Jane, "The Answer Was Always 'Yes!' " *Brunonia* (January, 1955), pp. 5–9.

Bell, Millicent, "The Black Sun Press." *Books at Brown,* 17 (1955), pp. 2–24.

Benét, William Rose, "Round about Parnassus." *The Saturday Review of Literature* (January 30, 1932).

Boyle, Kay, "Homage to Harry Crosby." *Transition,* 19–20 (June, 1930), pp. 221, 222.

———, *My Next Bride.* New York: Harcourt, Brace & Co., 1934.

Conroy, Jack, "Harry Crosby: In Memoriam." *The Rebel Poet,* 1 (January, 1931), p. 3.

———, review of *Transit of Venus* and *Mad Queen. Morada* (1931), p. 5.

Cowley, Malcolm, *Exile's Return.* New York: Viking Compass Edition, 1956.

Crane, Hart, "To the Cloud Juggler." *Transition,* 19–20 (June, 1930), p. 223.

Crosby, Caresse, *Poems for Harry Crosby.* Introduction by Stuart Gilbert. Paris: Black Sun Press, 1931.

———, *The Passionate Years.* Carbondale, Ill.: Southern Illinois University Press, 1968.

Cummings, E. E., "IX." *Poems 1923–1954.* New York: Harcourt, Brace & Co., 1954.

Fox, Hugh, "Harry Crosby: A Heliograph." *Books at Brown,* 13 (1969), pp. 95–100.

Gilbert, Stuart, "A Personal Note." *Transition*, 19–20 (June, 1930), pp. 224–227.

Jolas, Eugene, "Harry Crosby and *Transition*." *Transition* (June, 1930), pp. 228, 229.

Kahn, Sy, "Hart Crane and Harry Crosby: A Transit of Poets." *Journal of Modern Literature*, 1, pp. 45–56.

———, "The Slender Fire of Harry Crosby." In *The Twenties: Poetry and Prose*, edited by Richard E. Langford and William E. Taylor. Deland, Fla.: Everett Edwards Press, 1966. Pp. 1–6.

Kaiser, Stuart B., "Diary of the War." July 5, 1917–June 28, 1919. (Unpublished)

Lymington, Gerard, "Memoir." (Unpublished autobiography of the Earl of Portsmouth)

Minkoff, George Robert, *A Bibliography of the Black Sun Press*. Introduction by Caresse Crosby. Great Neck, N.Y.: Printed by the author, 1970. (A detailed inventory and description of all books of the Black Sun Press, as well as other books published throughout the years by the Crosbys)

Reed, Victor, "Reading a 'Sound Poem' by Harry Crosby." *English Language Notes*, 6 (March, 1969), pp. 192–96.

Sedgwick, William Ellery, "Obituary." *Class of 1922: Fourth Report*. Cambridge: Harvard University Alumni Association.

Smith, William Jay. "*Petits Chevaux*: The Twenties." *The New Republic* (February 9, 1963).

Soupault, Philippe, "Harry Crosby." *Transition*, 19–20 (June, 1930), p. 232.

Warren, Dale, "The Black Sun Press." *Publishers Weekly* (June 6, 1931), pp. 2714–16.

Wheelwright, John Brooks, "Wise Men on the Death of a Fool." *Hound & Horn*, 4 (Spring, 1931), pp. 401, 402.

(Note also the critical essays concerning Harry Crosby's work by D. H. Lawrence, T. S. Eliot and Ezra Pound that appear in *Chariot of the Sun*, *Transit of Venus* and *Torchbearer*.)

III. GENERAL BIBLIOGRAPHY

Alvarez, A., *The Savage God*. New York: Random House, 1972.

Amory, Cleveland, *The Proper Bostonians*. New York: E. P. Dutton & Co., 1947.

Auchincloss, Louis, *Edith Wharton: A Woman in Her Time*. New York: Viking Press, 1971.

Baker, Carlos, *Ernest Hemingway: A Life Story*. New York: Charles Scribner's Sons, 1969.

Baudelaire, Charles, *Les Fleurs du Mal*. Translated by George Dillon and Edna St. Vincent Millay. New York: Washington Square Press, 1962.

Beach, Sylvia, *Shakespeare and Company*. New York: Harcourt, Brace & World, Inc., 1959.

Beebe, Lucius, *Boston and the Boston Legend*. New York: Appleton-Century Co., 1935.

Bell, Millicent, *Edith Wharton and Henry James: The Story of Their Friendship.* New York: George Braziller, 1965.

Benson, Albert Emerson (editor), *Saint Mark's School in the War Against Germany.* Norwood, Mass.: Plimpton Press, 1920. (Privately printed for the school)

———, *History of Saint Mark's School.* Southboro, Mass.: Plimpton Press, 1925. (Privately printed for the Alumni Association)

Bergonzi, Bernard, *Heroes' Twilight: A Study of the Literature of the Great War.* New York: Coward-McCann, 1965.

Birmingham, Stephen, *The Late John Marquand.* Philadelphia: J. B. Lippincott Co., 1972.

Boyle, Kay, *Short Stories.* Paris: Black Sun Press, 1929. (See also McAlmon, Robert, *Being Geniuses Together*)

Breton, André, *Manifestoes of Surrealism.* Translated by Richard Seaver and Helen R. Lane. Ann Arbor: University of Michigan Press, 1969.

Cabot, Elizabeth, *Letters of Elizabeth Cabot.* Two volumes. Boston: Privately printed, 1905.

Callaghan, Morley, *That Summer in Paris.* New York: Coward-McCann, Inc., 1963.

Camus, Albert, *The Myth of Sisyphus.* Translated by Justin O'Brien. New York: Vintage Books, 1955.

———, *The Rebel.* Translated by Anthony Bower. New York: Vintage Books, 1958.

Cardinal, Roger, *Outsider Art.* New York: Praeger, 1972.

Charters, James, *This Must Be the Place.* As told to Morrill Cody. New York: Lee Furman, 1937. (The memoir of Jimmy the Barman)

Coolidge, Olivia, *Edith Wharton: 1862–1937.* New York: Charles Scribner's Sons, 1964.

Cowley, Malcolm, *A Second Flowering: Works and Days of the Lost Generation.* New York: Viking Press, 1973.

Crane, Hart, *The Bridge.* Paris: Black Sun Press, 1930.

———, *The Complete Poems and Selected Letters and Prose.* Edited by Brom Weber. New York: Anchor Books, 1966.

Crawford, Mary Caroline, *Famous Families of Massachusetts.* Boston: Little, Brown & Co., 1930.

Cummings, E. E., *The Enormous Room.* New York: Modern Library, 1934.

De Quincey, Thomas, *Confessions of an English Opium Eater.* Edited by Alethea Hayter. Harmondsworth, Middlesex: Penguin Books, 1973.

Dos Passos, John, *One Man's Initiation.* Ithaca: Cornell University Press, 1969.

———, *The Fourteenth Chronicle: Letters and Diaries of John Dos Passos.* Edited by Townsend Ludington. Boston: Gambit, 1973.

Farber, Maurice L., *Theory of Suicide.* New York: Funk & Wagnalls, 1968.

Farrar, Mrs. John, *The Young Lady's Friend.* Boston: American Stationers' Co., 1836.

Fitzgerald, Edward, *Rubáiyát of Omar Khayyám.* Garden City, N.Y.: Dolphin Books, 1969.

Ford, Hugh, *Published in Paris: American and British Writers, Printers, and Publishers in Paris, 1920–1939*. New York: Macmillan, 1975.

Fowlie, Wallace, *Rimbaud: A Critical Study*. Chicago: University of Chicago Press, 1965.

Fussell, Paul, *The Great War and Modern Memory*. New York: Oxford University Press, 1975.

Genthe, Charles V., *American Narratives: 1917–1918*. New York: David Lewis, 1969.

Gershman, Herbert S., *The Surrealist Revolution in France*. Ann Arbor: University of Michigan Press, 1969.

Glassco, John, *Memoirs of Montparnasse*. New York: Oxford University Press, 1970.

Hardwick, Elizabeth, *Seduction and Betrayal*. New York: Random House, 1974.

Hayter, Alethea, *Opium and the Romantic Imagination*. Berkeley: University of California Press, 1968.

Hemingway, Ernest, *A Moveable Feast*. New York: Charles Scribner's Sons, 1964.

Hoffman, Frederick J., *The Twenties: American Writing in the Postwar Decade*. New York: Free Press, 1962.

Horton, Philip, *Hart Crane: The Life of an American Poet*. New York: Compass Books, 1957.

Huddleston, Sisley, *Bohemian Literary and Social Life in Paris: Salons, Cafés, Studios*. London: George G. Harrap & Co., 1928.

Huysmans, Joris-Karl, *Against Nature*. Translated by Robert Baldick. Baltimore: Penguin Books, 1959.

Jolas, Eugene, "Frontier Man." (Unpublished autobiography)

———, *Secession in Astropolis*. Paris: Black Sun Press, 1929.

Josephson, Matthew, *Life Among the Surrealists*. New York: Holt, Rinehart & Winston, 1962.

Joyce, James, *Tales Told of Shem and Shaun*. Paris: Black Sun Press, 1929.

Kellogg, Grace, *The Two Lives of Edith Wharton: The Woman and Her Work*. New York: Appleton-Century Co., 1965.

Kenner, Hugh, *A Homemade World: The American Modernist Writers*. New York: Knopf, 1975.

———, *The Pound Era*. Berkeley: University of California Press, 1971.

Lawrence, D. H., *Sun*. Paris: Black Sun Press, 1928.

———, *The Escaped Cock*. Paris: Black Sun Press, 1929.

———, *The Letters of D. H. Lawrence*. Edited by Aldous Huxley. New York: Viking Press, 1932.

Le Gallienne, Richard, *From a Paris Scrapbook*. New York: Ives Washburn, 1938.

Lewis, R. W. B., *Edith Wharton: A Biography*. New York: Harper & Row, 1975.

Linscott, Robert N. (editor), *State of Mind: A Boston Reader*. New York: Farrar, Straus & Co., 1948.

Lubbock, Percy, *Portrait of Edith Wharton*. New York: D. Appleton-Century Co., 1947.

Lymington, Gerard, *Git Le Coeur*. Paris: Black Sun Press, 1928.

———, *Spring Song of Iscariot*. Paris: Black Sun Press, 1929.

McAlmon, Robert, *Being Geniuses Together*. Revised and with supplementary chapters by Kay Boyle. Garden City, N.Y.: Doubleday & Co., 1968.

MacLeish, Archibald, *Einstein*. Paris: Black Sun Press, 1929.

———, *New Found Land*. Paris: Black Sun Press, 1930.

Marks, Harry, *The Black Sun Press: 1930*. New York: Privately printed, 1930. (Catalogue)

Paul, Elliot, *The Last Time I Saw Paris*. London: Cresset Press, 1951.

Peabody, Richard R., *The Common Sense of Drinking*. Boston: Little, Brown & Co., 1931.

Peckham, Morse, *The Triumph of Romanticism*. Columbia: University of South Carolina Press, 1970.

Poe, Edgar Allan, *The Fall of the House of Usher*. Illustrated by Alastair. Introduction by Arthur Symons. Paris: Éditions Narcisse, 1928.

Powel, Gretchen and Peter, *New York 1929*. Paris: Black Sun Press, 1930. (A book of photographs priced at one hundred dollars; the only copy I have seen is at the New York Public Library)

Pritchett, V. S., *Midnight Oil*. New York: Random House, 1972.

Putnam, Samuel, *Paris Was Our Mistress*. Carbondale, Ill.: Southern Illinois University Press, 1970.

Rimbaud, Arthur, *Complete Works*. Translated by Paul Schmidt. New York: Harper & Row, 1975.

Rogers, W. C., *Ladies Bountiful*. New York: Harcourt, Brace & World, 1968.

Sartre, Jean-Paul, *Baudelaire*. Translated by Martin Turnell. New York: New Directions, 1967.

Schopenhauer, Arthur, *Selections*. Edited by DeWitt H. Parker. New York: Charles Scribner's Sons, 1928.

Seaburg, Carl, *Boston Observed*. Boston: Beacon Press, 1971.

Shattuck, Roger, *The Banquet Years: The Origins of the Avant-Garde in France: 1885 to World War I*. New York: Vintage Books, 1968.

Stein, Gertrude, *Paris France*. New York: Liveright, 1970.

Stengel, Erwin, *Suicide and Attempted Suicide*. Harmondsworth, Middlesex: Penguin Books, 1969.

Tomkins, Calvin, *Living Well Is the Best Revenge*. New York: Viking Press, 1971.

Unterecker, John, *Voyager: A Life of Hart Crane*. New York: Farrar, Straus & Giroux, 1969.

Valéry, Paul, *Masters and Friends*. Translated by Martin Turnell. Princeton: Bollingen Foundation, 1968.

Weber, Brom (editor), *The Letters of Hart Crane*. New York: Hermitage House, 1952.

Weeks, Edward, *My Green Age*. Boston: Atlantic Monthly Press, 1973.

Wharton, Edith, *A Backward Glance*. New York: Appleton Century-Croft, 1934.

Wickes, George, *Americans in Paris*. Garden City, N.Y.: Paris Review Editions, 1969.

Wilde, Oscar, *The Birthday of the Infanta*. Illustrated by Alastair. Introduction by Harry Crosby. Paris: Black Sun Press, 1928.

————, *The Portable Oscar Wilde*. Edited by Richard Aldington. New York: Viking Press, 1971.

Wilson, Edmund, *Axel's Castle*. London: Fontana, 1961.

————, *The Twenties*. Edited by Leon Edel. New York: Farrar, Straus & Giroux, 1975.

————, *The Wound and the Bow*. London: University Paperbacks, 1961.

Woroszylski, Wiktor, *The Life of Mayakovsky*. Translated by Boleslaw Taborski. New York: Orion Press, 1970.

Index

TITLES IN SERIES